BEN JONSON'S WALK TO SCOTLAND

At the heart of this book is a previously unpublished account of Ben Jonson's celebrated walk from London to Edinburgh in the summer of 1618. This unique first-hand narrative provides us with an insight into where Jonson went, whom he met and what he did on the way. James Loxley, Anna Groundwater and Julie Sanders present a clear, readable and fully annotated edition of the text. An introduction and a series of contextual essays shed further light on topics including the evidence of provenance and authorship, Jonson's contacts throughout Britain, his celebrity status, and the relationships between his 'foot voyage' and other famous journeys of the time. The essays also illuminate wider issues such as early modern travel and political and cultural relations between England and Scotland. It is an invaluable volume for scholars and upper-level students of Ben Jonson studies, early modern literature, seventeenth-century social history and cultural geography.

JAMES LOXLEY is Professor of Early Modern Literature at the University of Edinburgh. He has published widely on Renaissance poetry and drama, and also on issues in contemporary literary theory. His publications include *Royalism and Poetry in the English Civil War* (1997), *Ben Jonson* (2002) and *Shakespeare, Jonson and the Claims of the Performative* (with Mark Robson, 2013).

ANNA GROUNDWATER lectures in British and Scottish History at the University of Edinburgh. Her publications include *The Scottish Middle March, 1573 to 1625: Power, Kinship, Allegiance* (2010) and *Scotland Connected: The History of Scotland, Britain and the World at a Glance* (forthcoming, 2014). She is on the councils of the Society of Antiquaries of Scotland, the Scottish Medievalists and the Scottish History Society, and is a fellow of the Royal Historical Society.

JULIE SANDERS is Professor of English Literature and Drama at the University of Nottingham and Vice Provost (Teaching and Learning) at the Ningbo China campus. She has edited plays by Ben Jonson, Richard Brome and James Shirley, and was a contributing editor to *The Cambridge Works of Ben Jonson* (2012). Her other publications include *The Cultural Geography of Early Modern Drama, 1620–1650* (2011), which won the British Academy Rose Mary Crawshay Prize for international women's scholarship in 2012.

BEN JONSON'S WALK TO SCOTLAND

An Annotated Edition of the 'Foot Voyage'

*

James Loxley
Anna Groundwater
Julie Sanders

CAMBRIDGE
UNIVERSITY PRESS

CAMBRIDGE
UNIVERSITY PRESS

University Printing House, Cambridge CB2 8BS, United Kingdom

One Liberty Plaza, 20th Floor, New York, NY 10006, USA

477 Williamstown Road, Port Melbourne, VIC 3207, Australia

4843/24, 2nd Floor, Ansari Road, Daryaganj, Delhi - 110002, India

79 Anson Road, #06-04/06, Singapore 079906

Cambridge University Press is part of the University of Cambridge.

It furthers the University's mission by disseminating knowledge in the pursuit of education, learning and research at the highest international levels of excellence.

www.cambridge.org
Information on this title: www.cambridge.org/9781108438780

First published 2015
First paperback edition 2017

A catalogue record for this publication is available from the British Library

Library of Congress Cataloging in Publication data
Ben Jonson's walk to Scotland : an annotated edition of the 'foot voyage' / edited by James Loxley, Anna Groundwater and Julie Sanders.
    pages   cm
Includes bibliographical references.
ISBN 978-1-107-00333-0 (hardback)
1. Jonson, Ben, 1573?–1637 – Travel – England.   2. Jonson, Ben, 1573?–1637 – Travel – Scotland.   3. Literature and society – Great Britain – History – 17th century.   4. Cultural geography – Great Britain.   5. England – Foreign relations – Scotland – Early works to 1800.   6. Scotland – Foreign relations – England – Early works to 1800.   I. Loxley, James, 1968– editor.   II. Groundwater, Anna, editor.   III. Sanders, Julie, 1968– editor.
PR2638.B56   2015
822'.3–dc23

                                                          2014024240

ISBN 978-1-107-00333-0 Hardback
ISBN 978-1-108-43878-0 Paperback

CONTENTS

ILLUSTRATIONS

ACKNOWLEDGEMENTS

We have incurred innumerable debts during the course of writing this book –
indeed, without the generosity, enthusiasm and kindness of those mentioned
here we would barely have been able to get started. We are deeply grateful to
the depositor for permission to reproduce the text of the 'Foot Voyage', and to
the staff of Cheshire Archives and Local Studies, particularly Liz Green, for the
invaluable assistance rendered to this project. We would also like to acknowledge the substantial financial support provided by the Arts and Humanities
Research Council, which enabled us to undertake the work necessary to bring
the edition and accompanying essays to completion much more quickly, and
much more thoroughly, than would otherwise have been the case. Heartfelt
thanks are due especially to Ian Donaldson and Martin Butler, whose interest,
support and assistance have been indispensable from the outset. Frances
Henderson gave us crucial assistance with early modern shorthand, Tracey
Mooney created a superb map of three early seventeenth-century journeys for
us, and Natasha Simonova did much to bring the index together. Sarah Poynting,
Sarah Stanton and Rosemary Crawley played vital roles in getting the project
started, keeping it going and seeing it through to publication. Anna is especially
grateful for Bob Younger's vital help and support, without which archival visits
would have been much more difficult to make. Julie would like to thank John
Higham, not least for getting the walking boots muddy for real. James is deeply
grateful to Joanna Loxley, who has not only put up with the sometimes over-
bearing presence of Ben Jonson in her life for many years but also offered
innumerable brilliant suggestions and much sagacious advice along the way.

Our work has also benefited immeasurably from the generosity with their
time, skills, knowledge and expertise of so many friends and colleagues. Their
willingness to answer questions, look over material and make suggestions has
been enormously important; in fact, we couldn't have done without it. In this
connection, we would like to thank Michael Bath, Peter Beal, Martin Bennett,
Mark Brayshay, Michael Brennan, Stephen Daniels, Katherine Duncan-Jones,
Kenneth Dunn, Eve Equi, Heather Falvey, Chris Fleet, Eugene Giddens, Julian

Goodare, Mark Goldie, Ralph Hanna, Margaret Hannay, Gabriel Heaton, David Hitchcock, Ann Hughes, Tom Hughes, Andy Kesson, Emelye Keyser, Stephen Knight, James Knowles, Sally-Beth MacLean, Joseph Marshall, John McGavin, Andrew McRae, Jemima Matthews, James Merryweather, Catriona Murray, Diana Newton, Patricia Panek, Alan Radford, Jamie Reid-Baxter, Nicola Royan, Matthew Steggle, Catherine Stevens, Crosby Stevens, Laura Stewart, Daniel Storza Smith, Sebastiaan Verweij, Katie Wales, Adrian Woodhouse and Henry Woudhuysen. We are also very grateful to Oliver Edwards and Brian Mains, of the Royal Grammar School, Newcastle, to John Ives, church-warden of St John the Baptist, Muston, to Francis Withers, lay minister at St Mary's, Oxted, and to Revd Susan Blagden, rector of St Dunawd, Bangor Monachorum, for their patient assistance with our queries along the way.

Audiences at the universities of St Andrews, Bath Spa, Edinburgh, Exeter (Cornwall campus), Keele, Manchester, Nottingham, Oxford Brookes, Sheffield Hallam, Sussex and Teesside Universities, the Society for Renaissance Studies, Leicester Literary and Philosophical Society, and the London Renaissance Seminar have all commented helpfully on aspects or versions of this work in progress, while the expert assistance of librarians and archivists in the institutions we have visited during the course of our research has been invaluable. Thanks are due in particular to staff at the National Library of Scotland, the National Records of Scotland, the National Archives, the University of Nottingham Library, the Borthwick Institute, Lambeth Palace Library, Guildhall Library, Yorkshire Archaeological Society, London Metropolitan Archives, Durham University Library, and the record offices of Leeds and Sheffield (WYAS), Bradford, Doncaster, Durham, Edinburgh, Flintshire, Huntingdon, Lincoln and Stamford.

The cover image from 'Landscape with Travellers and Peasants on a Track', by Jan Brueghel the elder, is copyright the owner and the National Gallery, London, and is reproduced by permission. The page image from the Aldersey manuscript at Figure 1 is reproduced by permission of Cheshire Archives and Local Studies and the depositor, to whom copyright is reserved; Figure 2 is reproduced by permission of the British Library; Figure 4 by permission of the National Library of Scotland; and we are grateful to Cambridge University Library for permission to reproduce Figure 5. The epigraph on p. 107 from Robert Macfarlane, *The Old Ways: A Journey on Foot* (2012) appears by kind permission of the author.

A NOTE ON NAMES

This edition provides a modernised text of the 'Foot Voyage', in the belief that the task of comprehending the difficult aspects of the account – which is for the most part a matter of understanding names and references or making sense of elliptical, abbreviated or compressed passages – should not be made any harder than necessary by the preservation of archaic habits of spelling and punctuation which differ from contemporary practice. At the same time, we have corrected the most obvious and least consequential scribal errors, while indicating substantive changes in the collations. Where required, such corrections have also been discussed or mentioned in the notes. An annotated transcription of the account that preserves the spelling, punctuation and scribal features evident in the Aldersey manuscript has been published in the online edition of *The Cambridge Works of Ben Jonson*, and may be consulted there.

However, place and proper names present a special challenge for the modernising editor, and the 'Foot Voyage' is particularly rich in both. With place names, emendation in line with current practice would be a matter of standardisation as much as a matter of modernisation – it is often the case that one spelling in a language of a particular town or city's name is now used to the exclusion of alternatives, even though this spelling may well be as archaic as any others. With personal names, one spelling may well appear to predominate, but often there are plenty of variants of a single name in use across the centuries and still amply in evidence today. So here again, only more obviously, to emend would be to standardise rather than to modernise, or to assume that the latter process is nothing other than the former.

This is a potential problem, because the 'Foot Voyage' is in large part the record of a journey through a not yet thoroughly standardised terrain and is to this extent shaped by, and revelatory of, the experience of cultural encounter – what Jonson himself calls 'discovery'. The profusion of names is one of its most striking features, and these are obviously a source of interest, or at least a focus of attention, for the writer – the linguistic sites, indeed, for all his encounters. We see him carefully noting variations and pronunciations ('Worsop', 'Bozers', 'Curos'), registering the linguistic geography of particular forms (from southern 'bridge' to northern 'brigg') and – most obviously in the list of Forth harbour towns with which the account concludes – attempting to wrap his pen around lists of names he has clearly never encountered before and certainly not seen written down. The account's idiosyncrasies in the writing of names are revelatory of this attention to the singularities of place and the particularities of the people living there. But they are just as revelatory of the limitations of any such attempt to capture those singularities – of the traveller taking his own locality with him into the experience of encounter. To pursue what we might call comprehensive modernisation – which in this instance definitely needs to be understood as much spatially as temporally, and thus more obviously as standardisation – would erase this layer of the text, and would remake it in the image of a cultural norm, or balance of forces, that is alien to it.

Given this, the text perhaps calls for a process of conservative, or what might even be called strict, modernisation. That is to say, orthographic archaisms can be avoided, without pursuing standardisation of other aspects. In this way, obstacles to textual intelligibility can be filtered out, while evidence of encounter, of attention to the proprieties or singularities of place – a vital element, in fact, in what is intelligible about this text – is retained. The text in our edition, therefore, has been prepared in accordance with the following principles for the treatment of place and personal names.

1. We have modernised obviously archaic doubled consonants or vowels, terminal 'e', and other similar features (e.g. 'Wentfoord', 'Warde', 'wandswoorth').
2. We have standardised names in instances where any difference between the spelling in the text and more usual forms appears to be solely orthographic (e.g. 'Rede', 'Cackstone', 'Bamborough'), or where the pronunciation indicated by the original spelling is consistent with authoritative modern pronunciation of the name (e.g. modern spelling 'Boulmer' for 'Boomer' in the 'Foot Voyage', 'Coquet' for 'Cocket', and 'Kirkcaldy' for 'Carcadhy'). Significant differences from the original spelling have been indicated in the collations and/or the notes.
3. We have substituted standard forms for spellings resulting from what would appear to be scribal errors ('Kerbon', where 'Curwen' or a similar variant would be expected).
4. Where there is more than one spelling used in the text, we have regularised to the form closest to modern usage.

5. However, we have made a presumption in favour of retaining the original spelling – subject to point 1 above – where one or more of the following are known or probable:

   a. it is a variant in use both in and beyond the early modern period (e.g. 'Withrington', 'Foster', 'Nysam') or reflective of distinctive and attested local, regional or national usage (e.g. 'St Andros', 'King-gorn', 'Kill gorn')

   b. it is plausibly an authorial error or inaccuracy, probably stemming from unfamiliarity (e.g. 'knights hall' for 'Kneesall', 'wymb' for both '-weem' and 'Wemyss', 'Biggs' for 'Gibbs', 'Eathertonne' for 'Adderstone', 'Cobersmith' for 'Cockburnspath')

   c. indications for pronunciation suggest a difference from the modern standard (e.g. 'Worsop', 'Pomfret')

   d. no referent is known, and no standard can be readily inferred (e.g. 'Hoord', 'Pelen').

Both points 2 and 5c depend on the notion of a 'modern standard' pronunciation, which can only problematically be invoked as a control: what is 'standard' from one perspective is a 'local variant' from another. For our purposes, therefore, this is taken to mean a pronunciation widely and currently in use by people familiar with the name. On some occasions, such as the need to choose between the account's 'Carcadhy' and standard 'Kirkcaldy', points 2 and 5b might be thought to conflict. In such instances, we have opted for standardisation if no significant difference in pronunciation can reasonably be inferred, or if the original spelling includes distracting archaisms. In some instances of personal names, in particular, the process of strict modernisation required under point 1 above has produced what we might call a 'synthetic' form, neither standard nor original (e.g. 'Nesbick' for standard 'Nisbett' or 'Nesbitt' and original 'Nesbicke'), but this has only been permitted where the synthetic form is itself an attested variant, and the emendation has been signalled in the collations or notes.

ABBREVIATIONS

AC   Venn, J. and J. A. Venn. 1922–7. Eds. *Alumni Cantabrigienses. . .from
           the Earliest Times to 1751*. 4 vols. Cambridge. Inc. in *ACAD: A
           Cambridge Alumni Database*. http://venn.lib.cam.ac.uk/Documents/
           acad/intro.html

AHCD   Longstaffe, William. 1858. *The Acts of the High Commission Court
           within the Diocese of Durham*. Surtees Society, 34.

Alch.   *The Alchemist*, in *The Cambridge Works of Ben Jonson*.

AO   Foster, Joseph. 1891. Ed. *Alumni Oxonienses: The Members of the
           University of Oxford, 1500–1714*. www.british-history.ac.uk

AShS   Wickham Legg, L. G. 1904. Ed. *A Short Suruey of Twenty-six Counties
           Observed in a Seven Weeks Journey begun on August 11, 1634, by a
           Captain, a Lieutenant, and an Ancient, all three of the Military
           Company in Norwich*. London.

Barriers   *The Speeches at Prince Henry's Barriers*, in *The Cambridge Edition of
           the Works of Ben Jonson*.

BI   Borthwick Institute, University of York.

BL   British Library.

Bodl.   Bodleian Library, University of Oxford.

BR   Dodds, Edwin and Herbert Maxwell Wood. 1905. Eds. *The Registers
           of Berwick-upon-Tweed in the County of Northumberland*. Vol. I:
           Baptisms, 1574–1700. Newcastle.

BRO   Berwick Record Office.

BT   Brereton, Sir William. 1844. *Travels in Holland, The United
           Provinces, England, Scotland and Ireland*. Ed. Edward Hawkins.
           Chetham Society.

CALS   Cheshire Archives and Local Studies.

CB   Camden, William. 1610. *Britain, or A Chorographicall Description of
           the most Flourishing Kingdoms, England, Scotland, and Ireland
           [Britannia]*. Trans. Philemon Holland. London.

CBP	Bain, J. 1894–6. Ed. *The Borders Papers: Calendar of Letters and Papers Relating to the Affairs of the Borders of England and Scotland*. Edinburgh.
CCED	*Clergy of the Church of England Database*, King's College London. http://theclergydatabase.org.uk/
CCROH	Cambridgeshire County Record Office, Huntingdon.
CELM	Beal, Peter. Ed. *Catalogue of English Literary Manuscripts*. https://celm2.dighum.kcl.ac.uk/
CL	McClure, N. E. 1939. Ed. *The Letters of John Chamberlain*. Philadelphia.
CP	Cokayne, George E. 1887–98. *Complete Peerage of England, Scotland, Ireland, Great Britain and the United Kingdom. Peerage*. 8 vols. London.
CRO	Cumbria Record Office.
CSPD	Green, M. A. E. et al. 1856–1947. Ed. *Calendar of State Papers, Domestic Series, 1603–1704*. London.
CWBJ	Bevington, David, Martin Butler and Ian Donaldson. 2012. Eds. *The Cambridge Edition of the Works of Ben Jonson*. Cambridge.
DA	Doncaster Archives.
DCRO	Durham County Record Office.
Disc.	*Discoveries*, in *The Cambridge Edition of the Works of Ben Jonson*.
DQS	Fraser, C. M. 1988. *Durham Quarter Sessions Rolls, 1471–1625*. Surtees Society, 199.
DSL	*Dictionary of the Scots Language*. www.dsl.ac.uk
DUL	Durham University Library.
EBBA	*English Broadside Ballad Archive*, University of California at Santa Barbara. http://ebba.english.ucsb.edu/
EBR	Wood, Marguerite. 1931. *Extracts from the Records of the Burgh of Edinburgh, 1604–1626*. Edinburgh.
ECA	Edinburgh City Archives.
EDD	Wright, Joseph. 1898–1905. *The English Dialect Dictionary*. 6 vols. London.
EMI	*Every Man in his Humour*, in *The Cambridge Edition of the Works of Ben Jonson*.
EMO	*Every Man out of his Humour*, in *The Cambridge Edition of the Works of Ben Jonson*.
Epigr.	*Epigrams*, in *The Cambridge Edition of the Works of Ben Jonson*.
ERO	Essex Record Office.
ES	Chambers, E. K. 1923. *The Elizabethan Stage*. 4 vols. Oxford.

ESRO   East Sussex Record Office.

FES   *Fasti Ecclesiae Scoticanae: The Succession of Ministers in the Church of Scotland.* 11 vols. Edinburgh.

FMG   Clay, John. 1894–6. Ed. *Familiae Minorum Gentium.* 4 vols. Harleian Society, 37–40.

For.   *The Forest,* in *The Cambridge Works of Ben Jonson.*

FRO   Flintshire Record Office.

H&S   Herford, C. H. and Percy Simpson. 1925–52. Eds. *Ben Jonson.* 11 vols. Oxford.

HALS   Hertfordshire Archives and Local Studies.

HMCL   Royal Commission on Historical Manuscripts. 1893. *The Manuscripts of the Earl of Lonsdale.* London.

HMCM   Royal Commission on Historical Manuscripts. 1885. *The Manuscripts of Lord Muncaster.* London.

HMCMH   Royal Commission on Historical Manuscripts. 1902. *The Manuscripts of Colonel David Milne Home.* London.

HMCMi   Royal Commission on Historical Manuscripts. 1911. *The Manuscripts of Lord Middleton.* London.

HMCMK   Royal Commission on Historical Manuscripts. 1930. *The Manuscripts of the Earl of Mar and Kellie.* London.

HMCP   Royal Commission on Historical Manuscripts. 1891–1931. *The Manuscripts of the Duke of Portland.* London.

HMCR   Royal Commission on Historical Manuscripts. 1888–1905. *The Manuscripts of the Duke of Rutland.* London.

HMCS   Royal Commission on Historical Manuscripts. 1883–1976. *The Manuscripts of the Marquess of Salisbury.* London.

HMCSa   Royal Commission on Historical Manuscripts. 1940–66. *The Manuscripts of Major-General Lord Sackville.* London.

HN   Bateson, Edward, et al. Eds. 1893–1940. *A History of Northumberland.* Newcastle.

HP04   Thrush, Andrew and John P. Ferris. 2010. Eds. *The History of Parliament: The House of Commons, 1604–1629.* www.historyofparliamentonline.org/research

HP09   Bindoff, S. T. 1982. Ed. *The History of Parliament: The House of Commons, 1509–58.* www.historyofparliamentonline.org/research

HP58   Hasler, P. W. 1981. Ed. *The History of Parliament: The House of Commons, 1558–1603.* www.historyofparliamentonline.org/research

HR   Dendy, Frederick. 1901. Ed. *Extracts from the Records of the Company of Hostmen of Newcastle-upon-Tyne.* Surtees Society, 105.

Informations	'Informations. . .to William Drummond', in *The Cambridge Works of Ben Jonson*.
KE	Shaw, William Arthur. 1906. Ed. *The Knights of England*. 2 vols. London.
	King's Ent. Part of the King's Entertainment, in *The Cambridge Edition of the Works of Ben Jonson*.
LA	Lincolnshire Archives.
LIA	*The Records of the Honorable Society of Lincoln's Inn. Admissions*. 1896. Vol. I. London.
LJ	*Journal of the House of Lords*. Vol. II: *1578–1614*. www.british-history. ac.uk/
LMA	London Metropolitan Archives.
LP	Lambeth Palace Library.
MAR	Boyle, John and Frederick Dendy. 1895–9. Eds. *Extracts from the Records of the Merchant Adventurers of Newcastle-upon-Tyne*. 2 vols. Surtees Society, 93 and 101.
NA	Nottinghamshire Archives.
NCR	Copnall, H. H. 1915. Ed. *Nottinghamshire County Records of the 17th Century*. Nottingham.
NHA	Nichols, John. 1971. *The History and Antiquities of the County of Leicestershire*. 8 vols. Wakefield.
NLS	National Library of Scotland.
NP	Nichols, John. 1828. *The Progresses, Processions and Magnificent Festivities of King James the First*. 4 vols. London.
NRO	Northumberland Record Office.
NRS	National Records of Scotland.
ODNB	*Oxford Dictionary of National Biography*. www.oxforddnb.com
OED	*Oxford English Dictionary*. www.oed.com/
PA	Parliamentary Archives.
Pan's Ann.	*Pan's Anniversary*, in *The Cambridge Edition of the Works of Ben Jonson*.
PP	Taylor, John. 1619. *The Pennyles Pilgrimage*. London.
RCAHMS	Royal Commission on the Ancient and Historical Monuments of Scotland. www.rcahms.gov.uk/
REED Camb	Nelson, Alan. 1989. Ed. *Records of Early English Drama: Cambridge*. Toronto and London.
REED Ches	Clopper, Lawrence M. 1979. Ed. *Records of Early English Drama: Chester*. Toronto.

REED Cumb   Douglas, Audrey and Peter Greenfield. 1986. Eds. *Records of Early English Drama: Cumberland, Westmorland, Gloucestershire*. Toronto.

REED Lanc   George, David. 1991. Ed. *Records of Early English Drama: Lancashire*. Toronto and London.

REED Newc   Anderson, J. J. 1982. Ed. *Records of Early English Drama: Newcastle-upon-Tyne*. Toronto and Manchester.

RGI   Foster, Joseph. 1889. Ed. *Register of Admissions to Gray's Inn, 1521–1889*. London.

RIBA   Royal Institute of British Architects, Library Drawings Collection.

RMS   Thomson, J. M., P. J. Balfour, J. H. Stevenson and W. K. Dickson. 1882–1914. Eds. *The Register of the Great Seal of Scotland*. 11 vols. Edinburgh.

RPCS   Buron, J. and David Masson. 1877–98. Eds. *The Register of the Privy Council of Scotland, 1545–1625*. 14 vols. Edinburgh.

RPS   *Records of the Parliament of Scotland to 1707*. University of St Andrews. www.rps.ac.uk/

SA   Sheffield Archives.

SP   Paul, Sir James Balfour. 1904–14. Ed. *The Scots Peerage*. 9 vols. Edinburgh.

STS   Scottish Text Society.

Tilley   Tilley, Morris. 1950. *A Dictionary of the Proverbs in England in the Sixteenth and Seventeenth Centuries*. Michigan.

TNA   The National Archives, Kew.

TWRO   Tyne and Wear Record Office.

Und.   *The Underwood*, in *The Cambridge Edition of the Works of Ben Jonson*.

UNL   University of Nottingham Library.

VCHC   Elrington, C. R. and A. P. M. Wright. 1973 and 1978. Eds. *A History of the County of Cambridge and the Isle of Ely*. Vols. v and vi. Victoria County History. www.british-history.ac.uk/

VCHE   Powell, W. 1966. Ed. *A History of the County of Essex*. Vol. v. Victoria County History. www.british-history.ac.uk/

VCHHe   Page, William. 1912. Ed. *A History of the County of Hertford*. Vol. iii. Victoria County History. www.british-history.ac.uk/

VCHHu   Page, William, Granville Proby and S. Inskip Ladds. 1932 and 1936. Eds. *A History of the County of Huntingdon*. Vols. ii and iii. Victoria County History. www.british-history.ac.uk/

VCHM   Baker, T. and R. Pugh. 1976. Eds. *A History of the County of Middlesex*. Vol. v. Victoria County History. www.british-history.ac.uk/

VCHN	Page, William. 1906–10. *A History of the County of Nottingham.* 2 vols. Victoria County History. www.british-history.ac.uk/
VCHYC	Tillot, P. M. 1961. *A History of the County of York: The City of York.* Victoria County History. www.british-history.ac.uk/
VCHYER	Allison, K. J. 1969. Ed. *A History of the County of York, East Riding.* Vol. I. Victoria County History. www.british-history.ac.uk/
VCHYNR	Page, William. 1914 and 1923. *A History of the County of York North Riding.* 2 vols. Victoria County History. www.british-history.ac.uk/
WID	Greenwell, W. 1860. Ed. *Wills and Inventories from the Registry at Durham.* Vol. II. Surtees Society, 37. Wood, Herbert. 1929. Ed. *Wills and Inventories from the Registry at Durham.* Vol. IV. Surtees Society, 142.
WP	Cooper, J. P. 1973. Ed. *Wentworth Papers, 1597–1628.* London.
WR	Walker, John. 1948. *Walker Revised. Being a revision of John Walker's Sufferings of the Clergy during the Grand Rebellion, 1642–60.* Ed. A. G. Matthews. Oxford.
WSA	Wiltshire and Swindon Archives.
WYAB	West Yorkshire Archive Service, Bradford.
WYAL	West Yorkshire Archive Service, Leeds.
YAS	Yorkshire Archaeological Society, Leeds.
YG	Cliffe, J. T. 1969. *The Yorkshire Gentry from the Reformation to the Civil War.* London.
YML	York Minster Library.

INTRODUCTION:
JONSON'S 'FOOT VOYAGE' AND THE
ALDERSEY MANUSCRIPT

A discovery

Ben Jonson's walk from London to Edinburgh has caught the imagination and provoked the curiosity of many since it was first mooted in June 1617, a year before he set off. The journey itself was not the adventure it might have been before the Union of the Crowns, but that a celebrated and, frankly, weighty poet should choose to attempt it on foot was certainly remarkable. Most importantly, the expedition produced the encounter between Jonson and William Drummond recalled in the latter's notes of his guest's conversation and opinions, or 'informations'. The views, jests and anecdotes set down there illuminate Jonson's poetic principles, his views of his contemporaries, and the account he chose to give of himself. They are particularly beguiling for allowing us to imagine that we are hearing Jonson speak off the record, as it were, and that we can catch his conversational tone even through Drummond's editorial compressions and sometimes pursed lips. The *Informations* also provide us with glimpses of the journey itself, including Jonson's irritation at being followed – mocked, he thought – by Taylor, and his purchase of a pair of shoes at Darlington, which he 'minded to take back that far again' (ll.514–15). Such snippets have been combined with a sparse patchwork of other sources to build up an outline picture of Jonson's walk and his possible motives for undertaking it. We also know from Edinburgh records that Jonson was made a burgess of the city, and that a dinner was held there in his honour in September 1618. In his *Pennyles Pilgrimage* Taylor records meeting his fellow poet at the house of John Stewart in Leith, while Jonson's correspondence with Drummond and a dedication inscribed in a book presented to a Scots courtier reveal the names of some of his other hosts.[1] From such diverse and, in some cases, fragmentary sources, scholars such as David Masson, Ian Donaldson and

---

1 *CWBJ*, Letter (e), Letter 14; Knowles, 2006, 267; *CELM*, JnB 758.

James Knowles have crafted an intriguing picture of the king's poet, at the height of his fame, comfortably berthed in the capital of James's first realm in the autumn and winter of 1618–19.[2]

Such convincing critical accounts are all the more impressive given that we have always recognised that we ought to know rather more than we do. Among his notes on his guest's works, Drummond recorded that Jonson was planning 'to write his foot pilgrimage hither, and to call it *A Discovery*' (l.317). Unfortunately, this narrative does not survive, and may indeed never have been completed. Jonson must at least have had it in draft, however, since in his 'Execration Upon Vulcan' (*Und.* 43) he noted the loss of 'my journey into Scotland sung, / With all the adventures' (ll.94–5) in the 1623 desk fire that consumed some of his papers. This particular loss has become one of those gaps in the literary record that tantalise all the more for being so clearly labelled.

Unknown to scholars until recently, however, a record of the journey did survive the centuries, preserved from fire and other threats among the papers of the Aldersey family of Aldersey Hall in Cheshire.[3] These papers, now held in Cheshire Archives and Local Studies, include a manuscript containing a 7,000-word account entitled 'My Gossip Joh[n]son / his foot voyage / and myne into / Scotland', detailing Jonson's travels as far as his investiture as an Edinburgh burgess. Almost as surprising as the discovery of this account, though, is the fact that Jonson did not write it; it is instead the work of a previously unsuspected travelling companion. Influenced, perhaps, by the still-restless spectre of ungentle Ben, we have been used to thinking of Jonson journeying unaccompanied: 'I'm off to Scotland soon', he informs Shakespeare in Edward Bond's 1973 play *Bingo*; 'Walking. Alone. Well, no one would come with me.'[4] Solitariness has more reasonably been inferred from the absence of any references to a companion in the known sources. But they, by and large, fail to detail the journey, instead providing glimpses of Jonson's stay in Scotland. Until the 'Foot Voyage' account came to light, the only surviving pieces of evidence from the walk itself appeared to be a brief poetic exchange with a 'Mr Craven', recorded in a manuscript collection associated with William Cavendish, Duke of Newcastle, and another poem apparently presented to Jonson along the way, first noted by Mark Bland in 2004.[5]

2 Masson, 1893; Donaldson 1992; Knowles, 2006.
3 The discovery was first announced in Loxley, 2009.
4 Bond, 1974, 30.
5 Bland, 2004, 378 and 397.

The 'Foot Voyage', then, is undoubtedly a major addition not just to our knowledge of this episode but to our broader understanding of Jonson's life and the history of the period. Among much else, it can illuminate local and family histories all the way along the great north road, contribute information to the architectural history of buildings as far apart as Worksop Manor and Culross Abbey House, add significant detail to the industrial history of the English midlands and the Fife coast, shed light on the social and cultural practices of mobility and hospitality, and furnish us with informative sidelights on the high political dynamics of James VI and I's conjoined kingdoms. But it also raises a series of questions, some of which still remain unanswered, or at least open. Who was this companion? How did this account come to be written? What relation does it bear to Jonson's own writings and papers? How did this copy come to be kept among the papers of a Cheshire gentry family with no known connection to the leading writer of his age or his literary world?

In this introductory essay we focus on the manuscript witness, addressing the status of the surviving text, the provenance of the manuscript in which it is found, and – as far as is possible – the question of authorship, in order to provide a detailed context for our annotated edition of the 'Foot Voyage' itself. The three essays which follow the edited text invoke a more expansive notion of context, in an attempt to begin the process of assimilating the 'Foot Voyage' into our critical accounts of Jonson's life, writing and times. We certainly do not claim to have completed that process: there is no doubt much more to say, and much that we have overlooked. The fascinations of the walk persist, as they did, no doubt, for Jonson himself: this, perhaps, is why he came to speak of 'adventures', and of his journey as 'a discovery'. In the 'Foot Voyage' we find him unexpectedly sprung to life, startling us with discoveries of our own.

The manuscript and the account

The manuscript containing the account of the 'Foot Voyage' was deposited in the Record Office at Chester in 1985 by Mrs Beatrice Aldersey, as just one item in a large collection of papers ranging in date from the sixteenth to the twentieth centuries (ref. CR 469). This supplemented an earlier collection (ref. CR 69) deposited in March 1954 by Mrs Aldersey's late husband, Captain Ralph Aldersey. The Alderseys had for some generations been based at Aldersey Hall, just over 7 miles south-east of Chester, although the grand house itself had clearly become more of a burden than an asset by the early twentieth century; it had for a while been adapted for use as a horticultural college before being demolished some years after the end of the Second World War.[6]

The manuscript containing the 'Foot Voyage' account is in many ways an unremarkable document. It is an unpaginated, unfoliated quarto, 20.2cm by 15.5cm, bound presumably early in its history using a basic stitch along the fold. This binding remained intact until the manuscript was disbound for conservation in December 2012. Gatherings 1 and 8 are each formed from a sheet of paper watermarked with a single-handled, crowned pot, initialled 'I VA'; a sheet of paper from a stock with a watermark of very similar design, but different proportions and dimensions, was used in a letter to Nathaniel Bacon dated 30 January 1615.[7] The four leaves of the first quire are blank and still unopened, though substantially damaged, while the final leaf of the eighth has been reduced to a stub. Quires 2–7 are formed from sheets of a higher-quality paper with a Basel crozier, post horn and fleur de lis watermark, which also incorporates the letters R, G and D. The watermarks for sheets 2, 4 and 6 are close to identical in size, shape and positioning in the sheet; those of sheets 3, 5 and 7, however, while featuring the same elements, not only differ in the detail of proportion and arrangement but also show a pronounced stretching of the right-hand edge and a flattening of the lower section. In its undistorted portions, this watermark very closely resembles that of a paper stock used for a letter from John Hunt to Walter Bagot dated 6 September 1619.[8] Despite their differences, however, in both of the batches of this paper used in the Aldersey manuscript the G is contiguous with the framing shield, whereas in the Bagot letter it connects to the central crozier itself. Basel crozier watermarks of this sort are associated with paper manufactured in France as well as in Switzerland, and many with these elements originated with the Durand papermakers of western France.[9] Heawood judged paper with such watermarks to be 'much used in England, for both books and writing, between 1620 and 1650', although, as the Bagot letter shows, it was clearly available and in use before then.[10]

---

6 The copy of Bridgeman and Earwaker, 1899, acquired by the National Library of Scotland, contains, among other loosely inserted cuttings and letters relating to the family, a brochure for the horticultural college dating from 1931.

7 Now Folger MS L. d. 203.

8 Now Folger MS L. a. 544.

9 Gaudriault, 1995, 120–1.

10 Heawood, 1930, 273.

The persistence of a residual tie connecting the inner and outer bifolia of each gathering, evident when the manuscript was disbound in 2012, showed that the six sheets of Basel crozier paper were folded into individual quires and then opened, and that the arrangement of each quire was preserved by the scribe as he wrote. The outermost gatherings of pot paper were perhaps added at this point to act as makeshift boards, and the fact that some characters in the text are obscured by the rudimentary stitching applied to the manuscript confirms that this took place after the writer had done his work. It seems likely that the manuscript first circulated in this form, and a clear pattern of folding around the spine suggests that it was reasonably well read, or at least thumbed, by its early possessors.

The account of the walk begins with a title, 'My Gossip Iohson his Foot Voyage and Myne into Scotland', on 2.1, the first leaf of the second gathering (though the first of crozier paper), then continues over 18 leaves to 6.2v.[11] It is followed by some brief additional passages on 6.3, comprised of snatches of dialect, a jest and some supplementary notes on the properties of the healing well that the travellers visited at Pettycur in Fife (see 'Foot Voyage', Appendix 1). Leaf 6.3v is blank, then followed by 'Canesco or the sleu doggs Language', a carefully entitled and intriguing account of the commands used by masters of bloodhounds in the Scottish and English borders, on both sides of 6.4 (Appendix 2); this in turn is followed on 7.1 by antiquarian observations concerning two prominent events in York's ceremonial history and some heraldic details at the west door of the Minster there (Appendix 3). The single hand in which the account and these additional sections are written is assured and accomplished, with regular and consistent flourishes, while many of the proper names and some important, unusual or Latin words – 'Tomb', 'Epitaph', 'poetica licentia' – are written in full or in part in an elegant italic. Although there is no sign of the paper being ruled, and the neatness of the writing fluctuates somewhat, the text is for the most part consistently organised on the page. Spacing between lines is regular throughout; a wide left-hand, and negligible right-hand, margin are constant between 2.1 and 4.1v, after which a narrower left margin and slightly more generous right are consistently used. The use of catchwords, of customary contractions including 'lre' for 'letter', the relative infrequency of corrections or overwriting, and the recurrent deployment

---

11 As it is unpaginated and unfoliated, we have here assigned numbers to gatherings, and then to leaves within those gatherings, in accordance with the structure of the manuscript.

of line fillers also indicate the well-trained hand of a practised, quite probably professional, copyist.

Consistent with this interpretation, several instances of eyeskip, 'reverse' eyeskip and other transcription errors strongly suggest that the text of the 'Foot Voyage' preserved in the Aldersey manuscript is a fair copy; coupled with the evidence of the hand itself, this might reinforce the view that we are looking at a scribal rather than authorial rendering of the account. While other textual evidence is not completely conclusive, on balance it supports the former hypothesis. For example, the text includes some marginal and interlineal additions in the same hand that might at first appear to be authorial emendations. The three marginal notes, however, lack insertion points or carets in the main text, and so might instead be faithfully and scribally reproduced from a precedent version or copy in which they were already marginal. (In this edition we have incorporated them at an appropriate point into the main body of the text, while noting their original position in the collations.) Some of the interlineal additions clearly supply omissions made by the copyist, but while others are not inconsistent with the possibility of authorial intervention, they are also usually susceptible of other interpretations. On 2.4v, for example, a passage that concludes 'And carryed down the Markhams etc.' is followed by the abbreviated note, 'Mr Richardson, Mr Carnaby; m. & n. etc' (see modernised text, ll.136–7). This could plausibly be read either as an authorial addition, or the subsequent revision of a deliberate exclusion; however, it also makes sense as the scribal correction of an accidental omission. On only one occasion, in the appended 'Canesco', do we have strong evidence for our writer acting as more than a copyist. On 6.4, the ungrammatical phrase 'then he goeth pisses, or doeth his businesse' has been altered by erasures and interlineal additions to the somewhat less euphemistic, and still ungrammatical, 'then he goe pisse, and shitt' (modernised text, App. 2, l.3). Yet while such intervention might suggest an authorial hand at work, and is certainly more difficult to explain as a scribal correction of merely scribal error, it is also consistent with a scribe assuming, on this occasion, an editorial role. On its own, it provides insufficient support for the suggestion that the Aldersey manuscript contains a holograph copy of the 'Foot Voyage'. If further evidence were needed, we could point to errors in the surviving text that its author would surely have been unlikely to make – perhaps the most spectacular of these is the phrase 'Galeard of Maw' (modernised text, l.549), which substitutes an intriguing dance for John Gall or Gaw, laird of Maw.

There are other features of the text which indicate that it stands at some not easily definable distance from its original. For example, on 2.3v the insertion 'now Lord Mansfield' immediately follows the first mention of 'Sir William Candishe' (modernised text, ll.97–8). Since this is seamlessly included in the text as copied here, it would seem plausible that the phrase was added in a previous redaction of the text. Cavendish assumed this title in November 1620 and was elevated to the earldom of Newcastle in 1628, so we are clearly justified in saying that the version in the Aldersey manuscript dates from at least two, and perhaps as many as ten, years after the events it records. It is, in fact, most probably a copy of an intermediate version itself no older than late 1620. In addition to such an interpolation, the forty-eight separate instances on which the account resorts to 'etc', usually rendered 'ec', signal sometimes abrupt elisions. On 2.1, for example, while the travellers are in Hertfordshire, we meet 'Blitheman *Master* of Arte who *etc*' (modernised text, l.7), with no indication of what has here been omitted; on the road between Ayton and Cockburnspath, in southern Scotland, we learn that the travellers 'hired a guyde, having also Sir Will*iam's* man *with* vs and the king [./] *etc*' (modernised text, ll.490–91), which makes little sense unless 'king' here is a truncated possessive – the king's huntsman, or something similar. More usually, these elisions do not cut across syntax or sense in quite so disruptive a fashion, and can come to seem more like an authorial tic than indicators of significant cuts to the text; nonetheless, they are plentiful enough to suggest that a fuller or more extensive redaction stands behind the surviving account. It is not possible to say whether this is a faithful copy of an already abbreviated text, or one in which some abbreviation has been undertaken.

We can nevertheless offer some conjectures on the processes of its composition from the text as we have it. The 'Foot Voyage' is written almost entirely in the past tense and shows some signs of having been written up only after the journey itself had been completed. When, for example, the author declares 11 September 'the tediousest day's journey in the whole voyage' (ll.492–3), we might think that such a judgement could only be pronounced retrospectively, and would belong to a process of final composition postdating the events described. Yet such moments are few and far between, and even this instance might instead be read as a judgement formed in relation to his experience of the days between 8 July and 10 September, rather than from a position retrospective to the entire adventure. For the most part, the account's narratorial position is maintained at a close distance to the events related, concerned to capture the outline of what unfolded each day, without allowing itself a narratorial position removed from the daily sequence. It is, to that extent, a strongly paratactic piece of writing. At some of the more static moments, this sequence blurs: of the walkers' four-day stay in Newark we learn something about the company they kept, and that 'here were fireworks and bull-baiting' (l.87), but little of the order in which events occurred. The account of their visit to Belvoir is similarly affected, although this time the cause might have been a bout of illness suffered by the writer, for which treatment was subsequently sought at Newark. There is also a stark lacuna at York, when Jonson leaves his companion in their lodgings and accompanies Sir Arthur Ingram to Bishopthorpe – its protagonist absent, the narrative is for the most part suspended.

In its general adherence to chronological order, and the proximity of narrative standpoint to the daily rhythm of events, the 'Foot Voyage' is similar to other more or less unheralded travel writings of the era which were not printed at the time. Lexically, stylistically and in its choice of interests, it is perhaps closest to the surviving travel journals of Sir William Brereton, which record a journey undertaken through the Low Countries in 1634, and a voyage through northern England, Scotland and Ireland the following year.[12] Brereton was a Cheshire baronet, and at times his phrasings and tone are suggestively similar to those of the 'Foot Voyage' – his journal, too, for the most part, is 'a plain, unimpassioned statement of what he saw and observed'.[13] Both journals share some stylistic and grammatical irregularities, such as 'abrupt changes of construction'.[14] However, unlike the author of the 'Foot Voyage', Brereton is loquacious and detailed, while his judgements of Scotland tend to the severe.

Brereton's journals and the 'Foot Voyage' differ significantly both from well-known and other, more obscure accounts of domestic travel in the early seventeenth century – John Taylor's prose narratives, for example, or the 'Relation of a Short Survey of 26 Counties' undertaken by three members of 'the Military Company' at Norwich in the summer of 1634 – in their general lack of rhetorical self-consciousness.[15] The latter, for example, sports with the military metaphors licensed by its author's soldierly status. But, while rare, such rhetorical flourishes are not entirely absent from the writing of Jonson's companion. When he resorts to simile in describing the appearance of onlookers gazing down on the

---

12 *BT*; first identified as his by Edward Hawkins in his edition of 1844.
13 *BT*, vi.
14 *BT*, vi.
15 *AShS*; Chandler, 1999, is a useful modern anthology of Taylor's travel narratives.

poet's formal entry into Edinburgh – 'the windows also being full, everyone peeping out of a round hole like a head out of a pillory' (ll.527–8) – the use of a comically effective figurative ornament is all the more striking for its infrequency. (Compare, too, Brereton's more prosaic remarking of the 'boards' lining the fronts of houses on the High Street, 'wherein are round holes shaped to the proportion of men's heads'.)[16] Similarly, the stylistic élan and wry humour with which episodes of clerical drunkenness at Bottesford and Tollerton are recounted suggest a literary talent that is elsewhere suppressed or absent, and with which Taylor and the author of the 'Short Survey' are either better endowed or more liberal and confident in deploying.

For all its differences, the 'Short Survey' does offer an insight into how such travel journals were composed in its description of the three travellers taking notes in Lincoln, 'for feare our memories should beguile vs of our mornings sight'. As its editor remarks, 'appeal is frequently had to "day-notes,"…in case the reader should be dissatisfied with the information given in the completed work'.[17] Brereton's journals, too, include 'references to another book, which may have been the original journal, or possibly a different work altogether'.[18] It is reasonable to suppose that the author of the 'Foot Voyage' also relied on such aides-mémoire, and that the stylistic and syntactical irregularities it shares with Brereton's journal derive from a similarly unpolished compositional process. Given that they are mentioned in the narrative, both Brereton's and the military travellers' notes were intended for preservation, and there is some evidence that the same was true of the 'Foot Voyage'. The additional passages included in the Aldersey manuscript, clearly copied at the same time and presumably from the same or a closely related source, preserve observations and details from the journey which were not incorporated, or even drawn on, in the narrative itself. It was perhaps this supplementary quality that ensured their preservation: they show the diversity of what could catch the travellers' attention, and raise the question of exactly whose attention was being caught. As we have noted, the account is mostly silent on the companion's activities during Jonson's sojourn with the archbishop of York, Tobie Matthew, at Bishopthorpe, yet one of the appended passages consists substantially of details from York's history of archiepiscopal hospitality – it is perhaps probable that these were gleaned by the companion from his own sources, or from an unrecorded visit to the minster, but the possibility

16 *BT*, 102.
17 *AShS*, 8, xx.
18 *BT*, vi.

that Jonson himself garnered them from his learned and generous host
should not be ruled out. It is, in fact, this double perspective that truly sets
the 'Foot Voyage' apart from other journals of the time. It is a traveller's
tale, to be sure, but unusually it keeps a sustained focus on another
traveller rather than recounting, as its primary subject matter, the narra-
tor's own experiences and impressions of the places visited. Hence, perhaps, the relative paucity of local detail in the main account, and its relative
brevity – hence, too, its silence when Jonson leaves the picture at York and,
again, during the companion's final week in Edinburgh.

If the central presence of 'my gossip' serves to organise the account, the
picture of Jonson that emerges from it is nevertheless a product of the
companion's own emphases. It is striking how little attention is paid to
Jonson's conversations or to any 'informations' – to use Drummond's
term – that he might have imparted along the way. There are no direct
quotations, and only some fragments of reported speech. Jonson's comment on Sir William Cavendish's exceptional riding ability is the most
compelling of these, given its relation to *Und.* 53 (discussed below), but
otherwise we learn only of the occasional toast uttered: dining at Durham,
Jonson 'entreated that *poetica licentia* he might propose a health, which
was the king's' (ll.370–1), a repetition of a performance he had previously
given at Welbeck, and probably a version of the grace that survives in a
number of manuscript copies and is dated in one to 1618.[19]

Provenance

The 'Foot Voyage' account and additional passages are not the only
contents of the Aldersey manuscript. While leaves 7.2–7.3 are blank, 7.3v
to 8.3v, reversed, contain the first ten chapters from the book of Job written
out in the system of 'short writing' or 'tachygraphy' devised by Thomas
Shelton and published in a long succession of works and editions beginning in 1626. The notes from Job are initially written neatly and carefully
with ruled margins and title lines, longhand chapter headings and fully
numerated verses, although these features are omitted on later pages.
There are some idiosyncratic departures from Shelton's prescribed
forms, particularly concerning the placing of the tittle used to indicate a
plural 's': in the manuscript this is invariably inscribed to the left of the
word it is modifying, instead of to the right, hence enabling the use of a

19 *CWBJ*, 5.346–7.

tittle placed on the right of a word to denote a silent terminal 'e' – an apparently unique, but hardly helpful, adaptation. Some of the short forms for whole words in the biblical transcription, such as those for 'affliction', 'come' and 'one', for example, are found only in Shelton's later elaboration of his method, first published in his *Tachygraphy* in 1635, indicating that these lines were themselves written after 1635. In addition to the biblical verses, on both sides of 7.4 the writer has transcribed a version of the 'Table' for short forms of words that was first included in *Tachygraphy*, and frequently republished after that, corroborating the dating evidence to be derived from the biblical verses. Yet the writer also lapses into longhand for a few words on 8.3v, and his use there of a secretary 'h' suggests that this work was not undertaken much more than a few decades, perhaps only a few years, after its *terminus a quo*. The transcription of Job is then followed on the rest of 7.4 and 7.3v by a further short string of shorthand characters, and a final 15 lines of shorthand notes. All the shorthand verses and notes are penned in a different ink and hand from that in which the 'Foot Voyage' account is written. Crucially, too, they are spread across two gatherings – quire 8, one of the two binding sheets of pot paper, and the hitherto blank leaves of quire 7, which on its first leaf contains the last of the passages appended to the 'Foot Voyage'. And whereas the basic stitching has cut across some of the words of the latter, none of the shorthand text is obscured in this way.

The evidence marshalled so far suggests, therefore, that the Aldersey manuscript was created as a scribal separate containing the 'Foot Voyage' account and attendant passages, possibly consisting at first only of the twenty-four leaves on crozier paper in gatherings 2–7, although the enclosing sheets and stitching were presumably incorporated very soon after. The addition of the shorthand suggests that a seventeenth-century possessor reversed it, opened the eighth gathering, and began to use the hitherto unused 'binding' leaves of the manuscript for shorthand exercises, going beyond the sheet of pot paper and onto the leaves of crozier paper left blank in the seventh gathering by the 'Foot Voyage' scribe. From this, we can also deduce that this copy of the 'Foot Voyage' account, although produced as a reasonably high-quality scribal separate, sufficiently valued to be given the protection of a pot paper binding, and showing evidence of repeated early handling, came soon enough into the possession of someone who valued its blank leaves as much as, if not more than, its contents. While the evidence of damage by water, bookworms and mice suggests the manuscript was hardly prized thereafter, it was nevertheless preserved in the obscurity into which it had fallen.

This obscurity is not immediately dispelled by an examination of the collection of documents among which the 'Foot Voyage' manuscript was presumably kept, and with which it still remains. The bulk of both collections of Aldersey papers deposited at Chester had been calendared some decades prior to their division by J. P. Earwaker and C. G. O. Bridgeman for the extensive Appendix to the latter's *Genealogical Account of the Family of Aldersey of Aldersey and Spurstow Co. Chester*, privately published in 1899. The 'Foot Voyage' manuscript is not listed in the Appendix, but despite its extent this is clearly not a comprehensive catalogue of all items to be found in the family's papers. A manuscript containing the antiquarian William Aldersey's history of the mayors of Chester, for example, is described by Bridgeman in the course of his *Genealogical Account*,[20] but not listed in the calendar of family documents, and a number of the other items deposited in 1985, especially those only tangentially related to the history and genealogy of the Aldersey family, are similarly absent. Furthermore, the two deposits now at Cheshire Archives and Local Studies do not constitute the totality of the manuscripts accumulated by the family over the centuries. There are items calendared by Bridgeman and Earwaker, such as the Letters Patent granting the reversion of the Escheatorship of Cheshire to Thomas Aldersey (1600–75), which were not included among the items deposited in 1954 or 1985.[21] Twenty-seven books of sermon notes made, for the most part, by the son of this Thomas Aldersey (also called Thomas) in the latter half of the seventeenth century were sold at auction on 18 December 1986 and acquired by the Bodleian; they do not feature in Bridgeman and Earwaker.[22] It is possible that some of the manuscripts were neglected for parts of their history: while, as we have noted, the 'Foot Voyage' quarto suffered some minor damage, Mrs Aldersey suggested to David Mills that the manuscript containing the history of the mayors of Chester was rescued 'from a garden bonfire' by her father-in-law.[23]

In common with many similar collections, the Aldersey papers at Chester are largely an accumulated record of property transactions. Ranging across four centuries, they include the evidence of a great variety of such transactions, involving different generations and branches of this prominent Cheshire family, and other connections established by marriage over the years. The more personal papers

---

20 CALS, CR 469/542; see Bridgeman and Earwaker, 1899, 36.
21 Bridgeman and Earwaker, 1899, 135–6.
22 Now Bodl. MS Don. e. 155–63, ff.38–55. Cf. Sotheby's, 1986.
23 Mills, 1989, 10.

surviving from the sixteenth and seventeenth centuries, though, are focused on the lives and activities of the Alderseys of Bunbury and Spurstow, and most of the correspondence from this period belongs to this branch. The Thomas Aldersey responsible for the sermon notes features heavily in the letters preserved; he also left a spiritual meditation written in the professional hand of a scribe he employed elsewhere to write legal documents,[24] and a notebook – misleadingly calendared and catalogued as a commonplace book – containing what would appear to be his own somewhat pedestrian verse, the highlight of which is an acrostic in praise of Cromwell. Into the latter has been inserted a bifolium featuring a hitherto unrecorded copy of the text of Andrew Marvell's poem 'Clarendon's Housewarming' as it was printed in 1667, written in a precise and neat hand which is also used for fair copies of sermons in one of the Bodleian notebooks.[25]

There is little to connect the manuscript containing the 'Foot Voyage' with the other contents of the collection in which it is preserved – characteristic evidence of the circulating scribal separate.[26] It would nevertheless be reasonable to hypothesise that it owes its place in the collection to this man or his immediate family, even though the hand in which it is written bears no resemblance to any found elsewhere in the collection. A potentially significant detail is the use of the manuscript to write out biblical verses in shorthand. Two of the sermon notebooks are the work of a Flintshire clergyman and non-juror, Hugh Morris, who was rector of the parish of St Dunawd, Bangor Is-coed, for the brief period from 1687 until his exclusion in 1690.[27] One of these two note-books includes a fairly closely copied exposition of the system of short-hand first outlined in 1649 by Thomas Shelton in his *Zeiglographia, or a New Art of Short-Writing*,[28] his successor to the system outlined in *Short Writing* and *Tachygraphy*, and Morris uses shorthand characters in the sermons written out in both these notebooks. Some of Morris's sermons were preached at the church of St Mary the Virgin, Dudleston, in Shropshire, near Plas Yolyn and Cilhendre, the estates of the Edwards family in the seventeenth century;[29] Thomas Edwards of Cilhendre married Frances, Thomas Aldersey's aunt, in 1635, and surviving correspondence

24 'God's Mercies', CALS, CR 469/549; compare CALS, CR 469/289.
25 CALS, CR 469/546; Bodl. MS Don. f.53.
26 Heaton, 2010, 77.
27 Revd Susan Blagden, Rector, Bangor Monachorum, in private correspondence.
28 Bodl. MS Don. 162, ff.3–13.
29 See NLW, MSS 11430–81.

testifies to family connections both before and long after this alliance.[30] One of the Aldersey notebooks now in the Bodleian contains a dedication to 'Thomas Edwards', and the same name in both a secretary and an italic hand.[31] On the same leaf is written a string of shorthand characters, the letters 'a' to 'p' in the earlier, more popular Shelton system, and another of Thomas Aldersey's own notebooks shows him using the same system to take notes from sermons in 1661.[32] That the 'Foot Voyage' manuscript also demonstrates the devotional use of shorthand might, therefore, be imagined to account for its presence in the Aldersey papers, suggesting that this later Thomas Aldersey was behind its acquisition and preservation. However, the fragment of longhand on 8.1v of the Aldersey manuscript bears no resemblance to other examples of his writing; furthermore, the use of shorthand in the sermon notebook differs in several crucial respects from that in the Aldersey manuscript, featuring neither of the defining idiosyncrasies of the latter and forming a number of common words in a completely different way. There would appear to be no grounds for suggesting that this Thomas Aldersey is responsible for the repurposing of the Aldersey manuscript at some point after 1635; more broadly, such evidence cannot be used to identify the point at which the manuscript entered the family papers.

Further caution here is justified by the fact that some of the sixteenth- and seventeenth-century items in the Aldersey collections were clearly obtained many years later. A 1577 request for expenses from Thomas Shakespeare, messenger of the Queen's chamber, was acquired in 1792: it is endorsed 'This was given to Mr. Stokes by William Duncan, his hairdresser; who received it wrapt round some cheese or other necessary.'[33] Both the manuscript containing William Aldersey's history of the mayors of Chester and a sixteenth-century alphabetical list of knights' fees in Cheshire are endorsed 'J. Price Jes. Coll. Oxford', suggesting that they were once in the extensive antiquarian collections of John Price, a member of Jesus College from 1754 to 1783 and Bodley's Librarian from 1768 until his death in 1813; the endorsement matches other instances of his signature.[34] The contents of Price's own library were auctioned in 1814, and although they are not listed individually in the sale catalogue, it seems likely that these two items were incorporated into the Aldersey family

---

30 Bridgeman and Earwaker, 1899, Pedigree 1; NLW, MSS 11453E/132 and 11453C/255.

31 Bodl. MS Don. f.55, f.1.

32 Bodl. MS Don. f.42, ff.2–8.

33 CALS, CR 469/541.

34 CALS, CR 469/544; *ODNB*; Price's signature can be found on the title page of the copy of Alexander Luders' *Essay on the Use of the French Language* in the library of Trinity College, Oxford, call number U.3.11(3).

papers only after that date.[35] It is not impossible that the 'Foot Voyage' manuscript also entered the family collections as late as the nineteenth century, although the lack of any equivalent endorsement, and indeed of any signs of acquisition or intermediate ownership beyond the seventeenth-century shorthand notes, make it more likely that it came into the family's possession fairly early and remained undisturbed thereafter. To this extent, it is a quietly persistent anomaly, and its origins and earlier existence remain amenable only to conjecture. Nevertheless, the fact that it was preserved in this particular collection necessarily focuses attention on the collectors. If we cannot say precisely when and how it came into their hands, we can still explore the possible overlap between their world and the milieu in which a manuscript account of Jonson's walk to Edinburgh might be expected to circulate.

The Aldersey family

In the sixteenth and seventeenth centuries a number of branches of the Aldersey family were playing notable roles in the commercial and civic life of Chester, Cheshire and London. William Aldersey (c.1513–77) of Middle Aldersey served as MP for Chester in parliaments under Edward VI and Mary I; long involved in the government of Chester, he obtained a charter for the incorporation of the city's Merchant Adventurers, becoming the first master of the Company, and was elected mayor in 1560. His prominence in the city's political life was not without peril: he was later involved in disputes with his fellow aldermen over the extent of the respective jurisdictions between civic and county courts, and was even briefly disfranchised on two occasions.[36] Two of his sons, Fulk and John, also served as mayor of the city, in 1594 and 1603 respectively; John's son William was elected to the same honour in 1613.[37] William Aldersey of Picton and Chester was another mercantile member of the extended family who assumed a high civic role, being elected mayor in both 1595 and 1614; he was also a noted antiquary, particularly admired for his research into the history of Chester.[38]

Perhaps the most notable Aldersey of the later sixteenth century, however, was Thomas (1521/2–98), a younger son of the Bunbury and

---

35 T. King, 1814a; T. King, 1814b.
36 *HP09*; Barrett, 2009, 83–5.
37 Bridgeman and Earwaker, 1899, Pedigree 2.
38 *ODNB*, William Aldersey; Bridgeman and Earwaker, 1899, Pedigree 1; CALS, CR 469/542; Mills, 1989, 3.

Spurstow branch who moved to London and became a richly successful merchant and citizen, a prominent member of the Haberdashers' Company, and sat as an MP in 1572, 1584, 1586 and 1589. He acquired the rectory of Bunbury and endowed a grammar school there, run by the Haberdashers; by the terms of his will he left further money to support a preaching ministry in the parish, perhaps in an effort to counter the persistent recusancy for which the parish was then known, and which encompassed even his elder brother's heir, Randall Aldersey.[39] He was a client of the elder Cecil, a strong advocate for mercantile interests and a man with a godly interest in social reform.[40]

In 1554 Thomas Aldersey married Alice Calthorpe, whose brother was to serve a term as lord mayor of London in 1589.[41] The couple had no children, however, so he chose his nephew as his heir: not the recusant Randall, but his younger brother, John (c.1541–1616), who had been apprenticed to his uncle in London and was made free of the Haberdashers in 1568.[42] In 1574 John married Anne Lowe, whose brother, Thomas, had also been apprenticed to Thomas Aldersey and was made free of the Company in 1572.[43] John Aldersey prospered as a London merchant and his uncle's heir: by the first decade of the seventeenth century he had a residence in the parish of St Pancras, Soper Lane, and owned estates in Essex and Surrey.[44] His monument in St Mary's church, Oxted, records that he and his wife had seventeen children; seven – two sons and five daughters – were living when he made his will in January 1614.[45] Samuel, their eldest surviving son, was baptised at St Mary Magdalen, Milk Street, on 16 May 1581, and, like his father and great-uncle, became a successful merchant.[46] He was made free of the Haberdashers by patrimony in 1601 and spent the first decade of the seventeenth century trading as a merchant adventurer in Germany.[47] The five children he had with Mary van Oyrle, daughter of a merchant of

39 Wark, 1971, 84–5, 138–9; Calthrop, 1916, 23–6.
40 *ODNB*; *HP58*.
41 *ODNB*.
42 LMA, CLC/L/HA/C/007/MS15857/001, f.104v.
43 LMA, CLC/L/HA/C/007/MS15857/001, f.109v.
44 'Elizabeth Alderson' married William Pitchford at St Pancras on 24 March 1600, while her sister, Margaret, married Charles Hoskins in the same church on 20 April 1602; both women stood godmother at a baptism there in March 1604. 'Robert Bushe, servaunt vnto Mr John Aldersey' was buried in St Pancras on 5 June 1607. However, the family's links to the parish go back further: Alice Aldersey, wife of Thomas, was godmother at a christening held in 1583. See Bannerman, 1914–15, 140, 145, 295, 445–6. Rylands and Beazley, 1918, 10–11.
45 TNA, PROB 11/128/242.
46 Clarke, 1942, 21.
47 LMA, CLC/L/HA/C/007/MS15857/001, f.146v; PA, HL/PO/PB/1; *HMCSa*, 2.138–40, 143, 147, 153, 164–5, 181; Baumann, 1990, 328.

Nuremberg and Antwerp, were the subject of an act for naturalisation in 1628, the year of their mother's death.[48] In his later life he was one of the founders of the Massachusetts Bay Company and acted as Treasurer for the Feoffees of Impropriations, a company of the godly aiming to acquire church livings in pursuit of their ideal of an effective preaching ministry.[49] His second wife was the sister of Charles Offspring, rector of St Antholin's and a leading clerical member of the Feoffees, and the widow of Daniel Elliott, a Merchant Taylor and one of the scheme's prominent supporters; Aldersey's daughter, Anne, married Robert Eyre, son of another of the group's members.[50]

Samuel's surviving sisters, meanwhile, married into the London and home counties gentry. Elizabeth became the wife of Thomas Coventry in 1610, after the death of her first husband, William Pitchford; in a hagiography of Coventry she is described as 'a citizen's widow, beautifull rich yong and of good fame'.[51] Dorothy's first husband was Sir Thomas Hoskins of Oxted, and her second Sir Henry Capel of Hadham, Hertfordshire.[52] Margaret married another Hoskins, Charles, while Mary was first married to Thomas Westrowe, a grocer and an alderman, subsequently to Sir Norton Knatchbull of Kent and finally to Sir Edward Scott of Scott's Hall, also in Kent.[53] At Samuel's death in 1633, the family's civic importance was acknowledged in a suitably grand funeral procession 'from Haberdasher Hall to St Stephens Church in Coleman streete on Thursday the 25th of July': among the mourners were Coventry, by now the Lord Keeper, aldermen, divines and physicians, as well as 'poore men in gownes 2 and 2 to the number of 106'.[54] He was buried in the chancel of St Stephen's, the church of a notably godly parish, 'his Hatchments and Ensignes proper to his name and estate hanging over him'.[55]

By the 1630s, then, the Alderseys of Bunbury and Spurstow had established a prominent place for themselves in the mercantile and civic life of the capital, and were reaping the social rewards. At the same time, the family circuits connecting London merchants and Cheshire gentry were reinforced by participation in the life of the universities and Inns of Court. John Aldersey and his son-in-law, Sir

48 ODNB, Anne Eyre; PA, HL/PO/PB/1.
49 Calder, 1934, 13; Calder, 1957, 30, 54 and 79; Grell, 2011, 290–2.
50 Calder, 1957, xiv; Bridgeman and Earwaker, 1899, Pedigree 1; CCED, Person ID 44534; ODNB, Anne Eyre.
51 See note 44 above; ODNB, Thomas Coventry; BL, MS Stowe 619, f.54v.
52 Bridgeman and Earwaker, 1899, Pedigree 1.
53 See note 44 above; Bridgeman and Earwaker, 1899, Pedigree 1; HP04; Rylands and Beazley, 1918, 11.
54 BL, MS Add 71131J.
55 Stow, 1633, 869.

Thomas Hoskins, were specially admitted to the Middle Temple in 1607, 'by the assent of Mr Jermy, Reader, and other Masters of the Bench'.[56] Samuel's younger brother, William, matriculated as a pensioner from St John's, Cambridge, in 1612, took his BA at Trinity in 1615–16, became a Fellow in 1618 and was awarded his MA the following year. In 1622, Thomas Aldersey (1600–75) – grandson of Randall, and heir to the Bunbury and Spurstow estate – was enrolled at Gray's Inn; he had been admitted as a pensioner to Queens' College, Cambridge, in 1619, and studied there alongside his cousin, Charles Hoskins the younger, son of Sir Thomas and Dorothy.[57] It would appear that he and his younger brother, another John (1605–56), subsequently capitalised on the family connection to the Lord Keeper, residing in Coventry's London house during the later 1620s and early 1630s, while Thomas, perhaps with Coventry's assistance, secured a reversion of the Escheatorship of Cheshire in 1629.[58] Thomas's son, heir and namesake, born in 1635, attended Oxford – where he began the practice of making the sermon notes now held in the Bodleian – before moving to Gray's Inn to start a career in the law; he was called to the bar in 1663.[59]

The Aldersey family's involvement in the central institutions of early Stuart England provides several possible points of contact with the circles in which Ben Jonson moved and thrived. Their increasing immersion in the life of the Inns of Court, for example, must have brought them during Jonson's later years into contact with many of his friends and connections, as must their growing proximity – via Thomas Coventry – to the hinterland of the royal court. At the same time, Jonson's sustained relationship with London's civic institutions, as Bricklayer, citizen, poet and chronologer, would allow for association in that area. On one occasion, the connection becomes temptingly close. In 1604, Jonson was contracted by the Haberdashers' Company to provide some now lost speeches for the lord mayor's pageant. Since Anthony Munday also received payment 'for his paines', it has been suggested that Jonson displaced him as writer of the entertainment.[60] Interestingly, Jonson's speeches were spoken to celebrate the mayoralty of Sir Thomas Lowe, John Aldersey's brother-in-law – there is, though, no evidence in the surviving records to suggest that the commission either brought Jonson

56 Martin, 1904–5, 2.475. A 'John Alderson, gen.' was admitted to Lincoln's Inn in 1595, although this might not be a reference to Aldersey: Lincoln's Inn, 1896, 119.
57 RGI, 166; AC.
58 CALS, CR 469/379–80; Bridgeman and Earwaker, 1899, 135–6.
59 Fletcher, 1901, 445.
60 CWBJ, 2.499–500; Robertson and Gordon, 1954, 64.

and the Alderseys into direct contact, or arose from an already existing relationship.[61] One might anyway imagine that the family's predominant religious sympathies over several generations – Randall Aldersey's recusancy notwithstanding – would have made a friendship between them and Jonson somewhat unlikely, but this is not necessarily an entirely dependable assumption.

The North Wales connection

Such shared circles mitigate the distance between Jonson's London and the Cheshire of the Aldersey family. However, it is also possible to trace a more concrete, though still at several points conjectural, association. As Mark Bland has detailed, Jonson had a strong connection early in his career to several individuals and families from North Wales, including Sir John Salusbury of Lleweni, Sir Edward Herbert and Hugh Holland. These relationships can be attested not only through Jonson's own writings (see, for example, *Epigr.* 106, 'To Sir Edward Herbert', and the 'Ode ᾽Αλλεγωρικη' prefaced to Holland's *Pancharis* of 1603), but also through such evidence as Holland's commendatory poem for the 1605 quarto of *Sejanus* and Jonson's autograph copy of his 'Ode to James, Earl of Desmond', which survives in a folio manuscript once owned by Sir John Salusbury.[62] As Bland stresses, these circles also took in other families apparently without a demonstrable or direct connection to Jonson, especially the Thelwalls of Plas Y Ward and Bathafarn. Edward Thelwall of Plas Y Ward hosted Edward Herbert during the latter's unsuccessful attempt to learn Welsh at the beginning of the 1590s, and married, as his third wife, the mother of John Salusbury (he was her fourth husband).[63] In the preceding generation Simon Thelwall, Edward's father, had married into a junior branch of the Salusbury family, thus cementing the connection that his son's marriage reaffirmed.[64]

But Jonson's link with this North Wales milieu extended beyond the last years of Tudor rule, as Bland notes.[65] Holland, the Salusburys and

---

61 Unsurprisingly, close links between the families were maintained: the register of St Pancras, Soper Lane, records that Sir Thomas Lowe stood godfather for Thomas, son of Sir Thomas Hoskins and Dorothy Aldersey, in March 1606, while Margaret Hoskins acted as godmother (Bannerman, 1914–15, 146).
62 Bland, 2000, 44–8; *CWBJ*, 2.413.
63 *ODNB*, Edward Herbert; Woudhuysen, 1996, 319; *HP04*; Bland, 2000, 48, 52, 54.
64 *HP58*.
65 Bland, 2000, 57, 78.

the Herberts were lifelong connections, and we find the Thelwalls re-
entering the picture later, too. Most notably, when Sir Henry Herbert
secured a reversion of the Mastership of the Revels in 1629 – behind
Jonson in the queue for the formal position, but nevertheless a role he
had been exercising in practice since 1623 – he did so in a partnership
with one Simon Thelwall. This man has proved somewhat elusive, and
attempts to identify him have not been helped by the fact that there were
at the time – as Gerald Aylmer ruefully recorded in a different connection – at least four men of this name from Denbighshire families.[66] An
equal hindrance has been a widespread tendency to conflate, in part, the
Plas Y Ward and Bathafarn Thelwalls, and make brothers of men who
were in fact cousins in the expansive early modern sense of the word.[67]
N. W. Bawcutt has convincingly suggested that the likeliest candidate
here is a younger relative of Simon Thelwall, seventh son of John Wynn
Thelwall of Bathafarn. This Simon, born around 1561, was a lawyer,
proctor of the court of arches and MP for Denbigh Boroughs in 1593;
he married Ann Biggs of Woodford in Essex and settled there, thus
becoming neighbour, late in life, to Henry Herbert. Some of his brothers
were well connected, with the most prominent, Eubule Thelwall
(c.1557–1630), attending Westminster, taking degrees from Cambridge
and Oxford, and then joining Gray's Inn at the age of 30 to pursue a
swiftly successful legal career. He was knighted in 1619 and became
president of Jesus College, Oxford, in 1621.[68] Another brother, Bevis,
was 'sometimes a mercer, than a page of the bedchamber, and now a
knight', as Chamberlain put it in 1623.[69] By the end of James's reign Sir
Bevis was clerk of the great wardrobe, and a fourth brother, Ambrose –
whose name reflects the family's patronage connection to the
Elizabethan earl of Warwick and his countess, Anne Dudley – appears
to have been a yeoman of the robes, so the Bathafarn Thelwalls were
perhaps well placed to acquire further courtly offices.[70] Yet, as Bawcutt
notes, this Simon could not have been Herbert's partner in the Revels,
since the man concerned was named in post-1660 legal disputes over the
control of the London theatre; even one of the notably long-lived
Thelwalls would have been unlikely to have managed a century.[71] In
fact, his will reveals that Simon of Woodford died in 1630, but he had a

66 Aylmer, 1961, 255.
67 See Bland, 2000, 54; Woudhuysen, 1996, 319; Bawcutt, 1996, 37.
68 *ODNB*, HP04.
69 *CL*, 2.535.
70 TNA, LC 2/6, ff.21, 45, 50; *ODNB*, Sir Eubule Thelwall.
71 Bawcutt, 1996, 37.

namesake nephew, the younger son of his brother Richard, of Llanbedr Hall, a mile from Bathafarn.[72] This Simon was probably born around 1601; he may have studied at Oxford before being admitted to Gray's Inn in 1619, two years after his cousin Daniel, Richard's son and heir.[73] Treasury books indicate that both Herbert and Thelwall were the subjects of money warrants in connection with the Mastership of the Revels as late as 1671; while the younger Simon's date of death is as yet unknown, rival candidates from the Plas Y Ward branch – Edward's son and great-grandson – appear to have died in the 1650s and 1660s.[74]

The identification of this man with Henry Herbert's partner is of particular significance here because of an intriguing letter written on 22 August 1637 by Simon Thelwall of Gray's Inn to a relation in North Wales. The letter is preserved in the Rhual manuscripts at Flintshire Record Office and was calendared, along with the rest of the correspondence in this collection, by B. E. Howells. It has also been cited by Mark Bland, although he mistakenly attributes it to Edward Thelwall.[75] Among other pieces of news and family business, the writer informs his addressee that 'your ould freind Ben Iohnson the poet died at westminster one friday last'.[76] If this Simon were indeed the joint holder of the reversion of the Mastership of the Revels with Herbert, then the news of Jonson's death would have been of significant personal relevance, as the poet's reversion had priority over their own. Yet it is just as significant that Thelwall should identify his correspondent as an old friend of Jonson, because this is not someone whom we would otherwise have reason to associate with him.

Thelwall's letter was addressed to Evan Edwards, a gentleman of some means living at Rhual, near Mold, and perhaps then engaged in building the handsome house still standing there. Edwards was born around 1594, the eldest son of Thomas ap Edward and his wife Alice, and his own brief autobiography gives a concise précis of his career:

> Evan their eldest sonne was att the age of 17 putt to be a Clerke in the Exchequiour att Chester, att the age of 19 he was prefered to Sir Euble Thelwall [by him admitted of] Graies Inn where he contynued till he was 22 & then was preferd to be secretary to Richard Earle of Dorset where he contynued [14 yeres] while the Earle lived: After abou[.] his age of 35 he was

---

72 TNA, PROB 11/158/322, 11/158/357; HP04.
73 AO; RGI, 142, 146.
74 Shaw, 1908, 901; Griffith, 1914, 274.
75 Howells, 1967, 222–3; Bland, 2004, 398.
76 FRO, MS Rhual D/HE/457.

made Baron of the Exch of Chester by <the> K. Ch. his Letters patente Anno Cha. Primo.[77]

Some details are perhaps passed over here, as Edwards was admitted to Gray's Inn for a second time in August 1619, on the same day as the son of Bevis Thelwall, and he also seems to have sat for Camelford in the Sackville interest in the parliament of 1627.[78] His connection to the Thelwalls and, indirectly, to the Herberts, was further reinforced by his marriage in May 1620 to Joan, daughter of Simon Thelwall of Woodford. With her he had six children, three of whom were baptised at Woodford between 1627 and 1630; three of Sir Henry Herbert's children were also christened in the same church between May 1626 and December 1628.[79] Edwards' eldest son, Thomas, was born and baptised at Blackfriars in April 1625, with Sir Bevis Thelwall and the elder Simon Thelwall named as godfathers.[80] Edwards clearly spent some time at Gray's Inn as late as 1630, as a letter addressed to him at Sir Eubule Thelwall's lodgings at the inn demonstrates.[81] The connection was sustained once he left London and its environs for Flintshire, with his brother-in-law, Daniel Thelwall, promising in March 1633:

> I liue so retiredly at woodford that my life may be very well compared to yours but that you liue farther of, & my cosen Simon is the only constant newes-monger, but when I heare anythinge worthy the communicatinge vnto you I shall let you know it.[82]

Edwards' house at Rhual, moreover, was a mere 5 and 6 miles, respectively, from the Thelwall estates at Bathafarn and Llanbedr Hall.

How, then, might this Flintshire gentleman have become an 'old friend' of Ben Jonson? Clearly, Edwards' long-standing and intimate connection with the Thelwalls, and their link in turn with the Salusburys and the Herberts, might be thought to provide enough of a route. Edwards' important place in the household of the earls of Dorset, however, is most likely relevant here too. Despite the implication of the awkward phrasing in his autobiographical note, Edwards in fact served both the third earl, Richard Sackville, who rewarded him with a bequest of £100 in his will, and Richard's brother Edward, who succeeded to the

---

77 FRO, MS Rhual D/HE/658. Edwards writes of himself in the third person.
78 *RGI*, 156; *HP04*; see also MS Rhual D/HE/666, which includes this detail in a brief biographical note written after Edwards' death.
79 FRO, MS Rhual D/HE/658; Bawcutt, 1996, 6.
80 FRO, MS Rhual D/HE/658; *HP04*.
81 FRO, MS Rhual D/HE/742.
82 FRO, MS Rhual D/HE/455.

earldom in 1624.[83] According to Daniel Thelwall, Sir John Sackville, cousin and retainer to both earls, still maintained a friendly interest in Edwards in 1637; as late as 1657, when he was in severe financial difficulties, Edwards hoped his former service to the family might be enough to solicit assistance from the third earl's erstwhile countess, Lady Anne Clifford. (He was to be disappointed.)[84] Jonson addressed the fourth earl, before his elevation, in a fine poem of thanks (*Und.* 13), so it is plausible that he met and befriended Edwards when he too joined the network of Sackville clients. There is certainly evidence to suggest that another of the poet's friendships may have begun in this milieu, although it is usually traced to Oxford: Brian Duppa, who was to edit the celebrated volume of elegies, *Jonsonus Virbius*, in 1638, served as chaplain to the third earl of Dorset in the late 1610s and early 1620s, received books as gifts from him and derived his first two livings from a stipulation in the earl's will.[85] The inclusion in *Jonsonus Virbius* of an elegy by Lord Buckhurst, the fourth earl's son and heir, would seem to be an acknowledgement of both Duppa's and Jonson's links to the family.[86] Certainly, Duppa and Edwards were well known to each other: in the third earl's lifetime they were seated among the senior servants at the parlour table when the Knole household dined, while Edwards' papers preserve two letters from Duppa addressing him as his 'worthy friend', and asking him to intercede with the earl on his behalf.[87] These letters most probably date from 1618 and 1630, indicating too that theirs was no shortlived acquaintance.[88]

Evan Edwards, then, links the North Wales gentry with whom Jonson was acquainted and the Sackville circles within which he also moved. But

83 ESRO, SAS-RF/12/38, and see Sackville documents witnessed by Evans and dated 1624 and 1625; ESRO, SAS-RF/12/41, SAS/G23/8 and SAS-M/1/234.
84 FRO, MS Rhual D/HE/458, D/HE/477. Edwards is twice mentioned by name in Clifford's 'Knole Diary', once in connection with a disturbance at Appleby in August 1616, and again in passing in an entry for February 1617 (see Clifford, 2003, 42 and 51). Although at least one other man of the same surname was to be found among the lower ranks of the third earl's retainers, the secretary is undoubtedly the person meant.
85 Donaldson, 2011, 354–5; Bodl. MS Rawl. D 1386, f.204; ESRO, SAS-RF/12/38. Some modern biographers erroneously suggest that Duppa's patronage by the Sackville family began with the fourth earl, or only in the later 1620s; see, e.g., *ODNB* and Isham, 1951, xx–xxi.
86 Duppa, 1638, 10.
87 Sutton, 1902, 225; Heal, 1990, 161–2; FRO, MS Rhual D/HE/741–2.
88 FRO, MS Rhual D/HE/741–2. The later letter is written from Christ Church and dated 29 November, but no year is given. However, Duppa's discussion of Donne's ultimately mortal illness and the possible distribution of his clerical offices suggests that it was penned in the winter of 1630. The portion of the earlier letter on which the date has been written is damaged, but close inspection suggests either 1618 or 1628; since it is also endorsed 'Mr Duppa', and the cleric received his DD in 1625, the earlier date is more likely.

at what point in their careers did the paths of Jonson and Dorset's secretary coincide? It is possible that Edwards was among the 'Company at Dorset House' who escorted the earl to court to see *The Golden Age Restored* on 1 January 1616, although this would not, of course, indicate any personal connection with the masque's author.[89] For Simon Thelwall, writing in 1637, Jonson is Edwards' old friend, suggesting that any bond would date from the 1620s at the latest. Jonson's 'Epistle to Sir Edward Sackville' has been dated by its most recent editor to the early 1620s, which might be taken to suggest that Jonson's connection with the family and its household officers was then either fresh or at its strongest.[90] This period coincides with Evan Edwards' deepest involvement with the Sackvilles, and with Duppa's greatest dependence on the family's patronage. It also overlaps the period in which the surviving copy of the 'Foot Voyage' was written, and – given that the manuscript is probably a scribal separate – was most likely in limited circulation. It would not stretch the bounds of speculation too far to suggest that a copy or two came into Sackville circles, and that one was kept by Jonson's Flintshire friend. Given this date range we could also tentatively ask whether the characters who populate the antimasque hastily rewritten for performance in February 1618 might not owe something to the Welsh Inns of Court circles with which Edwards was connected – one of these figures, after all, is a Welsh attorney named Evan.

No evidence has yet been found of a direct link between Edwards or his Thelwall relatives and the Aldersey family among whose papers the manuscript containing the 'Foot Voyage' eventually came to rest, although there undoubtedly would have been contact. As we have seen, Thomas Aldersey, the Bunbury and Spurstow heir, attended Gray's Inn in the early 1620s, while his son of the same name, who accumulated the bulk of the seventeenth-century papers in the collection, was admitted in 1654 and made his legal career there.[91] Throughout this period, the Bathafarn, Llanbedr and Woodford Thelwalls were a permanent fixture at the Inn. Yet any interaction need not have occurred only in London. As his autobiographical notes relate, Edwards secured a reversion of the post of Baron of the Exchequer at Chester in the first year of Charles's reign, and he had returned to Rhual – itself only 11 miles

89 Clifford, 2003, 29.
90 *CWBJ*, 7.107.
91 *RGI*, 269.

west of the city – to take up this role by 1633.[92] Around the same time, Thomas Aldersey returned home to become, eventually, Escheator of Cheshire, and it is more than plausible to imagine their lives, in these palatinate offices, intertwining. What is more, Evan Edwards' younger brother, William, was a Chester merchant, serving as alderman, sheriff and mayor for the city from the 1620s to the 1640s.[93] The brothers owned a 'faire house' on Foregate, named – interestingly enough – 'the Globe'; in his civic role, William Edwards hosted John Taylor at Chester during the water poet's 1639 journey through the midlands to Norfolk and the north of England, and was thanked in the ensuing pamphlet for the 'good and friendly entertainment' he provided.[94] Unlike his brother, whose actions as a commissioner of array at the outset of the civil wars led to his financial troubles, William Edwards was more sympathetic to the godly and parliamentarian cause, serving as a recruiter MP for Chester and helping to secure a relatively mild composition settlement for his brother, although he was subsequently excluded in Pride's Purge.[95] Throughout William's career, members of the extended Aldersey family maintained their presence, too, in Chester's civic life, coming into regular contact and, indeed, occasional dispute, with him.[96] If the county roles of Escheator and Baron of the Exchequer undertaken by their respective heads did not foster communication between the families, their joint participation in Chester's civic life certainly did. Here too, then, we have a variety of routes along which the manuscript account of Jonson's 'Foot Voyage' might have travelled. It is worth noting, though, that tracing such routes would still leave us needing to find a place in the history of the manuscript's transmission for the addition of the shorthand biblical verses, which cannot be securely associated with any of the Alderseys or, indeed, any other potential agent in this process.

Jonson and the Aldersey manuscript

Much of the preceding discussion has assumed that this third person narrative of his grand walk was initially of interest to, and circulated among, Jonson's own network of friends, patrons, followers and acquaintances, and that one copy, at least, emerged from those circles

92 FRO, D/HE/658, D/HE/455; *HP04*.
93 CALS, CR 469/542.
94 J. Taylor, 1639, 28; CALS, ZA/F/34/29, ZCHB/3, ff.161–2.
95 *HP04*.
96 TNA, CHES 14/52, ff.4v, 7.

to find an eventual home in Cheshire. It might be objected, however, that the processes of editing, copying, circulation and preservation which have left the surviving artefact where it now is could have gone on independently of any such network, and that the writer's intimacy with Jonson need not have extended even to a subset of the poet's many contacts. If this was the case, it would be pointless to plot plausible channels along which the manuscript might have been passed between Jonson's immediate circle and the Alderseys. However, the assumption of an origin within Jonson's orbit for the account is not unreasonable, nor obviously unwarranted. Who more than such people would have a direct interest in the details of the expedition? And from where did Jonson's companion, the account's author, come, if not such a network?

There is also some further, though far from robust, evidence that might be cited in support of the hypothesis of a Jonsonian origin. The hand in which the surviving copy of the account is written, as we have said, is accomplished, and probably professional; it provides some of the evidentiary support for the suggestion that the manuscript is a scribal separate. It is also a fairly distinctive hand, featuring as it does some relatively unusual features. Most prominent among these is the consistent use of an elaborate, leftward-curling, often looped, otiose initial stroke for the letters 'w' and 'v'. These flourishes are at their most expansive in obviously majuscule forms, but they are clearly apparent throughout (Figure 1). Interestingly, such distinctive forms are also deployed in a very well-known presentation manuscript of *The Masque of Blackness*, now in the British Library, which Jonson has signed but is otherwise in the hand of an unknown amanuensis (Figure 2).[97] There are in fact a number of consistent similarities between the two hands, encompassing the obvious – and potentially misleading – areas of letter forms and ligatures and the less immediate aspects of proportion, spacing and the spatial relationship to each other of adjacent letters. Such a range of similarities might encourage us to the view that the same scribe was responsible for both texts, were significant differences between the hands not also evident. At a basic level, the hand of the Aldersey manuscript is looser than that of *Blackness*, and shows greater variety within its secretary script – a change in slant at the beginning of the final paragraph, for example, is visible on the page image reproduced here, suggesting perhaps that the scribe rested briefly between penning these two paragraphs, and was not overly concerned to ensure complete

97 BL, MS Royal 17B xxxi.

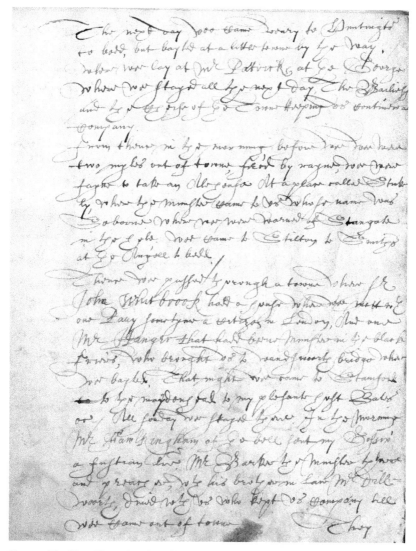

Figure 1 The 'Foot Voyage' in the Aldersey manuscript, CALS, CR 469/550, showing 2.2v.
© Cheshire Archives and Local Studies and the depositor.

consistency of appearance between them once he resumed his task. It is
also a noticeably more mixed hand than that of *Blackness*, using a greater
number of italic forms more often. There are some striking and, at first
glance, absolute differences: as can be seen in the page images

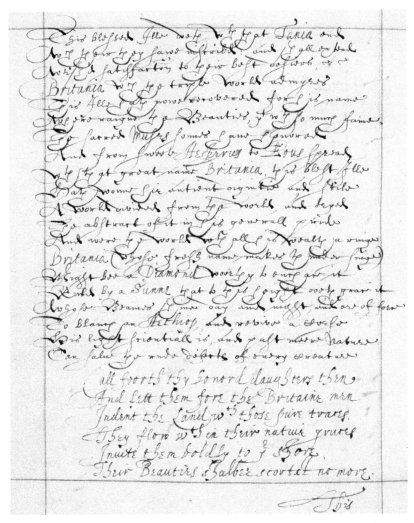

Figure 2 *The Masque of Blackness* presentation manuscript, BL, MS Royal 17B xxxi, showing f.6v. © British Library Board.

reproduced here, for example, the descender on the medial and final minuscule 'y' of the *Blackness* scribe curls to the left, looping only if forming a ligature, whereas the equivalent stroke in the Aldersey manuscript lacks any such curl, and if anything arches slightly to the right, although it too loops if beginning a ligature. The initial 'y' used by the writer of *Blackness* sometimes has a flourish to the left on the first stroke, as in the distinctive 'w' and 'v' forms shared by both, and a pronounced leftwards, then rightwards, loop on the descender, whereas the 'Foot Voyage' scribe uses a consistently italic form for initial 'y' without any kind of flourish and with a simple leftward loop. Similarly, a clear difference in the writing of minuscule secretary 'h' can be seen: in the *Blackness* manuscript the letter is often formed with a particularly rounded lower arc, whereas in the Aldersey manuscript this is usually flattened, or directed downward, and the angle between it and the stem of the letter is correspondingly larger. On occasion, the upper part of the arc is almost continuous with the stem. Such differences might be enough to rule out the possibility that the same scribe was responsible for both pieces of writing.

The problem for any such conclusion, however, is that none of the differences are as absolute as they at first appear. For example, the curling descender on the medial and final 'y' of *Blackness* is also found, on occasion, in the Aldersey manuscript, and the initial italic 'y' characteristic of the latter is found on at least one occasion (f.7v, final line, 'your') in the former. The more relaxed, less geometrically precise arc on the secretary 'h' found in the Aldersey manuscript also features, on occasion, in the *Blackness* hand (Figure 2, 'light', 8 lines up), while the more careful forms that predominate in the latter have their equivalents in the former (Figure 1, 'the', l.5). The picture is further complicated by the evidence presented by another manuscript containing a copy of a Jonson poem written in a similar hand. The likeness between the presentation manuscript of *Blackness* and the scribal copy of Jonson's commendatory poem for Thomas Palmer's *The Sprite of Trees and Herbs* was first pointed out by Percy Simpson in an article of 1895 and mentioned in the subsequent Oxford edition of Jonson's *Works*, but has not been the subject of further scholarly attention; the resemblances are indeed strong, and the suggestion that the same scribe was responsible for both appears sound.[98] There are, though, some significant differences between the hands – most strikingly, the formation of 'sl' and 'st' ligatures. But if such differences can occur within the same hand across these two manuscripts – and if they are, in that case, evidence of a single scribe's flexibility and capability – then might the differences between *Blackness* and the Aldersey manuscript be similarly interpreted?

It is not easy, perhaps not even possible, to settle such a question on the available evidence. The presumption of identity between the hand of

---

98 The manuscript of Palmer's treatise is BL, MS Add 18040; Jonson's poem occurs on f.10. See Simpson, 1895, 243–4; *H&S*, 11.125.

the Palmer manuscript and that of *Blackness* depends on the balance of similarities and dissimilarities, which can itself be more easily assessed given the fact that these are both presentation copies of works by Jonson and can be dated to within seven years of each other.[99] By contrast, at least sixteen years separate *Blackness* and the Aldersey manuscript, and the latter does not have the features typical of a presentation copy; it is also, of course, not a work by Jonson. Consequently, the significance of likenesses and differences between them becomes harder to assess. So although we might reasonably entertain the possibility that the same scribe was responsible for both, we should do so only with the fragility of the evidence for such a view duly acknowledged.

The thought, nonetheless, gives rise to possible implications. It might support the view that the Aldersey manuscript emerged from Jonson's milieu, or suggest that Jonson himself knew the 'Foot Voyage' text and was even in some way involved in the production of this and perhaps other copies. If either of these latter possibilities were the case, then a rather striking moment in the account, noted above, might appear especially significant. One morning with the Cavendishes at Welbeck, we are told, 'Sir William rid his great horse, which he did with that readiness and steadiness, as my gossip say they were both one piece' (ll.197–8). This directly parallels Jonson's own rather more erudite and elegant recollection of the moment, as it appears in *Und.* 53:

> When first, my Lord, I saw you back your horse,
> Provoke his mettle, and command his force
> To all the uses of the field and race,
> Methought I read the ancient art of Thrace,
> And saw a centaur, past those tales of Greece;
> So seemed your horse and you both of a piece!
>
> (ll.1–6)

Perhaps the likeness here is simply a matter of two separate recollections of Jonson's reaction to a display of equestrian mastery, but it is also possible that this is an instance of direct influence. The poem might just predate, and so shape, this moment in the 'Foot Voyage', although the surviving text of the latter was, as we have established, probably written before 1628 and the former cannot have been written until 1625, when the grand 'stable' at Welbeck mentioned in l.13 was completed; the poem, moreover, was not printed until the posthumous second folio of Jonson's

99   *The Sprite of Trees and Herbs* dates from 1598–9, the BL copy of *Blackness* is a pre-performance script, probably from December 1604: *CWBJ*, 2.506 and *CWBJ* online, *Blackness*, 'Textual Essay'.

Works and does not appear to have had a wide manuscript circulation.[100]
But the influence, if any, might actually run the other way: if Jonson was
familiar with the 'Foot Voyage', then he could have taken his cue for the
address to Cavendish from his erstwhile companion's recollection of his
conceit. He apparently told Drummond that he composed his verses
'first in prose, for so his master, Camden, taught him' (*Informations*,
l.293), so it would not seem implausible, in this instance, for him to have
begun this poem from a prose note of his observations made by his fellow
walker. Given that he lost his own account of his grand pilgrimage in the
study fire of 1623, he might then have sought out or commissioned a copy
of the version written by his companion, or one he possessed already
could then have assumed a new importance for him. His description of
the lost work in his 'Execration Upon Vulcan', which identifies it specifically as 'my journey into Scotland *sung*' (*Und.* 43, l.94; emphasis ours),
might, indeed, implicitly distinguish it from the more rudimentary prose
account produced by his companion.

Questions of authorship

Who, then, was this companion? If the Aldersey manuscript is a scribal
separate, as we have suggested, then any external evidence that can be
gleaned from it is of little use in answering such a question. The internal
evidence of the account is not overly helpful, either. It is unsigned, and
the writer makes no attempt to indicate his identity. His description of
Jonson as 'my gossip' stresses their intimacy, but does not necessarily
help to define it with any real precision. 'Gossip' is a term of various
signification, included by Thomas Blount among the 'hard words' he
deemed worthy of a definition in his *Glossographia* of 1656. He there
gives it only the meaning most obviously authorised by its etymology:

> Our Christian Ancestors (understanding a spiritual affinity to grow between
> the Parents and such as undertook for the Child at Baptism) called each other
> by the name of *Godsib*, which is as much to say, as they were *Sib* together, that
> is, of Kin through God: And the child in like manner called such, his God-
> Fathers or God-Mothers.[101]

---

100 *CWBJ*, 7.201. Only four MS copies survive, one of which reproduces its text of the poem from
    John Benson's 1640 edition of the 'Execration Upon Vulcan' and other epigrams. See *CELM*,
    JnB 85–8.
101 Blount, 1656, sig. [S5].

In his second edition he broadens the kinship relation to 'a Cousen before God', to some extent acknowledging the looser deployment of the term that his focus on its roots occludes.[102] In fact, 'my gossip' could also mean one's own godparent, or a close friend with whom no formal spiritual association existed; it was also used to speak particularly of female friendship in an often dismissive fashion, and by the early seventeenth century was well on its way to its currently dominant meanings.[103] In Jonson's *Cavendish Christening Entertainment*, for example, the term is used in its proper sense (ll.10, 16, 26); in *A Tale of a Tub*, though, Clench and Medlay use it to address or speak of other characters without necessarily implying formal kinship (2.2.48 and 140; 3.1.79), while the 'gossips' of *The Staple of News* are characteristic instances of its gendered, and somewhat derogatory, meaning. Sometimes, it appears to be used with other relational terms to invoke an erotic, or eroticised, relationship. The duke of Buckingham repeatedly addressed the king as 'dear dad and gossip' in their intimate correspondence of the mid 1620s, an appellation that James echoed in signing himself 'your dear dad and Christian gossip' and returned when addressing Buckingham as 'my sweet Steenie and gossip' or 'my sweet gossip'.[104] At their most literal these addresses simply acknowledge that the king was godfather to Buckingham's eldest child, Lady Mary Villiers, who had been christened on 30 March 1622 (all the letters in which the correspondents address each other as 'gossip' appear to postdate this event), but the adjective 'sweet' and the conjunction of this title with other appellations clearly intensify the bond.[105] The relationship between our writer and his gossip, therefore, might be understood in any of these ways. Only one other personal bond is mentioned in the account: the author records the travellers' meeting at Tadcaster with 'my gossip-in-law', a Mr Richardson, but neither the name nor the relationship as described constitute strong leads. While there were indeed, and unsurprisingly, residents of Tadcaster with the surname Richardson at this period, little is known of them (one was a brewer).[106] This man may anyway have been travelling himself. It is not impossible that he is the Edward Richardson encountered, in passing, at Welbeck – the fact that the writer appears to be unfamiliar with both the Richardsons of Bawtry and the

102 Blount, 1661, sig. T1v.
103 *OED*, Gossip *n.* 2, 3, 4.
104 Bergeron, 1999, 179–219; 150, 162, 173, 158.
105 *ODNB*, Mary Villiers.
106 Tadcaster Historical Society, 2005, 105, 130–1, 139.

Richardsons of Durham would seem to rule them out. The very unusual formulation 'gossip-in-law', mingling the languages of spiritual and legal affiliation, complicates rather than clarifies: while it might suggest that he is the husband of one of the writer's gossips, it is also susceptible of other interpretations. What is more, Edward Richardson married the wife who eventually survived him only after 1626, and his will contains no evidence either of a prior marriage or of any children.[107]

Nonetheless, further internal evidence does allow us to create some elements for a profile of the author. The fact that both travellers were made honorary burgesses of Dunfermline in September – the relevant burgh records have long since disappeared – suggests that Jonson's companion was male and of sufficient age to have such a title conferred upon him. Surviving records show that the honour was bestowed on advocates, courtiers, gentlemen and the higher servants of the nobility in the surrounding years, so we might expect the companion to have been of similar status.[108] His inclusion in most of the festivities along the way and his evident literacy suggest that he may well have been more than a menial retainer, and the fact that Bishop Neile at Durham entreats the companion to prevail on Jonson to dine with him on St Bartholomew's day indicates that others saw the two men as something better than master and humble servant, too. But the writer appears, nonetheless, to have been in some crucial dimensions Jonson's inferior: after all, Neile's kindness to him is remarked because it is remarkable, implying that he was not so generously treated by the travellers' other hosts. Furthermore, he may not have accompanied Cavendish and Jonson to Bolsover, while he is excluded from the poet's visit to Archbishop Matthew at Bishopthorpe during their visit to York. Here, he spends some of the time instead with Edmund Sheffield's steward – perhaps, then, he had a not entirely dissimilar standing in his relationship with Jonson. There is, too, a consistent vein of deference running through the account. The companion's careful recording of the fact that Jonson 'discovered his love and care of me' at Newark, 'for he would not eat till he had sent for Doctor Hunton and Webster his apothecary, to confer about an infirmity I was troubled with' reveals a degree of deferential regard at the heart of his affective investment: he seeks, but is not assured of, the 'love and care' of this charismatic figure. So the fact of their intimacy would appear to be especially valuable, and deserving of record, to the writer – and the proof

107 Willis, 1755, 55; TNA, PROB 11.175.
108 Shearer, 1951, 60, 73, 163, 152, 158, 164.

that Jonson reciprocates in some regard is carefully noted too. By the same token, there is a note of melancholy abandonment, followed by redemption, in his stormy tribulations south of Durham:

> Here a great gate was blown down upon me.
>   By the way I lost my gossip, and came muck wet to Mr Dearham's at the King's Arms where I found my gossip accompanied with Mr Richardson and other gentlemen
>
>   (ll.341–4)

The extraordinarily persistent use of the possessive 'my gossip' to denote Jonson appears, from this viewpoint, rather more than an unimaginative tic: each of its ninety-one iterations – by contrast, the poet's proper name is used on only seven occasions – frames him through the particular bond to which the account is itself a kind of enduring testimony, however indistinct one party to that bond now is. Whether the source of the deferential investment thus insisted on is a disparity in age or a less quantifiable distinction we are not yet in a position to say.

Such deference could usefully be characterised as filial – we might recall, here, the coupling of 'gossip' with such terms in the correspondence of Buckingham and James, which David Bergeron rightly suggests 'taps into intimate, personal terms, even familial terms' – and in this sense would be entirely consistent with Jonson's paternal self-presentation in his later years.[109] The widespread tendency for parents to seek baptismal sponsors among their elders also meant that the 'siblings' thus created could vary substantially in age, as the otherwise profoundly different cases of James and Buckingham, on the one hand, and Edwards and his senior Thelwall relatives, on the other, both demonstrate. We know that Jonson did accrue followers, of course, and eventually cultivated for himself the character of father to a tribe of literary sons. His relationship with Richard Brome appears to have begun with the latter very clearly in Jonson's service, as the Induction to *Bartholomew Fair* makes clear (l.6), but developed into the kind of friendship shaped by pedagogy that he also seems to have had with Nathan Field.[110] In the title of the poem Jonson wrote for the 1632 publication of Brome's *The Northern Lass* he described him as 'My Old Faithful Servant, And (by His Continued Virtue) My Loving Friend', and went on to call Brome's period in service his 'prentice-ship' (l.10).[111] Indeed, Jonson's status as a Bricklayer enabled him to take

109 Bergeron, 1999, 128.
110 Donaldson, 2011, 103, 106; *ODNB*.
111 *CWBJ*, 6.389.

apprentices: records show that one young man, John Catlin, was inden-
tured to him for eight years in 1612.[112]

It is worth considering the possibility, then, that his companion might
have come from among this group of younger, deferential writers and
actors. A major objection to any such suggestion is that our writer fails to
show a developed interest in any literary or intellectual dimension to the
social exchanges that took place on their walk, and we might reasonably
expect one of Jonson's literary or theatrical 'sons' to have taken greater
note of exactly this aspect of his master's activities. Furthermore, it seems
doubtful that a genuinely menial servant or apprentice would be as privy
to Jonson's social exchanges with the nobility and gentry as our writer
seems to have been, and someone in such a position would be unlikely to
have been made an honorary burgess of Dunfermline. But the condition
of service was common, of course, and far from the only determinant of
rank: despite his apparent origins in poverty, and his clear status as
Jonson's 'man', Brome's name is still prefixed with the honorific 'Master'
in the Induction to *Bartholomew Fair* – an acknowledgement of gentle
status which is unlikely to be entirely ironic or mocking.[113] And while the
writer of the 'Foot Voyage' does not seem, on this evidence, to have
possessed an accomplished literary mind, there are – as we noted above –
flashes of stylistic and rhetorical talent, which are most evident in the
depiction of characters and incidents rich with comic potential. In this
connection, it is perhaps worth mentioning that on a few distinctive
occasions the phrasal idiosyncrasies of the 'Foot Voyage' are replicated,
or at least echoed, in Brome's dramatic works. The punning reference to
the 'shake-rag errant, with his two doxies' (l.3) on the road to Tottenham,
for example, resonates with the mention of 'errant, downright beggars' in
A Jovial Crew, as well as the use, later in the same play, of the relatively
uncommon term 'shake-rag' itself.[114] The pun on 'errant' is hardly
surprising, however, so it would be unwise to make too much of this
alignment. More noteworthy, perhaps, is the coinage in the same play of
the phrase 'beggars in law' to denote the wives of importunate, or beggarly,
courtiers (1.1.53), which echoes, in the logic of its formation, the unusual
term 'gossip-in-law' found in the 'Foot Voyage' (l.290). Brome

112 Kathman, 2004, 20.
113 For Brome's humble origins, see *ODNB* and Steggle, 2004, 13–15; in his 1630s lawsuit with
    Salisbury Court, Brome described himself as a 'gentleman'. Steggle raises the possibility that
    the mention of Brome in the Induction to *Bartholomew Fair*, either in part or in its entirety,
    might be a later interpolation and cannot be taken as definitive evidence for Brome's relation-
    ship with Jonson or his status in 1614: 2004, 15.
114 Brome, 1968, 2.1.165, 3.1.403. Further references to this edition are included in the text.

also exploited the applicability of the 'in-law' suffix to unexpected terms in *The New Academy*, where Matchill deduces his own status as Valentine's 'Master-in-law' from the latter's use of 'Mystresse' to address Matchill's wife – although such formulations are far less rare than those involving ungendered or non-relational nouns.[115] If we were tempted to speculate in this direction, however, Brome's later relationship with William Cavendish and his use of a Nottinghamshire setting for *A Jovial Crew* might come to seem significant.[116]

Such resemblances and details, however, are ambiguous, indeterminate or fleeting – even advanced together they are very unlikely to provide much support for identifying Brome as Jonson's walking companion, or for seeing the elder poet not just as his master and teacher but as his gossip. Too little is known of the detail of Brome's life, and the gulf between the style and focus of the 'Foot Voyage' and those of his accomplished dramatic writing might still be thought too wide. Perhaps, then, our writer should be sought instead in the kind of circles in which Evan Edwards and his Thelwall relatives moved; perhaps – as there is nothing to prove otherwise in the papers he left to his descendants or in the records of the Sackville family – we can even imagine Edwards cementing his friendship with Jonson on the road to Edinburgh in the summer of 1618. As such possibilities multiply, however, any attempt to settle on a more determinate profile inevitably falters. There is the temptation, too, to seek for answers or solutions in places where accessible evidence abounds, rather than where such answers might more plausibly, but less promisingly, be sought – it is possible, of course, that the Edwards connection looks plausible only because it is one that we can document from the surviving sources with a tempting degree of thoroughness. Our three contextual essays here explore the ways in which the 'Foot Voyage' has opened a window onto Jonson's life at the height of his fame and in the execution of one of his most distinctive feats; it has given us detailed and vivid new insights into the character and times of the most celebrated writer of his age. It has also, in passing, shed light on the landscape through which he walked, on many of the people he encountered along the way, and on what it meant to undertake a walk such as this in the first place. But, until new evidence or new lines of enquiry emerge, the account looks likely to keep many of its own secrets and to confine us to speculation or guesswork, however sober or informed, about its origins, occasion and purpose.

115 Brome, 1659, sig. [K8].
116 Steggle, 2004, 150–1, 162–3, 165–7; Sanders, 2011, 109.

My gossip Jonson
his Foot Voyage and mine
into Scotland

*

MY GOSSIP JONSON HIS FOOT VOYAGE AND MINE INTO SCOTLAND

We set out of London on Wednesday the eight of July and reached that night to Tottenham High Cross, where we lodged at the Bear etc. By the way thither we met with the shake-rag errant and his two doxies etc.

From thence to Waltham, where my Lady Wroth came to my gossip etc. with Mr Ed Kerry, Mr Harbert and 5

1–2. **Tottenham…the Bear:** Tottenham 'was often known as Tottenham High Cross, from the medieval wayside cross in High Road' (*VCHM*); the 'decayed and rotten' wooden cross was replaced with 'a new one built of brickes' around 1600 (Bedwell 1631, sig. D3). No record of a Bear inn, tavern or alehouse has been found: a 1619 survey of the manor of Tottenham recorded premises called the Bull-head, the Three Conies, the Angel and the Swan, but this list is unlikely to be exhaustive (LMA, MS ACC/0695/009, 38, 40, 43, 76). 2–3. **shake-rag errant:** 'A ragged, disreputable person', rogue or beggar (*OED*, Shake-rag *n.*; Wilkins, 1668, 264 and 'Alphabetical Dictionary'); 'errant' suggests both vagrancy and wickedness. Cf. Richard Brome, *A Jovial Crew*: 'stark, errant, downright beggars' (2.1.165). 3. **doxes:** Variant of 'doxy', 'Vagabonds' Cant for the unmarried mistress of a beggar or rogue' (*OED*, Doxy *n.*[1]). 4. **Wroth:** Mary (c.1587–1651/3), daughter of Robert Sidney, earl of Leicester; highly accomplished writer, performer in court entertainments and patron to some of her most distinguished contemporaries. Jonson addressed several poems to her (*Epigr.* 103, 105; *Und.* 28), and she was the dedicatee of *The Alchemist* in both the 1612 quarto and the 1616 folio. She was married to Sir Robert Wroth in 1604, and widowed ten years later. She lived principally at Loughton Hall, some 6 miles across Epping Forest from Waltham Cross, while her kinsman Lord Edward Denny, later a sharp critic of her romance *Urania*, resided at Waltham Abbey, 2 miles from the main north road

(*ODNB, VCHE*). 5. **Kerry…Harbert:** The Sidney and Herbert families were extensively intertwined, and Mary Wroth was romantically involved with her cousin, William Herbert, earl of Pembroke, so 'Mr Harbert' is probably another kinsman. Candidates include two notable brothers of Jonson's friend, Sir Edward Herbert, subsequently baron of Cherbury, who were recipients of Pembroke's patronage. George Herbert (1593–1633) was then a Fellow of Trinity College, Cambridge, and could have been in Waltham Cross on 7 July, as could Henry Herbert, if he was not then in France, where he spent at least some of this year. Henry (c.1594–1673) was to take over the duties of Master of the Revels from Sir John Astley in 1623; his country residence was at Woodford, 4 miles from Loughton (*ODNB*, William Herbert; Herbert, 1941, 364–9; Brennan, 1988; Hannay, 2010, 252–3). It is harder to identify a plausible Mr Edward or Edmund Carey/Cary/Carew: this might be a relative of Sir Edward Cary of Aldenham, Hertfordshire, who died in London on 18 July 1618 (*HP58*). He was the father of Henry Cary, First Viscount Falkland; Jonson addressed poems to both Henry and his son Lucius, the Second Viscount (*Epigr.* 66; *Und.* 70). Aldenham is about 14 miles west of Waltham Cross, but Sir Edward's family, too, were related to Lord Denny, so a Cary presence in eastern Hertfordshire is not implausible. A son named Edward was born to Sir Henry and Lady Elizabeth Cary in 1616 but appears to have been shortlived; no other family members of this name are known, although the Aldenham parish register records

Title: Jonson] Iohson MS   3. errant] errant, MS

[39]

Mr Powell, etc. There also came to us two Cambridge men, one fellow of Q College called Holmes, and Blitheman Master of Art who etc.

Thence to Hogsdon, where a lunatic woman met us by the way and went dancing before us, and a humorous tinker of whom we could not be rid etc. There also three minstrels thrust themselves upon us, asking 10 whether we would hear a merry song, which proved to be the life and death of my Lord of Essex. This forenoon it thundered and rained, which stopped us from setting forwards till towards the evening. Then we came to Ware, to Mr Cross's, where Sir Robert Mansell, Sir Arnold Harbert,

the burial of a 'Mr. Edward Carey Gent.' in 1639 (*ODNB*, Elizabeth Cary; Brigg, 1902, 133, 149). The first name could be an error, however, in which case this might be another member of Sir Edward's family; a further possibility is Thomas Carew (1594/5–1640), who entered the service of Sir Edward Herbert before travelling with him to Paris in 1619 and was himself related to Lord Denny through his grandmother, Martha Denny (*ODNB*, Thomas Carew, Sir Matthew Carew, Martha Carew). The surname is not uncommon, and other candidates might be found in the ample family of Henry Carey, Baron Hunsdon, and elsewhere. **6. Powell:** Mary Wroth's maternal grandmother was Gwenllian Powell, so 'Mr Powell' is probably a relation – perhaps the poet, writer and lawyer Thomas Powell (d. c.1635), whose first work, *Loves Leprosie*, was published with a dedication to Robert Sidney in 1598, or the John Powell, of Oriel College, Oxford, who was awarded his MA on 4 July 1618 and is the addressee of an epigram in William Gamage's *Linsi-Woolsie*, first published in 1613 (*ODNB*, Thomas Powell; *AO*). Powell wrote a commendatory verse for Gamage's volume, which also contains epigrams to Mary Wroth, her husband, her sister, members of the Herbert family and Jonson himself. The minor poet and translator John Polwhele, who was influenced by Jonson and wrote in praise of Herbert, is a further possibility, although he was in all likelihood too young in 1618 (Bodl., MS Eng. Poet. f.16, ff.10–11; Moul, 2010, 199). **7. Holmes:** William Holmes (d. 1653) matriculated from Queens' College, Cambridge, in 1607; he took his BA in 1611, his MA in 1614, and was elected Fellow in 1617. Later vicar of Meldreth, Cambridgeshire, and Raunds in Northamptonshire; sequestered 'for several great misdemeanours' during the civil war (*AC*; *CCED*, Person ID 28126; *WR*, 280). **7. Blitheman:** John Blitheman

or Blythman (b. c.1592), probably of Royston; matriculated from Queens' in 1608, took his BA in 1612 and his MA in 1615 (*AC*). **8. Hogsdon:** Variant for Hoddesdon, 5 miles north of Waltham Cross. **9. humorous:** Capricious, fantastic, odd; alternatively, peevish, ill-humoured (*OED*, Humorous *adj.* 3a, 3b). **10–11. song…Essex:** Probably either 'A lamentable new Ballad vpon the Earle of Essex his death' (*EBBA* 20044, 30130) or 'A lamentable Ditty composed upon the death of Robert Lo[rd Devereux] / late Earle of Essex' (*EBBA* 30124, 32221, 32617), which were printed together as a broadside in the early seventeenth century; a surviving edition of the 'lamentable Dittie' bears a 1603 imprint (*STC* 6791). Other possibilities include the tetrameter verses beginning 'O England now lament in teares' (BL, MS Tanner 306, f.192; Morfill and Furnivall, 1873, II.245–9). **14. Cross's:** John Cross (d. c.1635) is recorded as an 'innholder' at Ware, and as possessing a wine licence, during this period. His will is dated 1635, and in 1636 John Taylor mentions that 'Wil: Cross' keeps the Crown at Ware, an inn mentioned in a source of 1603 (HALS, DE/Cm/38061; ERO, D/ABW 53/28; TNA, E 163/17/22; Taylor, 1636, 42; *VCHHe*). **14. Mansell:** Sir Robert Mansell (c.1570–1652) began his rise as an officer in the navy during the 1590s, and subsequently became a naval administrator and an assured and long-standing operator at the Jacobean court. Although he prospered through his office he also harboured commercial ambitions and by 1615 was a member of Lord Zouche's glassmaking sydicate. He sold the treasurership of the navy in the spring of this year and was appointed vice-admiral of England – a high-ranking sinecure – in May. Mansell also tilted in the Barriers for *Hymenaei* (*HP04*; *ODNB*; *CWBJ*, 1.clii). **14. Harbert:** Sir Arnold Harbert or Herbert (by 1574–c.1649) was a gentleman

6. Powell, etc.] Powell etc, MS   6. men, one] men. One MS   7. Holmes] Homes MS
7. Master] Mr MS   8. way] way, MS   9. us,] vs MS   10. us,] vs MS
11. song,] song MS   14. Cross's,] Crosses. MS

and Mr Rice came to us and Sir Thomas [sic] subscribed 10 pieces etc. 15
Here my fat hostess commended me with a token. Thence to Puckeridge
to the Falcon, where we dined, where mine host Holland gave my gossip
a forest bill etc. That night we came to Dick of Buntingford's to bed.

The next day we went to the church, where Sir John Skynner met us,
offering us the entertainment of his house etc. Here we met with Gin. 20

pensioner of James VI and I, knighted at
St Andrews in July 1617 during the king's visit
to Scotland. A servant of George Home, earl
of Dunbar (see l.532), until his patron's death
in 1611, he transferred his allegiance thereafter
to Thomas Howard, Earl of Suffolk, whose son
and heir, Theophilus, held the post of lieutenant of the band of gentlemen pensioners
and married Dunbar's daughter in 1612 (BL,
MS Add 34,122 B; *KE*; *ODNB*; *HP04*). **15. Rice:**
Probably Henry Rice (c.1590–c.1651), Mansell's
nephew via his sister Elizabeth. She had married Walter Rice of Newton, Carmarthen-
shire, an Elizabethan gentleman pensioner
retained and knighted in 1603, but whose
family estates had been dispersed following
a number of attainders during the sixteenth
century. In 1612, Sir Walter transferred
his estates in Pembrokeshire to Henry, his
eldest son, whose court connections helped
him to an agreement with his father's creditors
in 1617; a few years later, Mansell attempted
to secure an advantageous marriage for his
nephew (*HP58*; *HP04*; Meyrick, 1846, I.210–
11). **15. Thomas:** A slip – Sir Thomas was
Mansell's elder brother, the heir to the family's
estates and a baronet from 1611; he was a bearer
of the canopy at Prince Henry's funeral in 1612
(*HP04*). **15. subscribed...pieces:** 'Subscribed'
here suggests that the enterprise of the walk
had a commercial dimension, as George
Garrard had suggested in 1617 (Donaldson,
1992, 14); a 'piece' is a gold 'Unite' worth
22s. **16. token:** A copper tavern token, issued
by the innkeeper and redeemable in their es-
tablishments; worth a farthing or halfpenny,
and usually given as change (*OED*, Token *n*.
11a, Tavern *n*. C4; Williamson, 1889, xxii).
Cf. *EMI* (Q), 1.3.34, (F), 1.4.38. **17. Falcon...
Holland:** Thomas Holland kept the Falcon,
one of several inns in Puckeridge and still in
business; Taylor describes him as 'mine old
acquaintance...and my loving and auncient
hoste' (HALS, HAT/SR/84, 141; *PP*, sig.
G2). **18. forest bill:** A woodman's bill-hook
(*OED*, Forest *n*. C2). **18. Dick of
Buntingford's:** A 'Richard Hantler' of Buntingford is described as 'inholder' in the Layston parish memorandum book in 1621 and was

a prominent figure in the administration of the
town. He was listed as the previous owner of
some of the estate of one Samuel Harris in
1661, which included the George inn at Buntingford (Falvey and Hindle, 2003, 45–6, 53,
55–6, 60, 117–18). **19. Skynner:** Buntingford
benefited from a charity established by one
Henry Skynner in the mid sixteenth century,
but his son John died in the early 1570s without heirs. A John Skinner or Skynner (c.1579–
1669) was a prominent figure in Hitchin, 10
miles west of Buntingford, but was never
knighted (Chauncy, 1826, II.173; Metcalfe,
1886, 93; TNA, PROB 11/330/68; Falvey and
Hindle, 2003, lxxii, 82–5, 104–5, 107). This
may, therefore, be an error for Sir John Caesar
(1597–1647), younger son of Sir Julius Caesar,
Master of the Rolls, and former chancellor of
the exchequer, ally and client of the earl
of Salisbury. Sir Julius had purchased the estates of Hyde Hall and Reed, north of Buntingford, in 1612 and was to settle them on Sir John
in 1625. Both properties would have been relatively convenient stopping places for anyone
travelling between Buntingford and Royston.
Sir John had been knighted in Edinburgh during James's 1617 visit (*VCHHe*; *ODNB*, Julius
Caesar; Granger, 1824, V.83–4; *KE*). **20. Gin:** If
a proper noun, as the use of an initial majuscule 'G' and italic in the manuscript might
indicate, then possibly a member of the
Gynne family resident in the parish of Anstey,
3 miles north-east of Buntingford (A. King,
1996, 146); also occasionally encountered
as a diminutive name for a woman: cf. *Comedy
of Errors*, 3.1.31. However, if an unusual
common noun, for which both an initial
majuscule letter and italic script are also used,
this is perhaps a reference to the juniper-
flavoured distilled spirit 'genever', which
was well enough known in England by the
early seventeenth century to be mentioned
punningly in the *Merry Devil of Edmonton*
(printed in 1608; sig. C2) and Massinger's
The Duke of Milan (1623; sig. B1; 1.1.11).
The distilling of spirits was a growing industry, and, by the 1620s, 200 London households were said to be dependent on the
trade (Clark, 1983, 95). The abbreviated

16. Puckeridge] Puckridge MS
20. Here we met with Gin] Marginal addition; no insertion point in the text MS

There my gossip contributed two pieces to the newly erected chapel wrought by the means of Mr Strange the minister etc.

The next day mine host would needs bring us out of town towards Royston, but left us not till he brought us through, where we lay at Mr Atkinson's at the Talbot. Here the maids and young men came out of town to meet us etc. 25

The next day my father Atkinson with his household, *vide*, his two son-in-laws and his son, brought us on the way, first to Erthington, where we baited, and after to Caxton, the King's Arms, where we met with oyez, and I fell out with mine hostess etc. And brought us the next day two miles of the way. 30

The next day we came weary to Huntington to bed, but baited at a little town by the way. Where we lay at Mr Patrick's at the George where we stayed all the next day, the bailiff and the chief of the town keeping us continual company. 35

From thence in the morning; before we were two miles out of town, frecked by rain, we were fain to take an alehouse at a place called Stukeley, where the minister came to us whose name was Seabourne;

name has not hitherto been recorded this early. **21–22. chapel...Strange:** Alexander Strange (c.1570–1650) was vicar of Layston, the parish containing Buntingford, between 1604 and 1650. He is especially notable for his schemes for the relief and employment of the poor, and for his construction of a new chapel of ease to replace the inconvenient parish church of St Bartholomew. Dedicated to St Peter, the chapel was begun in 1614 and completed, after many years of fundraising, in 1628. It cost £420 to build (Falvey and Hindle, 2003, xv, 13, 344). **24. Royston:** Seven miles north of Buntingford; a market town that was home to lodgings built for James VI and I in the early years of his English reign, and frequently used by the monarch (*VCHHe*). **25. Atkinson's:** Nicholas Atkinson held a wine licence for Royston between 1616 and 1620, and is described as 'innholder' in contemporary recognizances (TNA, E 163/17/22; HALS, HAT/SR/141). A part of the 'King's Lodgings' was built on a garden formerly belonging to the Talbot (*VCHHe*). **28. Erthington:** Arrington, also known as Ermington, 6 miles north of Royston on Ermine Street, where there were a number of inns (*VCHC*). **29. baited:** Rested briefly, took refreshments (*OED*, Bait *v.*[1] 7a). **29. King's Arms:** In 1619,

John Layer of Shepreth described Caxton as 'a small village, but well known for that it is a post town and hath Innes for the receipt of travellers'. Hostelries in this period include the Crown, White Hind, Red Lion and George at Caxton, but this list is not exhaustive (W. M. Palmer, 1927, 37–8, 46, 49, 51; *VCHC*; TNA, E 163/17/22). **30. oyez:** A clamour; here, of acclamation (*OED*, Oyez *n.* A). **33. town:** 'By the way' suggests Papworth Everard, half way between Caxton and Huntingdon; 'town' need not suggest a settlement of any size (*OED*, Town *n.* 3). **33. Patrick's:** The George is a long-established inn, part of the current building dating from the early seventeenth century; in 1598 it was in the possession of Sir Henry Cromwell. A William Patrick lived in the parish of All Saints, in which the George was located, in the 1620s and 1630s, and a man of the same name is listed as alderman in a new charter of 1630 (*VCHHu*; CCROH, H26/27, p.7; CCROH, AH28/46/1). **34. bailiff:** The borough of Huntingdon was governed by bailiffs and twenty-four burgesses until the 1630 charter created the offices of mayor and aldermen (CCROH, H26/17). **37. frecked:** Freckled, sprinkled. **38. Seabourne:** James Seabourne, ordained priest in 1617 and appointed vicar of Great Stukeley in January 1618 (*CCED*,

21. pieces to] pieces, to MS   27. day my] day, My MS   36. morning;] morning MS
37. frecked] frec'd MS   38. Stukeley] Stukly MS   38–9. Seabourne; where] Seborne where MS

where we were warned of Stangate in the Hole. We came to Stilton to Smith's at the Angel to bed.

Thence we passed through a town where Sir John Whitbrook had a house, where we met with one Pavy, sometime a citizen in London, and one Mr Hanger that had been minister in the Blackfriars, who brought us to Wandsworth bridge where we baited. That night we came to Stamford to the Maidenhead to my pleasant host Bates etc. All Sunday we stayed there. In the morning Mr Folkingham of the Bell sent my

40

45

Person ID 102406). **39. Stangate:** Stangate Hole, 4 miles north of Great Stukeley; with Shooter's Hill in Kent proverbially notorious for 'robberies that are committed daily', and a haunt of the highwayman Gamaliel Ratsey. He was executed in 1605 but was sufficiently well known to be recalled in *The Alchemist* (?Skinner, 1604, sig. D4; Anon., 1606, sig. I1v; Anon., 1605, sig. D4v; *Alch.*, 1.1.99). **40. Angel:** A prominent inn on Ermine Street in Stilton, owned in 1618 by Robert Apreece (*VCHHu*); 'Smith' was presumably his tenant, although the name is not recorded in this connection. **41. Whitbrook:** Sir John Whitbrook (d. 1619) was knighted in 1604, and acquired the manor and advowson of Water Newton, the 'town' mentioned here, in 1610. Cited in 1612 as a recusant, and held in the Fleet prison from May 1617 at the latest; subsequently involved in a prison riot by 'elite recusants'. He was stabbed and killed by a fellow prisoner at the Fleet in September or October 1619 (*NP*, 1.439; *VCHHu*; *CSPD, 1611–18*, 120; A. Harris, 1879, 29–42; *ODNB*, Alexander Harris; *CL*, 2.267). **42. Pavy:** Unidentified, but plausibly a relation of Salomon Pavy, the boy actor included in the printed cast list for *Cynthia's Revels* and *Poetaster* and movingly elegised by Jonson after his death in 1602 (*Epigr.* 120). **43. Hanger:** John Hanger (1579–1638) studied at Trinity and Corpus Christi before his ordination in 1604; he was rector of Water Newton from 1606–29 and of the adjacent parish of Stibbington from 1613. He married his wife Mary in 1611, but she died in November 1618, the same month as their infant son; in 1619 he married Jane, widow of Peter Edwards, and presumably lived with her at Stibbington Hall, which features a plaque with the initials I. E. and I. H. and the date 1624. A 'Mr Handser' was mentioned as the minister of St Anne's, Blackfriars, in Jonson's citation for recusancy in 1606, and charged with certifying his and his wife's 'diligent & ordinarie' church attendance. This Mr Handser has been identified with a 'John Handclir' appointed to St Anne's in 1605 (CCROH, HP76/1/1/1; *CCED*, Person ID 69995; *AC*; *VCHHu*; *H&S*, 1.221, 223); it is likely that these are both references to Hanger. **44. Wandsworth bridge:** Wansford Bridge, 2½ miles from Water Newton on the old north road; a stone bridge was constructed in the final decades of the sixteenth century, to replace an earlier wooden structure. **45. Bates:** Taylor stayed with Mr Bates at 'the signe of the Virginitie (or the Maydenhead)' at Stamford on his southwards journey from Scotland in October 1618. The will of John Bate, innholder of Stamford, was proved on 8 November 1630 (*PP*, sig. G2; TNA, PROB 11/158/419). **46. Folkingham:** William Folkingham (b. 1575) took on the lease of the George, one of the grandest and most important inns in Stamford, in 1616, and became the town's postmaster in January 1618. He was also the author of *Brachigraphy, Post-Writ, or, the Art of Short-writing*, entered in the Stationers' Register on 10 July 1620; the first edition was probably published later that year, with an 'Address to the Reader' amply demonstrating its author's literary style. In *Pan's Anniversary*, performed for Twelfth Night 1621, Jonson perhaps recalls him in referring to 'a great clerk, who (they say) can write, and it is shrewdly suspected that he can read too; and he is to take the whole dances from the foot by brachygraphy, and so make a memorial, if not a map of the business' (*Pan's Ann.*, ll.106–9). The Bell on Butcher Row is mentioned in a source of 1728, but no corroboration of Folkingham's involvement with an inn of this name has been found; it is perhaps an understandable slip, since the equivalent inn at Stilton, where the travellers had spent the previous night, was (and is) called the Bell (E. Butler, 1951, 160; WSA, 9/30/23; TNA, Pipe Rolls,

39. Hole. We] hole, wee MS   42. house,] house MS   42. Pavy,] *Pauy* MS
43. Blackfriars] blacke Friers MS   44. Wandsworth] wandswoorth MS
46. Folkingham] *Fawlkingham* MS

gossip a fustian letter. Mr Barker, the minister there and preacher, with his brother-in-law Mr Dillworth dined with us, who kept us company till we came out of town.

They with Mr Folkingham brought us to Witham to Mr Arthur Cropper's, postmaster, eight miles off, where we lay. Where the gentle-woman would give no reckoning, but the bounty of my gossip made it dearer than an inn etc.   50

Thence to Belvoir castle to my Lord of Rutland's where was then my Lord Willoughby, and where I was very ill. Here my gossip gave to the   55

AO 1/1952/20, f.3; Rogers, 1983, 77; VCHHu). 47. **fustian:** Inaptly high-sounding or bombastic (OED, Fustian adj. 2a); cf. EMO, 3.1.131–2: 'Prithee let's talk fustian a little and gull 'em, make 'em believe we are great scholars.' 47. **Barker:** Thomas Barker (b. 1572) of Hambleton, in Rutland, was appointed perpetual vicar of All Saints and rector of St Peter's, Stamford, in 1601. He matriculated from Trinity College, Cambridge, in 1589 (CCED, Record IDs 98900, 98901; AC; AO). 48. **Dillworth:** John Dilworth (b. 1584) of Lancashire became rector of Hargrave, Northamptonshire, in 1610 and vicar of Brigstock, Northamptonshire, in 1616; Hargrave is 10 miles, and Brigstock 15 miles, south of Stamford. Alice, daughter of John Dilworth, was baptised at All Saints in December 1618 (AO; CCED, Person ID 133939; LA, PAR/1/ 1). 50. **Cropper's:** Arthur Cropper was the postmaster at South Witham. In 1637 his son James was recorded as having inherited the role from his widowed mother some four or five years previously (TNA, Pipe Rolls, AO 1/1952/ 20, f.3; CSPD, 1637, 331, 418–19). 54. **Bever... Rutland's:** Belvoir Castle, in Leicestershire, the seat of the earls of Rutland, about 12 miles north-east of South Witham. Belvoir was the favourite property of Francis Manners (1578–1632), the sixth earl, who had succeeded to the title on the death of his brother Roger in 1612, and it was visited frequently by James VI and I; Gypsies Metamorphosed, commissioned by the marquis of Buckingham to celebrate his marriage to Rutland's daughter, Catherine, received its second performance there on 5 August 1621. The fifth earl's wife, Elizabeth, daughter of Sir Philip Sidney, had been a regular performer in court masques, Jonson's patron and the addressee of several of his poems (Epigr. 79, For. 12, Und. 50); to Drummond,

Jonson described her as 'nothing inferior to her father...in poesy' (Informations, ll.159– 60), detailing too her sometimes difficult relationship with her husband (Informations, ll.277–9). She died less than a fortnight after him in 1612. With his brother, the sixth earl had been involved in the Essex rebellion of 1601. He became a Catholic after his second marriage in 1608 to the recusant Cicely Hungerford, but was nevertheless appointed a privy councillor in 1617 and accompanied the king on his return to Scotland that year. The sixth earl commissioned an impresa from 'Mr Shakspeare' and Richard Burbage in 1613, for use in that year's accession day tilt, also tilted in A Challenge at Tilt, and possibly danced in The Irish Masque at Court (ODNB, Roger Manners, Francis Manners; HMCR, 4.494; CWBJ, 1.cli). 55. **Willoughby:** Probably Robert Bertie (1582–1642), later first earl of Lindsey, whose family seat of Grimsthorpe castle is 15 miles south-east of Belvoir. Peregrine Bertie, Willoughby's father, had in his later years been an associate and supporter of the earl of Essex. Willoughby was a 'close friend' of Rutland, and they were both made Knights of the Bath together at the creation of Prince Charles as duke of York in January 1605; gifts and resources were often exchanged between them, and Willoughby was a regular visitor to Belvoir. Like his friend, Willoughby danced or tilted in Jacobean entertainments, including Hymenaei and its Barriers, and Prince Henry's Barriers. In the spring and summer of 1618, the pair were cooperating as lieutenant and deputy-lieutenant in arrangements for militia musters and as commissioners of sewers for Lincolnshire (Hammer, 1999, 286–7; Honeybone, 2008, 170; KE; HMCR 4.478–9, 496, 500, 510, 514, 522; ES, 3.378–9; CWBJ, 1.cli,

48. Dillworth dined with us, who] Dillwoorth, dined wth vs who MS   50. Arthur] Ar MS
51. postmaster] interlineal addition with caret MS   51. off, where] off where MS
54. Belvoir Castle] Bever castle MS   55. Willoughby] Willowby MS
55–6. Here...crown] Marginal addition; no insertion point in the text MS

lowest scullion in the house half a crown. There the earl subscribed 30 pieces and my Lord Willoughby 10. Captain Stratford fetched me up to the castle etc.

From thence we were brought by Captain Stratford, Mr Marks and another gentleman of my lord's to Bottesford, three miles off Belvoir, where lie all the earls of Rutland entombed. But by the way, the earl, my Lord Willoughby, and Sir Robert Willoughby, being a hunting and spying us on our journey, galloped over to us and the earl bid God send us well on our pilgrimage.

At Bottesford, a grave and reverent man called Doctor Fleming gave us great entertainment. And an honest parson Surcot beneficed hard by

60

65

clv–clvi; LA, 10ANC/*Lot 355/1; LA, Spalding Sewers, 449/1). **57. Stratford:** Captain Stratford is listed among the household at Belvoir at the time of the fifth earl's funeral in 1612, and as acting for or accompanying the sixth earl in subsequent years (*HMCR*, 1.444, 4.487, 505–6). **59. Marks:** Andrew Marks was a musician, and a member of the household of both the fifth and sixth earls. He is mentioned in Rutland accounts in connection with the acquisition and repair of instruments (*HMCR*, 4.470, 487, 507, 513, 518–19). **60–1. Bottesford... entombed:** The choir of St Mary the Virgin in Bottesford, a little more than 3 miles north of Belvoir, houses elaborate funeral monuments to the earls of Rutland. That of the first earl and his countess was erected in 1543, with memorials to the second, third and fourth earls and their consorts following over the next fifty years; a payment of £100 'in full payment for the finishing of the monument erected at Botesforth for the late Earle Roger of Ruttland' was made in 1619 to the sculptor Nicholas Johnson or Janssen. Payment for indentures for the making of the tomb and an advance of £50 to the sculptor feature in the previous year's accounts, while the sixth earl is recorded as discussing it with the rector of the church in 1615, so it is likely that it was under construction when Jonson visited (Mowl, 1993, 28–36; *HMCR*, 4.504, 512, 517). **62. Willoughby:** The only 'Sir Robert Willoughby' known to be living in 1618 was not knighted until December; he would appear to have come from a junior branch of the family, very distantly related to the Berties, with lands at Turner's Puddle in Dorset (*CSPD, 1580–1625*, Add., 533; *KE*). Given that Lord Willoughby's first name was Robert, it is possible that the account here is mistaken, in which case this could be another

Willoughby knight – perhaps Sir Percival, of Wollaton, 18 miles west of Belvoir, or his son, Sir Francis. Sir Percival appears to have had a cousin and brother called Robert (his paternal grandfather's name), but there is no evidence that either of these men was knighted (*HMCMi*, 562, 609; *HP58*; *HP04*; *AO*). **65. Fleming:** Samuel Fleming (1548–1620), admitted to Cambridge as a King's scholar in October 1565, having previously attended Eton; ordained in 1576, he attained his BD in 1580 and was appointed rector of Bottesford the following year. From the 1590s, he was described as 'Doctor Fleming', although no record of a doctoral degree survives. At Cambridge he was tutor to the future Sir John Harington, who later recalled his defence of 'humane learning', specifically the study and use of rhetorical ornament, against the criticisms of 'the precise sort, that would have the word and church all goe naked' (*AC*; *CCED*, Person ID 24186; Miller, 1959, 67; Harington, 1804, II.207). He served the third earl of Rutland as chaplain from at least 1586 and performed the same role for the three earls following. His brother, Abraham, was a prolific writer and the editor-in-chief for the 1587 edition of Holinshed's *Chronicles*; Samuel himself may have written an unpublished history of the reign of Queen Mary (*ODNB*, Abraham Fleming; Painting Stubbs, 2011, 91–126; Miller, 1959, 57, 79). In March 1619, in his capacity as a justice of the peace for Leicestershire, Fleming joined Rutland and Lord Willoughby in examining the 'Belvoir witches' convicted of bringing about the death of two of the earl's children (Anon., 1619). **66. Surcot:** John Surcot (d. 1633), rector of Muston from the late sixteenth century (*NHA*, 2.288–9).

59. Marks] Markes MS   **60.** Bottesford] Botsfoord MS
60–1. off Belvoir, where] of Bever where MS   **62.** Robert Willoughby,] *Rob Willowby* MS

would not part from us till he had made us taste of all the ale thereabouts, and not contented so waylaid us at the town's end with a pail full of ale, which when he had emptied, we made low courtesy to his red nose, and parted etc.

Thence we came to a town two miles off called Stanton, to   70
one Mr Aston's who married Mr Stanton's widow, and who held his land by tower guard: that is, was bound upon any occasion when the earl should call him to maintain that tower which was called by his name Stanton's tower, in which tower my gossip and I lay. There my gossip gave to the gentlewoman of the house a piece, to her daughter half a   75
piece, and to every servant in the house two shillings. From thence one Draper would needs go along with us to Newark etc., where we had purposed to lie at Mr Atkinson's, the postmaster's, but Wamble of the Hart subtly anticipated us etc.

67. **ale:** Traditionally, brewed without hops and flavoured with herbs or spices; already identified as a country drink by the early seventeenth century ('Gallobelgicus', 1629, sig. C2; Clark, 1983, 96). 69. **courtesy:** Courtesy, curtsy: 'the customary expression of respect by action or gesture', especially to a superior; a bow (*OED*, Courtesy *n.* 8). 71. **Aston's... widow:** Elizabeth Disney (c.1566–1634) was the widow of William Staunton (c.1563–1602); as her second husband she took Thomas Aston, who had been her 'menial servant', and by him had a daughter, Faith – presumably the recipient of Jonson's generosity here. They lived a mile north-west of the church of Staunton in the Vale at Staunton Grange, a property in which she had a life interest. In 1619, Aston was cited for non-attendance at church and failure to take communion at Easter. After his death, Elizabeth married a third time (*NHA*, 3.704; Staunton and Stenton, 1911, 42–3; BI, V/1619/CB, f.339v). 74. **Stanton's tower:** According to William Burton, the Stauntons 'held [their] lands...by the tenure of *Castle gard*, by keeping and defending a Tower in the Castle of *Beluoire*, against any assault or invasion: which Tower to this day, is called *Staunton Tower*'. Staunton Tower, 'the most important portion' of Belvoir castle, was rebuilt by the Manners family in the sixteenth century (Burton, 1622, 9; Eller, 1841, 325). 77. **Draper:** A William Draper of Bottesford was coadjutor of Newark between 1606 ad 1614, but does not appear in the records after that date (*HMCR*, 4.469; NA, DC/NW/3/1/1, ff.123, 125, 131v, 133, 136v). Just possibly the occupation rather than the name of this fellow traveller, in which case see l.78

below. 77. **Newark:** In 1609 Newark was said to be 'a great thoroughfare towne and a post town, and the Kinges Majesties subjects doe usually travell from the north parts into the south parts through the said town, and lykewyse back again'. The 'neat Market place' at the heart of the town was described in a 1634 account as 'in a manner 4. Square, euery way ascending to the Crosse standing in the midst: the Buildings round about are fayre, and straight, exchange like, both walkes, and shops, with Trading well stor'd, and with hansome Creatures well furnish'd, such as were able to refresh weary Trauellers' (Samuels, Henstock and Siddall, 1996, 22; *AShS*, 11). 78. **Atkinson's:** The Atkinsons were a substantial Newark family, with tombs in the choir of the parish church. Taylor's 'George Atkinson' is an error for Gilbert Atkinson, postmaster in 1617 and 1618; he was later an Alderman and, by 1627, kept the White Hart inn (C. Brown, 1879, 302; *PP*, sig. G1v; TNA, Pipe Rolls, AO 1/1952/20, f.3; Samuels, Henstock and Siddall, 1996, 24). 78–79. **Wamble of the Hart:** The White Hart was one of the grandest and oldest inns in Newark, located in the south-west corner of the market square and distinguished by its ornately decorated fifteenth-century front range. This building is now the office of the Nottingham Building Society, but wall decoration dating from the early seventeenth century is still visible on its interior timbers. In 1618, it was leased and kept by a draper, William Wombwell, who also served as a coadjutor in the town between 1615 and 1624 (Samuels, Henstock and Siddall, 1996, 24; NA, DC/NW/3/1/1, ff.139v–160).

69. courtesy] curtesie MS   70. off] of MS   72. guard: that] guard That MS
74. gossip] goss MS   77. etc.,] etc MS   78. postmaster's,] Poastmasters

Here my gossip discovered his love and care of me, for he would not eat 80
till he had sent for Doctor Hunton, and Webster his apothecary, to confer
about an infirmity I was troubled with etc. We stayed here from Friday till
Tuesday. Here Mr Mun Mason the preacher, and the aldermen with other
gentlemen of the country, especially the Markhams, still kept us company.

81. **Doctor:** Anthony Hunton (d. 1624), BA at
Christ's, Cambridge 1578/9, MA 1582; licensed
to practise medicine, 1589; he was also preacher at Newark, where he was buried. He translated Jacques Guillemeau's *Worthy Treatise of
the Eyes*, first published in 1587 or 1588 when
he was a 'Student in Physicke'; the second
edition of 1622 has a dedication to Francis,
sixth earl of Rutland, and additions by Richard Banister of Stamford. Hunton attended
on the families of both the fifth and sixth earls
(BI, Probate Register, 38, ff.343–4; *AC*;
Poynter, 1947, 174–5; *HMCR*, 4.409, 461, 478,
522). 81. **Webster:** A Henry Webster was an
assistant on the corporation of Newark council
from at least 1603, alderman in 1603–4 and
1613–14, and in 1618 was both an assistant
and a justice of the peace. 'Henry Webster,
of Newark, poticarie' is mentioned in Rutland
accounts for 1588 and was among the retainers attending the funeral of the fifth earl
in 1612; in 1595 'Mr Docter Hunton and Mr
Harrye Webster' received 30s for 'commynge to
Belvoyre to her Ladyship' (NA, DC/NW/3/1/1,
ff.107v, 109, 111, 125, 133, 141v–142, 143; *HMCR*,
4.394, 409). 83. **Mr Mun Mason:** Edmund
Mason (d. 1635), of Egmanton, Nottinghamshire, 10 miles from Newark, who received his
BA from Clare College, Cambridge, in 1594/5,
proceeded to his MA in 1598 and then took up
a fellowship at Pembroke. He was ordained in
1608 and subsequently held a number of livings in the Midlands, including Ordsall, near
Retford, which was then in royal patronage,
and the parish church of St Mary, Newark, to
which he was appointed in 1618. By 1604, he
counted Nathan Field and Francis Beaumont
among his associates; in 1615, he played several
parts in the performance of George Ruggle's
neo-Latin satire *Ignoramus* before the king and
Prince Charles, a production for which Clare
College was the sponsor. Mason was tutor to
the prince, probably prior to his appointment
at Ordsall in 1614, and from at least 1621 a
chaplain-in-ordinary at court: his *Sermon
Preached at Oatlands* was published in 1622 by
royal command. His fellow royal chaplain, Richard Corbet, celebrates Mason as 'a man whose
Tongue and Life is eloquent' in his account of a
visit to Newark in *Iter Boreale*, a commendation

that also stresses his conformity. Mason's ecclesiastical advancement (he eventually became
dean of Salisbury) led to his resignation as
vicar of Newark in 1628; he presented a 'black
wand' to the Corporation that was still in its
possession three centuries later (*ODNB*; *CCED*,
Person ID 30908, Record ID 77092; Kelliher,
2000; *REED Camb*, 530, 955; Corbet, 1955, 39;
W. H. Mason, 1915, 154–5). 84. **aldermen:**
Under the charter granted to Newark in 1549,
a corporation of one alderman and twelve
assistants was created. This was formally
changed only 1625, when King Charles issued
a new charter naming the 'alderman' as 'mayor',
and the 'assistants' as 'aldermen'. The use of the
plural here may indicate that the terminology of
the new charter was in use prior to its issuance;
an additional charter of 1604, which appears to
speak of 'aldermen', may account for or reflect
the uncertainty (C. Brown, 1879, 65, 87,
100). 84. **Markhams:** The principal branch of
the Markham family had their seat at Cotham,
Nottinghamshire, 4 miles south of Newark,
and were an important presence in the town:
the early sixteenth-century Markham chantry
chapel is prominently situated on the south
side of the high altar in St Mary's. The children
of Robert Markham (1536–1606) included Gervase (c.1568–1637), the writer, and Francis
(1565–1627), both author and soldier. Sir Robert Markham (1563–1609), the eldest son, inherited a declining estate, and managed only to
hasten the process. The family's principal seat
and some of the rest of their lands were acquired by Sir Charles Cavendish of Welbeck by
1616. Three of Sir Robert's sons, John (b. 1590),
Robert (b. 1596) and Alexander (b. 1601), are
described as 'of Newark upon Trent' in papers
dated 1618, perhaps suggesting that they were
prominent among the Markhams mentioned –
given Gervase Markham's subsequent undertaking of a foot voyage of his own, walking
from London to Berwick in 1622, it is possible
that he too was of the company here and took
his inspiration from a direct encounter with
Jonson's progress (*ODNB*, Gervase Markham;
D. Markham, 1854, 44; NA, DD/P/8/105; DD/
P/8/108; NA, DD/P/8/111). However, the reference may be to the Ollerton branch of the
family, founded by Thomas Markham

80. me, for] mee. For MS 84. country,] cuntrey MS 84. Markhams,] Markhams MS

Here Twentyman of the Saracen's Head and Peet Quint made good 85
sport. Mr James Stewart and Sir Davy Wood lighted as we came there.

(c.1523–1607), uncle to Robert – Ollerton is 12 miles north-west of Newark, in the direction Jonson was to travel, and members of this family were to provide hospitality and company in the days to come. Thomas Markham was a longtime servant of Queen Elizabeth, and for many years an associate of Gilbert Talbot, seventh earl of Shrewsbury, and his wife, Mary Cavendish. His wife Mary (see below, l.162), whom he married around 1567, was daughter and heiress of Rice Griffin of Northamptonshire. Through his sister Isabel or Isabella he was uncle to Sir John Harington, who not only addressed him in the 'Apologie' appended to *The Metamorphosis of Ajax* in 1596 but presented him with a large paper copy of the work. Harington was known to Jonson, and a kinsman of the latter's patron, Lucy Russell, countess of Bedford; Bedford's circle also included her aunt, Lady Bridget Markham (d. 1609), wife of Sir Anthony Markham (d. 1604) of Sedgebrook, head of a junior branch of the family. Sedgebrook is 10 miles south of Newark, so it is just possible that some members of this family were among the company at Newark (*Informations*, ll.26–8; *ODNB*, Lucy Russell; C. Markham, 1913, 1.148–50). Thomas Markham's daughter, Elizabeth, married Edward, son of Ralph Sheldon of Beoley, who may also have been known to Jonson: a man of this name is the addressee of *Epigr.* 119 (though there credited with a knighthood, which Sheldon of Beoley did not possess; the addressee of this poem is more probably Sir Ralph Shelton, of Norfolk). A 'Sheldon' is also named as one of the protagonists of 'The Famous Voyage' and has sometimes been identified as a member of the Beoley family (*HP58*; *Epigr.* 119 and 133, *CWBJ*, 5.190; Blomefield, 1806, v.269; *KE*). In the 1590s, the Ollerton and Cotham branches of the Markham family found themselves on different sides in a county feud between the earl of Shrewsbury's adherents and the family of Sir Thomas Stanhope. The fortunes of the Ollerton Markhams took a turn for the worse when Thomas's heir, Sir Griffin (c.1565–c.1644), was exiled and disinherited as a result of his participation in the 1603 'Bye Plot', an affair in which two of his younger sons, the twins, Charles and Thomas, were also implicated. Thomas was succeeded by his third son, George. Many members of this branch of the family, including Sir Griffin, George and the younger Thomas, were recusants; their brother, Robert, left for the English College in Rome in 1594, although he appears to have been providing intelligence for Essex within the year, while another Catholic sibling, William, was a protagonist in the attempted flight of Arabella Stuart in 1611. In a letter to his nephew of 1600, their father mentions that he has been meeting with friends 'twice or thrice a week' at the Mermaid in Bread Street, London – the party included 'my brother, Sheldon his sonne' and a Mr Catesby, who may be the Gunpowder plotter with whom Jonson was recorded as dining in 1605 (*ODNB*, Griffin Markham; C. Markham, 1913; *NCR*, 149, 153, 156; Harington, 1962, 23–4, 58; Tighe, 1986; LP, MS 708, f.43; Hammer, 1999, 181–2; Steggle, 2012). **85. Twentyman:** John Twentyman owned and kept the Saracen's Head, the second of Newark's principal inns. He shared his forename both with his father (d. 1593) and with his eldest son (b. 1587). In 1603 he delivered a scholarly Latin address to the king on his journey south, so pleasing James that Twentyman 'became a great favourite, and was always near his Royal person in his numerous hunting excurs[i]ons' in the area. A coadjutor from at least 1596, he was elected assistant in 1605 and alderman in 1609. The following year he served as coroner and continued as an assistant until 1622 (NA, DD/1440/74/2–3; *NP*, 1.88–9; NA, DC/NW/3/1/1, ff.86, 114, 123, 152v). **85. Peet Quint:** Something of a puzzle, though clearly a name. 'Quint' is found as a surname, while 'Peet' and 'Pete' are recorded, but only rarely, as an abbreviation for Peter at this period. 'Peter Quint' and close variants are just as uncommon, Shakespeare and Henry James notwithstanding. But while 'Peet' is encountered as a surname in the Newark area, the addition of 'Quint' would then make little sense unless used in an analogous fashion to 'Charles Quint' to indicate the fifth in a series of holders of this name. Most simply, this is perhaps an error for Peter Key (d. 1620), assistant when Twentyman was elected alderman in 1609 and a fixture in the town's civic leadership throughout this decade (NA, DC/NW/3/1/1, ff.125, 127, 129, 131, 133, 136, 139, 140–4, 146–9). **86. Stewart:** A James Stewart is recorded as receiving money from the king 'for service' in 1605 and 1608, and a man of the same name was a member of the royal household in 1617 (TNA, E 101/627/14, f.24; BL, MS Add 58,833, f.22; TNA, LS 13/168, 359). **86. Wood:** Sir David Wood was

85. Twentyman] twenty man MS

Here were fireworks and bull-baiting.

From Newark, Mr Markham with the chief of the town brought us to Canton, where a dinner was provided for us.

From thence we went to Knights Hall, where Mr Thomas Mason   90
overtook us, and with the rest of the company brought us to his brother-in-law's house, Mr Hartopp's, where we had a little banquet, and from thence went to Rufford where the countess gave us extraordinary grace and entertainment. Where the next day was hunting and a stag killed,

knighted in 1604 and was later caught up in the Overbury case when it was alleged that Frances Howard, while countess of Essex, had sought to induce him to murder Sir Thomas Overbury, with whom he was at odds. He has been identified as a member of the queen's household and as servant to the earl of Richmond, a title conferred in 1613 on Ludovick Stuart, duke of Lennox, the son of the young James's favourite, Esmé Stuart, and elder brother to Jonson's patron of the same name, who succeeded him to the dukedom; Lennox was an important courtier over many decades, spanning James's Scottish and British reigns. Wood was the addressee of a 'Dogrell' poem written by William Fowler (KE; CSPD, 1611–18, 319; ODNB, Thomas Overbury; LJ, 30/5/1614; ODNB, Ludovick Stuart; W. Fowler, 1914, I.320). 87. bull-baiting: A nineteenth-century bull-ring or bear-baiting post can be found on the north-eastern side of the market place, presumably a replacement for an earlier structure. 89. Canton: Caunton, across the Trent, 5 miles north of Newark, and west of the main north–south road. 90. Knights Hall: An error for Kneesall, 4 miles north-west of Caunton. At the western end of the village is Old Hall Farm, a substantial, and unusual, sixteenth-century brick-built hunting lodge with terracotta newel staircase and window and door surrounds. Its striking presence may account for the mistake (Summers, 1972). 90. Mason: The elder brother of Edmund Mason and heir to the family property at Egmanton, 3½ miles north of Kneesall. He was admitted to Gray's Inn in 1598, and was probably the Thomas Mason who matriculated from Clare College, Cambridge, around 1590, and received his MA from Pembroke in 1598 (RGI, 94; AC). 92. Hartopp's: Bridget Mason married Samuel Hartopp (d. 1636), of Burton Lazars, Leicestershire, who also held leases in Kneesall – he is mentioned as one of

the chief 'owners' of the village in 1612. A Mr Hartopp sent a buck to the funeral of the fifth earl of Rutland in 1612 and was given 12s 6d (TNA, PROB 11/171; Trollope, 1890, 168; Thoroton, 1790, III.136; HMCR, 4.487). 92. banquet: More probably 'a slight repast' or a course of sweetmeats than a feast (OED, Banquet n.¹ 2, 3a). 93. Rufford: A former Cistercian monastery and substantial estate just within the north-east boundary of Sherwood Forest, as that was established in the sixteenth century. The manor and liberty of Rufford were acquired by the earls of Shrewsbury after the Dissolution, and remained with the family until the 1620s. During its occupation by Gilbert and Mary Talbot it was described by Sir John Holles as an 'asylum' for 'obstinate recusants' (BL, MS Add 74,291; Mastoris, 1998, 81, 91; HMCP, 9.47–9). 93. countess: Lady Jane Ogle (1566–1625) was the eldest daughter and heiress of Cuthbert, seventh Lord Ogle, of Bothal, in Northumberland. She married Edward Talbot (1561–1618) in 1583; her younger sister, Lady Catherine, married Sir Charles Cavendish of Welbeck, further cementing the relationship between their respective families. Counted as a Protestant in a 1606 report on the religious affiliations of the Northumbrian gentry, Jane Talbot became countess of Shrewsbury in 1616, when her husband succeeded his brother, Gilbert – with whom he had long quarrelled – as the eighth earl. After Edward's death in February 1618, and despite a legal dispute over the property with his brother's heirs, she remained in residence at Rufford (HMCS, 19.3; NA, DD/SR/225/157–64). She also continued to oversee her husband's estates around Pontefract, in Yorkshire, and her own Ogle inheritance at Bothal. Jonson wrote an epitaph on her death (CWBJ, 5.715). Richard Andrews praised her generous provision of 'Almes' in a poem of the early 1620s, and the charity and hospitality 'which

and hawking at the poult, by Mr Thomas Westby of Anfield. We stayed   95
all day the next day. My lady gave the charge of my gossip to
Mr Young who was sent thither by Sir William Candish – now
Lord Mansfield – to stay for him and attend him to Welbeck. All
my lady's gentlemen were wholly attendant on us: Mr Cookson, her
solicitor, Mr Wright, gentleman usher, Mr Selby, gentleman of the   100
house, Mr Washendon, her chaplain; all which brought us to
Edenston, where Pilkinton etc.

she at *Rufford* every day did show' were
commemorated by William Sampson in *Virtus
Post Funera Vivit* (BL, MS Harl. 4955, f.67v;
Sampson, 1636, 12). **95. poult:** Game birds
(*OED*, Poult *n.*[1] 1). **95. Westby:** Thomas Westby (d. 1659) of Ravenfield, near Rotherham
in Yorkshire, which was among the estates
of Rufford Abbey acquired by the fourth earl
of Shrewsbury at the Dissolution, and in which
Edward Talbot maintained a particular interest. His kinsman George Westby lived at Car-
burton, around 5 miles north of Rufford (*FMG*,
3.528; *VCHN*; NA, DD/4P/46/21; UNL, AN/
PB/341/5/9; Dugdale, 1854, 174). **97. Young:**
Possibly Thomas Young, who witnessed documents relating to the transfer of property
between the seventh earl of Shrewsbury and
Sir Charles Cavendish in 1609 (NA, DD/P/
6/1/21/4). **97. Candish:** William Cavendish
(1593–1676), son of Sir Charles Cavendish
of Welbeck and his wife, Lady Catherine
Ogle. Entered St John's College, Cambridge,
in 1608; created Knight of the Bath in
June 1610, ahead of the investiture of Henry,
Prince of Wales, and tilted in *Prince Henry's
Barriers* earlier that year and *A Challenge at
Tilt* in 1613/14. He travelled with Sir Henry
Wotton's embassy of 1612 and sat as MP
for East Retford in the 1614 parliament. Sir
Charles Cavendish – stepbrother to Gilbert
Talbot – was widely suspected of sharing
the Catholicism of his sister, Mary, who was
Gilbert's wife. He died in April 1617, and
William married for the first time in 1618.
According to the biography written by his
second wife, Margaret Cavendish, he then
'lived, for the most part, in the Country,
and pleased Himself and his neighbours
with Hospitality, and such delights as
the Country afforded'. His position as

executor for Gilbert Talbot's will helped
him to achieve ennoblement as Viscount
Mansfield in 1620; he was made earl
of Newcastle in 1628. A keen horseman,
poet and dramatist, he was addressed
by Jonson in two epigrams (*Und.* 53, 59) and
described as his 'best patron' aside from
the king. For him Jonson also wrote
a christening entertainment and two masques, *The King's Entertainment at Welbeck*
(1633) and *Love's Welcome at Bolsover*
(1634). Cavendish preserved some of their
correspondence from the early 1630s
(*CWBJ*, Letters 16–19). Jonson's late plays
were shaped by Cavendish's views and preoccupations; Cavendish's own writing, in
turn, was heavily influenced by Jonson
(*ODNB*; M. Cavendish, 1667, 4; UNL, Pw 1/
570–91; *HP04*; N. Rowe, 1994). **99. Cookson:**
Henry Cookson acted for the countess for a
number of years, and looked after her interests in the flurry of property suits following
the deaths of Gilbert and Edward Talbot
(NA, SR/207/112, DD/P/25/1 and SR/207/
112; Cooper, 1973, 109–12). **100. Wright:** A Mr
Wright is mentioned in contemporary accounts relating to the Shrewsbury estates, but
without further identifying detail (UNL, Pw
1/572, 575, 578). **100. Selby:** The countess
made a particular mention of a 'Marie Selby'
in a memorandum to her will of 1625 (BI, Probate Register, 39, f.187), who may have been a
relation to the Mr Selby here. **101. Washendon:**
Possibly a member of the Washington family of
Adwick, near Doncaster, of whom both Bartholomew and Phillip were clerics (*CCED*, Person
IDs 128139, 16009; *AC*; *AO*). **100. Edenston:** An
archaic variant for Edwinstowe, a village
in Sherwood Forest, nearly 2 miles north
of Rufford. **102. Pilkinton:** Unidentified.

97–8. Candish – now Lord Mansfield – to] Candishe now Lord Mansfield to MS
99. us:] vs. MS   99–100. Cookson, her solicitor,] Cookson hir solliciter MS
100. Wright,] Wright MS   100. Selby,] Selby MS   101. Washendon,] *Washendon* MS
101. chaplain; all] chaplin, all MS

From thence to Welbeck where my gossip made fat Harry Ogle his mistress.

Here besides all other open entertainments Sir William Candish 105 showed us all his house, with the pleasures and commodities thereof.

Among the rest he showed us his father's library, which besides the neatness and curiosity of the place, the books were many and of especial choice. Then he brought us to his room of evidences, in handsomeness equal to the other with boxes all about it, where were all the spoils Sir 110 Charles had brought away from Sir John Stanhope. Who with thirteen well-appointed, armed with pistols, swords, and staves, two of them being fencers which had took the sacrament to kill him, set upon him,

103. **Welbeck:** Former abbey and chief seat of Sir Charles Cavendish. It was acquired by the Shrewsbury Talbots in 1584 from Richard Whalley, whose family had held it since the Dissolution, in favour of Gilbert Talbot, subsequently seventh earl of Shrewsbury. In 1597, the earl obtained a second lease of Welbeck and immediately made it over to his brother-in-law, Sir Charles Cavendish, and Lady Catherine Ogle, and it was bought outright for them in 1607. Improvements were planned following this purchase, but only partially implemented. Welbeck was again the focus of expansion and development in the early 1620s, when William Cavendish oversaw the construction of a substantial Riding House (Turberville, 1938–9, I.14–16, 37; Worsley, 2002, II.122–4). 103. **Harry Ogle:** 'Henry Ogle of Welbeck, gent' (c.1559–1635) was described as 'servant and cousin' in elegies William Cavendish wrote for him. Ogle was an important figure in the retinue of both Sir Charles and William, a trusted retainer and receiver of lands. He was possibly also the author of verses in the Newcastle manuscript signed 'H. O.' and addressed to Richard Andrews, a physician and poet with connections to both branches of the Cavendish family and to Donne (NA, DD/P/8/128; UNL, PwV25, ff.32, 34; Worsley, 2007, 10, 15; BL, MS Harl. 4955, f.163; Kelliher, 1993, 159). 104. **mistress:** Possibly a suggestion that Jonson bestowed the role of mistress of the house on Ogle when Sir William left Welbeck in his guest's hands (see below, l.130). Given its privileged position some way ahead of the narrative of Jonson's temporary reign,

the identification of Ogle as Jonson's mistress may imply a more intimate relationship between the two men. 109. **room of evidences:** The 'evidence house' or 'evidence room' at Welbeck contained important deeds and papers, and also functioned as a treasury to keep money and other valuable items. Surviving John Smithson drawings for closets or business rooms, possibly drawn for Welbeck, may give an indication of the layout for a room such as this (NA, DD/2P/24/73 f.2; UNL, PwK 2893; Worsley, 2002, I.86–7; RIBA, 29132–4; Woodhouse, 1999). 110–111. **spoils…Stanhope:** On 18 June 1599, Sir Charles Cavendish was ambushed at Kirkby-in-Ashfield, Nottinghamshire, by a group of armed men led by Sir John Stanhope. This was the last, and one of the most violent, episodes in a long-running feud initiated by Gilbert Talbot and Stanhope's father, Sir Thomas, which had drawn in many of the parties' clients and relations; Cavendish and Sir John had been sharply at odds since a Nottinghamshire election of 1593 (MacCaffrey, 1960). A 'declaration' of this 'fowle outrage' written two days later from the Cavendish perspective, and surviving in two slightly varying versions, largely accords with the narrative here in factual details, but lacks any mention of the vengeful 'fencers', 'hired or professional swordsman' (OED, Fencer n. 1b; UNL, Pw 1/424). 112. **well-appointed:** i.e. well-equipped men. 113. **took the sacrament:** Took communion together to solemnise their intention. In this context, the resort of evil or treasonous conspirators: cf. CSPD, 1591–4, 551; Shakespeare, Richard II, 4.1.328, 5.2.97–9.

104. mistress] Mrs MS   105. William] Will MS
106. house, with the pleasures and] house wth the pleasures, and MS
107. library, which] library wch MS   111. Stanhope] Stanhop MS
112. well-appointed, armed] well appointed armd MS

having but Mr Harry Ogle, his groom and page in his company. Being first shot as he lighted off his horse through the groin and into the buttock, after which wound he slew those two that had sworn his death, and made himself master of their weapons, another left dead and all the rest hurt and put to flight.

The weapons that he brought away were these: two pistols, a staff with two pikes in it, a rapier that reached to my nose, and a basket hilt sword as long as that, another sword with a great basket hilt dagger. And there was the cudgel which Sir Charles had bastinadoed Sir John with before, and upon it written, 'the staff that Sir John Stanhope was beaten with'.

Here Mr Lukenell, who had been tutor to Sir William and now read the mathematic to his brother Mr Charles, gave my gossip a little wheel of his own invention, which driving it before you, would show how many miles, poles or yards you went, and the just distance from town to town according to our measured miles.

The next day after dinner, Sir William with my old Lady Candish and his own lady went to Rufford, and resigned the whole house to my gossip etc., commanding his steward and all the rest of the officers to obey my

115

120

125

130

---

116. **wound:** Sir Charles's injuries were still the topic of medical correspondence in December 1599 (LP, Talbot MS 709, f.33). 119–121. **weapons…dagger:** The version of the 'declaration' acquired by Chamberlain lists 'two rapiers, two pistolls, one sword and dagger, all which are safely kept by Sir Charles'; the other, in the Portland Collection, omits the sword and dagger. The 'staffe with two pikes in it' may be that mentioned in the 1599 accounts as belonging to an unfortunate keeper, 'whom Stanhope that morning tooke with him as he found him in his parke without bootes or weapon but a pike staffe which he had' (CL, 1.77; UNL, Pw 1/424). 122. **bastinadoed:** Beaten with an implement such as a cane or stick (OED, Bastinado v. 1). 124. **Lukenell:** Henry Lukin (1586–1630), an important servant in the Cavendish household involved not only in tuition but also in architecture and surveying; eventually given the tenancy of a family property. The evidence here of his role as a teacher of mathematics and his acquaintance with Jonson suggests that he might be portrayed in the figure of the 'Mathematician' who features in the *Cavendish Christening Entertainment*, as Herford and Simpson speculated (Worsley, 2002, 1.72–3;

H&S, 10.700). 125. **brother Mr Charles:** Charles Cavendish (c.1595–1654), younger brother of Sir William; a 'great master' of mathematics, he became a noted collector of mathematical works and a patron or correspondent of philosophers and mathematicians, including Thomas Hobbes, Walter Warner, William Oughtred and Marin Mersenne. He was knighted during the king's visit to Welbeck on 10 August 1619 (ODNB; Aubrey, 1898, 1.153). 125. **wheel:** A surveyor's wheel. 127. **poles:** A measure of distance: standardised at 5½ yards, but varying between regions (Zupko, 1985, 309–10). 129. **old Lady Candish:** Catherine Cavendish (c.1569–1629), Sir William's mother. Following the death of her sister, Jane, countess of Shrewsbury, in 1625, she successfully petitioned the king for her right to the title Baroness Ogle. She was the subject of an epitaph by Jonson (CWBJ, 6.315) incorporated into a design for a funeral placard or more permanent memorial preserved in the Newcastle manuscript. She may have inspired the character of Lady Loadstone in *The Magnetic Lady* (BL, MS Harl. 4955, f.55; CWBJ, 6.407). 130. **his own lady:** William Cavendish's marriage to Elizabeth Bassett (d. 1643), the widow of Henry

---

114. company. Being] company, Being MS   115. off] of MS   117. master] Mr MS
119. these: two] these. Two MS   123. written, 'the…with'] written the…wth MS
123. Stanhope] Stanhop MS   124. Lukenell,] *Lukenell* MS   124. William] *Wil* MS
129. Candish and] *Candish*, and MS   131. etc., commanding] etc / Commaunding MS

gossip in all things, which authority he did as freely put in execution. For that afternoon he commanded a buck to be killed, and made Mr George Markham his woodman, who with the two twins were come of purpose to meet us; he gave the keeper his fee and sent half a buck to Sir Thomas   135 Brudenell. That night he commanded the wine cellar to be thrown open, and carried down the Markhams etc. Mr Richardson, Mr Carnaby; m. & n. etc.

Howard, third son of the earl of Suffolk, is unlikely to have taken place prior to June 1618; it is noted, as news, by Chamberlain in a letter of 24 October that year, in which she is rightly described as 'a great heyre' (CL, 2.174; Worsley, 2002, I.127). A mention by Chamberlain, in a letter dated 25 October 1617, to 'Sir William Cavendish' having a son might seem to suggest an earlier date for the marriage, but this is a reference to William's cousin and namesake, the heir to the earl of Devonshire, whose own eldest boy was born on 10 October that year (ODNB). Despite being styled 'Lord Cavendish' from around this time, the Devonshire heir is referred to as 'Sir William' here, and again in a letter of 31 January 1618 (CL, 2.107, 133; on both occasions, McClure's gloss is in error). **133. buck:** A mature male fallow-deer, at least 5 years old; a stag (see l.94 above) is a red deer (Gascoigne, 1575, 235–6). **133–134. George…twins:** George Markham of Ollerton and his brothers, Thomas and Charles. Ollerton is 7 miles south-east of Welbeck. **134. woodman:** A huntsman or forester, evoking the legal and political offices of forest government. **135. keeper:** An officer responsible for a forest or park. **136. Brudenell:** Sir Thomas Brudenell (1578–1683) was born into an uncompromisingly Catholic family, and maintained this religious allegiance throughout his life. In 1593, he enrolled at Caius College, Cambridge; his father died six years later. According to a marginal note in the 'Liber Brudenellorum', a compilation of family information made by Thomas himself, he married Mary Tresham on 12 October 1605, a month and a day after the death of her father, Sir Thomas, and two days prior to the induction of her brother, Francis, into the Gunpowder Plot. His wife was niece to Ralph Sheldon; Brudenell himself was a friend of the recusant Mary Talbot, countess of Shrewsbury. Following the death of his uncle in 1606, Brudenell took up residence on the family estates at Deene Park in Northamptonshire, 10 miles south-west of Stamford. He angled unsuccessfully for a Knighthood of the Bath in 1610 (but

became one of the first baronets the following year), was knighted in 1612 and was made Baron Brudenell in 1628; the title of earl of Cardigan was conferred on him in 1661, in recognition of his loyalty to the Crown during the civil wars. He had strong antiquarian interests, counting Sir Robert Cotton among his friends, and built up a great and still extant library on foundations laid by his father-in-law; the collection includes a presentation copy of *The Elements of Armorie* by Edmund Bolton, also a friend and commender of Jonson. Brudenell does not feature among the addressees of any of Jonson's works, but the 'Catholic supper party' attended by Francis Tresham and Jonson, among others, on or around 9 October 1605 might have had some connection to the Brudenell–Tresham wedding and thus testify to their obviously warm relationship (Barker and Quentin, 2006, 44–137; Wake, 1954; ODNB, Francis Tresham; Croft, 2000, 264, 275–7; HMCP, 9.49; H&S, 11.578). **137. Richardson:** Edward Richardson (d. 1637), agent for William Cavendish in his negotiations as executor of the seventh earl of Shrewsbury's will and on other business. He was the stepbrother of Sir Ralph Winwood, who served as secretary of state from 1614 until his death in October 1617, and was co-executor for Gilbert Talbot's will with Sir William Cavendish. Richardson was knighted at Welbeck alongside Charles Cavendish on 10 August 1619 (NA, DD4P/46/6; CL, 2.260; ODNB, Ralph Winwood; TNA, PROB 11/175). **137. Carnaby:** William Carnaby was born around 1593 and was a cousin of Sir William Cavendish through his maternal grandmother; his family estates were in Northumberland, including property at Bothal, and he served as justice of the peace after 1621 and MP for seats in the county. He was witness to Cavendish deeds and indentures between 1617 and 1619, and was knighted at Welbeck on the same day as Edward Richardson and Charles Cavendish (HP04; DD/P/8/111, 114, 170; NP, 3.560). **137. m. & n.:** An opaque abbreviation.

132. execution.] execution; MS   133. killed, and] kyll'd. And MS   135. us; he] vs, hee MS
135. buck] booke MS

On Sunday my gossip reigned wholly and gave entertainment to all comers. The officers came to know his pleasure and what he would command. Diverse gentlemen dined with him; Mr Steward with other 140 gentlemen would not be persuaded to sit but wait. Whilst we were at dinner Mr Carnaby comes from Rufford with commendations to my gossip from all the ladies and Sir William Candish, and with a commission to lay all the doors open to Mr Jonson, and that my lady resigned all power and authority to him to do what he pleased. The house was his; 145 and withal to entreat him they might have as good cheer as he could make them when they came home.

After dinner, by the entreaty of the Markhams and a desire my gossip had to see Sir Thomas Brudenell (who had come over to him but that some business he had then in hand stayed him), my gossip prepared to 150 walk to Worthingsop, alias Worsop, accompanied with Mr Lukenell with his wheel, which he drave before him to show us the secret and use thereof, and Mr Young and Mr Thomas Markham, who gave his man his horse and went himself on foot with us.

In the meantime my gossip gave order to the keeper to kill a buck next 155 morning.

Also pig-face put on, but for some private reason against my gossip's will.

---

140. **Steward:** Probably the 'steward' of l.131. **151. Worsop:** Worksop, a small market town nearly 4 miles north of Welbeck; the name is sometimes given a trisyllabic form, such as 'Workensop' (CB, 550–1). Worksop Manor stands a mile to the west of the town; in the late 1570s or early 1580s the sixth earl of Shrewsbury instigated an extensive remodelling and enlargement of an existing hunting lodge on the site, under the direction and to the designs of Robert Smythson. The resulting building was strikingly tall and extensively glazed, a 'lantern and skyscraper of a house' (Girouard, 1983, 110). William Cavendish spent some of his childhood here, in the care of Gilbert Talbot, and in 1604 formally welcomed Prince Charles to the house during the prince's journey south. The manor was settled on the earl's daughters in 1604, although he and Mary, his countess, retained the title during their lifetimes. In 1617, the Worksop properties were conveyed to Sir William Cavendish, presumably in his capacity as executor of Gilbert's will. The imprisonment in June 1618 and subsequent punishment of Mary Talbot – a consequence of her entanglement in the fate of Arabella Stuart – led eventually to the confiscation of the estate (Turberville, 1938–9, 1.44; HMCP, 2.118; SA, ACM/SD/411, 887, ACM/W/151; NA, DD/P/36/1). In a poem from the first half of the 1620s, Richard Andrews describes the Cavendish/Talbot era at Worksop as 'past', and identifies its current owner as Thomas Howard, earl of Arundel, the husband of Aletheia, the seventh earl of Shrewsbury's youngest daughter (BL, MS Harl. 4955, f.67v; ODNB, Thomas Howard). **157. pig-face:** A pig's head; the elliptical syntax is unhelpful, but this and l.163 suggest a joke either at Jonson's expense or, just possibly, set up by him (see OED, Against prep. A 14).

138. entertainment] entertayment MS
140. command. Diverse gentlemen] comaund [Mr S] Divers gent MS
143. William] Wil MS   144. Jonson] Iohnson MS   145. his;] his, MS
149. Brudenell] Brudnell, MS   150. him),] him) MS
151. Worthingsop, alias Worsop,] Worthingsop alias Worsop] MS
153. Markham,] Markham MS   156. morning.] morning MS

As we passed through Welbeck a herd of huge grown stags made towards us as if they came to entertain us.

At Worsop Sir Thomas Brudenell stood ready to entertain us, and Mrs Markham, mother of the twins, gave us a very hearty welcome, and very wittily (for some former rude offence of his) pinched pig's-face.

We were first brought up to the great chamber, the floor whereof fell down when the king was there, a wonderful fair room; then to the king's chamber, far beyond that, and after to the gallery, who for the bigness and beauty thereof exceedeth most that I have seen. It is fourscore and fifteen of my paces long. There are some eight large windows, in which are set the coats and arms of all the dukes, earls and barons of England.

The house is as goodly as I have seen both for the height, situation and form of building. It stands in a park which is eight miles about, furnished with the tallest, straightest and largest oaks that ere I saw, and hath had in it at one time 1,500 deer; eleven hundred died in the great snow.

160

165

170

---

162. **Mrs Markham:** Mary Griffin (c.1540–1633) married Thomas Markham of Ollerton by 1565. The marriage joined the Markhams to the Brudenells: Robert Brudenell, Thomas's father, was an uncle on her mother's side, though born within a few years of her; hence Mary Markham and Thomas Brudenell were cousins, and he had passed some of his childhood at the Markhams' property in Kirby Bellars, Leicestershire (C. Markham, 1873; C. Markham, 1913; Wake, 1954, 104; Barker and Quentin, 2006, 44–5). Gervase Markham's brother, Francis, described her as 'a great inheritrix, wise, virtuous and very religious (in her religion which is Popish)'; in 1592 she was said to be 'a great perswader of weake women to popery', although Queen Elizabeth's loyalty to Thomas Markham ensured that neither he nor his wife were penalised for her Catholicism (Tighe, 1986, 41, 34). She and her husband were long-time servants and associates of the seventh earl and countess of Shrewsbury, and Mary Markham was in charge at Rufford when it was searched by Sir John Holles in 1611 (HMCP, 9.47–9). 163. **pig's-face:** It is unclear who is pinched – perhaps the head prepared in l.157, but the mention of a 'former rude offence' suggests that the epithet has been transferred to Jonson or another member of the party. 164. **great chamber:** On the first floor of the house, 63ft by 33ft (RIBA, 29244). 164. **floor:** A mishap affecting James's visit in either April 1603 or April 1617; here probably defective ceiling plaster rather than

a serious structural fault, hence insufficiently consequential to warrant a mention in surviving accounts of those journeys (OED, Floor n.[1] 2b; NP, 1.84–8; 3.268). 165–166. **king's chamber:** Otherwise undocumented, although its existence can obviously be inferred from royal visits. 166. **gallery:** The second-floor gallery at Worksop was 'famous all over England' for its size and position in the house, although no other record of its armorial glazing survives. It measured 212ft by 36ft; hence, the writer's pace was about 27in (68.5cm) (Girouard, 1983, 113; RIBA, 29244). 171–173. **park... snow:** In his 1636 'Survey of Worksop' John Harrison noted that 'this Parke is well adorned with timber, & not meanely furnished with Fallowdeare, the number of them at this present is about eight hundred' (SA, ACM/W/26; White, 1904, 132). The hard winter of 1614–15 was described as the 'great snow' in The Cold Yeare (1615) – although this pamphlet recycles some of the contents of The Great Frost (1608), which recounts earlier tribulations – and Tobie Matthew, archbishop of York, recorded in his diary for early 1615 that there was 'Wonderful Frost and Snow above Seven Weeks together, never the like Seen in England, with exceeding great Fluddes of Water by the Thawe'; the Belvoir accounts for this year include payments to two men on April 27 'for chardges brozeing [i.e. browsing] wood for his Lordshipp's dearre at Belvoire, donne in the greatte snowe' (YML, MS Add. 18,111; HMCR, 4.503).

---

163. pig's-face] Piggs-face MS   164. chamber,] chamber MS   164. floor] flower MS
165. room;] room, MS   168. are] as MS   171. about,] abo<..> MS   173. 1,500] i500 MS
173. deer; eleven] deere, eleuen MS

On Monday we made ready to depart in the morning, but the importunity of Mrs Markham, the knight and her sons (my gossip withal 175 hearing that Sir William would not come home till night) stayed us till after dinner. In the meantime we all walked over to Worsop town where we visited the old and ruinous abbey founded by Lord Lovetoft, who lieth in the church with Lord Furnivall and Nevell. And in the chapel we found kine. Here stuck the arrow etc.   180

There (because my gossip had seen some fine cans at Belvoir) [he] would needs seek out the Welsh goldsmith that made them, meaning to buy some of them, among which we met with one of a yard long, which we measured out in liquor with London measure to those that lighted in our company.

After dinner we took our leave, and the knight and Mr Thomas 185 Markham brought us more than halfway to Welbeck.

Presently upon our return the ladies came, whom Mr Jonson welcomed to his house, and at supper bid them want nothing, for if they did

---

175. the knight: Sir Thomas Brudenell.
178–179. abbey...chapel: Worksop Abbey or Priory was at the centre of the town in the early modern period; it was associated especially with its founder, William de Lovetot, and his descendants; the church also housed monuments to Gerard de Furnival and later members of his family, including Sir Thomas Nevill, lord high treasurer, who died in 1407. After the Reformation the parts of the church not in parish use, including the lady chapel in its south-eastern corner, fell into disrepair, but Camden records that 'the West part of the Church standeth still passing faire to be seene with two towre steeples' (Eddison, 1854, 26–45; White, 1875, 20–33; *CB*, 551). The church and its gatehouse were substantially restored in the nineteenth and twentieth centuries. **180. kine:** Cows, cattle (*OED*, Cow *n.*[1] 1b). **180. arrow:** Perhaps a reference to otherwise unrecorded folklore relating to Robin Hood – monastic foundations play a prominent part in many such stories, although Worksop Priory is not mentioned in any known instances. Robin's selection of his burial place by firing an arrow from a priory gatehouse, which might be recalled here, does not feature in an extant narrative of his death from earlier than the eighteenth century; Kirklees Priory in the West Riding has been identified as the grave site since the early sixteenth century. Nonetheless,

Worksop sits at the northern tip of Sherwood Forest and to the south of the Barnsdale where the early 'Gest of Robyn Hode' – with which Jonson is likely to have been familiar – is located, and many places in the vicinity have relevant associations; Cavendish, too, had a strong interest in the subject (Dobson and Taylor, 1976, 22, 302–3; Knight 2005, 140–2; Raylor, 1999, 425). A piece of a human skull from the medieval period distinguished by an embedded arrowhead is still preserved in the church, and sometimes said to be that of a Sherwood forester; it may not have been displayed here, however, until the nineteenth century (B. Harris, 2006, 434). **181. cans:** Drinking vessels (*OED*, Can *n.*[1] 1a); cf. *EMI* (Q), 2.2.47: 'two cans of beer'. **182. goldsmith:** Unidentified; the goldsmiths named in the calendared Rutland accounts for this period worked out of London. **184. London measure:** Weights and measures varied considerably across the Stuart kingdoms, and attempts at standardisation were only systematically pursued after 1660; 'London measure' was proverbially generous (Hoppit, 1993, 92–4; Tilley, M798). Cf. William Cavendish, *The Triumphant Widow*: 'here's a Boule of Sack to you, here give me the Can that measures Ale by the Yard, *Derby* measure, Sir, here's this Can of Sack to you, Sir' (W. Cavendish, 1677, 26–7). **184. lighted in:** Chanced into (*OED*, Light *v.*[1], 10e).

---

176. William] *Wil* MS   183. them, among] them among MS
186. Markham brought] Markham, brought MS
187. came, whom Mr Jonson] came whom Mr *Iohnson* MS

it was not his fault. Chafed at the table for lights, and checked the waiters because there was no more new bread, which freedom of his mingled with a great deal of mirth much delighted the ladies.

The next day Sir William Candish carried my gossip to see Bolsover, alias Bozers, castle, on which Sir Charles had built a delicate little house etc. As also to meet one Smithson, an excellent architect, who was to consult with Mr Jonson about the erection of a tomb for Sir William's father, for which my gossip was to make an epitaph.

The next morning Sir William rid his great horse, which he did with that readiness and steadiness, as my gossip say they were both one piece. That day Sir George Che<.>r and his mother and his lady, Doctor

190

195

189. Chafed: Fumed, showed irritation (*OED*, Chafe *v.* 10a). **189. checked:** Reproved, reprimanded (*OED*, Check *v.*[1], 11). **192. Bolsover:** Bolsover, in Derbyshire, 6 miles west of Welbeck. 'Bozer' is a local pronunciation; it is used by George Aglionby in his poem 'On Bolsover Castle' (BL MS Harl. 4955, f.188). **193. castle:** The Little Castle was under construction from late 1612, on land acquired by Sir Charles Cavendish from his brother-in-law, Gilbert Talbot; the building and an initial fitting-out of the interior had been completed by the time of Sir Charles's death, and it is possible that Jonson's 1618 masque, *Pleasure Reconciled to Virtue*, helped to shape its decorative scheme (Girouard, 1983, 234–42; Hughes, 2010, 2; Worsley, 2002, I.125–6). **194. Smithson:** Building work on the Little Castle was directed by John Smithson (d. 1634), son of Robert, who was both an architect and an important figure in the management of the estates of both Sir Charles and his son, although he lived outside the household from 1615. In the autumn of 1618 he travelled to London on Sir William's business and possibly in his company, and made a series of architectural studies which influenced his subsequent practice (Girouard, 1983, 234–42, 248–51; Worsley, 2002, I.57–9, 72–3, 125–6). **195–196. tomb…epitaph:** The 'epitaph' is 'Charles Cavendish to his Posterity' (*CWBJ*, 5.350); it is inscribed on the monument erected in the Cavendish chapel at St Mary's, Bolsover, itself constructed in 1618 (Worsley, 2002, I.59–60). There, and in BL, MS Harl. 4955, f.54v, the poem prefaces a tabulation of Sir Charles's virtues by Henry Lukin; this is in turn followed by a further prose epitaph attributed, in the manuscript, to Jonson. **197–198. horse… piece:** Cf. *Und.* 53, probably written after the construction of the Riding House at Welbeck

in 1622–3, and prior to Cavendish's elevation to the earldom of Newcastle in 1628: 'When first, my lord, I saw you back your horse, / Provoke his mettle, and command his force / To all the uses of the field and race, / Methought I read the ancient art of Thrace, / And saw a centaur, past those tales of Greece; / So seemed your horse and you both of a piece!' (ll.1–6). **199. George Che<.>r…lady:** The name is unclear. Possibly Sir George Chute (1586–1649), his mother, Elizabeth, and Anne Barnham (d. 1655/6), his second wife. Sir George was a son of George Chute, of Bethersden in Kent and St Giles, Cripplegate, whose will was proved on 18 May 1618. The younger George pursued a military career, like his eldest brother, Sir Walter (c.1574–1617), and was knighted in 1608; by 1617 he was a gentleman pensioner and courtier, again following in his brother's footsteps (TNA, PROB 11/131/ 345, PROB 11/257/462; HP04; BL, MS Add 34,122 B; Pearman, 1889, 61–2). In the 1614 parliament Sir Walter Chute sat for East Retford, a Nottinghamshire constituency, probably as a result of the patronage of Sir John Holles, whose family seat was Haughton Hall near Bothamsall, 7 miles east of Welbeck. Holles counted the elder George as his 'antient ould frend' and interceded with him on his sons' behalf in 1616 (HP04; Seddon, 1975, I.111). Jonson's epitaph on Elizabeth, daughter of Sir George and Lady Anne (*Und.* 35), who was baptised at St Giles on 18 December 1623 and died on 18 May 1627, is inscribed on a brass plate in the church of St Andrew at Sonning, in Berkshire (LMA, P69/ GIS/A/002/MS06419/002; *CWBJ*, 7.151). Another possibility is Sir George Chaworth (c.1569–1639), his wife Mary (d. 1646) – the daughter of Sir Thomas Kniveton and Jane

Waterhouse and his wife, and Mrs Purpoint came to Welbeck, and my   200
gossip at dinner began the king's health. The cobweb could not be pissed
down.

That night Mr Bates, a good scholar, and the pleasant tell-tale, led
with the fame of my gossip came thither to see him; who the next

Leche, half-sister and gentlewoman to Bess of Hardwick – and his mother, Jane. George attended Trinity College, Oxford, in 1586 and entered Gray's Inn in 1605 after receiving his Oxford MA. A kinsman of Roger Manners, fifth earl of Rutland, he was a servant to Lady Arabella Stuart by 1603 and a courtier to King James soon afterwards; his main seat in Nottinghamshire was at Annesley, nearly 14 miles south of Welbeck. Around 1616, John Smithson drew up plans for alterations to another Chaworth property, Wiverton Hall. Chaworth was prominent enough at court to carry the banner of the union in the funeral of Queen Anna in 1619, and another at the funeral of King James in 1625. He sat in the parliaments of 1621 and 1624, before purchasing a viscountcy in 1628 (*HP58*; *HP04*; Pevsner, 1979, 383; RIBA, 29243, 29245; *NP*, 4.1046; TNA, LC 2/6, f.62). **200. Waterhouse...wife:** Tobias or Toby Waterhouse (d. c.1646), son of Gregory, of Siddal near Halifax; took his BA from Trinity College, Cambridge, in 1596/7 and an MA in 1600, the year after he was appointed to a fellowship. He gained a BD in 1607 and his doctorate in 1612. By 1618, his livings included the rectories of Kirkby-in-Ashfield, a Cavendish manor 12 miles south of Welbeck, and Whitwell, Derbyshire, only 3 miles to the west of the Cavendish home; he was sequestered for delinquency during the civil war (*AC*; *CCED*, Person ID 29937; *FMG*, 3.849; *WR*, 294–5). He married Elizabeth Copley of Southill, Bedfordshire, at All Saints, Hertford, in April 1612, the same month that he was presented to the rectory of St Lawrence, Whitwell; a memorial plaque in the church for their young son, Toby, suggests that he was born in December 1618. In 1619, Waterhouse was cited for 'seldome preaching and neuer catechising on the saboath dayes' at Kirkby (HALS, DP48/1/1; *HMCS*, 21.360; BI, V/1619/CB, f.353v). Waterhouse's prosperous cousin, Robert, of Shibden Hall, near Halifax, served as lawyer to the sixth and seventh earls of Shrewsbury (*HP58*; Lister, 1917, 285, 288; LP, MS 701, ff.41, 65, 91). **200. Mrs Purpoint:** Gertrude Pierrepoint or Pierrepont (c.1588–1649) was the daughter of Henry Talbot, younger brother of the seventh and eighth earls of

Shrewsbury. In January 1601, she married Robert Pierrepont (1584–1643), son of Sir Henry Pierrepont, whose family was strongly Catholic and related to the Cavendishes; Robert served in that year's parliament as a Shrewsbury nominee at the very young age of 17, and subsequently held various county offices. In addition to their seat at Holme Pierrepont, near Nottingham, the family had a secondary residence at Hodsock, 7 miles north-east of Welbeck. Some sources credit Robert Pierrepont with a knighthood, but he in fact remained 'Esquire' until created Viscount Newark in 1627; he became earl of Kingston-upon-Hull the following year. He was a cousin of Francis and Sir John Beaumont, and had been the former's contemporary at Oxford and the Inns of Court. The design for Sir Henry Pierrepont's tomb at Holme Pierrepont was undertaken by John Smithson around 1615 (*HP58*; *ODNB*; *NCR*, 4, 8, 13, 110, 133; Kelliher, 2000, 12; Girouard, 1962, 52; RIBA, 29209). **201. began...health:** A toast or a grace; perhaps the lines Jonson composed between 1617 and 1619 (dated 1618 in Bodl., MS Rawl. poet. 26, f.1v) surviving in a number of manuscript versions (*CWBJ*, 5.346–7). This dinner took place on 5 August, the anniversary of the Gowrie conspiracy of 1600, an alleged plot to kill the king hatched by John Ruthven, Earl of Gowrie, and his brother, Alexander. James's deliverance from this danger was commemorated annually in both Scotland and England, and Jonson's gesture probably acknowledges the occasion (K. Brown, 1994, 72). **201–202. cobweb...down:** In the absence of other explanations, perhaps a contest conducted by the men in the party. **203. Bates:** Henry Bates (d. 1636), matriculated from Trinity College, Cambridge, in 1611; took his BA in 1614/15 and his MA in 1618. A friend and client of Sir William Cavendish and his namesake cousin, the earl of Devonshire, and chaplain-in-ordinary to King James and King Charles; called 'Mr Bates of the North' in a 1625 list of James's chaplains. The jocular and gossipy tone of his correspondence suggests that he might aptly be described as a 'pleasant tell-tale' (*AC*; TNA, LC 2/6, f.43; BL, MS Add 70,499, ff.118, 139,

morning promised to bring him to Hodsock to Sir Gervase Clifton's, but 205
we rose so early we left him behind us. There we found my Lady
Wentworth and her three brothers, Mr John, William and Robert. We
stayed only dinner, and after many courtesies done to my gossip by Sir
Gervase at his departure he offered him a buck.

That night we came to Bawtry where Mr Richardson, chief and 210
commander of all the town, was prepared to entertain us.

He hath the impost for wines and weighing of the lead. In this place is
the greatest trade of lead in Christendom or the world. It is brought

---

141v, 162). **205. Hodsock...Clifton's:** Sir Gervase Clifton (1587–1666) inherited estates
at Clifton, near Nottingham, and Hodsock
while still an infant. Long a ward, he was
taken under the wing of the seventh earl of
Shrewsbury – who commended his 'rare and
excellent wit' – and entered St John's College,
Cambridge, in 1603. He acquired a baronetcy
in 1611, and sat for Nottinghamshire in the
parliament of 1614, probably as Shrewsbury's
nominee – he helped to carry the canopy at the
earl's funeral in 1616. In 1612 he married Pene-
lope Rich, daughter of the earl of Warwick and
the first of his seven wives, but she died the
following year. The hospitality he offered to
everyone from 'the king to the poorest beggar'
was celebrated by his friend, the antiquary
Robert Thoroton. An occasional poet himself,
Clifton was also a friend and patron of artists
and writers, including John Marston, Francis
Beaumont, John Smithson and Thomas
Hobbes; Michael Drayton wrote an elegy on
his first wife. He also played a role in Marston's
Castle Ashby entertainment of 1607 and may
have performed in *Gypsies* in 1621 (*HP04*;
Hobbes, 1997, 820–3; Girouard, 1962, 50–1;
RIBA, 29205; Tricomi, 1977, 203; Burke and
Coolahan, 2005, 125; Seddon, 1980, 33–4;
Jonson, 1970, 330–1). The Clifton house at
Hodsock was Hodsock Priory – never, in fact,
the home of a religious order, but a moated
manor house with a large, brick, sixteenth-
century gatehouse (Pevsner, 1979,
144). **206–207. Lady Wentworth:** Lady Margaret Clifford (d. 1622), daughter of Francis
Clifford, Fourth Earl of Cumberland, who
married Sir Thomas Wentworth, later Earl of
Strafford, in 1611; elder sister to Frances (d.
1627), who married Clifton as his second wife
in September 1615 (*HP04*; *ODNB*, Thomas
Wentworth). **207. brothers:** Here, probably,
brothers-in-law: William Wentworth (c.1595–
1644), entered the Inner Temple with his eldest

brother, Thomas, in 1607, and matriculated
from St John's College, Cambridge, in 1609;
resident at the Inner Temple in 1619 and called
to the bar in 1620; John (d. 1625), admitted to
the Inner Temple in 1611 and matriculated
from St John's a year later; Robert, admitted
to the Inner Temple in 1616 (*AC*; Cooke, 1868,
110, 124, 139; *WP*, 120–1). **208. courtesies:** Presumably, hospitable and respectful treatment,
but, if qualified by 'at his departure', perhaps
see note to l.69 above. **210. Bawtry:** Bawtry,
a market town on the great north road, and
a significant port at the furthest navigable
point on the River Idle. This river linked the
mining industries of the Midland counties, by
way of the Trent and Humber, to the port of
Hull and beyond (*VCHYER*). Part of the
manor of Bawtry was leased from the Crown
by Jane, countess of Shrewsbury, and her kinswoman Catherine Widdrington (SA, CM 1680,
1696). **210. Richardson:** Richard Richardson
(d. 1623), prosperous gentleman, merchant
and Shrewsbury bailiff. His two surviving
sons were Lindley, his heir, and Gilbert – the
latter's name demonstrating the family's Talbot connections (SA, CM 1679, 1758; BI, Probate Register, 37, ff.511–12). **211. was prepared:**
i.e. had made preparations. **212. impost:**
Weighing was an essential stage in lead transactions, and Bawtry was 'the main internal
market for Peak lead'. The town's pre-
eminence in this area had been established
by the sixth earl of Shrewsbury, whose own
operation – 'stretching as it did from his ore
purchases in the Peak to the sale of lead
at Rouen' – was unmatched by any of his
Derbyshire competitors (Kiernan, 1989, 237,
255). The Bawtry trade was controlled by
a succession of Shrewsbury servants, including
Richardson; around 1617 he built a new weigh-
house, and his assertion of a monopoly over
lead-weighing at 8d or 9d a fother (see l.212
below) caused some dispute with other Bawtry

---

207. William and Robert] *Wil* and *Rob* MS   210. Bawtry] Batry MS

hither by wains; every wain carrieth a fodder, and eight pigs makes a
fodder, every pig weighing 24 pounds. There hath been taken five   215
pounds a day for mere weighing, and 100,000 pounds a year for lead.
These are conveyed by catches to Stockwith, and there taken into keels,
and so carried to Hull and all places. The wains that brings these to
Bawtry carries all other commodities back into Derbyshire and
Nottinghamshire, for this town serves them with wine, flax and other   220
commodities, having warehouses for the laying in of such commodities.
Here we had great entertainment, where we stayed all the next day, being
Friday. Here Mr Baldwin that keeps the countess's house at Pomfret, and
Mr Babthorpe that keeps the park met us. Here four deans, hearing of
my gossip's being there, came to see him.   225

merchants (Kiernan, 1989, 235–7). **214. wains:**
Large, open, usually four-wheeled carts, especially useful for carrying heavy loads; wagons
(*OED*, Wain *n.*¹ 1a). **214. pigs:** A measure of
weight for lead or iron; of no standardised
dimension, but usually around ten times greater than 24lbs; Ray's definition would give
200lbs (Zupko, 1985, 299). **215. fodder:** Also
'fother', in general use, 'a cartload', but 'relates
properly to Lead, and signifies a certain weight,
Viz, 8 piggs or 1600l [i.e. pounds]' (Ray, 1674,
19); elsewhere given as equivalent to 19.5cwt, or
2,184lbs (Zupko, 1985, 151–3; *OED*, Fother *n.*
2a). **217. catches:** Sturdy, shallow or flat-
bottomed vessels suitable for navigating inland
waters (*OED*, Catch *n.*²) **217. Stockwith:** East
and West Stockwith face each other across
the Trent at its confluence with the
Idle. **217. keels:** Larger river-going or coasting
vessels (*OED*, Keel, *n.*² 1a). **220. wine, flax:**
Two of the most common commodities im-
ported through Hull, in increasing volumes,
from the Low Countries, France, Spain and
the Baltic (*VCHYER*). **223. Baldwin:** John
Baldwin, servant to Edward Talbot, eighth
earl of Shrewsbury, and subsequently to his
widow. His father, Thomas, of Diddlebury,
Shropshire, had been for many years servant
to George Talbot, the sixth earl, who died in
1590. John was left £50 in Edward Talbot's will
(Grazebrook and Rylands, 1889, 23; SA,
WWM/StrP./20/216; NA, DD/4P/46/21; BI,
Probate Register, 40, f.262). **223. house at
Pomfret:** The sixth earl of Shrewsbury settled
his lands at Pontefract on Edward Talbot in
the 1560s; the New Hall, dated 1591 over the

porch, was built to a Smythson design, and
visited by King James in April 1617 (White,
1904, 339–40; Girouard, 1983, 172–5; *NP*, 3.270;
K. Taylor, 1998, II.18). **224. Babthorpe:** Brian
Babthorpe (d. 1621), who was left £100 in Edward Talbot's will; his own records a bequest
to 'my honorable Ladie and *Mistress* Jane
Countesse of Shrewsbury' (NA, DD/4P/46/21;
BI, Probate Register, 36, f.600). **224. four
deans:** Probably acting for the archdeaconries
of Pontefract and Doncaster, rather than
Ainsty or Craven. Lawrence Wilson (b.
c.1553), dean of Pontefract, was curate of Hor-
bury, in the parish of Wakefield (*CCED*, Person ID, 123048, Record ID, 183018; BI,
Archbishop's Court, Com.Bk. 1, f.50, 51v, 54).
Thomas Pullein (d. 1627), also dean of Pontefract, was born in York, matriculated from
Christ's College, Cambridge, in 1583, and took
his BA and MA from Oxford in 1587 and 1589/
90, respectively; he was vicar of Pontefract
from 1597 and of nearby Darrington from
1610, and served as chaplain to Tobie Matthew,
Archbishop of York. The plague sermon he
delivered at York Minster in 1604 was printed
four years later, with a dedicatory epistle to the
city's mayor and aldermen (C. Pullein, 1915,
182–4; *AC*, *AO*, *CCED*, Person ID 121656; BI,
Institution Act Book 3, f.497 insert; T. Pullein,
1608; BI, Archbishop's Court, Com. Bk 1, ff.43,
54v). William Wilkinson (?1578–1623), dean of
Doncaster, was rector of High Hoyland from
1604 until his death. He may have matriculated
at Oxford in 1595, receiving his MA in 1601
(*CCED*, Person ID 135497; *AO*; BI, Archbishop's Court, Com. Bk. 1, ff.51v–52). Richard

214. wains; every] waynes every MS   216. 100,000] 100000 MS   219. Bawtry] Batree MS
219–20. Derbyshire and Nottinghamshire] Darby shiere, and Notingham shier MS
222. day,] day MS   224. Babthorpe] Babthrop MS

That night after supper we set on towards Doncaster, conducted thither by Mr Richardson and his two sons, Mr Wright that married his kinswoman, and the master of the Crown with a bagpipe playing before us.

We came at one of the clock at night to the Hind to Mr Carver's, an   230
alderman and a justice of peace, which Mrs Lovet his neighbour took very grievously because she looked to have had [us], having been by other gentlemen spoken to before and willed to prepare for our entertainment.

The next morning one Sir Thomas Bland, hearing of my gossip's   235
being there, desired his acquaintance, whom my gossip invited to dinner with another gentleman with him.

After dinner my gossip went to visit Sir William Anstrudder who had invited him to dinner etc. There we found a long table full of

Winter (d. 1632), dean of Doncaster, matriculated from Trinity College, Cambridge, in 1588, taking his BA in 1591/2 and his MA in 1595. He was schoolmaster at Doncaster before being ordained and appointed to the rectory of Sprotborough in 1596 (*AC*; *CCED*, Person ID 122928; BI, Archbishop's Court, Com. Bk 1, f.53). **226. Doncaster:** Market town and staging post on the great north road. **227. Wright:** Possibilities include the John Wright who is listed among 'my good friends' in Richard Richardson's will, or Henry, who occupied lands at Austerfield, just north-west of Bawtry (SA, CM 1680, 1688, 1692; BI, Probate Register, 37, ff.511–12). **228. Crown:** One of Bawtry's main inns, already known as such by the 1550s (TNA, C 1/1474/54–5). The 'Master' is unidentified. **230. Carver's:** William Carver (d. by 1640), 'inhoulder', a burgess and alderman from 1610, including in 1618–19; mayor in 1613 and 1622; listed as a justice of the peace as late as 1631. The White Hind was leased from Emanuel, Lord Scrope. Doncaster already had at least five inns in the mid sixteenth century, and their number increased with the development of road traffic; the inns' busiest day was Saturday, when the market was held – Jonson arrived at one o'clock on Saturday morning (Brent and Martin, 1994, I.193, 200–5, 234; DA, AB6/2/16, f.2v; Barber, 1994, 72–3; TNA, E 163/17/22). **231. Lovet:** Elizabeth Levett was the widow of Richard, alderman, postmaster and holder of a wine licence. He died on 11 February 1618, leaving her 'all my goods lands tenements and hereditance' in Doncaster

(Brent and Martin, 1994, I.220, 247; TNA, E 163/17/22; BI, Probate Register, 35, f.95). **235. Bland:** Sir Thomas Bland, of Kippax Park, just north of Castleford, a manor purchased by his father in 1595. Knighted in 1604, Sir Thomas was married to Katherine, daughter of Sir John Savile, later Baron Savile of Pontefract; he succeeded his father in December 1612. Philip Massinger dedicated the 1632 quarto of *The Maid of Honour* to 'my most honour'd friends' Sir Thomas Bland and Sir Francis Foljambe, acknowledging 'that you have beene, and continued so for many yeeres (since you vouchsafed to owne me) Patrons to me and my despised studies' (Carlisle, 1826, 31–6; YAS, MD335/13/2/1; Massinger, 1632, sig. B2). **238. Anstrudder:** William Anstruther of Anstruther, Fife (d. 1649); a courtier to James in Scotland, he followed his master to England, was knighted at the coronation in 1603, and served in the bedchamber and privy chamber. He helped to carry the canopy at the queen's funeral in 1619. His younger and better-known brother, Sir Robert (1578–c.1644), was a noted courtier and diplomat; Robert married Mary, daughter of Sir Robert Swift of Yorkshire, and Taylor records meeting him at his father-in-law's house at Wheatley, 1½ miles from the centre of Doncaster, in October 1618. Wheatley eventually descended to Sir Robert Anstruther, and is presumably where Sir William entertained Jonson (*KE*; TNA, *SP* 14/90/118; TNA, LC 2/5, LC 2/6, f.40; *ODNB*, Robert Anstruther; B. Burke, 1859, 52).

226. Doncaster] Donckester MS   228. master] Mr MS
232. grievously because] greivously, because MS   235. Bland] *Blan* MS
238. William] *Wil* MS

gentlemen and ladies, and came time enough to the banquet. In the   240
meantime came riding in coach my Lord of Buccleuch, who made very
much of my gossip. Among the rest there was a justice of peace with
whom my gossip made good sport.

That night with much ado to get away we came to Skelbrooke to
Mrs Copley's, where she and the gentleman her son gave us great welcome,   245
being sent to before by the countess of Shrewsbury to that purpose.

Here we drank at Robin Hood's well.

240. **gentlemen:** Possibly including John Craven (d. 1646), a member of a Doncaster family who matriculated from St John's College, Cambridge, in 1588, before moving as a scholar to Trinity; he took his BA in 1593/4 and his MA in 1597, before appointment in 1604 as vicar of Harworth in Nottinghamshire, 7½ miles south of Doncaster. In 1616, he married Dorothy, widow of Anthony Armitage; both Anthony and his elder brother, William, featured prominently in Doncaster's governing gentry. 'Mr Craven' held property in Doncaster itself and also had a lease by 1618 on Hexthorpe Hall, about a mile to the west (*AC*; Train, 1961, 90–1; Blagg, 1914–15, III.42; *FMG*, 3.894; Brent and Martin, 1994, I.216–17, 256; DA, AB6/2/16, f.4v, 12v; *CCED*, Person ID 116252). He was probably the writer of the verse address 'To Master Ben Jonson in his Journey By Master Craven', to which Jonson composed an extempore response (*CWBJ*, 5.349) – the poems are known only from the Newcastle manuscript, a compilation of poetry associated with or of interest to William Cavendish and his family; Harworth was a Shrewsbury living, close to Bawtry and Worksop, and Craven had been chaplain to Gilbert Talbot, Cavendish's uncle. He was also a friend of Richard Richardson of Bawtry, another Shrewsbury client, and supervisor of his will (BL, MS Harl. 4955, f.47v; LP, MS 3201, f.237; BI, Probate Register, 37, ff.511–12). **241. Buccleuch:** Walter Scott (d. 1633), second Lord Buccleuch and head of the Scott kindred; his landholdings covered a large part of the central Scottish Borders. He was noted for his military career in the Low Countries and his suppression of crime in the Borders; Jonson alludes to his reputation in the Windsor text of *Gypsies*, where his fortune is told (431–45). Created first earl of Buccleuch in 1619, 'his profusion and hospitality embarrassed his estate' (*SP*, 2.234); he also amassed a significant library, with over 850 volumes

listed by Sir John Scot of Scotstarvit in 1634. By October 1618 he was at Branxholme, near Hawick, and planning to spend the winter at Crichton Castle, 11 miles south of Edinburgh (NRS, GD224/935/22; NRS, GD224/906/58, no. 1; Knowles, 2006, 270–1). **243. good sport:** If John Craven was also a justice of the peace, this might refer to his poetic exchange with Jonson, but no evidence of him acting in this capacity has been found; other possibilities include Sir Robert Swift, owner of the house in which the 'banquet' may well have occurred (TNA, C 181/2, f.255v; DA, DZ/MZ/63). **245. Mrs Copley's:** Jane Copley (c.1572–1626), widow of John (d. 1615), whom she married in 1588. Her eldest son, Godfrey (c.1589–1648), matriculated from Magdalen College, Oxford, in 1606; after entering Lincoln's Inn he became a barrister in 1614, and served eventually as recorder for Doncaster and Pontefract; his brother, Thomas (1597–1628), emigrated to Connecticut. Members of the family had served the Talbots, and their interests, for many years (*AO*; J. Hunter, 1828–31, I.22, II.458; Bodl., MS Eng. misc. c.275; BI, Probate Register, 39, ff.15v–16; LP, MS 701, f.109). **247. Robin Hood's well:** At the side of the north road near Skelbrooke; later graced with a stone cover by Vanbrugh (Hey, 1981, 140–2). In the 1630s, and probably earlier, the well was overseen by a keeper, and travellers were able to make use of a dish on a chain when drinking (Brathwaite, 1638, sig. S1). 'Being thirsty, we tasted a Cup at Robin Hood's Well, and there according to the vsuall, and ancient custome of Trauellers, were in his rocky Chaire of Ceremony, dignify'd with the Order of knighthood, and sworne to obserue his Lawes: After our Oath we had not time to stay to heare our Charge, butt discharg'd our due Fealtie Fee, 4d. a peece to the Lady of the Fountaine, on we spur'd with our new dignitie to Pomfret' (*AShS*, 13).

241. Buccleuch] MS *Buckleugh*   246. Shrewsbury] Shrewsberry MS
247. Here…well] Marginal addition; no insertion point in the text MS

On Sunday after dinner Mr Copley and his man came on foot with us over Barnsdale to Wentbrigg. And the next day came again and met us at Pomfret where my gossip had by the countess of Shrewsbury a buck given him, a side of which he sent to Mrs Copley, and the rest he ate with the aldermen of the town, among which was Mr Pellen, the minister and preacher, and another gentleman of that name. And Mr Wakefield, an alderman and a good scholar. We lay at Mr Tatham's, an alderman, to whose house we came the back way because all the town was up in throngs to see us. And there was dancing of giants, and music prepared to meet us. And notwithstanding we took a byway to escape the crowd and staring of the people yet a swarm of boys and others crossed over to overtake us, and pressed so upon us, that we were fain to present our pistols upon them to keep them back, and made them believe we would shoot them to get passage etc.

The next day we visited the castle and whatsoever tasted of antiquity in the town. There we saw the chamber where Richard the third was

249. Barnsdale...Wentbrigg: Barnsdale was previously a forest; the name, and area, were for a long time as strongly associated with Robin Hood as Sherwood (Phillips, 2000, 203–7). The north road descended from Barnsdale to cross the Went at Wentbridge, halfway between Skelbrooke and Pontefract; 'Wentbrigg' is the northern form of the name. **250. Pomfret:** Pontefract, 'an ancient corporation' and the largest market town in the area. Notable also for its imposing castle, to which substantial repairs were made in 1618–20; a lease of the park was held by the earls of Shrewsbury from 1585, although the castle and honour of Pontefract was included in the jointure of Queen Anna in 1603. Edward Talbot and Jane Ogle maintained the Shrewsbury interest in the town from the 1590s, with the New Hall one of their chief residences (*AShS*, 13; Roberts, 1990, 24; SA, ACM/SD/275; G. Fox, 1827, 162; NA, DD/4P/28/82, DD/P/6/1/5/5). **252. Pellen:** See note to l.224. **253. another gentleman:** Perhaps Edward (d. 1619), also of York, whose father's will was witnessed by Thomas Pullein in 1605 (C. Pullein, 1915, 182–4). **253. Wakefield:** Joshua Wakefield (c.1570–1651), matriculated from St John's College, Cambridge, in 1587. Served as mayor of Pontefract in 1604 and 1613. Both Wakefield and his father, Edward, who sat for Hull in the 1586 parliament, had dealings with Edward Talbot and Jane Ogle (*AC*; G. Fox, 1827, 57; *HP58*; NA, DD/4P/28/82, DD/P/6/1/5/5; LP, MS 706,

f.156). **254. Tatham's:** William Tatham, mayor of Pontefract in 1608, 1615, 1616 and 1632; holder of a wine licence throughout this period (G. Fox, 1827, 57, 81; TNA, E 163/17/22). **256. giants:** Processional giants, of the kind used in towns and cities across England in midsummer and other festivities. Although the practice was widely suppressed after the Reformation, the ceremonial use of these effigies continued for several decades in cities including Newcastle and Chester (*REED Newc*, xv, 26–7, 92, 99, 113; *REED Ches*, liii, 162, 198–9, 299). The Pontefract giants may have been housed in the castle in the early seventeenth century: 'we view'd the spacious Hall, which the Gyants kept' (*AShS*, 14). **262. antiquity:** Perhaps including the parish church of All Saints, begun around 1300, with its distinctive double staircase, and the ruins of the Cluniac Priory of St John, adjacent to the castle – although much of the stone from its buildings had been reused in the construction of New Hall, and Camden remarked that 'there is scarce any rubbish now remaining' of its buildings (Bellamy, 1965, xxii, 49; *CB*, 696). **263–264. Richard...murdered:** Correctly, Richard II, who was imprisoned in Pontefract Castle in December 1399 and had died by 17 February 1400. The account of his murder by Exton is common to familiar sources, including Holinshed and Shakespeare. The writer's confusion perhaps arises from Richard III's association with Pontefract, as recalled by Camden: 'heere King Richard the

murdered and where H the 8th was c by Culpeper.

Then we were brought to Mr Frank, an Alderman, whose wife had   265
had three children at a birth, his wife then being nine and forty and
himself above three score when they were gotten, which all three were
then living. And in the same year he had a mare brought forth three
foals. And another woman was brought abed of five children within
three quarters of an year. And he at whose house we lay said his mother   270
was brought abed of him when she was forty nine, and his wife's mother
of his wife when she was threescore.

This night my gossip invited the whole town to his venison, and the
wine came to 41s, which my gossip paid.

The next morning Mr Tatham, Mr Wakefield, Mr Thwaites,   275
Mr Wilkinson, Mr Ward, aldermen, and Mr Wamble of Wamble, and
Mr Baldwin, keeper of the new house in the park and a great lover of
antiquities, who with the fat keeper brought us to Ferrybrigg,
where we met with Captain Robert Hazell and Captain Jaques etc.

Third caused Antonie Earle *Rivers*, King Edward the Fifth his Vnkle by the mothers side, and Sir *Richard Grey* Knight, halfe brother to the same King by the mothers side, both innocent persons, to loose their heads' (*CB*, 696). **264. H the 8th:** Henry VIII. **264. c by Culpeper:** According to a standard interpretation, Henry VIII was 'cuckolded' at Pontefract Castle in August 1541, when his queen, Catherine Howard, admitted Thomas Culpepper into her chamber. **265. Frank:** John Frank (d. 1622), mayor in 1600 and 1614; married to Dorothy Balne, of Balne, North Yorkshire, about 9 miles east of Pontefract. Four sons and six daughters survived infancy; their daughter Anne married William Wakefield, the son of Joshua. In 1617, Frank bought a very substantial house in the 'Naute market' or cattlemarket, now the Cornmarket, an area in which a number of aldermen had their principal dwellings (G. Fox, 1827, 57; J. Burke, 1833–8, II.576; Dugdale, 1854, 3, 218; Heslop, 1993, 7–8, 11–15). **275–276. Thwaites...Wamble:** Richard Thwaites (d. 1620), mayor on four occasions between 1585 and 1611; William Wilkinson (c.1560–c.1635), mayor in 1619, married to Mary Ward, daughter of Robert; therefore in all probability related by marriage to Leonard Ward, mayor in 1618 and 1634 (the mayoral election took place in September; hence,

Ward is correctly styled alderman here); William Wombwell (1565–1622) of Wombwell, 12 miles south of Pontefract, 'a man of great extravagance with a taste for litigation' (G. Fox, 1827, 39, 56–7; Dugdale, 1854, 52, 180; J. Foster, 1875, 365; *YG*, 378). **278. fat keeper:** Either Brian Babthorpe, keeper of the park, who with John Baldwin had joined the travellers at Bawtry, or perhaps the Robert Wilson identified as 'keeper of the castle' accompanying Baldwin at York (see ll.303–4 below). **278. Ferrybrigg:** Ferrybridge, 2½ miles beyond Pontefract, where the north road towards York crossed the River Aire. **279. Hazell:** Captain Robert Hasell is identified as 'the first Inventor and profeser' of a plan, originally proposed in 1620, to build and operate an amphitheatre in London capable of staging a wide range of public spectacles; nothing more is known of him (Hotson, 1949, 34). **279. Jaques:** 'Captain Jaques' is a name given to Jacomo di Francisci, who played a shadowy role in Ireland and the Low Countries in the 1580s and 1590s, apparently working for Sir Christopher Hatton and serving in Sir William Stanley's regiment; he has even been proposed as the model for Jaques in *As You Like It* (C. Nicholls, 1992, 230, 245; Enos, 2004, 137–9). As the man met here is later styled 'Mr' (l.33 below), it is possible that the military

265. Frank, an Alderman, whose] *Franc* an Alderman whose MS   **271.** wife's] *wives* MS
275. Tatham] *Tateham* MS   **275.** Thwaites] *Thwaytes* MS   **276.** Ward] *Warde* MS
277. Baldwin,] Baldwin MS   **278.** Ferrybrigg] ferry brigge MS   **279.** Robert] *Rob* MS

Who rid fair and soft with us till we came to Sherburn, where all the pins   280
are made, and is called the great cherry town, for here we had cherries in
the middest of August.

Here was at the same time a great match at bowls where Sir Robert
Hengate, Fulgiam, Darcy and diverse other knights and gentlemen met.

Here Mr Wentford, Garlington and Witham, hearing of my gossip's   285

title is an error: the name was not uncommon in Yorkshire and elsewhere, and, given the context, a connection to Francis Jaques, author of the Caroline play *The Queen of Corsica*, might be plausible (Dugdale, 1854, 162; Leech, 1947; Jaques, 1990). **280. fair and soft:** Proverbial: gently, slowly (*Tilley*, S601). **280–281. Sherburn... cherries:** Sherburn-in-Elmet, nearly 6 miles beyond Ferrybridge. Cf. *Barnabee's Journal*: 'Thence to Sherburn, dearly loved, / And for pinners well approved, / Cherry tenths the pastor aimeth / More than souls which he reclaimeth' (Brathwaite, 1638, sig. [S5]). **284. Hengate:** Robert Hungate (d. 1619), of Sand Hutton, 7 miles north-east of York; his family resided at Saxton, 2 miles north of Sherburn; admitted to Lincoln's Inn in 1567, and became a counsellor-at-law. Although from an often Catholic family, Hungate was distinctly Protestant. His bequests included money to establish a hospital and free school at Sherburn, and to support a preaching minister in Saxton and Sand Hutton (*LIA*, 75; BI, Probate Register, 36, ff.255v–60). **284. Fulgiam:** Probably Francis Foljambe (1590–1640), heir to substantial estates at Aldwark, near Sheffield, and Walton, in Derbyshire following the death of his elder brother in 1612. He also possessed the manor and hall at Steeton, just south of Sherburn, and is described as 'of Steeton' in a conveyance made between 1617 and 1622. An associate of Sir Thomas Wentworth, he became a baronet in 1622 and was elected to parliament for Pontefract in 1626; he was also a patron of Massinger, a relationship attested both by a surviving autograph poem and by Massinger's dedication of his *Maid of Honour* to Foljambe alongside Sir Thomas Bland. The latter's Kippax estate was only 4 miles west of Steeton (*HP04*; Johnston, 1835; NA, DD/FJ/1/276/7; *CELM*, MsP 9; Massinger, 1632, sig. B2). **284. Darcy:** Perhaps John Darcy (c.1602–24), son of John, Third Baron Darcy of Aston, near Sheffield, the stepson of Isabel Darcy; Godfrey Foljambe, Francis's cousin, had been her first husband. Described by Chamberlain

as 'a very proper and hopefull yonge gentleman', and a supporter of Sir Thomas Wentworth; returned to parliament for East Retford in 1624 shortly before his death from smallpox (*HP04*; *CL*, 2.555; *ODNB*, Isabel Wray). Possibly, however, an error for Henry Darley (1595/6–1671), of Buttercrambe, 2 miles east of Sand Hutton, who in 1619 married Ralph Hungate's daughter and heiress, Margery; the Darleys were 'one of the leading Puritan families in Yorkshire' (*HP04*; *YG*, 272). **285. Wentford:** Possibly Christopher Wandesford (1592–1640), or his brother, John (1593–1665), of Kirklington, north Yorkshire, although the family seat is 30 miles north of Sherburn. Schooled with Thomas Wentworth, Christopher became his lifelong friend and political associate. He attended Clare College, Cambridge, 1607–11, was admitted to Gray's Inn in 1612 and first entered parliament in 1621, on Wentworth's patronage. John entered Gray's Inn in 1613 and was called to the bar only four years later; a good friend of John Selden, he sat for Richmond in the parliament of 1624 (*HP04*; *ODNB*; Toomer, 2009, 584–5). Their brother, Michael (1597–1637), was admitted to Gray's Inn on 10 August 1618, so is unlikely to have been at Sherburn the following day (*AC*; *RGI*, 152). Alternatively, one of the younger brothers of Sir Thomas Wentworth (see. ll.206–7, note). **285. Garlington:** Perhaps Nicholas Girlington (c.1591–?1637) of South Cave, 26 miles east of Sherburn. He was doubly related to Francis Foljambe: his great-aunt, Anne Girlington, was the mother of Isabel Darcy, while Francis Foljambe's aunt, Troth Foljambe, was the daughter of William Tyrwhitt and Isabel Girlington. In the 1620s, he was suspected of recusancy (J. Hall, 1892, 22; Maddison, 1902–4, II.404; *ODNB*, Isabel Wray; *HP58*; J. Foster, 1875, 284; *YG*, 243). **285. Witham:** Possibly a member of the family who lived at Ledston Hall, in the parish of Ledsham, 4 miles south-west of Sherburn, until the 1620s. Henry Witham (1581–1625) was another associate of Sir Thomas Wentworth, the latter playing a part in the management of the family's property

283. Robert] *Rob* MS   **284.** Darcy] *Darcie* MS   **285.** Wentford] Wentfoord MS
285. Garlington] *Garlington,* MS

passing along, crossed of purpose to meet him, gentlemen dwelling thereabouts.

That night we came to Tadcaster to Mr Barker's at the George, where my gossip was prevented for the charge by Sir Thomas Bland etc.

That night came my gossip-in-law Mr Richardson who gave us a 290 gallon of burnt wine. For by reason of some difference between the Tavern and the house [where] we lay we could get no wine at supper for money, but my gossip Richardson's power prevailed at midnight.

On Wednesday by six of the clock we set forth from Tadcaster, and our two friends errant still keeping us company, who although they rid 295 we could not be rid of them. And by nine we reached York, where we took Mr Kay's at the George in Cunny Street, the famous

and eventually acquiring Ledston Hall for himself. In 1617, Witham obtained permission to travel to France for three years; if he was abroad in 1618, the Mr Witham at Sherburn may have been one of his younger brothers, Edward (b. 1585) or Thomas (b. 1586), both of whom were living in 1617; alternatively, he might be their cousin, Cuthbert Witham (d. 1655) of Garforth, 3 miles west of Ledston (J. Foster, 1875, 310, 593; SA, WWM/Str P/2/20, 15; Parsons, 1834, I.276–7; YG, 77; Brigg, 1917, 86; Clay, 1906, 26, 35; TNA, PROB 11/251/262). **288. Tadcaster…George:** Tadcaster, a market town 6 miles north of Sherburn well known for its brewing industry, and the site of a well-known bridge crossing the River Wharfe on the way to York. The Barkers were a long-established local family; the George had been a Tadcaster inn since the early sixteenth century at the latest (Tadcaster Historical Society, 2005, 101–6, 122–5, 128–31, 138; Bogg, 1904, 33–4). **289. prevented:** Anticipated (OED, Prevent v. I 1a). **290. gossip-in-law Mr Richardson:** An unusual formulation. 'In-law' denotes forms of kinship created by marriage rather than consanguinity; in the early modern period, this included the relationships now indicated by 'step-' (OED, -in-law comb. form); 'gossip', used strictly, denotes spiritual kinship, so this conjoins the legal and the spiritual: a 'gossip-in-law' would thus be a relation by marriage to the writer's gossip, or a gossip to the writer's legal relation. A similar formative process can be seen in the phrase 'master-in-law', used by Richard Brome in The New Academy and by William Rowley (or a possible co-author) in A New Wonder, a Woman Never Vexed to denote the husband of a character's mistress (Brome, 1659, sig.

[K8]; Rowley, 1632, 40); cf., too, Brome's coinage of the phrase 'beggars-in-law' to mean the wives of importunate or beggarly courtiers (A Jovial Crew, 1.1.53). If the 'Foot Voyage' here follows this pattern, then Mr Richardson would be the husband of another of the writer's gossips. Given that the term 'gossip' could be used less strictly, however, the phrase may simply indicate a relation by marriage to the writer's friend, or friend to the writer's legal relation. **291. burnt wine:** Either wine heated and flavoured, such as 'muld Sacke', or a distilled drink akin to brandy (from the Dutch 'brandewijn', burnt or distilled wine) (OED, Burnt adj. 5, Brandy n. a; Dekker, 1615, sig. A2v; Coles, 1677, sig. E2v). **295. friends errant:** Jaques and Hazell. **296. York:** Nine miles east of Tadcaster, 'the second City of England, the fairest in all this Country, and a singular safegard and ornament both, to all the North-parts. A pleasant place, large, and stately, well fortified, beautifully adorned as well with private as publike buildings, rich, populous, and to the greater dignity thereto it hath an Archiepiscopall See' (CB, 701); also, the seat of government for the north of England. **297. Kay's…Street:** Thomas Kay (d. 1624), merchant and inn-holder, was one of the chamberlains of York in 1605 and sheriff in 1613; he succeeded John Bilbowe as host of the George on Coney Street around 1606 (BI, Probate Register, 39, ff.338–9; Cook, 1909, 92; Drake, 1736, 365; TNA, E 163/17/22; Davies, 1880, 64). One of the best-known inns in the city, the George had a 'wide gateway and spacious inner quadrangle'; above the gateway, there was a decorated plaster front featuring 'a grotesque figure of a seated Bacchus, grasping an overflowing cornucopia in each hand'. Kay

289. Bland] Blane MS   **291.** burnt] burnd MS   **294.** Tadcaster, and] Todcaster. And MS
297. Kay's] Keis MS

ordinary. Where we were no sooner housed but diverse came to see and welcome us, among whom was Mr Haynes the minister and Mr Bartholomew Chaworth. Before we went to dinner, Sir Arthur 300 Ingram sent to my gossip telling him he hoped he would take none other house but his whilst he was in town, etc.

The next morning Mr Baldwin of Pomfret and Mr Wilson, keeper of the castle, came over of purpose to see us.

was also commemorated in John Taylor's account of his voyage to York in an old wherry, buying the poet's boat prior to Taylor's return, by road, to London: 'He entertain'd me well, for which I thanke him, / And gratefully, amongst my friends I'le ranke him' (*VCHYC*; Davies, 1880, 67; J. Taylor 1622, sig. [B7v]). **298. ordinary:** An inn with meals provided at a fixed price (*OED*, Ordinary *n.* 12c). **299. Haynes:** Thomas Haynes (d. 1620), vicar of St Martin's, Coney Street, from 1614 (*CCED*, Person ID 118173; Cook, 1909, vii, 90). **300. Chaworth:** Bartholomew Chaworth (d. 1635) was brother to Sir George (see above, l.199), and entered Gray's Inn in 1601; it is likely that he matriculated as a pensioner from Trinity College, Cambridge, in 1598, although he may then have been in his mid to late 20s. The address 'To Mr B. Chaworth' was added to James Howell's poem 'On my Valentine Mrs *Francis Metcalf* (now Lady *Robinson*) at York' in the second edition of *Epistolae Ho-Elianae*; the poem probably dates from 1629 (G. Marshall, 1871, 128; Cook, 1909, 95; *RGI*, 102; Ball and Venn, 1911–16, II.205; J. Howell, 1650, 158). **301. Ingram:** Sir Arthur Ingram (c.1565–1642) was the son of a London tallow-chandler with Yorkshire roots and connections. He studied civil law at Cambridge, and rose to prominence both as a merchant and as a manager of the commercial affairs of the earl of Suffolk and the earl of Nottingham, two of the most prominent members of the Howard family. His well-developed court connections and sharp business practices ensured his own enrichment, although his speculative ventures almost resulted in his ruin on at least one occasion. From 1609, he represented a succession of different constituencies in the early Stuart parliaments. He is named among the company of wits which met regularly at The Mitre tavern, and included John Donne, Christopher Brooke, John Hoskyns, Richard Martin and Lionel Cranfield. Rebuffed in his attempts to secure court office in 1615, he concentrated on the estates in Yorkshire he had begun to build up in 1607: he had acquired the position of secretary to the Council of the North in 1613, and subsequently purchased a lease of the Crown's rights in the alum industry. His prosperity survived the Howards' fall from favour, and he built himself an impressive house in York while continuing to accumulate land, office and influence in the county; by 1625, his estates yielded between £4,000 and £5,000 a year (*ODNB*; *HP04*; Upton, 1961; O'Callaghan, 2007, 3; *YG*, 95). He has been suggested as the model for the character of Merecraft in *The Devil is an Ass*; if so, he was either unaware of or untroubled by this portrayal (Prestwich, 1966, 98; Donaldson, 2011, 340). **303–304. keeper of the castle:** Presumably Pontefract castle, rather than York, given the company. In July 1618, Robert Wilson, 'Keeper of Pontefract Castle', was granted £3,000 and timber from the duchy of Lancaster for repairs (*CSPD, 1611–1618*, 554). He was possibly related to the Dionis Wilson who witnessed Brian Babthorpe's will, while John Baldwin later bequeathed his watch to Martha, wife of 'Diunis' or 'Dinnis' Wilson of Pegsworth in Northumberland, and perhaps Babthorpe's widow (BI, Probate Register, 36, f.600, and 40, f.262). Pegsworth or Pegswood was part of the barony of Bothal, and therefore the property of Jane, countess of Shrewsbury (NA, DD/P/6/4/2/1; TNA, E 41/43/ii). 'Dionisius Wilson of Bottle, yeoman' was identified as one of the 'deputies of Edward Talbot, esquire' in a presentment of 1602 (NRO, QSI/1, f.25 (145)).

299. us, among] vs. Among MS   **300.** Bartholomew] *Bat* MS
302. town, etc.] towne. ec. MS   **303.** Wilson, keeper] *Wilson keeper* MS
304. castle, came] castle came MS

This day Mr Walter, my Lord President's steward, showed me the new 305
manor which the king hath new built where St Mary's monastery stood,
and carried me down into the cellar, which is the fairest, largest, and
fullest of light that I have seen. Two springs of excellent sweet water
rising in the middest thereof. The next day, being Friday, Sir Arthur
Ingram carried my gossip in coach to my Lord's Grace accompanied 310
with a Scotch gentleman, one Mr Lumsdale.

On Monday the 17th of August we parted early out of York, accompanied with Captain Hazell and his friend Mr Jaques, who would needs

305. Walter: Most probably a kinsman of Sir Robert Watter (d. 1612), twice lord mayor of York and posthumous benefactor of the city; his will mentions a brother, William, and a nephew, Christopher. Mr Walter was steward to Edmund, third baron Sheffield and later earl of Mulgrave (1565–1646), who was president of the Council of the North from 1603 until he sold the office to Emanuel, Lord Scrope, in 1619 (Hargrove, 1818, II.301–8; ODNB). **305–306. new manor:** The former St Mary's Monastery, retained by the Crown after the Dissolution and rebuilt as the residence of the president of the Council; James VI and I stayed there on his southwards journey in 1603 and is reported to have ordered its renovation; work began under Lord Sheffield after 1611 and by 1616 had already cost more than £1,000. This phase of construction continued into the 1620s. The 'noble stone vaults…which may be compared with anything of that kind in Britain' were known as the 'King's Cellar' and formed part of a range constructed to accommodate Henry VIII on his visit to York in 1542; they were subsequently incorporated into the later buildings (NP, 3.271; VCHYC; CSPD, 1611–18, 379; Davies, 1883, 2, 5; Drake, 1736, 577; Colvin, 1963–82, IV.355–64). **310. my Lord's Grace:** Tobie Matthew (1544–1628), archbishop of York from 1606. He attended Christ Church College, Oxford, in the 1560s, became a canon in 1570 and was appointed dean six years later. He was an orthodox Calvinist in his convictions and associated politically with the earl of Leicester. As dean of Durham from 1583, and bishop from 1594, he gained a reputation as an indefatigable preacher and an effective administrator, overseeing a border commission and taking action to suppress Catholicism. His political involvements continued after his promotion to York, and he cooperated closely with the gentry and magnates active in the Council of the North. He preached the sermon at the funeral of Gilbert Talbot, seventh earl of Shrewsbury, in 1616 and granted a lease of the site of the archbishop's residence to Sir Arthur Ingram in October 1618 (ODNB). In the summer of that year, Matthew was resident at his palace at Bishopthorpe, 2½ miles south of the city; on Sunday 16 August, during Jonson's visit, he preached at Bilbrough, just over 4 miles west of Bishopthorpe (YML, MS Add. 18,122). His monument in York Minster noted that 'his house was a perpetual scene of entertainment for the rich, and of charity for the poor' (Murray and Pattison, 2000, 49). **311. Lumsdale:** Thomas Lumsden (d. c.1625), gentleman of the privy chamber and pensioner until the end of James's reign; caught up in the Overbury affair in October 1615 when Sir Edward Coke was angered by a critical account of the proceedings against Richard Weston that Lumsden sent to the king – he was denounced in Star Chamber by Francis Bacon for this 'false, odious, and libellous relation', fined and imprisoned (TNA, LC 2/6, f.39v; CSPD, 1611–18, 168, 218–19, 321 and 326; Bacon, 1824, IV.453). In 1613, he was granted a reversion of the stewardship of Galtres (see l.314 below) with his fellow courtier William Ramsay (see l.502 below), and he later also held a foot forestership and the office of Master of the Game; with James Heatley (see l.518 below), he acquired the stewardship of Sheriff Hutton. By 1619, he may have been the possessor of a brick-built hunting lodge near Sutton on the Forest, 7 miles north of York. He was, however, 'a man with chronic financial difficulties' (Cowling, 1968, 178); at his death, Sir Arthur Ingram was his principal creditor and acquired his forest offices (CSPD, 1611–18, 210; TNA, E 214/1503; WYAL, WYL100/SH/A1/8A, WYL100/SH/A1/12; Cowling, 1968, 178–9,

305–6. Walter, my Lord President's Steward, showed me the new manor] *Walter* my L President Steward shewed me the new manner, MS
306. built where] buylt, where MS   **309.** day,] day MS   **309.** Friday,] Friday MS

bring us as far as the forest, our purpose being that night to go no further
then Sir Henry Francklin's, where Sir Edward Stanhope promised to   315
meet my gossip. But as we travelled, hearing it was out of our way and
desiring to take advantage of the fairness of the weather we resolved to go
on, and so baited at Tollerton, where Parson Rogers hearing of our
passing by rid after us and recovered us at mine host Thorton's; where
my gossip discharged two borracho bottles upon mine host and the   320
parson, to the downfall of the one, and so elevating the other that Mr
Parson would needs bring us on the way, where to show his love to my
gossip he fell off his horse and after ran leaping and dancing before us
halfway to Topliffe, where we went to Mrs Warcup's the famous good
hostess, where we stayed till Wednesday being shut up with rain.   325

189). **314. forest:** The Forest of Galtres, to the north of York, which had once extended as far as the city walls; by the early seventeenth century considerably diminished, though still with a stock of over 800 deer and covering around 7,600 acres. Full disafforestation took place in the 1630s (Cowling, 1968, 174–89). **315. Francklin's:** Sir Henry Frankland (d. 1622), of Aldwark, who may have matriculated from Lincoln College, Oxford, in 1582; he was knighted in 1607 and was married to Jane, daughter of Sir Charles Wren (see below, ll.367–8). Aldwark is by the River Ouse, 11 miles north of York, 3 miles to the west of the village of Tollerton, and 9 miles south of the travellers' revised destination (*AO*; *KE*; *VCHYNR*). **315. Stanhope:** Sir Edward Stanhope (c.1579–1646) owned property at Grimston, just south of Tadcaster, and at Edlington, near Doncaster; he entered Gray's Inn in 1593 and was returned as MP for the constituency of Scarborough in 1601. He inherited his estates on the death of his father in August 1603, shortly after he had been knighted, and served as sheriff of Yorkshire in 1615–16. He was cousin both to Sir John Stanhope, Sir Charles Cavendish's 1599 assailant, and Charles, Baron Stanhope, whose extravagantly annotated copy of the second folio of Jonson's *Works* contains the claim that he met the poet at Lyons during his journey to France with Wat Raleigh in 1612–13 (*HP58*; *HP04*; Donaldson, 2011, 302; Osborn, 1957, 16). Sir Edward Stanhope's wife, Margaret Constable, was the daughter of strongly Catholic parents, and her brother, Henry Constable (1588–1645), was the 'most substantial Catholic layman in the East Riding' (*ODNB*, Henry Constable, Viscount Dunbar; *YG*, 290).

Both Stanhope and Constable held forest offices in Galtres (Cowling, 1968, 178; *HP04*). **318. Rogers:** Henry Rogers (?1584–c.1657), graduated BA from St Edmund Hall, Oxford, by 1610 and MA by 1614; rector of St Denys with St George, York, from 1612, and of St Mary, Bishophill Senior, York, from 1614; ejected for scandal by the protectoral commissioners for the West Riding in February 1655; he then confessing himself old and 'readie as a ricke of corne to bee putt into the barne' (*AO*; *CCED*, Person ID 12451; TNA, PROB 11/271/43; *WR*, 398; Cross, 1967, 138). **319. Thorton's:** William Thornton was granted a licence for an alehouse in Tollerton in 1615 (TNA, DL 41/863, f.7). **320. borracho bottles:** Large wine-skins, associated with both Spain and excessive drinking. Cf. *Devil is an Ass*, 2.1.71 and Ford, Dekker, Middleton and Rowley, *The Spanish Gipsy*, 1.1.6; likewise ?John Heath, 'In Borachium': 'Borachio sayd, Wine made his head too light, / And therfore would not drinke it: yet last night / Carowsing healths, so heauy was his head, / He fell asleepe, and there was left for dead' (?Heath, 1619, sig. [B5v]). **324. Topliffe:** More commonly called Topcliffe, a customary staging post for travellers heading north from, or south to, York: indeed, in 1615 this small town had thirteen licensed alehouse keepers (TNA, DL 41/863, f.11v). **324. Mrs Warcup's:** Elizabeth Warcopp (d. 1622), holder of a wine licence for Topcliffe, and widow of Jasper Kettlewell (d. 1590), yeoman, and George Warcopp (d. 1599), gentleman. Both her husbands were reasonably wealthy, and her own will shows her to have held substantial property in and around the town (TNA, E 163/17/22; BI, Probate Register, 37, f.341).

315. Henry] Hen MS   **315.** Stanhope] Stanhop MS   **316.** travelled] travayled MS
316. way and] way, and MS   **319.** recovered us at] recoverd vs at Tollerton, [where] at MS
319. Thorton's;] *Thortons* MS   **320.** borracho] borrachoe MS

On Wednesday three of the widow's sons, the Kettlewells, and Seagerson her nephew with two others brought us to Sandhewton, where we shifted by reason of a huge shower overtook us.

That night we came to Northallerton, where we lay at Scarlett's the postmaster.   330

On Thursday we passed Lowsie Hill, Smitham and baited at Croft. We passed Croft bridge, going two miles about because we would not pass Nysam ferry. Then we passed Skerne brigg, Tees runs under Croft brigg, and we came through wet to Darnton where we lay at Glover's the postmaster's, son-in-law to the good woman of Topliffe.   335

Friday we stayed all day at Darnton.

On Saturday the 22th of August we took our journey towards Durham, between that and Ferry on the Hill my gossip met Sir Robert Mansell and Sir Arnold Harbert, who had expected a month his coming

---

326. **sons:** Elizabeth Warcopp's sons were John Kettlewell (d. c.1654), the eldest; Jasper (d. c.1653); and William (TNA, PROB 11/243/141, PROB 11/226/52). 327. **Seagerson:** No one of that name is mentioned in surviving family wills. A John Seager of York died in 1614 or 1615; this might perhaps be a reference to one of his kinsmen. 'Nephew' can also mean 'niece' or 'grandson' (TNA C 142/344/28; *OED*, Nephew *n*. 2a, 2b). 327. **Sandhewton:** Sandhutton, a village 4 miles north of Topcliffe. 329. **Scarlett's:** Thomas Scarlett or Skarlett succeeded Christopher Skarlett as the postmaster at Northallerton in 1618; in 1615, members of the family held three of this substantial market town's fifty-two alehouse licences (TNA, Pipe Rolls, AO 1/1952/20, f.3v; TNA, DL 41/863, f.40). It is 11 miles north of Topcliffe. 331. **Lowsie:** Variant name for Lovesome Hill, 4 miles north of Northallerton and 3 miles south of Great Smeaton (cf. Ogilby, 1675, 5). 332–333. **Croft bridge...Nysam ferry:** Described in the mid sixteenth century as 'the grete Bridge at Crofte', and consisting 'of sixe myghtye large pillars, and of seven arches of stone worke'; an alternative to the most direct route, which took travellers down Breakhorse Bank and across the Tees via the ferry at Nysam or Neasham 2 miles to the east. As its name suggests, the gradient of Breakhorse Bank made it unsuitable for coaches and wagons (*VCHYNR*; Ogilby, 1675, 5). 333. **Skerne brigg:** A crossing over the River Skerne, either at the point where it joins

the Tees just north of Croft, now Oxneyfield Bridge, or 2 miles further north on the eastern edge of Darlington. 334. **Darnton:** Darlington '*vulgo* [commonly known as] *Darnton*', 'large and well frequented, being a Post-Town, well Accommodated for Entertainment' (Ogilby, 1675, 16). 334. **Glover's:** Peter Glover (d. 1625), postmaster, also held a wine licence between 1616 and 1622. He occupied a house known as the Post House or Talbot Inn in the north-eastern corner of Post House Wynd (TNA, Pipe Rolls, AO 1/1952/20, f.3v E; 163/17/22; Atkinson, 1993, 35). He appointed his 'right trustie and deere beloved' brothers-in-law John and Jasper Kettlewell as supervisors to his will, leaving them each a gold Jacobus (BI, Probate Register, 38. ff.586v–587). 337. **22th:** 'Two and twentieth'. 338. **Ferry on the Hill:** Ferryhill, 11 miles north of Darlington, which 'commaunds a great part of the Country, and though soe wondrous high, yet there on the top thereof wee...borrowed a cup of refreshing health, from a sweet and most pleasant spring' (*AShS*, 24). 339. **Mansell... Harbert:** Previously encountered at Ware (see l.14 above). Both had northern interests: Mansell had acquired a monopoly for the manufacture of glass, developing a site for its production near Newcastle which was probably operational by April 1618 (*ODNB*; *HP04*); Harbert's patron, Theophilus Howard, Lord Walden, was lord lieutenant in the north, and held lands there through his marriage, while Harbert himself

---

331. Hill, Smitham] hill Smitham MS   333. brigg, Tees] brigge Teze MS
335. Topliffe] *Topleif* MS   336. Darnton] Darneton MS   339. Arnold] *Arnoll* MS

to Newcastle. We baited at Ferryhill at the blind woman's, where our host of Darnton met us. Here a great gate was blown down upon me. 340

By the way I lost my gossip, and came muck wet to Mr Dearham's at the King's Arms where I found my gossip accompanied with Mr Richardson and other gentlemen ready to bring him to my Lord of Durham's, where he supped. My lord using him with all the love and respect that could be, entreating to bring all his company next day to dinner, and to use no other house but his. Whither we all came the next day, being Sunday, where the plenty of meat, variety of dishes and state of service was such as I saw not the like since our coming forth. But that which exceeded all the rest was my lord's extraordinary and strange freedom and familiarity with my gossip, and his grace and favour for his sake to us. 345 350

At dinner was Sir George Conyers, Mr Archdeacon, Mr Chancellor,

had a lease in 1615 of lands in North Tynedale. His connections undoubtedly led to his election as MP for Morpeth in the parliaments of 1614 and 1625, a seat standardly in the gift of Lord William Howard of Naworth (*ODNB*, Theophilus Howard; TNA, E 367/1306; *HP04*). **340. blind woman's:** Unidentified. **342. Dearham's:** Possibly Robert Dearham of Durham, coroner of Darlington for the bishop of Durham (TNA, DURH 30/121/12, 14). No record of the King's Arms has been found. **344. Richardson:** Perhaps the Mr Richardson of Tadcaster, suggesting either that he had travelled alongside Jonson or was re-encountering him here. The author appears to distinguish between this man and John Richardson of Durham (see l.360 below). **344-345. Lord of Durham's:** Richard Neile (1562-1640), bishop of Durham from 1617 to 1628, lived in a grand residence in Durham Castle by the cathedral. Neile was a native of Westminster, educated at the college, and served as dean of the abbey between 1605 and 1608; Robert Cecil's patronage helped him to become royal chaplain and clerk of the closet from 1603, with privileged access to the king and control over preaching rotas at court. Neile was a leading figure in what became known as Arminianism, the clerical movement promulgating an increasingly controversial set of doctrinal, liturgical and ecclesiological positions which, with royal support, became dominant in the Anglican church during the later 1620s and 1630s –

Neile himself became archbishop of York in 1632. According to Peter Smart, a hostile witness, Neile's 'principall care and study was to enrich himself, and his kindred, Chaplains, creatures, and favourites, which he made non-Residents, and Tot-quots [holders of multiple livings], heaping upon them all manner of preferments'. A circle of high churchmen who formed the focal point for emergent Arminian thinking became known as the Durham House group, after the bishop's residence on the Strand in London (*ODNB*, Richard Neile and Durham House group; A. Foster, 2000, 162; Smart, 1643, sig. *2). **353. Conyers:** Sir George Conyers of Sockburn, from a family often sheriffs of the palatinate of Durham, was deputy-lieutenant under bishop Neile; listed as a Catholic and cited or convicted for recusancy several times between the 1590s and the 1620s (TNA, DURH 20/42–57, 84–98; DUL, MSP 2, pt 2, f.275; Forster, 1960, 149–50; Calthrop, 1916, 87, 97). His sister, Elizabeth, was married to Sir Thomas Riddell of Northumberland (see ll.396-7 below). **353. Archdeacon:** William Morton (d. 1620), justice of the peace, vicar of St Nicholas, Newcastle, from 1596 and archdeacon of Durham from 1603 (*CCED*, Location ID 232853; *DQS*, 345). **353. Chancellor:** Durham bishopric had two chancellors. The chancellor of the palatinate, with secular jurisdiction, was Sir Richard Hutton (d. 1639), receiver-general of the bishopric's revenues. He was also a member of the Council of the North

340. Newcastle] new castell MS   **340.** Ferryhill] Ferry hill MS
342. Dearham's] Dirrham's MS   **345.** Durham's, where] Durhams where MS
348. day, being Sunday, where] day being sonnday. Where MS   **353.** Conyers] *Conniers* MS

Mr Robson and others. All my lord's gentlemen, Mr Robson the
younger, steward to my lord, Mr Stephenson, gentleman usher, 355
Mr Legatt, Mr Pelen, gentleman sewer, showing themselves rather
attendants then otherwise to my gossip, brought him home every
night to his lodging, and staying with him till twelve or one a clock.
My lord's chaplains, Mr Perne and Mr Clarke, doing the like. After
dinner Mr John Richardson brought us to his father's who hath married 360

until 1619, recorder of York since 1608,
knighted in York in 1617, and king's justice in
the court of common pleas from 1617 to 1639,
these occupations keeping him from Durham
much of the time (*DQS*, 343). The chancellor of
the spiritual courts was Clement Colmore (d.
1619), who was admitted to Oxford in 1566 and
became a Fellow of Brasenose in 1578. He held
various rectories in the bishopric from 1584,
and was a JP since at least 1601, sitting at the
quarter sessions held in Durham on 8 July 1618
(BI, Probate Register, 34, ff.435–40; *DQS*, 293–
4, 340). The appellation 'Mr' here points to
Colmore. **354. Robson:** John Robson (c.1581-
1645), rector of Morpeth, 1610–43, and subsequently member of the Durham high commission, appointed by Neile to the sixth prebendary
of Durham cathedral in 1623. He was a chaplain
to James VI and I by 1620, and his eldest son was
the first to be baptised in the new ornamented
font that Neile installed at Durham (*HP04*; Tillbrook, 1987, 208; DUL, DDR/EA/ACT/1/4,
p.56). **354–355. Robson the younger:** Probably
Mr Robert Robson, under-sheriff of Durham
by 1621, sheriff from 1624 (DUL, MSP 92, f.25;
CCB/B/16/46). **355. steward:** The steward
listed for 1616–18 is Robert Cooper; the sentence may suggest that the younger Robson in
fact fulfilled this office (DUL, Handlist of
Officeholders). **355. Stephenson:** John Stephenson was appointed escheator of Durham
and clerk of the assize in September 1619; on
15 August 1618 he was paid £105 from the
bishopric revenues (DUL, DCD/B/AA/2, f.1v,
2; CCB/B/16/47, f.3). **356. Legatt:** Mr Thomas
Posthumous Legatt of Hornchurch in Essex,
who in October 1619 was granted a lease by
the dean and chapter of Durham of Powter
Close on the River Tyne; one of his guarantors
was the bishop's auditor, suggesting his closeness to the bishop's household. He may have
been involved with the Tyneside coal trade
(DUL, DCD/B/BA/9, f.613). **356. Pelen:**
Unidentified. **359. Perne:** Andrew Perne (d.
1640), one of Neile's chaplains, came with
him from his previous bishopric of Lincoln.

He took his BA from Peterhouse, Cambridge,
in 1596/7 and his MA in 1600; he was a Fellow
of the college from 1598 to 1621, and was made
vicar of Norton and rector of Washington
in Co. Durham in 1621; a member of the Durham House group, he instituted ceremonial
changes in northern churches (*AC*; *ODNB*,
'Durham House group'; DUL, DDR/EA/
ACT/1/4, pp.46, 47). Not to be confused with
his younger, godly namesake. **359. Clarke:** Gabriel Clarke (1589–1662), another member
of the Durham House group and a Neile pro-
tégé, marrying his patron's niece. He was
appointed archdeacon of Northumberland
in 1619, and then translated to Durham on
Morton's death in 1620; in 1619, he was granted
the rectory of Howick and, in 1620, that of
Elwick; in 1624, he was given the mastership
of Greatham hospital for poor people in Co.
Durham, succeeding to increasingly senior
prebendaries in Durham cathedral. He was
also a member of Durham's high commission,
and a justice of the peace (*ODNB*, 'Durham
House group'; A. Foster, 1976, 44–6; DUL,
DDR/EA/ACT/1/4, pp.18, 29, 30, 37, 55; Add
MS 226, p.170). **360. Richardson:** Mr John
Richardson, elder (d. 1640) and younger
(d. 1623), were both lawyers, admitted to
Gray's Inn in 1598 and 1605 respectively (Prest,
1986, 149–50, 337; *RGI*, 93, 110). Richardson senior was appointed the bishop's remembrancer
and solicitor in all courts in 1607, later becoming clerk of the chancery and escheator for the
palatinate of Durham. One of the previous
bishop's men, he fell foul of Neile's new administration and was sacked shortly after Jonson's
visit (*DQS*, 346; DUL, MSP 33 and 71; Tillbrook
1987, 222–3, n.41; A. Foster 1987, 189–90). After
Neile's translation to Winchester in 1628, however, he recovered his position, becoming escheator for Norhamshire in 1636 (DUL, MSP
25, f.10). He lived comfortably in a house on the
North Bailey of Durham (*AHCD*, 89). His son
may have been the John Richardson employed
to carry letters between Durham and York (BI,
ABP 3/4–9).

354. gentlemen,] gent MS   355. Stephenson,] Stephenson MS   355. usher,] vsher MS
359. chaplains,] chaplens MS   359. Clarke,] *Clerke* MS

with Mrs El. Vavasour, where we met with things worth the seeing. Mr Richardson entreated my lord for Mr Jonson's company to supper, but my lord by no means would spare him.

My lord spake to me to entreat my gossip to stay the next day, being Barthelmew day, saying I might prevail with him etc. I answered none 365 might better command him then his lordship, who had bound him by so many favours to be at his service. This day dined there Sir Charles Wren of Nottingham, a most violent Puritan with whom my gossip had a pleasant encounter, at which my lord laughed heartily.

Here my gossip entreated that *poetica licentia* he might propose a 370 health, which was the king's etc.; my lord did the like at supper etc. In the afternoon we visited the monuments, especially that of venerable Bede, and St Cuthbert bishop of the Holy Isle, where we heard the manner of

361. Mrs El. Vavasour: Correctly, Anne, daughter of Henry Vavasour of Copmanthorpe, Yorkshire, and a gentlewoman in Queen Elizabeth's bedchamber. She is known to have married a John Richardson by 1618, when she was sued by the heir of her deceased lover, Sir Henry Lee, for bigamy, being married already to John Finch – her impending legal trouble was reported by Chamberlain in a letter of 8 August. The memory of her 1580 liaison with Edward de Vere, seventeenth earl of Oxford, was sustained through her association with the lyric 'Sitting alone upon my thought in melancholy mood', sometimes attributed to Oxford; she was also credited with verses that accompany the lyric in one manuscript (*ODNB; CL*, 2.164; Folger MS V.a.89, 8–9; May, 1980, 79–81; Marotti, 1995, 57–8). **365. Barthelmew day:** St Bartholomew's Day, celebrated on 24 August, was a traditional time for markets and fairs, and the celebrated fair at Smithfield was the setting for *Bartholomew Fair*, first staged in 1614. It also marked the anniversary of the massacre of thousands of Protestant Huguenots in France in 1572. **367. Wren:** Sir Charles Wren of Binchester (d. 1621), knighted in 1607, was the constable of Durham castle from 1606, steward of Raby and Brancepeth castles, and a justice of the peace from at least 1606 to 1617. His wife was the daughter of John Thornhaugh, of Fenton, Nottinghamshire (*DQS*, 348–9; DUL, CCB/B/21/29; ACC Add MS 924/5, p.3; ACC Add MS 924/3; *WID*, 4. 147–9). He was pardoned for the killing of one Robert Ratcliff in a duel in 1589; in 1608, the earl of

Shrewsbury's agent, Henry Sanderson, wrote that Wren 'bloweth the same bellowes' as another notable Puritan, probably Gilbert Frevile of Bishop Middleham (DUL, MS 924/2; LP, MS 702, f.63). **368. violent Puritan:** cf. *Disc.* 43–6. **370. poetica licentia:** Poetic licence, 'a priuiledge giuen to Poetrie' (Harington, 1591, sig. ¶4). **371. health:** As at l.201, perhaps the verses composed between 1617 and 1619 (*CWBJ*, 5.346–7). **372. Bede:** The Venerable Bede (c. 673–735) was a monk and historian in the monastery at Jarrow, whose *Ecclesiastical History of the English People* (c. 731) was first printed in Strasburg after 1474, and then in numerous sixteenth- and seventeenth-century editions. Bede was initially buried at Jarrow, but subsequently re-interred in the Galilee chapel of Durham cathedral in a blue marble tomb; this was dismantled following the Reformation, and the remains buried more simply under two of the original marble stones in 'ye bodye of the church and lyeth now over against the estmost Toumbe of the Neivell' (*ODNB*; J. Fowler, 1903, 44–6, 103–4, 225, 233–5, 286–7). Bede's reputation was much associated with the Northumbrian saint Cuthbert, whom he commemorated in his *Life of Cuthbert*. **373. Cuthbert...Isle:** St Cuthbert (635–87) was the prior of the monastery on Lindisfarne, 'the Holy Isle', a small island joined to the Northumbrian coast. He spent many years as a hermit on the more remote island of Inner Farne, in later life becoming a bishop in Northumbria before returning to Inner Farne, where he died. Following Viking attacks, his body was

361. Vavasour, where] *Vavasor.* Where MS   362. Jonson's] *Iohnsons* MS
364. day,] day MS   365. day,] day MS   365. answered, none] answeard not MS
371. etc.; my] ec, my MS   373. Cuthbert] *Cutberd* MS

his translating thither, with the discourse of the cow which stands in the side of the church, the town taking the name of Dunholmes thereupon. 375

On Tuesday morning, the waits and cornets came to our lodging. Mine host brought us to Chester where Mr Tibalds, a physician, and another townsman came to us, and from thence kept us company to Newcastle. By the way my gossip bought a salmon and a salmon trout etc. Mine host was [a] drunken, disordered fellow, but she a good wife. 380

We had by the way a full sight of that stately and well seated castle of Lumley.

We came that night to Newcastle where my gossip lay at Carr's, and I at widow Wallace's. My gossip was invited the next day to

carried to Chester-le-Street in about 875, where it remained for a century; after further travels, he was eventually interred east of the high altar in Durham cathedral in 1104. The much-visited shrine was dismantled after the Reformation and the body reburied in a plain grave behind the altar, reputedly still uncorrupted. Despite the Reformation, St Cuthbert remained important to the secular and ecclesiastical communities of Durham and to the regional identity of England's north-east. During his period in office, Richard Neile made efforts to 'restor[e] many of [Durham's] traditions and customs' (Newton, 2013, 440, 447–53; J. Fowler, 1903, 69–75, 286). **374. discourse… cow:** Cuthbert's final resting-place was reputedly chosen when the monks searching for a suitable site followed two milkmaids looking for a dun or brown cow to Dun Holm, a rocky peninsula in the River Dee, where the cathedral was then built. An account of 1593 described how 'a monument of a milke maide milkinge hir koue' was erected 'on the outside of the north-west turrett of the Nine Altars' of the new cathedral, which though 'defaced by the weather…to this day is there to be seene'; it was replaced by the current monument around 1775 (J. Fowler, 1903, xiv–xv, 66, 71, 74, 254). **376. waits:** Here, both wait-pipes or shawms and the waits, 'a small body of wind instrumentalists maintained by a city or town at the public charge' (*OED*, Wait *n.* 8a). The earliest surviving record for the Durham waits dates from March 1618 (*REED Lanc*, 178). **376. cornets:** Horns; metonymically, their players. **377. Mine host:** Presumably Robert Dearham of The King's Arms. **377. Chester:** Chester-le-Street, nearly

6 miles north of Durham; 'chiefly one streate of very meane building' (Leland, 1906–10, I.74). **377. Tibalds:** Mr Anthony Theobald, *alias* Tebald (1587–1635), graduated from Emmanuel College, Cambridge, in 1591 and lived in St Mary-le-Bow, Durham (*AC*). **380. Mine host:** Possibly Richard Fletcher, who had a wine licence for Chester-le-Street in 1616–22 for £2 (TNA, E 163/17/22); given that Dearham appears to have accompanied the travellers to Chester, perhaps a reference to him. **382. Lumley:** Lumley Castle, ancestral home of the ancient Northumbrian family of that name, 'a stately pile of Building, and a Parke, sweetly situated vpon a fine ascent of the Riuer Were' (*CB*, 742; *AShS*, 30–1). **383. Newcastle:** Situated on the north bank of the River Tyne; approached from the south across a bridge of eight arches, on 'the left hand whereof standeth the Castle: after that, a steepe and vpright pitch of an hill risith: on the right hand you have the Mercat place, and the better part of the City in regard of faire buildings…It is adorned with foure churches, and fortified with most strong walls that have eight gates in them, with many towres' (*BT*, 85; *CB*, 809–10). **383. Carr's:** Leonard Carr owned the Nag's Head, an inn in Sandhill described by travellers in the 1630s as 'the fairest built inn that I have seen', and a 'stately, prince-like, freeston inn'. Carr was a prosperous wine-merchant, and member of the Merchant Adventurers and Hostmen Guilds in Newcastle (*BT*, 89; *AShS*, 32; *MAR*, 2.225; Welford, 1884–7, III.34, 325). **384. widow Wallace's:** Unidentified; in 1600, Hugh and James Wallace rented houses in Sandgate near Sandhill (Welford, 1884–7, III.135–6).

375. church, the] church. The MS   377. Tibalds, a physician,] Tibalds a *Phisition* MS
379. Newcastle] new castle MS   382. Lumley] Lomley MS   383. Newcastle] new castle MS
384. Wallace's] *Walleses* MS

Mr Maddison the mayor to dinner, and was most lovingly used by   385
Mr Boyd, that is in suit with the town for an impost upon coal.

My gossip went to the free school and gave the master a piece to buy a
book with.

On Thursday we were invited by Sir George Selby, where was at
dinner Captain Poor. And after dinner Sir John Fenwick came.   390

385. Maddison: Lionel Maddison (c.1530–1624) was an affluent Merchant Adventurer and Hostman, with interests in the coal trade. He held a number of civic offices, and although then in his late 80s was elected mayor for the third time in 1617. There is an elaborate monument to him and his immediate descendants in the church of St Nicholas, now Newcastle cathedral (Mackenzie, 1827, I.262; *MAR*, 2. 207). **386. Boyd:** Andrew Boyd, knighted in 1620, cupbearer to James VI and I. He was given £1,000 by the king in 1615; in 1623, James 'particularly desire[d]' his pension to be paid. His place at court led to a grant of the office of surveyor of coals at Newcastle in 1616; it was re-granted for life in 1619, with an annuity of £500 given to him in 1621 (TNA, LC 2/6, f.40v; *NP*, 4.611; *CSPD, 1611–18*, 277; *CSPD, 1619–23*, 624). It was a contentious office, his powers disputed by the corporation of Newcastle, and from 1616 onwards Boyd instigated enquiries by the Crown into alleged abuses of the coal trade by Newcastle merchants (*CSPD, 1611–18*, 351, 556; *CSPD, 1619–23*, 58, 235, 406, 443; *HR*, 62–3). He danced in *The Irish Masque at Court* and was the addressee of an admiring epigram by John Dunbar (*CWBJ*, 1.cxliv; Dunbar, 2013, Century 5, Epigram 33). **386. in suit:** engaged in a lawsuit **387. free school:** Newcastle enjoyed high levels of literacy, with several schoolmasters employed in the 1500s. In 1600, Newcastle's 'Great Charter' formally founded the grammar school, although it continued to be known as the 'Free School', to which all freemen of Newcastle were entitled to send their sons. It was initially housed in St Nicholas's churchyard, but moved to St Mary's Hospital in 1607 (Tuck, 1986, 3, 5, 11, 16). **387. master:** Robert Fowberry (d. 1622), the school's master since 1615; 'a learned and painfull man to indoctrinate youth in Greek and Latin' (Gray, 1649, 20). His inventory included a substantial library of 150 books (Tuck, 1986, 19–20; TWRO, MD/NC/FN/1/1/10, f.303; Welford, 1884–7, III.247). **389. Selby:** Sir George Selby (1556/7–1625), alderman, mayor of Newcastle four times between 1600 and 1623; another

merchant adventurer and hostman with substantial interests in the coal trade (*HP04*; Welford 1884–7, III.426) was MP for Newcastle in 1601 and 1604, and for Northumberland in 1614, and served as a justice of the peace on the Northumbrian commission; he held office in Durham too, both as justice of the peace and as sheriff from 1608 to 1625, and hosted King James at Newcastle in 1617 (NRO, QSI/1, f.161; *HP04*; *DQS*, 347; TNA, DURH 20/103). The family was suspected of Catholicism: his sister, a reported recusant, was the second wife of Sir William Fenwick of Wallington, and her children were 'brought up in papistry', while in 1619 Selby's daughter, Isabel, married Sir Patrick Curwen, son of another recusant, Sir Henry Curwen (see l.419 below) (*HMCS*, 19.3–5; *ODNB*, 'Selby family'). He lived in a mansion in Oatmarket, also – and still today – known as Bigg Market (*HP04*; Gray, 1649, 19; Baillie, 1801, 119). **390. Captain Poor:** Unidentified. Henry Poor served as captain on the continent and in Ireland in the later years of Elizabeth's reign; he was, however, a knight by 1599, and no connection to Selby or Newcastle has been found (LP, MS 615, pp.58, 90, 179, 534; LP, MS 624, p.233; Wernham, 1994, 312). **390. Fenwick:** Sir John Fenwick (c.1580–c.1658), the son of Sir William Fenwick and his first wife; Sir George Selby, with whom he apparently maintained a close relationship, was thus his step-uncle. He was brought up a Protestant but in 1617 was bracketed with known recusants in a report on the poor state of the Northumbrian ministry. Despite this, in 1618 he was named a recusancy commissioner pursuing Northumbrian Catholics. He was a prominent member of Northumberland's gentry, whose wealth lay in his estates at Fenwick, Wallington and Cambo; he served as justice of the peace and deputy-lieutenant for the county. He was also a member of the Middle Shires commission, helping to suppress crime in the Anglo-Scottish Borders, and sat as MP for Northumberland in the parliaments of 1624 to 1628. He held no civic office, but had inherited a house in Newcastle's 'Noutte-Market' (Welford, 1884–7, III.199, 213; *HP04*;

385. dinner, and] dinner. And MS   **387.** master] Mr MS   **390.** Poor] Poore MS
390. Fenwick] *Fenneck* MS

Mr Bonner, sheriff, carried us from thence to his house where we heard all kind of music, and gave us hullock of 40 year old. And brought my gossip to his lodging, accompanied with another alderman and Mr Chapman.

On Friday my gossip, being ill, kept his chamber all day. Mr Mayor 395 sent to speak with him next morning, and Sir George Selby, Sir Thomas Ruddall with Mr Sheriff presented him with a present of ten pieces for his viaticum.

On Sunday we made on towards Bothal castle, and touched at

NRO, QSI/1, ff.145–6, 161). **391. Bonner:** William Bonner (d. 1627), the sheriff in 1617–18, was another of the busy Merchant Adventurers, and a Hostman of long standing, apprenticed in 1589, and appointed as steward of the guild in 1616. Originally, one of the Hostmen's principal obligations was to look after important visitors, principally merchants, to the city (Welford, 1884–7, III.213, 220, 426; TWRO, GU.HO/1/1, pp.144, 150). **392. music:** The aldermen of Newcastle regularly accompanied the drinking of wine with musical entertainment; for instance, in 1622 the Barber Surgeons' guild spent 5s on music during their head meeting at Leonard Carr's inn, and another 14s on music, wine and tobacco on a separate occasion there. In July 1623, the Masters and Mariners spent £2 at St Peter's eve on wine and music, and a similar sum the following year (*REED Newc*, 151). **392. hullock:** A Spanish red wine advised for the entertainment of 'persons of credite' (*OED*, Hollock *n.*; Percevel, 1599, 243; Hakluyt, 1599, 440–1). **394. Chapman:** The elder Henry Chapman (by 1556–1623) was another of Newcastle's civic elite, an alderman and former mayor; he was one of the original Hostmen owning rights in the coal trade, a wealthy merchant who left £1,600 in jewels to his wife (Welford 1884–7, III.139, 142, 250). He was elected an MP for Newcastle in 1597 and 1604. His brother Matthew's son was also Henry (d. 1633); this latter was the chief beneficiary of his uncle's will and 'had taken over the bulk of the family business' by 1617 (*HP04*). Matthew Chapman's daughter, Mary, married William Bonner in 1597, and in 1612 their son was apprenticed to the elder Henry (*WID*, 2.7–8; *MAR*, 2. 234). **397. Ruddall:** Sir Thomas Riddell (c.1568–1650) had substantial interests in Newcastle's coal trade, his share valued at £1,000 a

year in 1620. An alderman, he was knighted in 1616 and elected MP for Newcastle in 1621, 1625, 1628 and 1640. In 1615, he and Sir George Selby were tasked with defending the Hostmen's interests at the privy council against the patent for the surveyorship of the coals granted to Andrew Boyd. He remained a vociferous opponent of Boyd in the 1621 parliament. He also held office in Northumberland, sitting regularly as a justice of the peace. His wife, Elizabeth, sister of Sir George Conyers (see l.353 above), was convicted of recusancy in 1615; Riddell himself was cited as a recusant office holder during the 1620s (*HP04*; TWRO, GU.HO/1/1, p.138; NRO, QSI/1, ff.145, 161, 168, 173). **398. viaticum:** Travelling expenses; cf. *EMI* (F), 1.2.75; also, the final communion received by the dying, 'the viage provision of Christen men departing oute off this world' (*OED*, Viaticum *n.* 2a); if this latter sense is also aimed at, perhaps a somewhat Scotophobic gesture. **399. Bothal castle:** A central element in the Northumbrian inheritance acquired by Jane, countess of Shrewsbury. Jane and her husband, Edward Talbot, resided at Bothal prior to his elevation to the earldom; Talbot was on the Northumbrian commission for the peace, and *custos rotulorum* for the county (NRO, QSI/1, ff.18, 146). On the countess's death in 1625, Bothal passed to her sister, Catherine Cavendish, and thus became part of the rapidly expanding Cavendish estates. Bothal was a substantial castle, described in 1576 as having a great chamber, seven bedrooms, a gallery, a prison, two towers, a chapel and other 'prittie' buildings, with 'faire gardinges and orchetts wharin growes all kind of hearbes and flowres, and fine appiles, plumbes of all kynde, peers, damsellis, nuttes, cherries' (Ogle, 1902, 333). The MS spelling of Bothal as Bottle reflects its local pronunciation (Hodgson, 1832, 144).

391. Bonner, sheriff,] *Bonner* Sherief MS   **392.** 40] 40tie MS
395. gossip, being ill,] gossip being ill MS   **399.** Bothal castle, and] Bottle castle. And MS

Three-mile Brigg at Tom Robinson's, called Tom the Fencer, who   400
served Sir Harry Withrington, and brought us to Mr Ingleby's by
Harford, by reason we were taken with rain by the way. And
brought his greyhounds and beagles with him, and to give us
sport hunted all the way.

On Sunday we stayed at Bothal. On Monday Sir Harry   405
Withrington came himself to fetch my gossip to his house, and young
Mr Carnaby with him, and quit his horses and went on foot with us,

400. Three-mile Brigg: Three-mile Bridge, where the road north from Newcastle to Morpeth crosses the Ouseburn. **400. Robinson's... Fencer:** Possibly the Thomas Robinson who appears in a 1637 list of Newcastle brewers, although the name is not uncommon; a professional swordsman (Welford, 1884–7, III.349). The area immediately to the north of the bridge is called Fencer Hill. **401. Withrington:** Sir Henry Widdrington (c.1567–1623) was a prominent Northumbrian landowner, educated at Gray's Inn from 1590, knighted in 1603, subsequently holding various county offices, including that of justice of the peace, sheriff and deputy-lieutenant. Elected MP for Northumberland in 1604, he was a member of the commission drawing up proposals for Union; he was returned again in 1614 and 1621 (*HPo4*, 6. 774–9; NRO, QSI/1, f.161). Widdrington's mother was Ursula Carnaby, whose sister, Catherine (d. 1623), had married Cuthbert, seventh Lord Ogle (c.1540–97); he was thus first cousin to Jane Talbot and Catherine Cavendish, and kinsman to Sir William Cavendish. After Sir Henry's death, his heir, William, eventually became Cavendish's ward; William – who was knighted in March 1632 – may well be the 'Mr Withrington' mentioned in Jonson's 1631 letter to Cavendish (BL, Harl. MS 4955, f.202v; *CWBJ*, Letter 15; *ODNB*, William, first Baron Widdrington). Sir Henry was accused of recusancy, allegations made credible by his marriage to Mary Curwen, from a notoriously Catholic family, and by his brother Roger's known faith (see l.443 below; *HMCS*, 19. 3–5; *CSPD, 1611–18*, 355, 362, 406). Widdrington was connected to many of the major Northumbrian families: in his will, he named Sir John Fenwick, Sir Henry Curwen, Sir William Lambton (see l.411 below), his brother Roger and his son-in-law William Riddell, son of Sir Thomas (see ll.396–7 above) as supervisors (*WID*, 4.165–9). He was thus able to call on a sizeable armed retinue, it being

claimed that 'the great thieves of the county are supported by Lord Howard of Walden and under him by Sir Henry and Roger Wodrington and Sir John Fenwick', 'all of whom are dependents or servants' of the Widdringtons; there was, a correspondent complained, an 'entire want of justice, because these men support each other' (*CSPD, 1611–18*, 456, 465). In the middle of August 1618, Widdrington was at Burntisland in Scotland, where he exchanged memories of the 1597 Azores campaign with John Taylor; he was probably then visiting the renowned well at nearby Pettycur (see l.559 below; *PP*, sig. D4). **401. Ingleby's:** Mr Ingleby was probably related to the Inglebys of Ripley, Yorkshire: David, son of Sir William Ingleby, was known to have been in Northumberland in the 1590s with his niece, the wife of Sir Ralph Grey of Chillingham (see l.420 below); his daughter, Ursula, married Robert Widdrington, of Plessey, next to Hartford (*CSPD, Add. 1580–1625*, 191–2, 365; Hodgson, 1832, 297–8; *CBP*, 2.452). **402. Harford:** There had been an ancient religious establishment at Hartford or Herford Bridge, 11 miles north of the Tyne on lands subsequently acquired by the Widdringtons (Hodgson, 1832, 267–8, 297, 302–3). **406. his house:** Widdrington Castle, 6 miles north of Bothal: 'an ancient Castle, which gave the name unto the *Withringtons*, Gentlemen of good birth, and Knights, whose valour in the warre hath beene from time to time remarqueable' (*CB*, 812). The castle had been in Widdrington hands since at least 1341; 'its battlements were built on corbules, and it had round projecting turrets at each corner', with a fine tower that was reputedly 'one of the richest and handsomest' in the north. On his journey south in 1603, James VI and I 'was most royally feasted and banketted' there, 'delighting himselfe with the pleasure of the parke' and conferring knighthood on its owner (Hodgson, 1832, 241–2; *NP*, 1.67–8).

400. Three-mile Brigg at Tom] three myle brigg at Thom MS   400. Tom] Thom MS
405. Bothal] Bottle MS   406. Withrington] *Withrington*, MS

Mr Carnaby the elder and Mr Johnson, the countess of Shrewsbury's chaplain, doing the like, and Mr Randall Fenwick doing the like.

My Lady Withrington being sent for to her only sister, my Lady 410 Lampton, wife to Sir William Lampton of Lampton by Lumley castle, lying then extreme sick, notwithstanding, my lady hearing my gossip Jonson was a coming would not stir till she saw him, deferring her going two days only to give my gossip entertainment. On Tuesday the first of September we were stayed by Sir Harry who carried us on hunting where 415 we killed a buck.

On Wednesday the second of September we parted from Withrington, Sir Harry accompanying us with Mr Randy Fenwick and Harry Curwen. But overtaken with thunder and rain, we were fain to take East Chevington, which Mr Edwards hath taken of Sir Ralph Gray, 420

---

408. Carnaby the elder: Ursula, Sir Henry Widdrington's mother, was the daughter of Sir Reynold Carnaby of Halton, near Hexham; the families were also connected by the marriage of Ursula's brother, John Carnaby of Langley, to Jane, daughter of Sir John Widdrington. This marriage produced William Carnaby (d. c.1623), presumably the elder Carnaby here, who was therefore first cousin to Sir Henry Widdrington and the Ogle sisters; he served on juries at Quarter Sessions held at Hexham and at Morpeth (HN, 10.408; NRO, QSI/1, ff.130v, 145–6, 153v). 'Young Mr Carnaby' is probably his son, William Carnaby of Farnham and Bothal, whom Jonson had met at Welbeck. The younger William also served on the jury at Morpeth in 1617/18, and was a justice of the peace by 1629 (NRO, QSI/1, ff.174, 184). **408. Johnson:** Mr Henry Johnson (d. 1648), rector of Bothal from 1609; cited by the House of Commons in 1646 for officiating after his sequestration (WR, 290). **409. Fenwick:** Randall Fenwick (d. c.1640) originally of Deanham, eldest son of Marmaduke Fenwick of Kirkharle. Fenwick was suspected of recusancy and, with Roger Widdrington, accused of complicity in the Gunpowder Plot (CSPD, 1611–18, 406; Forster, 1972, 198–9). He may also have been associated with Lord William Howard of Naworth, a wealthy recusant of north-east Cumbria, overseeing Howard's land and mill at Morpeth (Ornsby, 1877, 69–70, 99–100, 423–5). **410–411. Lady Withrington…Lampton:**

Mary (d. 1622), daughter of Nicholas Curwen of Workington in Cumbria, married Sir Henry Widdrington by 1607, while her sister, Jane, married Sir William Lambton of Lambton, Co. Durham. Jane died by 1625, and Sir William later married Widdrington's daughter, Catherine (HP04; BI, Probate Register, 39, f.187; SA, CM/1680, 1696). **419. Curwen:** Sir Henry Curwen (c.1581–1623) was the Curwen sisters' half-brother by their father's second marriage. They were a notoriously recusant family: in 1606, it was reported that Curwen was 'a papist, who has lately married the widow of Christopher Wright the traitor'; his mother, too, was suspected (HMCS, 19, 3–5). Despite this he was MP for Cumberland in 1621 (HP04). Around 1613, Curwen sold Thornthwaite in Westmorland to Lord William Howard of Naworth, and appears to have been part of a Howard network with the recusant Roger Widdrington and Randall Fenwick (Ornsby, 1877, 5, 27). **420. Chevington… Gray:** East and West Chevington, 2 miles north of Widdrington, were the jointure lands settled in 1608 on the wife of Sir Ralph Grey (c.1552–1623) of Chillingham; the Greys were intricately connected with many northern Northumbrian families. Despite accusations of recusancy against him, his wife and several members of his family, Sir Ralph, who was knighted in 1603, served as a justice of the peace and as MP for Northumberland in 1604, and was a member of the

---

408. Shrewsbury's] Shrewsberries MS   409. chaplain,] chaplin MS
409. Randall Fenwick] *Randell Fenneck* MS   411. William] *Wil* MS
412. notwithstanding,] notwthstanding MS   413. Jonson] *Iohnson* MS
413. deferring] differing MS   417. on] one MS   418. Withrington,] *Withrington* MS
418. Randy Fenwick] *Randee Fenneck* MS   419. Curwen] *Kerbon* MS
420. Ralph Gray,] *Raph Gray* MS

who is one of the king's huntsmen and who kindly brought us beyond
Hadston and Dogston, where Mr Francis Carnaby hath houses, and almost
to Warkwith where my Lord of Northumberland hath an ancient castle,
and where Coquet runs about it, where you shall have a salmon for xijd and
a salmon trout for vjd, and a gilse, which is like a salmon, for a groat. And
here was the strange hermitage. Here were we stroaken in with rain, where
we were fain to stay to dry ourselves. From thence we came to Alemouth

425

Union commission alongside Sir Henry Widdrington (NRO, QSI/1, f.161; HP04; HMCS,
19.3–5). In 1629, his son, William, Lord Grey
applied to enclose a substantial area of Chevington into a park (DUL, GRE/X/P50/6, 9;
HN, 5.376, 392). 'Edwards' is an error, the tenant of East Chevington being Edward Dodsworth (d. 1630), of Barton, in Yorkshire;
'several members of [of the family] seem to
have served the Greys of Chillingham in the
management of their estates' (HN,
5.402). 421. huntsmen: The syntax here is misleading: the reference is to Dodsworth, who held
his office until the end of the reign. 'Huntsman to
King James' was engraved on his tombstone in
Warkworth churchyard, the lettering visible as
late as 1899 (TNA, LC 9/97, f.97v; LC 9/98, f.30v;
LC 2/6, f.48; HN, 5.402–3). 422. Hadston...
Carnaby: Francis Carnaby (d. 1645) was the
younger son of William Carnaby the elder; he
acquired Togston, just to the north of Chevington, through the inheritance of his grandmother, Jane Widdrington; his brother,
William, owned the neighbouring Hadston.
Togston was also known as Dogston, which
would account for the MS spelling here (HN,
5.332–3, 10.408). 423. Warkwith...castle:
Warkworth Castle, on the River Coquet 6
miles north of Widdrington, a property of
the earls of Northumberland. Henry Percy,
the ninth earl (1564–1632), was incarcerated
in the Tower of London from 1605 until 1621,
accused of complicity in the Gunpowder Plot
(ODNB). The castle had fallen into disrepair:
when James and his entourage visited it in 1617,
accompanied by Sir Henry Widdrington, 'they
seamed to greve at the waste of it, everie one of
them commendinge it for the best sight that
every they had sene' despite the 'goates
and sheepe in everie chamber'; of the lion
carved in a crest on the tower the king joked,
'this lyone houldes upe this castle'. It

was leased to Sir Ralph Grey, although
the earl's anger over his neglect led to its
return to the custody of the earl's servants in
November 1618 (HN, 5.71–3). 424. Coquet:
The River Coquet, which loops round Warkworth Castle and flows into the North Sea at
Amble. The MS spelling here reflects aspects
of its pronunciation. 424–425. xijd... vjd:
Twelve pence... six pence. 425. trout...
gilse: Salmon-trout are sea-trout which resemble a salmon; a grisle – 'gilse' here is an error –
is a young salmon on its first return to the river
from the sea (OED, Grilse n. a). Salmon-trout
were said to be 'very goodly fish of an excellent
tast' (Avity, 1615, 350), while salmon, described
by Sir John Harington as a 'princely fish', was
a valuable commodity: in 1562, the annual
rental value of the Coquet's fishery at Warkworth had been nearly £23 (Harington, 1591,
44; HN, 5.115). 426. hermitage: The Hermitage
of the Holy Trinity lies to the west of the castle
in the cliff above the River Coquet, 'wonder-
fully built out of a rocke heawen hollow,
wrought without beames, rafters, or any peeces
of timber' (CB, 813); it consists of a fourteenth-
century outer chapel and an older inner chapel
with an adjacent dormitory lying above a
kitchen, and is ornamented with a number of
figures chiselled out of the stone in niches.
Until the Reformation the earls of Northumberland had employed a chaplain to hold
weekly services there (HN, 5.124–
35). 427. Alemouth: Alnmouth, a fishing village owned by the earls of Northumberland, 3
miles north of Warkworth. Previously a prosperous haven with burghal privileges, but
by 1614 'in great ruine and decay', 'the inhab-
itants there very poore', and absorbed into the
earl's domains. In 1567, thirty-two out of the
sixty adults resident in Alnmouth were involved in illicit brewing and baking (HN,
2.479, 481–2).

422. Hadston and Dogston] Hadsdon, and Doydsdon MS   422. Francis] Franc: MS
424. Coquet] Cocket MS   425. gilse,] Gilse MS   425. salmon,] Salmon MS

where we drank drink not made of malt, and thence to Boulmer where the
fishermen dwell in little bothies.

At Alemouth Mr Ephraim Armar met us with beer. And at Boulmer   430
Mr Henry Whitehead. By the way we saw the isle of Coquet which one
Blackman, a merchant, had taken etc.

By the way we saw Dunstanburgh castle, which had been one of the
goodliest in that country, and Long Houghton and Little Houghton
where Mr Roddam dwells, between whom and Sir Henry Withrington   435

428. drink…malt: Malted grain is the key fermentable ingredient in beer or ale. **428. Boulmer:** Another fishing village in the Northumberland estates, 2 miles up the coast from Alnmouth; the MS spelling here follows the still-current pronunciation. **429. bothies:** A bothy was a temporary or permanent building used to house workmen, including buildings 'near the fishings used by salmon fishers' (*DSL* SND1, Bothy *n.* 1 (2)). Expanding on comments made by Hector Boece, in his 'Description of Scotland' William Harrison suggested that 'Bothe' was an antique and widely used term for 'a little cottage' (Holinshed, 1577, 2.12). 'Salmon bothies' are found in coastal locations around Scotland. **430. Armar:** Ephraim Armorer rented a croft in Alnmouth called the Chinnies from the earl of Northumberland, with a dovecote, and 117 acres of arable land in the commons (*HN*, 2.485). He was from a north Northumbrian family; in 1618, his kinsmen Alexander and Thomas were the postmasters at Alnwick and Belford respectively (TNA, Pipe Rolls, AO 1/1952/20, f.4). He was associated with the Greys of Chillingham, witnessing a number of family agreements in the early 1600s; he appeared on the grand jury of the session at Morpeth in 1615 (DUL, GRE/X/P50/6, 7; NRO, QSI/1, f.136). **430. beer:** Brewed with hops, unlike ale; becoming the more popular drink at this time (Clark, 1983, 96–7). **431. Whitehead:** Henry Whitehead lived at Boulmer on lands leased from the earl of Northumberland's estates by his brother, George, the earl's unpopular agent. Henry had interests in a coalmine and in 1616, thanks to his brother, was leasing 352 acres of valuable oak-filled parkland from the earl at Acklington, west of Warkworth (*HN*, 2.402–4; 5.71–2, 373n, 379–80). In 1613, Ephraim Armorer petitioned the earl on behalf of the Alnmouth burgesses against George Whitehead's enclosure of common land at Longhoughton,

claiming that they had 'in peaceable manner entered into the same ground, and with their feete cast downe' a hedge, 'without vyolence to anye person whatsoever'. Whitehead countered with two Star Chamber suits; to the earl he complained, 'howe much I am abused by thesse contry people' (*HN*, 2.381–2, 386–7, 482–3). **431–432. Coquet…merchant:** Coquet island, lying in the mouth of the River Coquet east of Warkworth and Amble, was previously owned by the priory of Tynemouth, the medieval chapel still standing in 1609 when James VI and I granted the island to London speculators. Leland observed that the island 'standith apon a very good vayne of se coles, and at the ebbe men digge in the shore by the clives, and find very good [coal]' (Leland, 1906–10, iv.123, 5.140). In 1611, the island's owner, Sir William Bowes, leased it for twenty-one years to Francis Jessop and others with the right to extract at least 500 tons of good white building stone a year (*HN*, 5.322–4). Mr Blackman is unidentified – perhaps one of the lessees. **433. Dunstanburgh:** Dunstanburgh castle, 5 miles north of Boulmer; an impressive fourteenth-century edifice, already substantially ruined by the sixteenth century. **434. Long Houghton:** Longhoughton was another of the earl of Northumberland's domains, a mile and a half west of Boulmer; 'a very long towne' with many lesser tenants (*HN*, 2.370, 386–7). **434–435. Little…Roddam:** Little Houghton, a mile north-west of Longhoughton, was the seat of Mr Edward Roddam. Its substantial medieval tower was enlarged in the seventeenth century, perhaps by Roddam (*HN*, 2.404–8). He was married to Margaret, one of Sir Ralph Grey's daughters. He was also connected to the notoriously unruly Forster family, his grandmother Barbara being one of the Forsters of Adderstone. In 1611, the settlement on Roddam's marriage to Margaret was made with Matthew Forster of Adderstone (see

428. malt, and] maſuꞁlte. And MS   428. Boulmer] Boomer MS   429. bothies] bothes MS
430. Boulmer] Boomer MS   431. Coquet] Cocket MS
433. Dunstanburgh] Dunstenborough MS   434. country, and] cuntrey. And MS
435. Roddam] *Raddam* MS   435. Henry] *Hen.* MS

was irreconcilable bate. Which Brandling was extremely hated of all the country.

That night we came to Mr Randy Fenwick's and stayed there Thursday and Friday.

On Saturday the 5th of September we came away accompanied with   440
Mrs Fenwick, Mrs Gray and her maid, who brought us two miles on the way to a loan where her kine fed to give us a merrybub for our farewell.

From Fenwick Mr Roger Withrington undertook the guiding of us,

---

ll.445–6 below) and Sir Ralph Grey; Ephraim Armorer and another Forster, Mark, were witnesses (DUL, GRE/X/P50/7). **436. bate:** 'Contention, strife, discord' (*OED*, Bate *n*.[1] 1a); in 1607, there was an arbitration of the boundary between the lands of Craster and Howick, which may have adversely affected Roddam. The arbiters included Ephraim and Roger Widdrington; a dispute perhaps arose from this, though see note following (*HN*, 2.354). **436. Brandling:** Probably an abbreviated note referring to Robert Brandling of North Gosforth and Alnwick Abbey, 'a volatile individual' who 'constantly picked quarrels with rivals, neighbours and even his own family' (*HP04*). There was a violent altercation involving Brandling and the Widdringtons around 1613 (TNA, STAC 8/55/2). Just possibly, though, the unusual noun 'branling', agitation or disturbance, referring to the apparent feud between Widdrington and Roddam (*OED*, Branling *n*.). **438. Fenwick's:** Howick, about a mile north-east of Littlehoughton; the property of his father-in-law, Sir Edward Grey of Morpeth, younger brother of Sir Ralph, and 'reputed a church papist' (*HMCS*, 19.3). Randall Fenwick's brother-in-law was Philip Grey, Sir Edward's heir, for whom Jonson wrote an epitaph (*Und*. 16). Philip, who appears to have served Lord Howard of Naworth, lived at Howick until his death in late 1615: the administration of his will is dated February 1616, and in 1619 his estate paid £32 owing to Randall (DUL, DPRI/1/1618/G9; DPRI/4/11, ff.82v, 289v, 293; *HMCS*, 19.3; *WID*, 4.215–16, *HN*, 2.355n.). Recent editors have relied on the date of 1626 for the administration of his will given in *H&S*; however, this is not found in Joseph Hunter's *Chorus Vatum*, the cited source (*H&S*, 11.59–60; BL, MS Add 24,491, f.18v). When Sir Edward died in 1627 he left ownership of Howick to Philip's son, but Randall continued to live there (*WID*,

4.216). **441. Mrs Fenwick:** Randall's wife, Catherine, daughter of Sir Edward Grey. **441. Mrs Gray:** Either Margaret, Philip Grey's widow, or Catherine's unmarried sister, Elizabeth, who ultimately gained ownership of Randall's lands at Deanham (*HN*, 2.354–5; NRO, ZSW/173/3, 8). **442. loan:** Scots and Northern English: 'before the enclosing of fields, a strip of grass of varying breadth running through the arable part of a farm and frequently linking it with the common grazing ground of the community, serving as a pasture, a driving road and a milking place for the cattle of the farm or village' (*DSL* SND1, Loan *n*. 1; *EDD*, Loan *sb*.[2] 4). **442. merrybub:** Given the location and the presence of both maid and kine, probably a 'merrybowk' or 'merrybauk', a 'cold Posset' or syllabub, identified as a Derbyshire word by John Ray, but clearly in wider northern use; cf. 'sillibouk' for the variant ending (*OED*, Merrybowk *n*.; Sillibouk *n*.; Ray, 1674, 32). See *Sad Shepherd*, 1.7.26–7, where ewes' milk and cider syllabubs join a list of rustic foodstuffs. **443. Fenwick:** A slip for Howick; the village of Fenwick is 18 miles further north. **443. Roger Withrington:** Roger Widdrington of Cartington (c.1572–1642), Sir Henry's younger brother, a noted recusant suspected of involvement in the Gunpowder Plot and associated with Lord William Howard of Naworth, for whom he acted as agent in Northumberland (Ornsby, 1877, 203, 318, 335, 337; Bidwell and Jansson, 1992, 207). In 1616, William Morton, archdeacon of Northumberland, accused him of directing Thomas Percy's treason and of being 'a patron of al theeves and murderers' (PA, HL/PO/JO/10/13/3; Ornsby, 1877, 427–30). He was married to Mary, daughter of the recusant Francis Radcliffe of Dilston. In 1619, Roger and Mary were convicted of recusancy and fined £280; parliament heard a petition alleging many 'popish' offences in 1626 (TNA, E 377/25; Bidwell and Jansson, 1992, 207).

---

438. Fenwick's] *Fennecks* MS   **441.** Fenwick] *Fenneck* MS   **443.** Fenwick] *Fenneck* MS

and Mr Randy Fenwick, Mr Strange, Godfrey, and another of the Withringtons, brought us through to Eathertonne to Sir Mathew   445 Foster's. By the way we drank at Thomas Foster's at Brunton, and John Foster's at Newham, and came by Preston tower where Mr Harbottle dwells, and by Mr Mathew Foster's, whose sons killed Mr Swinhoe, a Justice of peace whom they had ticed out of his house for a wrong received from his son. We saw Bamburgh castle, where Sir   450 Claudius Foster dwells.

The Benedictine monk Thomas Preston used 'Roger Widdrington' as his *nom de plume* for works written in defence of the oath of allegiance (Forster, 1972, 196–205). In 1593, Widdrington's uncle left him £20 a year 'for the better maintenance of his studie and librarye', and he bought books for Howard of Naworth, who was himself connected to Sir Robert Cotton. His will included books and 'certaine Mathamatical Instruments' (*WID*, 2.225–6, *WID*, 4.287–90). **444. Strange:** The mother of Catherine and Elizabeth Grey was Catherine Strange, daughter of Roger le Strange of Hunstanton, so presumably one of their cousins. **444. Godfrey:** Unidentified. **445–446. Eathertonne ...Foster's:** Correctly, Adderstone, which is around 10 miles north of Howick; Sir Matthew Forster had sizeable landholdings in the area. Described by Leland as a 'towre apon the south syde of Lindis ryver' (Leland, 1906–10, v.64), Adderstone had been held by the Forsters since at least 1427, this line being the senior branch of the prolific and papist Forster family. Sir Matthew's great-uncle was Sir John Forster (d. 1602), the roguish warden of the Middle March. His wife was Catherine Grey, a daughter of Sir Ralph and sister of Edward Roddam's wife, Margaret. He was connected too to the Ogles through his great-grandmother Dorothy Ogle's marriage to Sir Thomas Forster of Adderstone. Sir Matthew was knighted by James in 1617 in Durham, and appointed as sheriff of Northumberland in 1620 (*HN*, 1.221, 223–4, 228–9, 232; *WID*, 2.302–4). **446–447. Thomas...Newham:** Thomas Forster (d. c.1648) of Brunton, 5 miles north of Howick, was the son of Cuthbert Forster, Sir Matthew Forster's brother. His first wife was Margaret, sister of John Forster of Newham, 4 miles to the north of Brunton; John was married to Thomas's sister, Grace. Thomas Forster's second wife was Jane, daughter of William Carr of Ford, whose sister, Margaret, married John Craster of Craster (see l.452 below). Thomas's provisions for his funeral, stipulating plenty of

wine, 10lb of spices and sugar, with tobacco and two dozen pipes, suggest he was a generous host (*HN*, 2.107–9, 112). John Forster was himself descended from the Tughal Hall line of Forsters, a junior branch (*HN*, 1.275–6). **447. Preston tower:** A medieval pele tower 1½ miles from Brunton, to the west of the route towards Newham. Preston had been in Harbottle hands since the early fifteenth century; in 1621, Nicholas Harbottle, the Crown lessee, was paying £8 52s 4d a year rent for a 'mancion howse' and 361 acres there; he had inherited from Ralph Harbottle by 1596 (*HN*, 2.322, 324–5). **448. Foster's:** This Matthew Forster lived at Fleetham, around 2 miles north of Preston, and west of Newham; his wife Elizabeth was probably aunt of John Forster of Newham (*HN*, 1.288). **448–450. sons...son:** Thomas Swinhoe (1554–1616) of Goswick, near Lindisfarne. He sat regularly as a justice of the peace for the county, the last recorded occasion being 6 June 1616 (NRO, QSI/1, f.153v). The origins of the feud are unknown, although a Thomas Forster of Crookletch was accused in 1606 of a clandestine marriage with Swinhoe's daughter (*HN*, 1.232). Swinhoe had a son, William, but he had died by 1607, so this may have been the settlement of a very old score. His own will was registered on 29 June 1616 at Berwick, and his alleged murderers indicted on the same day; the seven men charged included at least two of Matthew Forster's sons, Ralph and John. The indictment read that Ralph, 'with a sword worth 2s., gave [Swinhoe] a fatal wound near the right knee six inches long and three inches deep and another fatal wound above the left knee which severed his leg'; the victim languished until midnight before dying. Ralph received a pardon for the murder in November 1618; two years later, however, a Nicholas Forster was hanged for his part in the crime (BRO, ZHG/III/3; NRO, QSI/1, f.158; *CSPD*, *1611–18*, 590; *HN*, 1.190). **449. ticed:** Enticed. **450–451. Bamburgh... Foster:** Sir Claudius Forster (1578–1623), one

At Sir Mathew Foster's we met with Mr Craster of Craster, where we supped, and dined there the next day, being Sunday, where Sir Harry Withrington had stayed for us. And in the afternoon we set forward, brought on the way by Sir Mathew Foster, and through to Fenham by Mr Roger Withrington and another of the Fosters, to Mr Read's, who with his brother met us by the way. We came through Easington Grange, and through Clerke; we saw Belford. 455

Mr Thomas Carr, the lord of Ford, came to meet us. Monday the 7th we parted from Fenham, brought on the way by Mr Read and his brother. 460

of Sir John Forster's illegitimate children, and married to Sir John Fenwick's half-sister, Elizabeth. He was made keeper of Bamburgh Castle in 1603, as his father had been, and granted ownership of the castle and its lordship in 1610. Claudius was knighted at Newmarket in 1615; he served as sheriff of Northumberland in 1612, and occasionally as justice of the peace (*HN*, 1.53–5, vol. II, pt II.17; NRO, QSI/ 1, f.153v). 'Bamborow, sometyme a huge and great castle, one of the strongest in thos partes', had seen better days; 'it hath beene sore beaten with time, and the windes together, which have blowne by drifts an incredible deale of sand of the sea into the fortresses' (Leland, 1906–10, V.64; *CB*, 814). Later restored, it remains very prominent in the landscape. **452. Craster:** John Craster of Craster, a fishing harbour just to the north of Howick; the supper and dinner mentioned were held at Adderstone. Craster was married to Margaret Carr, sister of Jane, wife of Thomas Forster of Brunton (see l.446 above). In 1607, the demarcation between his lands and those of the Greys at Howick was adjudicated, with Matthew Forster as one of the arbiters; Craster was a co-witness with Forster too in April 1618 of the sale of Wooler to Sir Ralph Grey of Chillingham (*HN*, 2.175, 354; DUL, GRE/X/P34/11). **456–457. Read's...brother:** Sons of Captain Sir William Read of Fenham, who had died in 1616; those living in 1618 included William (b. 1592), Lancelot (b. 1603) and Robert (b. 1606). Sir William was the illegitimate son of the first Capt. Sir William Read (d. 1604), a renowned soldier who had served with his son in the Netherlands; Sir William the younger was probably knighted in 1586 by Leicester during the campaign. His aged father had hosted James VI and I on his southwards journey in 1603; the king's 'gracious speeches' had so pleased the old soldier that Read claimed to 'feele the warmth of youth stirre in his frost-nipt blood' (*CBP*, 1.272, 2.776; *NP*, 1.67). Fenham, 7 miles north of Adderstone, was a well-appointed house (Raine, 1852, 176–9). **457. Easington:** Easington Grange, 4 miles south of Fenham, was built in the sixteenth century on the site of a medieval tower. It was given to Nicholas Forster, another of Sir John's illegitimate sons, by his father's widow in 1606; by 1637 it had been inherited by another Forster, Thomas (*HN*, 1.232, 413). **458. Clerke:** Possibly a scribal error for Elwick, just north of Easington Grange; the manor of Elwick was also given by Sir John Forster's widow to Nicholas Forster of Fenham. However, Gabriel Clarke, bishop Neile's favourite, was confirmed in the rectories of Elwick and Easington in 1620, so the error is perhaps the result of transposition or compression (DUL, DDR/EA/ACT/1/4, p.30; Add MS 244, pp.204–6). **458. Belford:** A tower and village 1 mile southwest of Elwick (*HN*, 1.363). **459. Carr...Ford:** Thomas Carr of Ford (1577–1642) was married firstly to Isabella (d. c.1608), the daughter of Sir John Selby of Berwick (see l.473 below), and secondly to Jane, a widow of a Scottish Kerr of Greenhead (*HN*, 11.391). He had been a gentleman of the bedchamber to James, but had fallen out of favour with him by 1607. The family's fortunes were in decline, Carr selling the manor of Twizell to his father-in-law, Sir John Selby, in 1606, and subsequently the lordship of Ford to Thomas Bradford of Bradford (BRO, SANT/DEE/1/25/4/1; *HN*, 1.302–4).

452. Craster of Craster] *Crastor of Crastor* MS   453. supped,] sup'd MS
453. Harry] *Har* MS   456. Read's,] *Redes* MS   457. Easington] *Isington* MS
458. Clerke; we] *Clerke wee* MS
459. Thomas Carr, the Lord of Ford,] MS *Tho Carre* the Lord of Foord MS

We sent for drink from the mill. We were overtaken with a sharp shower, a mile and more on this side Berwick. Sir William Boyer's man was sent from his master who met us two miles off, telling my gossip his master entreated him to take none other house for his entertainment but his. And himself then being ridden to sit on commission with Mr Sayer and Mr Atkinson, left order that three culverins should be mounted and the bells rung upon my gossip's approach.   465

Sir William found us at supper and ran to my gossip and kissed him, with the greatest joy for his company that could be expressed.

As soon as we came we went about the walls to view the fortifications.   470

On Tuesday we went with Sir William to the chapel, where Mr John Jackson, brother to Sir George Jackson, and Mr Stephen Jackson, the

462. Berwick: Berwick-upon-Tweed, on the Scottish side of the Tweed, in English hands since 1482. Its burghal privileges were confirmed in a new charter of 1604, transferring the town from military to civic command (Raine, 1852, 145–54; Scot, 1888, 257). The Tweed had long been spanned by a wooden bridge; a project to build a new stone bridge of fifteen arches was begun in 1611 and largely completed by 1624 (*BT*, 94; Scot, 1888, 411–15; Colvin, 1963–82, IV.769–78). **463. Boyer's:** Sir William Bowyer (d. 1628), the well-travelled captain of Berwick's garrison since at least 1591, skilled in fortifications, and 'a man ready with his pen, and knowledge to make a pound go as far as any'; Taylor called him a 'worthy old Soldier and ancient Knight' (*CBP*, 1.443–4, 520; *PP*, sig. G1; Scot, 1888, 198–9). In 1605, he was knighted at Edinburgh and given a house in Berwick by the earl of Dunbar (see l.533 below), lieutenant of the Middle Shires, before 1611. Although the garrison was largely disbanded that year, he had a substantial pension of 10s a day (*HMCM*, 244; CRO, D PEN/216/f.58; NRS, RH15/19/80; *CSPD, 1611–18*, 64, 76). He was one of the elected Guild Brethren in 1618, and mayor of Berwick in 1620–3 and 1625; James took particular care that annual fees of £1,200 were paid to him between 1618 and 1620, when payment was delayed because Bowyer was English (BRO, B1/8, pp.1, 42; NRS, GD124/15/29/11; 124/10/141/2; 124/10/175). **465. commission:** Unidentified; possibly a meeting of the commission of the peace, or a meeting of the Middle Shires commissioners. **465. Sayer:** Perhaps Edmund Sawyer, knighted in 1625, MP for Berwick in 1628, an official in the exchequer and auditor from 1621. His only known connection with the town by 1618 was through Berwick's submission of accounts to the exchequer for the

bridge (*HP04*, 6.238–41). In 1623, however, he was granted the lease of a fishery in the Tweed, which he co-held with Sir John Selby (see l.474 below), and by 1628 was involved in a dispute over the manor of Ellington, near Bothal, suggesting he held lands there (TNA, E 367/1474; Scot, 1888, 430; TNA, E 134/3Chas1/Mich42). **465. Atkinson:** No Atkinsons are named among the Guild Brethren of Berwick, although there are several Atchinsons in the parish registers; possibly the 'James Atchesone' whose case was heard in the Court of Pleas, Berwick, January 1618/19 (*BR*, 1.56; BRO, C2/1 p.116). **466. culverins:** Either relatively small weapons capable of being handled by one person, or cannons of around 10ft in length and 5 in in bore (*OED*, Culverin *n*. a, b). **466. mounted:** Of cannon or guns, set up ready for use (*OED*, Mount *v*. 22a, b). **470. fortifications:** Brereton described them as 'the strongest fortifications I have met with in England, double-walled, and outworks of earth', with a broad moat and 'inner walls of invincible strength, stone wall within, and without lined with earth about twenty yards thick'; 'something in decay' by 1635 (*BT*, 95). **471–472. John…George Jackson:** The Jacksons were a prominent Berwick family of merchants. Sir George is perhaps a mistake for Sir Robert, who was mayor five times between 1605 and 1640, and custom-master in 1617 (Scot, 1888, 479; BRO, B1/8, p.1; BL, MS Add 58,833, f.34v). His brother, John (d. 1627), was an assistant preacher, whose annual salary, paid by the corporation of Berwick, was raised by £10 in 1616 to around £20. The chapel was in some disrepair, with 'a great necessitie of seats' in February 1619 (Scot, 1888, 354, 396; *BR*, 1.85). **472. Stephen Jackson:** Born in 1578, mayor from October 1617 to October 1618

462. mile and] myle, and MS   **462. Berwick**] Barwicke MS   **463.** master] Mr MS
463. master] Mr MS

mayor, preached. Mr Mayor, Sir John Jackson, Mr Parkinson, Mr Edwards and his son-in-law Mr Marrott, Sir John Selby with young Strudder came to meet my gossip. 475

We were invited by Sir George Jackson to supper, where my lady made wonderful much of us. The next day, being Wednesday, we were invited by Sir John Selby, who feasted us royally at Anne Miller's. We supped all at Sir William Boyer's. I brought Sir John to his lodging where I stayed all night, and where Captain Hoord with other gentlemen and I 480 drank hard.

The next day, being Thursday, in the morning the mayor with the aldermen brought my gossip burnt sack and claret for his welcome.

We dined with the lord of Carr at Steele's. After dinner we took our journey, brought out of town with all the knights, gentlemen, mayor and 485 aldermen; two miles out of town was wine ready, where Sir William had sent a company of musketeers who gave us a volley of shot. Sir William could not contain himself from tears when he took his leave. Sir John

---

(BR, 1.9; BRO, B1/8, pp.1, 42, 62). **473. John Jackson:** Probably the Sir John Jackson of Berwick who was father of Mary, Lady Carey (ODNB; Bodl., MS Rawl. D. 1308). Little is known of him; he would seem to be distinct from the Sir John Jackson (d. 1623), of Hickleton and Womersley, near Pontefract, who served as king's attorney of the Council of York between 1603 and 1608, and was recorder of Newcastle in 1607, but for whom there is no evidence of a connection with Berwick; he advised Jane, countess of Shrewsbury, in her dispute over Rufford in 1618–19 with Lady Grace Cavendish (TWRO, MD.NC/D/4/4/1, GU.MS/14; HP58; WP, 109, 201). **473. Parkinson:** Thomas Parkinson, an alderman since at least 1591, was a merchant of substance, agent for Lord Walden, and mayor four times between 1591 and 1619 (CBP, 1.433, 438; BRO, B1/8, pp.1, 7, 65–72; CRO, D PEN/216/f.16). **474. Edwards:** William Edwards was one of the elected Guild Brethren in 1618 (BRO, B1/8, pp.9, 42, 66). **474. Marrott:** Gregory Marriott, who married Edwards' daughter, Elizabeth, in 1609. Marriott was on the Guild Roll in 1618 (BR, 2.20; BRO, B1/8, pp.41, 65). **474. Sir John Selby:** Of Twizell Castle, knighted 1604, ex-soldier, local landowner, on the Guild Roll in 1618; Middle Shires commissioner, MP for Berwick in 1614, 1621 and 1625, and a justice

of the peace 1616–36 (NRO, SANT/DEE/1/25/4/1; BRO, B1/8, pp.42, 65; HP04). **475. young Strudder:** The Selbys and the Strothers were interconnected through marriage; 'young Strudder' could be John Strother, admitted to Gray's Inn in 1614, or William Strother (b. 1599), one of the Guild Brethren, and town clerk in 1618 (BR, 1.51; BRO, B1/8, pp.66, 70); a Sir John Selby and another John Strother of Alnwick were joined in an indenture over Elwick in 1635 (DUL, GRE/X/P43). **478. Anne Miller's:** Probably the wife or widow of Gregory Miller, whose daughter Anna was baptised in 1601 (BR, 1.54). **480. Hoord:** Unidentified. Following the Union of the Crowns, Berwick was substantially disgarrisoned; by 1616 it contained only '2. companyes & some old pencioners' (Bodl., MS Rawl. D. 696), and the captain may have been among this remnant. **484. lord of Carr:** A slip for Thomas Carr, 'lord of Ford' (see l.459 above). **484. Steele's:** Possibly the house of Mr Lawrence Steele, bailiff in 1609, one of the elected Guild Brethren in 1615, and on the Guild Roll in 1618; was pursued for non-attendance at church in 1617 (BRO, C2/1, p.51; B1/8, pp.9, 30, 41, 65). **486. two miles out of town:** The Anglo-Scottish border; the ceremonies here presumably mark its crossing.

---

480. stayed all] stayed, all MS   **483.** aldermen;] Aldermen, MS   **488.** tears] teares, MS

Selby brought us to Ayton to George Hume's, where Val West played his prank in drink. On Friday we hired a guide, having also Sir William's man with us and the king etc., who brought us to Cobersmith to Mr Arnot. They grew cousins; this was the tediousest day's journey in the whole voyage, for I had not slept two nights before etc. We passed by Dunglass.

490

Saturday the twelfth we came to Mr James Bayly of the Loghend. We came by Newtonlees, Mr Acheson's, provost of Dunbar. We saw

495

489. Ayton: 'A pretty castle placed on the side of a hill' (*BT*, 96). **489. Hume's:** George Home, laird of Ayton, was a member of the large and powerful Home kindred that proliferated throughout Berwickshire; it included Lord Home and George Home, earl of Dunbar. **489. West:** The prolific father of at least eleven children baptised between 1607 and 1626 at Berwick. He was the brother of John West, the London-based client of the correspondent John Chamberlain (*BR*, 1.67–98, *CL*, 2.166, 171). **490. guide:** The road between Ayton and Cockburnspath was notoriously in need of repair, crossing 'the largest and vastest moors I have ever seen', and 'made difficile by haggis [hags, overhanging banks of peat resulting from water erosion] …and mony louse stanes lyand in the way' (*BT*, 96; *RPCS*, 11.92–3). **491. the king:** Perhaps a truncated reference either to James's journey along this road in 1617 or to an unidentifiable royal servant in the travellers' company here. **491. Cobersmith:** Cockburnspath, 12 miles north-west of Ayton. The highly unusual spelling 'Cobersmith' is also found in another early seventeenth-century English source (though inaccurately glossed by its modern editor as Cambuskenneth): see *CSPD, 1640*, 208. **492. Arnot:** William Arnot (d. by 1627), postmaster of Cockburnspath, son of the former provost of Edinburgh, Sir John Arnot of Berswick (d. 1616), and brother of the merchant burgess James (NRS, CS96/1/149; *RMS*, 7. nos. 1235, 1428). Criticised in 1617 by the privy council for his failure to repair the road between Cockburnspath and Dunglass in preparation for King James's journey; in 1619, he was charged with mismanaging his office, being unfit for the post and overburdened

with debt – perhaps partly a result of the bountiful hospitality 'this plaine home-spunne fellow' afforded to travellers, including Taylor. This was despite receiving a healthy £800 for the year 1617–18 (*RPCS*, 11.92–3, 12.69, 82–3, 365, 369; *PP*, sig. F4v; NRS, GD124/10/148/2). **492. grew cousins:** Became familiar (*OED*, *Cousin n.* 5). **494. Dunglass:** The 'pleasantly seated' castle of Alexander, earl of Home, a mile north of Cockburnspath; damaged by English attack in 1548 and rebuilt by 1603; James stayed here on 13 May 1617 (RCAHMS, Canmore ID 58908; *BT*, 96; *NP*, 3.300–5) **495. Bayly…Loghend:** Lochend lies just to the west of Dunbar; 'fragments' now remain of a seventeenth-century house (RCAHMS, Canmore ID 57615). James Baillie (c.1585–1636), was one of the Receivers of Crown Rents, a client of the treasurer, the earl of Mar, and substantially responsible for the logistical arrangements for James's visit in 1617; knighted in 1621. He bought the lands of Lochend in 1614 and increased his landholdings in Dunbar in 1618, his pension between 1617 and 1620 being £1,500 per annum. He briefly hosted Taylor on the latter's southward journey (*RMS*, 7. nos. 1051, 1808; NRS, E/24/35, ff.29v, 36v; E24/36, f.27v; E24/38, f.27v; GD124/10/148; will, CC8/8/57, ff.590–8; *PP*, sig. F4). **496. Newtonlees… Dunbar:** John Aitcheson of Newtonlees, next to Lochend, was provost of the royal burgh of Dunbar by 1613; in 1617, he was the burgh's representative at the June parliament (*RMS*, 7. no. 841; *RPCS*, 10.573, 11.156n., 207n.) A John Acheson was 'generall of oure Coynehouse' (the Mint) in 1615, when he claimed £10,000 was owed to his late father (NRS, E17/1, f.13).

489. Ayton] Eton MS   490. William's] Will. MS   491. etc., who] etc. Who MS
492. cousins;] cousins, MS   492. tediousest] tediou'st MS   495. Loghend] loghend MS
496. Newtonlees, Mr Acheson's,] Newton lyes Mr Achesons MS

Tantallon, the earl of Angus's castle by Auldhame. Lord of Lotherdale that hath the fair house.

Monday we stayed at Auldhame.

Tuesday in the afternoon we parted, and came that night to North   500
Berwick brought on the way by Mr Alexander and Mr James Auchmuty, and merry Mr Fenton. That night came Mr William Ramsey and two gentlemen more from Edinburgh of purpose to meet my gossip etc.

497. Tantallon...Angus's: William Douglas, eleventh earl of Angus, and first marquess of Douglas (1589–1660), was granted a licence to travel on the continent in 1616 for up to three years, his fortunes clouded by persistent accusations of recusancy and his father's known Catholicism. He lived both at Douglas Castle in Lanarkshire and Tantallon Castle, an imposing stronghold on the sea-cliffs about 7 miles north-west of Dunbar (*ODNB*). **497. Auldhame:** Near Tantallon, where Taylor 'found both Cheere and Welcome not inferiour to any that I had had' (*PP*, sig. F4); the MS spelling here reflects local pronunciation. The home of the Auchmuty family, whose most notable member was John Auchmuty of Scoughall (by Auldhame), a groom of James's bedchamber; described by Chamberlain as one of 'the high dancers' appearing in Jonson's *The Irish Masque* of 1613; he danced in *Pleasure Reconciled to Virtue* in early 1618 and was named in *For the Honour of Wales* (l.140). In July 1618, Auchmuty was paid his pension for the Whitsunday term of £333 by the Scottish treasury (*CL*, 1.496; *CWBJ*, 1.cxliv; NRS, GD124/10/148/2). A year later, Jonson gave him a book in gratitude for 'the hospitable favours / I received of him in Scotland / and elsewhere'; as Master of the King's Wardrobe in Scotland from 1611, Auchmuty was responsible for Queen Mary's bedhangings, about which Drummond wrote to Jonson in July 1619 (*CELM*, JnB 758; Knowles, 2006, 267; *RPCS* 10.624–5, 12.501; *CWBJ*, Letter (f); Bath and Craig, 2010, 282–7). **497. Lord of Lotherdale:** John Maitland, second Lord Thirlestane, created viscount of Lauderdale in 1616 and earl of Lauderdale in 1624 (d. 1645); a privy councillor, though not present between 23 July and 3 November 1618. His sister, Anna, married Robert Seton, second earl of Winton (*SP*, 5.301–3; *RPCS*, 11.412, 460). **498. fair house:** Lethington, now Lennoxlove, by Haddington; altered and augmented many times over the centuries (RCAHMS, Canmore ID 56512). A

fragmentary note: the house would not have been visible from the route of the walk. **500–501. North Berwick:** The royal burgh, 3 miles west of Auldhame, incorporated by a charter of 1568; associated with a notorious witch-hunt, trials and convictions, between 1590 and 1597. **501. Alexander... Auchmuty:** Alexander and James Auchmuty, John's brothers. They too were members of the royal household: Alexander was a gentlemen pensioner, made an honorary burgess of Edinburgh at the king's banquet in June 1617, subsequently knighted, and a gentleman of the privy chamber by the end of James's reign (*PP*, sig. F4; BL, MS Add 34,122 B; ECA, SL141/1/3; TNA, LC 2/6, f.39v). James became a groom of the bedchamber and was knighted during Charles I's visit to Scotland in 1633 (BL, MS Add 28,844, f.17; TNA, LC 2/6, f.40; KE). **502. Fenton:** Probably John Fenton, the 'worthy Gentleman' who guided Taylor to Dunfermline; clerk of the green cloth for Scotland, keeper of the register of the comptrollery since 1582, the 'comptrollar clerk' at Holyroodhouse; acted as the king's commissioner in June 1619 when he was instructed to inquire into North Sea fishing (*PP*, sig. E1; TNA, LC 2/6, f.34; *RPCS*, 10.311; 11.clxvii, 387, 605–7; NRS, E23/17/12;). Cf. Jonson's letter of 10 May 1619 to Drummond sending salutations to several, including 'the beloved Fentons' (*CWBJ*, Letter 14). **502. Ramsey:** Probably William Ramsay, a groom of the bedchamber from at least 1605; he was a kinsman – perhaps even a brother – of John Ramsay (c.1580–1626), a royal favourite who was created viscount Haddington in 1606 and earl of Holderness in 1621, and for whose wedding in 1609 Jonson wrote the Haddington masque. John Ramsay's lands were in what is now East Lothian, between Edinburgh and Dunbar; between 1610 and 1623 he was appointed to several commissions for the peace in the constabulary of Haddington (*SP*, 4.300; *ODNB*, John Ramsay). William Ramsay was given £600 by the king in 1612 and £1,000

Wednesday, Sir John Humes told my gossip that his shearers had made a great suit to him to have a sight of him. So he walked up into the fields where was a number of them with a bagpipe, who no sooner saw my gossip, but they circled him and danced round about him. 505

Sir John Humes with his two sons brought us on the way. We purposed to go that night to Preston where Mr Ramsey was to meet us. But the earl of Winton waylaid us, and stayed us at Seton where we met my Lord Bothwell. 510

Thursday, the two earls brought my gossip on the way, and other gentlemen brought him through to Preston, where we parted at Hamilton's with a cup of sack.

two years later; 1612 was also the year in which he had a notorious altercation with Philip Herbert, earl of Montgomery during a period of high tension between English and Scots courtiers. A bill for his naturalisation alongside Sir Francis Stewart, one of Jonson's patrons, was supported by the earls of Nottingham and Pembroke in the Lords in 1614 (although Stewart was not in fact naturalised until 1624), and he was made an honorary burgess of Edinburgh with other courtiers during James's 1617 visit. He was in Edinburgh on 1 September 1618, when he acted as witness for a transaction between Haddington and his kinsman Sir George Ramsay of Dalhousie by which the latter became lord of Melrose (TNA, LC 5/50, p.36; BL, MS Add 58,833, f.23; CL, 1.340, 342; HP04, Francis Stewart; LJ, 9/5/14; NRS, GD124/10/124; ECA, SL141/1/3; Senning, 1983, 206; NRS, GD 224/308/19). Other candidates include several relations of Ramsay of Dalhousie, or even his heir: this William (c.1595–1672) succeeded his father in 1629, and was created first earl of Dalhousie at Charles I's coronation visit in 1633 (SP, 3.95–100, 9.63; ODNB; RMS, 7. no. 704). **504. Humes:** Sir John Home (d. 1639), a prominent member of the numerous Home kindred, the fourth son of Patrick Home of Polwarth; he inherited the barony of North Berwick in 1597 from his uncle, Alexander Home, a provost of Edinburgh in the 1590s. This included the 'mansion called Neuwark with the dovecot', where the travellers probably stayed, the meadows of Heugh, North Berwick Law and the 'public way from Northberwick to Balgone' (NRS, GD110/28, 180–1, 671, 1217; Lithgow, 1618, sig. E4v; NRS, GD110/208). **504. shearers:** Reapers, harvesters, especially in northern usage (OED, Shearer n. 1; EDD, Shear sb.² II 3 (2)). **508. two sons:** Sir John had three sons, Alexander, George and Patrick. George inherited, replacing his older

brother, Alexander, who had died by 1633 (SP, 6.8–9; NRS, GD110/795). **509. Preston:** An inland village 13 miles west of North Berwick; then distinct from Prestonpans, the coastal settlement just to its north (NLS, EMS.s.676). **510. Winton:** George Seton, third earl of Winton (1584–1650); inherited the earldom when his brother, Robert, surrendered it in 1607 on the grounds of insanity, and lived at Seton with his mother, Margaret Montgomerie. A diligent privy councillor, ally and nephew of Alexander Seton, earl of Dunfermline, the chancellor of Scotland (see l.552); Winton was with his uncle when Dunfermline died in 1622, taking charge of the great seal (ODNB, Alexander Seton; RPCS, vols. XI and XII; NLS, Adv MS 33.1.1, vol. IX, f.9; 33.1.1, vol. X, f.50). **510. Seton:** Seton Palace, a late sixteenth-century building with a tall, square tower, 2 miles east of Preston; James was the earl of Winton's guest here in 1617. The palace was demolished in the late eighteenth century (RCAHMS, Canmore ID 54940; NP, 3.306). **511. Bothwell:** Francis Stewart (1584–1639), styled Lord Bothwell, brother-in-law to Winton through his sister, Isobel; the son of Francis, first earl of Bothwell, a cousin of James VI and I whose honours and lands were forfeited as a result of his repeated rebellions. He subsequently went into exile. The younger Francis was rehabilitated in 1614, but not restored to his father's former title or estates. He fought a lengthy battle to regain lands from the earls of Roxburgh and Buccleuch, with only limited success (SP, 2.172–3; RMS, 7. no. 1099; NLS, Adv MS, vol. V, ff.19, 45, 54; NRS, GD224/175/17–19). **514. Hamilton's:** Sir John Hamilton of Preston lived in Preston Tower, a fifteenth-century tower house, to which he added two upper Renaissance-style storeys in 1626; two years later he built another house nearby, incorporating an older structure; both buildings

513. Preston, where] Preston. Where MS   **514.** Hamilton's] hameltons MS

We passed through Musselburgh, where my gossip grew exceeding 515
sick. On this side Edinburgh Mr Nesbick going to his house meeting my
gossip welcomed us, and would needs go back with him. And at the
town's end Mr William Ramsey, Mr Heatley, Mr Alexander Stewart, and
Mr Alexander Dunsire met us and brought us to Mr James Dowie's,
where we lay. The women in throngs ran to see us etc., some bringing 520
sack and sugar, others aquavitæ and sugar, etc.

On Friday all these gentlemen with others of the town brought my
gossip to the high cross, and there on their knees drank the king's health,
testifying in that place that he had performed his journey. My gossip also

survive (RCAHMS, Canmore ID 53671, 53682).
The absence of a title here, though, perhaps
suggests premises owned or occupied by another person of that name. **515. Musselburgh:**
A harbour town 3 miles west of Preston at
the mouth of the Esk. **516. Nesbick:** Probably James Nisbet (d. by 1622); his estate at
Restalrig and Craigentinny was then just to
the east of Edinburgh and is now in its sub-
urbs. Nisbet was a merchant burgess, elected
bailie in 1617–18, and again in 1619–20; married
to Marion Arnot, sister of William, the Cockburnspath postmaster. The Nisbets were a
prominent Edinburgh family, to whom Jonson
sent greetings via William Drummond in May
1619. Sir Henry, James's father, had been provest several times; his brother, William, provest
between 1616 and 1618, and again in 1622, was
knighted by James in 1617 – he later installed
decorative emblematic panels treating the five
senses at his house in Edinburgh, a topic also
handled by Jonson in the Windsor text of
Gypsies Metamorphosed. Patrick, a third
brother, presented the king with a finely
bound 'book of verses from the Colledge of
Edinburgh, with [a] litle speach in their
name' at Holyroodhouse during his 1617 royal
entry into the city (Geddie, 1908; M. Wood,
1931, 182; *CWBJ*, Letter 14; Bath, 2003, 4, 23, 242–
3; J. Adamson, 1618, 43; *NP*, 3.323; BL, General
Reference Collection C.24.a.19). **518. town's
end:** The Netherbow Port at the foot of the
High Street, an ornate stone gatehouse, rebuilt
in 1571, separating the burgh of Edinburgh
from that of Canongate; demolished in 1764,
its position is still marked on the road
(RCAHMS, Canmore ID 52153). **518. Heatley:**
A Mr Heatley was listed as a gentleman of
Prince Charles's privy chamber in 1619 and
1625; probably the James Heatley involved

with Thomas Lumsden (see l.311 above) as
steward and keeper of Sheriff Hutton, his interest in which he assigned to Sir Arthur Ingram (TNA, LC 2/5, LC 2/6, f.71; WYAL,
WYL100/SH/A1, ff.12, 14, 14A; WYL100/PO/9/
15). A James Heatley graduated from Edinburgh in 1614; described as 'Master of artes
and fellowe of the Kings Majesties Colledge at
Eddenburgh' in 1626, when he was admitted
as a deacon by Richard Neile (Laing, 1858; BI,
Subscription Book 2, f.92). **518. Stewart:**
Alexander Stewart, carver to King James;
given a grant of forfeitures totalling £800 in
July 1625 'in accomplishment of the late King's
intention' (TNA, LC 2/6, f.40v; *CSPD, 1625–6*,
59, 544). **519. Dunsire:** Alexander Dunsire,
gentleman usher quarter waiter for Prince
Charles at his accession; as 'the King's servant',
granted denisation in February 1628 (TNA, LC
2/6, f.72; *CSPD, 1627–8*, 578; *CSPD, 1629–31*,
67). **519. Dowie's:** James Dowie (d. 1631), burgess and guild brother (*EBR*, 147); described as
a 'writer [lawyer] in Edinburgh', in a transaction with Robert Hay (see l.568) in 1624.
His domestic goods and silverwork were estimated at £400 in 1639 (NRS, GD30/1198; CC8/
8/59, f.160). **521. sack...sugar:** Like other
wines, sack was often sweetened with sugar,
and was a customary welcome given by both
English and Scottish civic authorities to honoured guests (for instance at Doncaster in 1617:
DA, AB6/2/159, p.15). **521. aquavitae:** 'Water
of life', a distilled spirit; also known by its
Gaelic name, *uisge beatha*, 'whisky', of which
this may have been an early form (*DSL* DOST,
Aquavite *n.*; DSL DOST, Usquebay
n.). **523. high cross:** The mercat cross; by the
kirk of St Giles on the High Street, described
by Taylor as 'the goodliest Street that euer
mine eyes beheld', with buildings 'of squared

515. Musselburgh, where] Muscleborrough. Where MS   **516.** Edinburgh] Edenburrough MS
515. Nesbick] Nesbicke MS   **518.** Heatley] Hetely MS
518. Alexander Dunsire] *Al: Donseere* MS   **519.** Dowie's,] *Dowayes* MS

drank to the bailiff and aldermen and the whole people their health, they 525
being so thick in the street that we could scarce pass by them, they ran in
such throngs to have a sight of my gossip. The windows also being full,
everyone peeping out of a round hole like a head out of a pillory.

From thence we went up to the castle where we saw the great cannon,
the bore whereof was so big that one got a woman with child in it. We 530
also saw the earl of Crawford of Lindsay, where there have been thirteen
earls of the name. He lieth prisoner there, overthrown as it is said by the
subtlety of the lord of Dunbar etc.

On Saturday my gossip with the former gentlemen and me rid to
Culrose, called Curos, to Sir George Bruce, who hath wrought that 535

stone, fiue, sixe, seauen Storyes high' (*PP*, sig.
D2v). The cross is clearly visible on James
Gordon of Rothiemay's panoramic map of
Edinburgh, 1647. **525. bailiff and aldermen:**
English terms. The burgh council was headed
by a provest, with four bailies, and twelve other
members, who were only ever referred to as
burgesses, burgh councillors or magistrates.
The bailies in September 1618 were James Ainslie (see ll.583, 590 below), James Dalzell,
Alexander Pierson and David Richardson;
there was also a dean of guild, David Aiken-
head, and a treasurer, William Rea, other
council members including James Nisbet and
his brother-in-law, James Arnot. Edinburgh's
population was around 20–25,000, of whom 6–
8,000 were from burgess families; the burgh
council was usually drawn from an even smaller number of merchant burgesses (ECA, SL1/1/
13, p.2; Stewart, 2006, 23–58, 341). **528. round
hole:** Buildings on the High Street did not have
'fair glass windows'; they were instead faced
with boards 'wherein are round holes shaped
to the proportion of men's heads' (*BT*,
102). **529. great cannon:** The giant siege cannon known as 'Mons Meg', capable of firing
330lb gunshot over 2 miles, given to James II in
1457. It is still on display at Edinburgh Castle;
Taylor recounts the same legend about its 20in
(50cm) calibre (*PP*, sig. D2v). **531. earl of
Crawford:** David Lindsay, twelfth earl of
Crawford (1576–1620), a violent and spend-
thrift man, initially warded in 1610 for debt,
but allegations of his violence in the Crawford–Edzell feud led to his continued imprisonment. In 1612, it was advised that 'he is too
much subject to the counsaill of young and evill

disposed persones' to be released. Although
occasionally let out on surety of 20,000
marks, he remained imprisoned in the castle
until his death (*ODNB*; *SP*, 3.31–2; NLS, Adv
MS 33.1.1, vol. III, f.43, vol. IV, f.2; *RPCS*, 9.68, 74,
629, 662). **533. Lord of Dunbar:** George
Home, earl of Dunbar (d. 1611), treasurer of
Scotland, lieutenant of the Middle Shires, and
the king's chief enforcer in Scotland. He was
part of the powerful Home kindred in Berwickshire and East Lothian, and connected to
Home of North Berwick (see l.504
above). **535. Culrose, called Curos:** Culross,
'a Towne called the *Cooras*', on the north
coast of the Firth of Forth, about 20 miles
from Edinburgh (*PP*, sig. E1). Made a royal
burgh under a charter of 1592; a thriving settlement based around the complementary industries of coalmining, salt production and
ironworking (RCAHMS, Canmore ID 48027;
D. Adamson, 2008). **535. Bruce:** Sir George
Bruce of Carnock, or Culross (c.1550–1625),
son of Sir Edward Bruce of Blairhall; an en-
trepreneur, ingenious developer of coalmines
and saltpans, and burgess of Culross. He
owned the lands and barony of Carnock, 5
miles north-east of Culross towards Dunfermline. In 1621, his 'mony worthie and proffitable
workis' were recognised by the privy council,
the king ordering them to reward him (*ODNB*;
NLS, Adv MS 33.1.1, vol. X, no. 34). His house at
Culross, known as the 'Palace' as a result of
James VI's visit to it in 1617, was built in two
stages, in 1597 and 1611; it features extensive
decorative painting, including a chamber of
'iconographically sophisticated' emblems
(RCAHMS, Canmore ID 48021; Bath, 2003,

525. health, they] health they MS   526. them,] them MS   527. full,] full MS
531. Crawford of Lindsay] Craford of Lynsey MS   534. me] my MS   535. Bruce,] Bruse MS

famous coalmine into the sea; the mouth where [it] is first sank it is called the eye, and where it opens up into the sea the mot. The most strange and remarkable thing that ever I saw or read of.

We stayed there all Sunday; there preached Mr Robert Calvin in the forenoon and Mr James Edmonstone in the afternoon. We saw my lord's fair house, but not finished.   540

On Monday we rode to Kingcarron to see Sir George his salt pans, of which he hath two and twenty, and finds above 500 poor people at work, and pays every Saturday in the year 100 sterling for wages. There we saw

---

57–77). **536. coalmine…sea:** Sir George Bruce had amassed coalmines and saltpans around Culross from the 1590s; in 1610, he had a tack of (i.e. was entitled to a levy on) the customs of all imports and exports of salt and coal out of Culross and Torryburn in Fife; in 1614, he received a royal charter confirming his monopoly of the extraction of sea-coal, with the right to make salt (*RMS*, 7. no. 1038; NRS, GD236/2/4). The mine ran some considerable distance out under the Firth of Forth and was without any contemporary equivalents in England or Wales. It was frequently viewed by visitors: the king, Lord Walden and John Taylor had all recently admired 'this vnfellowed and vnmatchable work' (*PP*, sigs. E1–E3; D. Adamson, 2008). It was inundated during a great storm in 1625, but Bruce's heir continued his mining interests. **536–537. mouth… eye:** See *OED*, Eye *n.*[1] 20c; Scots, 'ee'. A shaft rather than an 'ingaunee', the inclined entrance to a drift mine (*DSL* SND1, Ee *n.* 1 (2) b; D. Adamson, 2008, 170). **537. mot:** The circular wall or 'moat', 15.5m in diameter, built around the entrance to the mine 400m offshore, which prevented inundation at high tide; the mine as a whole was known as the Moat Pit (D. Adamson, 2008, 161, 174–7). **539. Calvin:** Robert Colville (c.1560–1631), minister of Culross since 1593; a presbyterian, he was a signatory of the 1617 protestation to parliament against the king's attempts to introduce 'high-church' reforms (*FES*, 5.14). The Colvilles were intermarried with the Bruces, and, in October 1618, Colville witnessed a number of Bruce deeds at Culross (see below; NRS, GD15/536–40, 638). His sister-in-law, Elizabeth Melville, Lady Culross, the author of *Ane Godlie Dreame*, was a great admirer, writing of his plain and powerful preaching, and lamenting his death as 'a soir strok to this congregatioun' (Reid-Baxter, 2006, 525–8). **540. Edmonstone:**

Mr James Edmonstone (d. by 1665), master of the Grammar School, Stirling, and presented to St Ninian's in Stirling in 1624 by the king. Three of his sons also became ministers (*FES*, 4.313–14), one of them, Robert, holding the second charge of Culross from 1649. James is not listed as a minister for Culross. The sermons were presumably preached in Culross Abbey, remodelled for use as the parish church; officially designated as such in 1633. An aisle containing a grand monument to Bruce and his wife was later built here (Hallen, 1878, 252; RCAHMS, Canmore ID 48040). **540–541. my lord's fair house:** Edward Bruce, Lord Kinloss (1548/9–1611), Sir George's elder brother, began the construction of a Renaissance mansion next to the church in 1608. Kinloss was a lawyer for the Crown, and both an English and Scottish privy councillor. His death in 1611 probably slowed building; his second son, and heir, Edward, was killed in a 1613 duel with Sir Edward Sackville, the future fourth earl of Dorset. His third son, Thomas, succeeded his brother as Lord Kinloss and would have been in possession of the unfinished house in 1618 (Beveridge, 1885, 1.111; RCAHMS, Canmore ID 48054; *ODNB*). **542. Kingcarron:** Kincardine, 2 miles west of Culross on the Firth of Forth, and long known primarily for salt production. From 1597 Sir George Bruce had been acquiring the coalmines of Kincardine, which provided the fuel for the process of salt extraction. (Whatley, 1984, 7; NRS, GD15/248–59, 345; NRS, GD236/2/4). **543. two and twenty:** At his death, Bruce owned a 'veritable empire' of forty-four saltpans, including those at Kincardine, along the coast of the Forth (Whatley, 1984, 26). That the figure given here should be exactly half that number suggests, perhaps, an alternative way of counting them. **543. poor people:** Cf. Taylor: 'Many poore people are there set on worke, which otherwise through the want of

---

536. sea;] sea, MS   539. Sunday;] Sunday MS
541. house,] house MS

540. Edmonstone] Edmudstone MS

a rare waterwork. He spends three hundred load of coals a week in   545
making of his salt, and makes an hundred and ten ton a week.

After that we entered the mine etc.

At Sir George's was Mr Heskins, Sir G his son-in-law, Sir John
Preston, Mr Gall, laird of Maw etc.

We went by Blair and Sands, two gentlemen's houses; Sir   550
George Bruce brought us to Dunfarlin, the Queen's town, where
my gossip was with all grace received by my Lord Chancellor and

imployment would perish' (*PP*, sig. E2).
545. waterwork: Possibly the 'Egyptian wheel'
by which sea-water was drained from the coalmine, 'a devise like a horsemill' with 'a great
chaine of Iron, going downeward many fa-
domes, with thirty sixe buckets' (*PP*, sig. E2v);
perhaps, though, the system of channels created to supply seawater to the saltpans at Kincardine (Whatley, 1984, 16). **546. hundred and
ten ton:** cf. Taylor: 'he doth make euery weeke
ninety or an hundred Tuns of salt'. This figure
has been described as 'grossly over-estimated'
(*PP*, sig. E3; D. Adamson, 2008, 186).
548. Heskins: John Erskine of Balgownie, married to Bruce's daughter, Magdalen; Balgownie
House is at the western edge of Culross. Later
knighted, Erskine established a family burial
site within the abbey church (*SP*, 3.485; Hallen,
1878, 252–3). **549. Preston:** Sir John Preston of
Valleyfield, 2 miles east of Culross, the father of
Marie Preston; she was married to Sir George
Bruce's son, also George. On 1 October 1618, Sir
George granted part of the lands of the barony
of Carnock to his son in fulfilment of the
marriage contract between him and Sir John;
witnesses included Robert Colville. Like the
Bruces and Erskines, the Prestons had a family
vault at Culross Abbey church (*SP*, 3.485; NRS,
GD15/536–40; Hallen, 1878, 252). **549. Gall,
laird of Maw:** The MS reading, 'Galeard of
maw', is a scribal error for John Gaw or Gall,
laird of Maw, married to Marjorie Bruce. She
was perhaps the daughter of Robert Bruce, fiar
('owner') of Wester Kennet, entrusted to the
care of Gaw by Bruce in 1606. Alexander Gaw,
John's father, had received an act of parliament
in his favour excluding his three houses and
lands in Culross from the burgh's charter in
1594 (NRS, GD11/88, GD24/7/162; *RPS*, 1594/4/
75). **550. Blair and Sands:** Possibly Blair
House, near Carnock, 3 miles north-east of
Culross, or Blairhall, a mile nearer Culross,
the seat of Sir George's elder brother, Robert,
and Sandyknow, just north of Carnock; more
likely, however, a house on the site of Blair
Castle, a mile west of Culross on the road to

Kincardine, and Sands, now demolished, a
mile further west towards Kincardine
(RCAHMS, Canmore ID, 49444, 48026; *SP*,
3.474; NLS, EMS.s.382; Hallen, 1878, 248; Beveridge, 1888, 198, 200). **551. Dunfarlin:** Dunfermline, an ancient royal burgh; the abbey
there was the former burial place of Scottish
kings. The regality of Dunfermline was owned
by Queen Anna, and around 1594 she built a
house beside the abbey, 'a delicate and princely
Mansion' according to Taylor, and one of her
favourite residences. It was the birthplace of
Princess Elizabeth in 1596, Princes Charles in
1600 and Robert in 1602 (*PP*, sig. E1; Dennison
and Stronach, 2007, 30–2). Ebenezer Henderson, the town's nineteenth-century annalist,
noted that 'according to tradition, Ben Jonson
visited in August 1618' (Henderson, 1879, 277).
552. Lord Chancellour: Alexander Seton (1555–
1622), earl of Dunfermline from 1605, eminent
lawyer and administrator; lord chancellor of
Scotland from 1604 and the king's foremost
adviser and agent in the country after the
death of the earl of Dunbar in 1611. Studied at
the German College in Rome for several years
from 1571, though outwardly conformed on his
return to Scotland. 'A great humanist in prose
and poecie, Greek and Latine, well versed in
the mathematicks and had great skill in architecture and herauldrie', he was celebrated by
John Dunbar as 'the sweet beloved of the
Muse, glory of learned men, honour of peace,
and darling of your nation' (Maitland, 1829, 63;
Dunbar, 2013, Century 5, Epigram 41). He was
heritable bailie of the regality of Dunfermline
for Queen Anna, occupying a house close to
the abbey, in which capacity he was expected
to provide entertainment for important visitors. Dunfermline was uncle by marriage to
John Auchmuty, and built a fine house at
Pinkie, near Musselburgh, in 1613; Jonson
later asked William Drummond for details of
the emblematic decoration either of its long
gallery or on Queen Mary's bedhangings,
which may have been kept there after the
king's return to Scotland in 1617 – Dunfermline

549. Gall, laird of Maw] *Galeard* of Maw MS   550. Blair and Sands,] Blare and Sands MS
550. houses;] houses MS   551. Bruce] *Bruse* MS   551. town, where] town. Where MS

my lady with her brother. We found my lady shooting at butts. Here we drank hard, with some six more, and were made burgesses.

We lay at Mr Biggs, who used my gossip and his company with all freedom and full entertainment. We stayed with him all Tuesday.   555

Wednesday Mr Gibbs with his two sons, Barnaby and William, with his son-in-law Mr James Creeton brought us to Brunt Island; and so to the well at Pettycur, a mile beyond Brunt Island and some two furlongs

---

was responsible for the logistics of the visit. James Raith, whom Jonson singled out for a particular greeting in the same letter, was Dunfermline's attendant and secretary (*ODNB*; NRS, GD150/1976, E41/2; *CWBJ*, Letter 14; Seton, 1882, 115, 143, 158; Masson, 1893, 804; Bath, 2003, 79–103; Bath, 2007; Bath and Craig, 2010, 285–6). **553. my lady:** The chancellor's third and much younger wife, Margaret Hay (d. 1659), daughter of James Hay, seventh Lord Yester, who was contracted to him with a tocher, or dowry, of £20,000, or £2,000 annual rent from the lands of Yester (Harvey and Macleod, 1930, 336). She had two brothers: John Hay (c.1583–1653), eighth Lord Yester, who was to marry his brother-in-law Dunfermline's daughter, Jean, in 1624 and was created first earl of Tweeddale in 1646; and Sir William Hay (c.1594–1658) of Linplum in East Lothian. **553. shooting at butts:** Practising archery, probably in the 'faire Gardens, Orchards, and Medowes belonging to the palace' described by Taylor (*PP*, sig. E1). Customarily, at least, a masculine pursuit: cf. *Magnetic Lady*, 1.4.13; though see also *Love's Labour's Lost*, 4.1, for contrary evidence. The earl of Dunfermline was a keen archer throughout his life (Seton, 1882, 130–1). **554. made burgesses:** Made honorary freemen of the town. Dunfermline's burgh records for the years 1613–19 have not survived, but this honour was bestowed on advocates, courtiers, gentlemen and the servants of the nobility in the surrounding years (Shearer, 1951, 60, 73, 163, 152, 158, 164). **555. Biggs:** A slip for Gibb or Gibbs. According to Taylor, John Gibb (c.1550–1628) of Carriber and Knock was 'the oldest servant the king hath', his service since James's infancy recognised in a number of grants from the 1580s onwards. These included the office of keeper of the palace and yards of Dunfermline Abbey in 1585, confirmed by the queen in 1592, with the monks' portion of the abbey, and its revenues, where he had a house. Taylor also stayed here, where he described himself 'well

entertained' (*PP*, sig. E1; Gibb, 1874, I.313–14). Gibb went south with James in 1603 as a groom of his bedchamber; in 1605, he had a grant of £3,000 from recusancy forfeitures, and in 1610 the king added the revenues associated with the chapel royal of Stirling to the office of master of the chapel that he had already received. He accompanied James in 1617 and was made an honorary burgess of Edinburgh; he was knighted in 1624 (TNA, LC 5/50, pp.7–8; BL, MS Add 58,833, f.21; NRS, GD1/1056/1/1; ECA, SL141/1/3; Gibb, 1874, II.65). One of his sons, Henry (d. 1650), was a well-rewarded groom in Prince Henry's bedchamber from 1605, and of the king's from 1613; he was also an associate of the courtiers Ramsay and Lumsden, the latter in 1623 describing Gibb as his 'very good friend' (Gibb, 1874, II.154, 386; TNA, LC 5/50, pp.37, 99, LC 2/6, f.40; NRS, GD124/10/136; Seddon, 1975, I.67–8, 215). With James, his son and heir, John Gibb witnessed a baptism in Dunfermline on 4 October 1618 (Paton, 1911, 170). **557. Gibbs…William:** No Barnaby or William is recorded as a son of John Gibb; a Bernard Gibb was the father of several illegitimate children and, in 1627, cowitnessed a baptism with Sir John (Paton, 1911, 158, 178, 222). **558. Creeton:** Probably James Crichton of Abercrombie, near St Monans, in Fife; he was brother to William Crichton, ninth Lord Sanquhar and later earl of Dumfries, and nephew to John Crichton, eighth (sometimes styled sixth) Lord Sanquhar, who masqued in *Haddington* and was executed for murder in 1612. James married Agnes Graham in 1615; he was perhaps the 'Master Crighton' who entertained Taylor at his house in Dunfermline in August (Warrick, 1899, 39; *CWBJ*, I.cxlvi; Paton, 1911, 157; *PP*, sig. E1). **558. Brunt Island:** Burntisland, a port on the Firth of Forth; ferries crossed between here and Edinburgh's port, Leith. **559. well:** 'This latelie found, and newlie-knowne, and too-too long unknowne Well' or spring at the coastal town of Pettycur, beside Kinghorn (Barclay, 1618, sig.

---

553. butts.] buttes, MS   **557.** sons,] sonnes MS
559. Brunt Island] *Brunt*: MS

559. Pettycur] *Peticure* MS

on this side King-gorn. We passed by St Colm which stands upon an   560
inch as they call it, that is, a little island. We also passed by Aberdour, a
house of my Lord Murton's, successor of that Douglas which fought with
Percy, in Chevet chase. But his chief house is in Lough Lavin, a lake of
ten miles long and eight miles broad, in the middest whereof stands a
castle, and his new house upon the lake.   565
      On Wednesday night we came to Leith to Mr John Stewart's, who had
appointed my gossip his guest. We found there Mr Davy Drumman with

A4v). Taylor tells of the water's 'rare operation to
expell or kill diuers maladies' and its sweet taste;
William Barclay's tract outlining its 'Nature and
Effectes' was prefaced by a letter to his printer,
Andro Hart, dated 8 August 1618; Patrick Ander-
son's work on the same subject is headed by a
dedication to the earl of Mar dated 8 October
(*PP*, sigs. D3v–4; Anderson, 1618; Barclay, 1618, sig.
A2). **560. King-gorn:** Kinghorn, the most east-
erly of these three firth harbours. **560–561. St
Colm…inch:** Here, St Colm's Inch or
Inchcolm, with its ancient abbey; cf. Shakespeare, *Macbeth*, 1.2.61. **561. Aberdour:** Aberdour Castle, the 'seaside villa' of William
Douglas, seventh (sometimes given as eighth)
earl of Morton (1582–1648), who succeeded his
grandfather in 1606 and received a licence to
travel abroad with his cousin, the earl of
Angus, for up to three years in January 1617
(*ODNB*). A new east range at Aberdour, which
included a long gallery and comfortable lodgings complete with painted ceilings, is usually
dated to the 1630s but may have been begun
signficantly earlier (Macgibbon and Ross,
1887–92, II.474–6; McKean, 2004, 129–
30). **563. Chevet chase:** Morton's ancestor,
James, second earl of Douglas, had beaten the
forces of Sir Harry 'Hotspur' Percy at the battle
of Otterburn in Northumberland in 1388,
events recalled in the very well-known ballad
entered in the Stationers' Register in 1624 and
printed soon after under the title 'A memorable song vpon the vnhappy hunting in Cheuy
Chase, beweene the Earle / Pearcy of England,
and Earle Dowglas of Scotland' (*EBBA* 20279).
The earliest recorded notice of the ballad, as
'the hunttis of cheuet', is in *The Complaynt of
Scotlande* (1549), and it was already in print in
England by 1565. According to Joseph Addi-
son, 'Ben Jonson used to say that he had rather
have been the author of it than of all his works'
(A. M. Stewart, 1979, 51; A. Fox, 2000, 2–
3). **563–565. Lough…lake:** In 1606, Morton
had inherited the Lochleven estate from his
grandfather, the sixth earl, formerly Sir William Douglas of Lochleven. The sixth earl had

built the 'Newhouse of Kinross' on the loch's
side after 1546 to replace the island castle on
Loch Leven as his principal residence (*ODNB*;
NRS, GD29/564). **566. Stewart's:** Identified by
Masson as the master of the ship *Post of Leith*,
who in 1614 had been employed by the Crown
to ship ordnance to Orkney to suppress the
rebellion there. Masson also mistakenly described him as the water bailie of Leith, con-
flating a 1614 entry for him with a reference to
James Foirman. Foirman was water bailie in
1617 and 1618 but had died by June 1619; a
Robert Stevensoun was 'water baillie officer'
in Leith in October 1618 when he was deprived
for neglect of his office (*RPCS*, 10.clxviii, 344,
698, 700–1; ECA, SL1/1/13, pp.2, 81, 84, 129).
However, the John Stewart (d. c.1656) who
occupied a tenement owned by James Ainslie
(see l.583 below) near the King's Wark in Leith
was in fact the last Commendator of Coldingham Priory, a younger son of Francis, former
earl of Bothwell, and therefore kinsman to the
king; hence the presence in Leith of John's
elder brother, Francis, 'Lord Bothwell'. The
brothers were also related to Sir Francis Stewart, another great-grandson of James V and
dedicatee of *Epicene* in the 1616 folio. With
William Ramsay this John Stewart witnessed
Lord Haddington's transaction with Ramsay of
Dalhousie in Edinburgh on 1 September 1618.
He might also be the John Stewart who with
'Hary Levingstoun' was paid by the Scottish
exchequer as a royal usher during James's
visit of 1617. On Ainslie's death in 1623, he
appears to have owed his landlord £300; Sir
John Scot of Scotstarvit wrote in the 1650s that
'he now has nothing, but lives on the charity of
his friends' (*SP*, 2.171; *HMCMH*, 203–4; W. K.
Hunter, 1858, 74–5; NRS, RS25/2, f.301v; NRS,
RS25/4/254–5; Butler, 1995b; NRS, GD224/308/
19; NRS, E34/50/5, f.1; NRS, CC8/8/52, p.158;
Scot, 1872, 117). **567. Drumman:** David Drummond, one of James's gentlemen pensioners,
who had met Taylor earlier in Burntisland; he
was in James's train in 1617, when he was made
honorary burgess of Edinburgh, and was party

560. Colm] Com MS   **561.** Aberdour] Aberdore MS   **566.** Leith] Leeth MS

Mr Robert Hayes who came to the new well to seek remedy etc.

On Thursday Mr John Stewart with his wife went in coach with Mr Davy Drumman to Cobersmith, where he was to meet Mr Robert Hayes, and so to go to London. In the meantime he desired my gossip to use his house as his own, and to bid his friends as free to it, and to command his servants as his own. Which he accordingly did, inviting Mr Ramsey, Mr Alexander Stewart, Mr Heatley, and Mr Dunsire, and kept them all day. At night my Lord Bothwell came, whom my gossip welcomed etc. The next day he stayed for my gossip's company and hawked. On Friday night Mr John Stewart returned.

The same night my gossip arrived at Leith the town of Edinburgh sent to Mr Stewart to entreat him to bring Mr Jonson to the town, telling him they would (if it pleased him to accept thereof) make him burgess, and make him amends for his no fuller entertainment when he was there before, excusing the same by the absence of many of them.

570

575

580

to the contract between Haddington and Ramsay of Dalhousie witnessed by William Ramsay and John Stewart on 1 September 1618 (BL, MS Add 34,122 B; *PP*, sig. D4; ECA, SL141/1/3; NRS, GD224/308/19). Apparently a jovial courtier and poet – but not, as is sometimes asserted, the king's fool or jester – he was evoked in the equine figure of 'Davus Dromo' or 'Messe Davy' in George Ruggle's comedy *Ignoramus* at Cambridge in 1615 (*CL*, 1.587; *REED Camb*, 540–1, 954–5, ?Weldon, 1650, 92). He published three volumes of neo-Latin verse, including a 1608 *Epithalamion* for Haddington's marriage (Green, Burton and Ford, 2012, 117). He was the addressee of poems by Alexander Montgomerie and John Dunbar; William Fowler, the queen's secretary, described him as 'messt spreit in cariage, no girning in his face, / From falshood cleir' (Montgomerie, 2000, 1.102; Dunbar, 2013, Century 6, Epig. 85; W. Fowler, 1914, 325). In May 1619, he was granted the annual rent of £521 out of the lands of Spott in Berwickshire, but was no longer a pensioner. He was, however, still listed as a gentleman of the privy chamber in 1625 (NRS, RS71/1, bk 2. no. 217; NRS, GD45/17/68; TNA, LC 2/6, f.40). While Shaw asserts that 'David Dromond, a Scotchman' was knighted at Brougham in August 1617, Nichols gives no first name for the man thus honoured – the

contemporary evidence suggests he was not James's courtier (*KE*; *NP*, 3.392). **568. Hayes:** Robert Hay, a groom of the king's bedchamber from at least 1611, and subsequently of the wardrobe; commended in an epigram by John Dunbar for his humanity and modesty; involved in a 1613 Anglo-Scots stramash at court, when William Ramsay came to his defence (*CSPD, 1611–18*, 76; TNA, LC 2/6, f.45; Dunbar, 2013, Century 1. Epigram 42; *CL*, 1.445). He was younger, and possibly half-, brother to James, Baron Hay, who was created viscount Doncaster on 5 July 1618 and later raised to the earldom of Carlisle. James Hay was a notedly extravagant master of the robes and, from 1613, master of the great wardrobe, accumulating debts of £42,000 by the time he relinquished his offices in 1618. He staged Jonson's *Lovers Made Men* for the French ambassador in 1617. At the king's direction, Robert Hay received £10,000 out of the impost on wine in June 1617 (*SP*, 5.218–9; *ODNB*, James Hay; *CWBJ*, 1.cxlviii; *PP*, sig. D4; NRS, E21/84, f.74). Hay was with Drummond when Taylor met him at Burntisland; Taylor encountered them again at Newcastle on 1 October, seven days after Drummond's departure from Leith (*PP*, sig. G1v). **569. wife:** John Stewart's wife was named Margaret Home (*SP*, 2.171–2). **578. town of Edinburgh:** The burgh

568. Robert] *Rob* MS   **578.** Leith] Leeth MS   **578.** Edinburgh] Edenborough MS
579. Jonson] *Ihonson* MS   **580.** they] thew MS   **580.** thereof)] thereof MS

In the meantime Mr James Haynsley, one of the bailiffs and landlord to Mr Stewart (Mr Etsby being the other), came himself in person to invite my gossip, and with all solemnity, in the name of all the town 585 offered him the honour of burgess, and his house to remain in as long as he pleased. My Lady Sampleton, widow and a Hamilton, dined with my lord and my gossip, and after dinner sent to my gossip to entreat him to see her house etc.

On Saturday, we went to Edinburgh to Mr Haynsley to dinner, my 590 gossip being accompanied with Mr John Stewart and his wife, Mr W. R., Mr Heatley and Mr Alexander Stewart. Where my gossip was with all ceremony made burgess.

I lay at Effy Wilson's, her husband is called Thomas Robinson, from

council of Edinburgh. **583. Haynsley:** James Ainslie of Darnick (d. 1623), a wealthy merchant burgess of Edinburgh, burgh councillor, and elected bailie in 1617–18. In 1607, he bought the lands of Darnick for 12,000 merks, and he loaned money to several nobles. He owned lands as well as a tenement in Leith (NRS, CC8/8/52, ff.156–61; *RMS*, 6. no. 1994; NRS, GD40/1/360; NRS, GD150/671; NRS, RS71/1, bk 1. 121, bk 2. 300). **584. Etsby:** The other bailies in September 1618 were Alexander Pierson, James Dalzell, and David Richardson; they were replaced on 6 October by Alexander Clark, John Byres, George Foullis and David Mitchelson (ECA, SL1/1/13, pp.2, 80). 'Etsby' is perhaps a wayward rendering of 'Byres'. **587. Sampleton…Hamilton:** Probably the 'Lady Samuelstoun' who is recorded as owing James Ainslie £80 in 1623, and who was presumably a member of the Hamilton of Samuelstoun family (NRS, CC8/8/52, p.158). If so, the likeliest candidates are either Jean Home of Whitelaw, niece of the late George, earl of Dunbar, widow of William Hamilton of Samuelstoun and cousin to Elizabeth Home, wife of Theophilus, Lord Howard de Walden; or her mother-in-law, Margaret Carkettill, widow of Patrick Hamilton of Samuelstoun (d. 1613). Their connection with Francis and John Stewart – several members of the Samuelstoun branch were involved in the then earl of Bothwell's raid on Holyroodhouse in 1593, for which the family had a remission in 1613 – would support either of these identifications, although no further

evidence that Jean or Margaret possessed a title has been found (*SP*, 3.283–8; *RMS*, 7. no. 920). Another possibility is Joanna, Lady Sempill (d. 1638), widow of Robert, fourth Lord Sempill (d. 1611). He was her second husband; she had previously been married to Sir John Hamilton of Lincliff, cousin to James Hamilton, second marquess of Hamilton, and a royal favourite in James's later years (*SP*, 7.552–3; *ODNB*, James Hamilton; Cuddy, 1989, 120). **587–588. my lord:** Bothwell. **588. dinner:** On 16 October 1618, the burgh's treasurer was ordered to pay James Ainslie £221 6s 4d spent by him 'vpone the dennir maid to Benjamin Jonsoun' at his admission as burgess (ECA, SL1/1/13, p.85; Town Treasurer's Accounts, 1612–23, p.597). Ainslie owned a tenement on the south side of Castlehill, but was perhaps resident in the north-east parish of the city (ECA, Edinburgh Protocol Books, Alexander Guthrie, 1612–14, 19.109; Bailies' Accounts Extent and Unlaws from 1564 to 1689, p.597). **591. W. R.:** William Ramsay. **593. burgess:** On 25 September the burgh council ordered the dean of guild to make 'Benjamyn Jonsoun – Inglisman burges and gildbrother' an honorary burgess, a dignity conferred on James's retinue in 1617. Jonson was presented with a gilded burgess ticket, for which a scribe was paid £14 6s 8d (ECA, SL1/1/13, p.79, SL144/3, 1618–1619, 20 January 1619). **594. Effy …Robinson:** Euphame Wilson (d. 1645) married Thomas Robertson, a stabler, on 29 December 1608. Around 1618, they are recorded as

583. Haynsley,] Haynsley MS   584. other),] other) MS   587. Hamilton] Hamelton MS
588. gossip, and] gossip. And MS   590. Edinburgh] Edenborough MS
590. Haynsley] Hansley MS   590. dinner,] dinner. MS   594. Wilson's] Willsons MS

Saturday till the Monday sevenight after, which was the fifth of   595
November, at what time I parted from Edinburgh, and at Leith took
boat for Brunt Island, where I met with a ship bound for England,
the master whereof was John Gadd, and his brother mate. I lay at
Robert Clerke's.

The harbour towns upon the Fife: St Andros, Catten wymb, Crill,   600
Anster, Wymbs, Buck, Earth haven, Leven, Easter wymb, Culrose, Largo,
Wester wymbs, Desert, Kirkcaldy, Kill-gorn, Burnt Island, Aberdour,
Anderkethen upon Lowthen, Haymouth, Coldingham, White Cove,
Dunbar, North Berwick, Aberlady, Prestonpans, Musselburgh,
Fishrach, Leith, Cramond, Queensferry, Abercorn.   605

living in the south-east parish of Edinburgh; an account of 1629 says she kept her house in College Wynd, between the Cowgate and the university buildings on what is now Chambers Street. She was also a moneylender, and was owed substantial sums by various gentlemen at her death (Paton, 1905, 744; ECA, Edinburgh Stent Rolls, SL35/1/2; *HMCL*, 80; NRS, CC8/8/62, f.731). **595. sevenight:** Seven-night or sen-night; a week. **596. November:** A slip – October is meant. **598. Gadd:** John Ged the elder, burgess, was on the burgh council in 1617–18; on 1 October 1618, John Ged the younger, burgess, was elected. He appears on the council on 6 October, but not again until 23 February 1619, perhaps suggesting an absence from the town (NRS, B9/12/4, ff.25, 35v). **599. Clerke's:** Robert Clerke, skipper and burgess of Burntisland; he apparently died in June 1618, although his will was not registered until March 1619 (NRS, CC20/4/7, p.92). No heir of the same name is known, but the reference to Clerke's premises need not imply that he was still alive, or thought to be so by the writer. **600. Fife:** A slip for 'Forth'; the eastern section of its northern shore is in Fife. **600–605. The harbour towns...Abercorn:** On both coasts of the Forth. The southern harbours are listed from south and east to north and west; the northern

towns are not listed in geographical order. See Blaeu's 1654 *Atlas* of Scotland, and the 1642 manuscript map of Fife by James Gordon of Rothiemay on which Blaeu's is based (Blaeu, 1654 and 2006; NLS, EMS.s.676; NLS, WD3B/7 and 30; NLS, Adv MS 70.2.10). Among the northern settlements, St Andrews, Crail, Leven, East Wemyss, Culross, Largo, West Wemyss, Dysert, Kirkcaldy ('Carcadhy' in the MS), Kinghorn, Burntisland, Aberdour and Inverkeithing, adjacent to Letham Hill, are all readily identifiable. 'Catten wymb' is probably Pittenweem; 'Auster' is an error for Anster or Anstruther, which is divided into 'Easter Ansterrudder' and 'West Anster' on Gordon's map; 'Wymbs' is most likely Wemyss, marked as a separate coastal settlement by both Gordon and Blaeu; 'Buck' and 'Earth haven' are probably the result of a confusion between Buckhaven and Earlsferry or the adjacent Elie. The writer does not appear to have visited any of these settlements east and north of Burntisland. On the south coast of the firth, the places listed are Eyemouth, Coldingham, Cove or 'Whytecoaue', near Cockburnspath, Dunbar, North Berwick, Aberlady, Prestonpans, Musselburgh, Fisherrow, Leith, Cramond, Queensferry and Abercorn.

595. sevenight] seavnight MS   595. fifth] fift MS   596. Edinburgh] Edenborough MS
596. Leith] leeth MS   597. master] Mr MS   600. Fife:] fife. MS
600. Anster, Wymbs] Auster wymbs MS   602. Kirkcaldy] Carcadhy MS
602. Kill-gorn,] Kill gorne MS   602. Aberdour] Aberdore MS   603. Cove,] Cove MS
604–5. Berwick, Aberlady, Prestonpans, Musselburgh, Fishrach, Leith] Barwicke Abberleddy, Prestonpannes, Muscleborough, fishrach, Leeth MS
605. Queensferry] Queenes ferry MS

Appendix One
Brief additional passages

By my sal ye ha ill cappers here, that is, waiters, I ha get na drink since I sat down, rising up at the table and sitting down again.

Another coming on New Year's Day to a house, bid 'em treat him well for he vowed he had eat no flesh that year.

James Keys, bailiff of Kill-gorn, was cured of a pearl in his eye by this 5 water etc.

A girl avoided 70 odd stones as big as little peas. And my Lord of Murton six great confirmed stones.

---

1. **Sal:** Scots, 'Soul' (*OED*, soul *n*.). 1. **cappers:** Scots, 'Coppar', cupbearer (*OED*, Copper, *n*.²; *DSL* DOST, Coppar *n*.). 5. **James Keys:** James Key or Kay, skipper burgess of Kinghorn (NRS, GD26/3/708). 5. **pearl:** 'A corneal opacity or cataract' (*OED*, Pearl, *n*.¹, A 1b). 5–6. **this water:** The water of the Pettycur spring or well ('Foot Voyage', l.559); contemporary commentators note its curative effects on, among other complaints, 'clouds or blots which effuscate or dimme the *Cornea tunica*', and its help with 'auoyding of the grauell in the bladder', i.e. bladder stones (P. Anderson, 1618; Barclay, 1618, sig. [A6]; *PP*, sig. D3v–[4]). 7. **avoided:** Voided,

passed. 7–8. **Lord of Murton:** 'Foot Voyage', l.562; travelling abroad from the summer of 1617, and in Paris in the spring of 1618; not hitherto thought to have returned to Scotland until 1620, but his presence at Kinghorn was recorded on 15 August 1618. Writing that summer, William Barclay claimed that the water 'bringeth downe little stones from the kidneyes, and expelleth them also from the bladder' but 'it is not tried to haue force to diminish or demolish a conformed or solidated stone in the bladder' (*ODNB*; NRS, GD112/39/28/11; Barclay, 1618, sig. [A6]).

---

1. here, that is,] here that is MS   5. Kill-gorn,] Kill-gorne MS

Appendix Two
Canesco

Canesco, or the Sleu-dog's Language
Lurg if a Dog, Mellin if a Bitch

Title: 'Canesco' is pseudo-Italian, of sorts, for 'dogs' language'; there is perhaps a counter-ironic play here on 'dog's eloquence' meaning verbal abuse (*Und.* 33, 12), a phrase traceable to Quintilian (*CWBJ*, 7.148). 'Sleu dog' and 'lurg dog' are terms for a sleuth hound or blood-hound, with the former and its variants found in both northern English and Scots while the latter, of Gaelic derivation, more distinctively Scots in its usage (*OED*, Sleuth *n.*[2], 1b; *EDD*, Sleugh-hound *sb.*; *DSL* SND1, Sleuth *n.* In combs. 1; *DSL* DOST, Lurg-dog, Lurgg, *n.*; *OED*, Lurgg *n.*). Boece claimed that 'sleu-thoundis' were unique to Scotland, distinguishing them by their colour and markings ('Reid hewit or ellis blak with small spraingis of spottis'); Topsell too distinguishes 'the sluth-hound of *Scotland*' from the 'English Bloud hounde', suggesting – as the reference here to its being carried on a horse in front of its master (l.1) confirms – that the former was smaller than the latter (Topsell, 1607, 150–1). The behavioural qualities of the sleuth hound as described by Boece are nonetheless conso-nant with those ascribed to bloodhounds gen-erally (Boece, 1540, sig. Cii). By the mid sixteenth century their characteristic use on either side of the border was well known, with John Caius commenting: 'in the borders of England & Scotland, (the often and accus-tomed stealing of cattell so procuring) these kinde of Dogges are very much vsed and they are taught and trayned vp first of all to hunt cattell as well of the smaller as of the greater grouth and afterwardes (that qualitie relin-quished and lefte) they are learned to pursue such pestilent persons as plant theyr pleasure in such practises of purloyning' (Caius, 1576, 7; trans. Abraham Fleming – see 'Foot Voyage',

l.65n). An Anglicised version of Boece's account of the breed was included in the 'De-scription of Britain' by William Harrison pub-lished with Holinshed's *Chronicles*. In his *Historie of Scotland* John Leslie also described the vital role played by 'quick senting Slugh-hounds' in the pursuit of 'Cattaile-stealers' in a passage quoted by Camden, but earlier in the work he noted (in the Scots translation of James Dalrymple) how 'from the first sent quhilke the dog perceiues, eftir the crie of his Leidar, follow, rinn or gang vthir men sa fast as thay will, it moues him nathing, he is nocht drawin back, bot still followis the fute of the flier' (*CB*, 'Scotland', 18; Leslie, 1888–95, I.21; Leslie, 1675, 13–14). Following the Union of the Crowns, with the Borders redesignated the 'Middle Shires', sleuth hounds were ac-corded a vital role in their final pacification: a 1605 article of the Scottish privy council or-dered 'that in every parish there may be some lurgg dogges kept, one or moe, according to the quantitie of the parish, for following of pettie stouthes [i.e. thefts]', while a warrant of 1616 addressed to the provost marshal of Carlisle requested the implementation of an earlier royal order to provide for the maintenance of 'slough dogs' in each parish, in order to combat 'the increase of stealths daily growing both in deed and report among you on the borders' (*RPCS*, 7.744; Nicolson and Burns, 1777, I.131). In *Of English Dogges*, Caius notes how blood-hounds are trained to be 'acquainted with their masters watchwordes, eyther in reuoking or imboldening them' (Caius, 1576, 8); of what it spuriously calls the 'Suth-hound', a 1594 'Me-morial of the most rare and wonderfull things in Scotland' says, 'when as hee is certified by words of Art spoken by his master, what goods

He cries first, 'horse, Lurg,' then the dog leaps up before him, and there will sit upon the neck of the horse like an ape. Then he bids him 'ga down sir, and make ye for'd,' then he goeth piss and shit. Then he bids him cast for a fore gate of a night drift; then he leads him in a line of cord, and as soon as he sees him put down his head, he cries, 'is that it? Chalice   5 that.' Then he barks. Then he cries, 'chalice that, the caple, and the cawd arne' (that is, the horse shoes) that drives the cow with it. 'Turn tha woo'd. Go where she goes; put her tull a stall, and thous ha' blood on her.

are stolne, whether Horse, sheep or Neat: immediatly, hee addresseth him suthly to the sent, and followeth with great impetuositie' (?Monipennie, 1594, sig. K2v). These 'words of Art' constitute 'the sleu-dog's language'; but the term presumably also includes the dog's gestural and vocal responses, insofar as they communicate the progress of the pursuit. 'Mellin' is perhaps 'mailin', a diminutive or derogatory term for 'an untidy or slovenly woman' in use in the English borders (*EDD*, Mailin *sb.*); which may itself be an alternative form of Malkin, an 'untidy or sluttish woman', especially a 'servant or country girl'; in Scots, a proverbial female name, sometimes specifically an 'awkward, long-legged half-grown girl'. Also, a name for an animal, often a cat (cf. Shakespeare, *Macbeth*, 1.1.10), but in specifically northern English and Scots usage, a hare (*OED*, Malkin *n.* 1, 5; *DSL* DOST, Malkin, *n.*; *DSL* SND1, Maukin, *n.* 1, 2, 4). 1. **horse:** A command – 'to horse'. 3. **ga:** Scots and northern English: go (*OED*, Go *v.*; *DSL* DOST, Ga *v.*). 3. **make ye for'd:** There is probably a contraction here, attested in Northumbrian usage: thus, 'make ye for it', i.e. prepare for the pursuit (*EDD*, For *prep.*, *conj.* and *sb.* 2: Dial. contractions (7a); *EDD*, Make *v.*[1] II: Dial. uses 1 (6b); *DSL* DOST, Mak, Make, *v.*[1] 21b). 4. **cast...drift:** Cast about for the scent indicating the path of a herd (of cattle) moved at night (*OED*, Cast *v.* 60–1; *DSL* DOST, Gate *n.*[1] 1a, 3; *EDD*, Gate *sb.*[2] and *v.*[2] 1, 3; *DSL* DOST, Drift, Dryft, *n.* 1; *EDD*, Drift *sb.* and *v.* 2). 4. **in a line of cord:** 'Line' ('lyne' in MS) is possibly a variant of, or error for, 'lyme' or 'lyam': bloodhounds were 'limers' or 'lyme-hounds' (*OED*, Lyam | Lyme, *n.*, Limer *n.*[1]; Jesse, 1866, II.33; *Bartholomew Fair*, 1.3.10);

hence, the leash on which this kind of dog is kept by its handler during the pursuit. Cf. William Somervile's description of a borderer setting out to track reivers in *The Chace* (1735): 'In a line, / his faithful hound he leads' (Bk 1, ll.316–17). 5. **Chalice:** 'Challense' or 'challance', Northumbrian and Scots form of 'challenge', the cry of a hound on picking up the scent of its quarry (*OED*, Challenge *v.* 1c; *EDD*, Challenge *v.* and *sb.*; *DSL* DOST, Chalange, Chalance, *v.*). 6–7. **caple:** A horse; most common in Scots usage by this time (*OED*, Capel | Capul, *n.* 1; *EDD*, Caple *sb.*; *DSL* DOST, Capill, *n.*); the horse, or one of the horses, used by those driving the herd. 6–7. **cawd arne:** Cold iron, in specifically northern spellings (*EDD*, Cold *adj. sb.*[1] and *v.*; cf. Scots 'cauld'); as the text says, figurative for horse shoes and, by metonymic extension, the scent trail of the horse. 7–8. **Turn tha woo'd:** 'Tha' is a northern English form of 'thou' (*OED*, Thou *pron.* and *n.*[1]; 'wood' a possible contraction of 'with it' (*EDD*, With *prep.* I Dial. forms (21)); so 'turn thou with it', i.e. keep to the herd's trail in its twists and turns. 8. **put... stall:** Bring her to a stand; 'tull' is a northern English and Scots form of 'to' (*EDD*, Till *prep.* and *conj.*) 8. **thous:** A contraction, in northern English and Scots usage: 'thou shalt' (*EDD*, Thou *pers. pron.* and *v.* 2 (23)); with 'ha', then, 'thou shalt have'. 8. **blood on hir:** Perhaps a promise of visceral satisfaction should the pursuit of the thieves be successful (though not, of course, at the expense of the recovered cattle); with reference to the sleuth hound's particular attraction to the scent of blood, and reputation for violently apprehending fugitives (Boece, 1540, sig. Cii; Jesse, 1866, II.171–2).

3. for'd] ford MS   3. goeth piss and shit] goe[th and] pisse[s] ⌐and shitt⌐ MS
5. head, he cries, 'is] head; Hee cryes is MS   7. cow with it] cow ptre ∧ <.> ⌐wth it⌐ MS
8. woo'd] wood MS

Keep thee with thine awne cow and change her not. Is that she that
tha first fand? Keep tha with that and change her not, but go where she 10
goes. Shame, thief, he'll shame's both. Shame him that would shame thee
and me.'

Then when he comes among other beasts he cries, 'is tat hit, that tha
first fand?' It's a night drift, and he waps it in the day fewte, that is, when
other beasts crosseth the trod. Then when he is troubled with another 15
trod, he cries, 'hast it? Keep thee woo't then. That's thine awne bugle,
i'faith tha gar'st thy bugle blaw now. Gather't, gather't, and go thy way
wooth't, and change not that.'

---

9. **awne:** Northern English and Scots: own
(*DSL* DOST Awin, Awne, *a.*; *EDD*, Own,
adj.). 10. **fand:** Northern English and Scots:
found (*EDD*, Find *v.* I 2 *pp.* (2)). 11. **thief:**
'Rascal', addressed to the dog (*EDD*, Thief *sb.*
3), but probably also with reference to the
cattle-thieves. 13. **other beasts:** Different
herds or kinds of livestock, or their tracks
and traces. 13. **tat:** Northern English: 'that'
(*EDD*, Tat *dem. adj.* and *pron.*). 13. **hit:** Emphatic form of the pronoun 'it'; northern English and Scots (*EDD*, Hit *pron.* and *sb.*²). 14.
waps…fewte: If not an error, then 'wap' is
perhaps 'bark' or 'proclaim'; otherwise, to
throw or knock or strike with force, or to
shake, in a transitive usage more common in
Scots than English (*OED*, Wap *v.*¹ 1a, 2, *v.*³;
DSL DOST, Wap, *v.* 1, 2); a dog prone to
barking was known as a 'wappe', according
to Caius (1576, 34). 'Fewte' is the tracks or
traces of an animal (*OED*, Feute | Fewte, *n.*).
So, perhaps, the hound gives voice at the
scent of the stolen cow even when it is overlaid by more recent or daylight trails. 15.
other…trod: Clarifying the earlier use of 'day
fewte': 'trod' is track or trail (*OED*, Trod *n.* 1a;

EDD, Trod *sb.* and *v.*¹ 3; *DSL* SND1, Trod *n.*). Cf.
the 'hot trod': 'the pursuit of Border marauders
was followed by the injured party and his friends
with blood-hounds and bugle-horn, and was
called the *hot-trod*' (Scott, 1805, 308). 16.
woo't: A contraction: 'with it'. 17. **bugle…**
now: 'Bugle' is at its root a young bull, whence
comes 'bugle-horn', shortened to 'bugle', vessel
or wind instrument, and sometimes denoting
the cry of a bull or cow (*OED*, Bugle *n.*¹ 1, 2;
DSL SND1, Bugle, *v.*); bugle-horns were used
with bloodhounds in the pursuit of border
reivers (see l.15n above). 'Gar' is northern English or Scots for 'to cause' or 'make', while 'blaw'
is a spelling and pronunciation of 'blow' from
the same areas (*DSL* DOST, Gar, *v.* *EDD*, Gar *v.*
and *sb.*¹; *OED*, Blow *v.*¹; *DSL* DOST, Blaw *v.*.).
Hence, 'you're making your own bugle blow
now': the quarry is either literally audible, figu-
ratively audible in its traces, or – most likely –
punningly heard in a metaphor for the dog's
own barking, which, with the huntsman's horn,
indicates that the chase is on. 17. **Gather't:** A
contraction: 'gather it', recover the trail, or
catch the quarry. 18. **wooth't:** A contraction:
'with it'.

---

11. Shame, thief,] Shame theefe MS 14. fewte] fewle MS 15. trod,] trod. MS
16. woo't] woot MS 17. Gather't, gather't] Gathert gathert MS 18. wooth't] wootht MS

When the dog runs this way and that way he bids, 'turn tha woo'd', and airt it, that is, put it east, west, north or south.   20

This gentleman gave eight pounds for one of these dogs, and was offered for the same twenty whies, that is, steers of two years old.

20. **airt it...south:** Scots: directs it along a particular bearing, with especial reference to the points of the compass (*OED*, Airt *v.* 1; *DSL* SND1, Airt, Art, Airth, Ert *v.*). The master is methodically guiding the hound's efforts to recover the trail. **21. gentleman:** Presumably the owner from whom this 'dogs' language' has been gleaned. **21. eight pounds:** A 'slewe dog' stolen in 1590 from Catton in England by men from Liddesdale was valued at £10 sterling, whereas the horses taken were only valued at between 40 shillings and £5 (*CBP*, 1.347). The text describing 'Nithsdale' printed in Blaeu's 1654 *Atlas* of Scotland, which mostly reproduces Camden's description, adds a sentence valuing a sleuthhound at 100 crowns (Blaeu, 2006, 69). **22. whies:** Variant form, perhaps reflecting English orthographic habits, of northern English and Scots 'quey', a young cow which has not yet calved, a heifer up to 3 years old (*OED*, Quey *n.*; *EDD*, Quey *sb.*¹; *DSL* DOST, Quy, Quey, *n.*¹; Ray, 1691, 81). A steer is male – this is presumably an interpretive error on the writer's part.

20. airt] ert MS

Appendix Three
Notes on Bothal and York

At Bothal we saw the battle-axe with which Robert Ogle, the first baron, slew Sir Davy Dunbar in a single combat. Who wore the tod tail, that is, the fox tail, in his hat in token none durst encounter him.

Henry the third matching with Scotland, both of the kings met at the Bishop's Palace in York, where the bishop bestowed three score beeves 5 on them for a breakfast, all other charges being suitable thereto.

George Nevell, archbishop and brother to the earl of Warwick that carried a king on his sleeve, at his establishment in the see

1–2. **Bothal...tail:** A medieval Scottish knight, Sir David Dunbar, is said to have toured the country wearing a fox's tail in his cap as a challenge to all in single combat. On calling at Ogle Castle, in Northumberland, he was received by either Sir John or Sir Robert Ogle, but an argument broke out over dinner and Dunbar was slain with a pole-axe. Another tradition has it that Dunbar was killed by Sir Robert Ogle (d. c.1350) in 1346 at the Battle of Neville's Cross near Durham, and the battle-axe taken to Ogle where the Scottish king David II was briefly imprisoned. The axe was incorporated into the family crest displayed on the gateway to Bothal castle, under which the travellers doubtless passed (Ogle, 1902, 31, 34, 305, 348–9). 2. **tod:** fox; northern English and Scots (*OED*, Tod, *n.*[1] 1a). Cf. *Pan's Ann.*, in which Pan 'Driv'st hence the wolf, the tod, the brock' (l.217); and the mention of 'tods' hairs' in *Sad Shepherd* (1.4.28). 4. **Henry...Scotland:** The elaborate celebrations for the marriage of Henry III's daughter, Margaret, to Alexander III of Scotland, at York Minster on 26 December 1251, attended by many of the nobility and knights

of both kingdoms. 5. **bishop:** Walter de Gray (d. 1255), archbishop of York from 1215 until his death. His distinctive canopied tomb is in the south transept of York Minster. 5. **three score beeves:** 'This assembly of the Princes, cost the Archbishop right deerely, in feasting and banquetting them and theyr traynes. At one dinner it was reported he spent at the first course. lx. fat Oxen' (Holinshed, 1577, 727; cf. A. O. Anderson, 1908, 366–7). 7. **Nevell:** George Neville (1432–76), fourth son of Richard Neville, Fifth Earl of Salisbury; chancellor of England 1461–7, and archbishop of York from 1465 until his death (*ODNB*). 7. **earl of Warwick:** Richard Neville (1428–71), sixteenth earl of Warwick and eldest son and heir to the fifth earl of Salisbury, effective governor of England early in the reign of Edward IV, whom he had put on the throne, and later responsible for the restoration of Henry VI; in Shakespeare's words, a 'proud setter-up and puller-down of kings' (*3 Henry VI*, 3.3.157). 8. **establishment...see:** George Neville was enthroned as archbishop of York in September 1465.

1. Bothal] Bottle MS   1. battleaxe] Battle ax MS   4. Scotland, both] Scotland Both MS
5. York, where] York. Where MS   7. brother] (brother MS   8. sleeve,] sleeve) MS

strewed a thousand yards of cloth, which reached from St James, from
whence he passed to the minster, which was presently cut and divided by   10
the people. He spent three hundred quarters of wheat, as many tuns of
ale and 104 tuns of wine, the fowl and all other provision coming to an
equal rate.

The earl of Warwick was his steward and another earl his marshal,
and he had four marshals more, all knights. The earls with all ceremony   15
served him.

He sat in estate by himself, and on his right hand sat beneath him
three bishops, and on his left a duke and two earls.

At the west end of the minster on each side the gate are placed
two statues, the one on the right side with a huge stone in both   20

9–11. **strewed…people:** The chantry chapel of St James stood a short distance outside Micklegate Bar on the Tadcaster road; it was 'remarkable for being the place from which the archbishops of York begun their walk on foot to the cathedral, at their inthronization; the cloth which was spread all the way for that purpose being afterwards given to the poor' (Drake, 1736, 245; cf. YML, DC A1/2/1465). 11–13. **He spent…equal rate:** Neville's installation feast at Cawood Castle, an archiepiscopal residence, is 'one of the most quoted examples of conspicuous consumption in late medieval England' (Woolgar, 2001, 7). Some details of the meals eaten were printed in *The Boke of Cokery* in 1500, while a fuller account of the provisions consumed and the form of the occasion was published as *The Great Feast* in 1570; a later edition appeared in 1645. The eighteenth-century antiquarian Thomas Hearne printed an account taken 'out of an old paper roll' which accords with *The Great Feast* in matters of detail, but contains additional information; a variant text had already been printed by Thomas Gent in 1730. Other early manuscript accounts have also survived (Anon., 1500, sig. aii; Anon., 1645; Gent, 1730, 77; Leland, 1770, 2–14; Dobson, 1996, 229–30; Woolgar, 2001, 23–4). 11–12. **as many tuns of ale:** *The Great Feast* and Hearne give a figure of 300 tuns; Gent gives 330 (Anon., 1645, sig. A2; Gent, 1730, 77; Leland, 1770, 2). 12. **104…wine:** 100 tuns: *Great Feast* and Hearne; 104: Gent (Anon., 1645, sig. A2; Gent, 1730, 77; Leland, 1770, 2). 14. **earl…marshal:** Accounts concur in naming Warwick as steward, but either name a knight as marshal or omit this detail (Anon., 1645, 6; Gent, 1730, 77; Leland, 1770, 3). 15. **four marshals:** Hearne gives 'viii. other knyghtes for the Hall' in addition to the marshal (Leland, 1770, 3). 15. **earls:** Not corroborated in Hearne, the fullest surviving account. 17. **He…earls:** 'Estates syttyng at the high Table in the Hall. First the archbishop in his estate; upon his ryght hande the Bishop of London, the bishop of Durham, and the Bishop of Elye: upon the left hande the Duke of Suffolke, the Earle of Oxforde, and the Earle of Worcester' (Leland, 1770, 3). 20. **two statues:** Figures on the exterior of the minster, either side of the west door; they represent the families of Vavasour and Percy, who contributed stone and timber, respectively, to the construction of the minster from the earliest years of the present building. Both statues were recarved when the west front was restored between 1802 and 1816. Vavasour, holding the stone, is to the left of the west door; visual records

8–9. see strewed] sea. Strewed MS   12. 104] 100 4<.> MS   12. wine, the] wyne. The MS
14–15. marshal, and] martiall. And MS

his hands, and by him a scutcheon that bears or with a double
dancy sables, who represents Vavasour of Hazelwood, whose house
hath still endured without any accession by marriage or quartering
of coats though matched often with great houses, who in the book
of doomsday when there...   25

suggest that this positioning predates the
nineteenth-century restoration (S. Brown,
2003, 120). **21. scutcheon:** Heraldic
shield. **21–22. or...Hazelwood:** The arms of
Vavasour of Hazelwood, near Tadcaster. Usually described as 'or, a fesse dancettée sable' –
i.e. a yellow shield with a black, deeply serrated
bar across it. The fesse dancettée, or dancetty,
was sometimes termed 'dance' or 'dancy'; arms
with a similar ordinary are also described as
'double dancy' by Thoroton (Thoroton, 1790,
III.63; Boutell, 1863, 48; Purey-Cust, 1890, 316;
OED, Dancy *adj.*). **23–24. quartering of coats:**
The combination of different family coats of
arms within a single shield, often the result of
marriage between heirs. **24–25. book of
doomsday:** The Vavasours at Hazelwood are
mentioned in the Doomsday Book.

22. Vavasour of Hazelwood] Vavasor of Hazell wood MS   **25.** doomsday] dom<..>day MS

Contextual essays

✳

The literature of wayfaring is long, existing as poems, songs, stories, treatises and route guides, maps, novels and essays. The compact between writing and walking is almost as old as literature – a walk is only a step away from a story, and every path *tells*.

(Robert Macfarlane, *The Old Ways*, 2012, 18)

1
THE GENRES OF A WALK

'Shifting place and air'

In *A Jovial Crew*, perhaps his last play, Richard Brome presents an extraordinary picture of a gentleman given, in the strongest possible sense, to travel. Springlove is steward to the 'ancient esquire' Oldrents, charged with the responsibility of managing the latter's substantial estate; when we first meet him he is encumbered with books and papers, ready to present to his master 'a survey of all your rents / Receiv'd, and all such other payments as / Came to my hands since my last audit' (1.1.123–5). Yet the efficiency with which he has calculated Oldrents' income and expenditure is not a function of the pleasure he takes in his work; instead he is keen to complete his duties ten days early, around 25 April, so he can pursue his calling – figured in the play as the stirring song of nightingales and cuckoos, to which Springlove responds with a surge of emotion. He wants to travel, as he has been restrained from doing for the last year and a half – in fact, as he says, he needs to travel, and cannot be reasoned out of this drive:

> 'Tis the season of the year that calls me.
> What moves her notes provokes my disposition
> By a more absolute power of nature than
> Philosophy can render an accompt for.
>
> (1.1.166–9)

To Oldrents, rooted as he apparently is in his family lands, this is nothing more than a 'disease of nature', a 'running sore' or 'gadding humour', a worryingly pathogenic element in Springlove's constitution (1.1.156, 175). But for his steward, this disposition is nothing less than the 'predominant sway of nature...in me' (1.1.242–3). It cannot be suppressed or denied, however suspect and unnatural it appears to those, like Oldrents, who wish only to cleave to their home country.

In his defence of his wanderlust, Springlove cites 'pilgrimages, and /
The voluntary travels of good men' (1.1.207–8) as virtuous manifestations
of the same tendency. But such journeys, Oldrents objects, are funda-
mentally different. They are undertaken 'for penance, or to holy ends'
(1.1.209) – they are, in other words, anything but ends in themselves.
Springlove, though, avers that the 'sufferings' of pilgrims and penitents
'are much sweetened by delights, / Such as we find by shifting place and
air' (1.1.212–13). In his eyes, even such devotional or corrective travel is
affected by the pleasures of shifting place. There are echoes here, perhaps, of such arguments for the educational virtues of travel as could be
found in works including Justus Lipsius's *A Direction for Travailers*
(translated and augmented by Sir John Stradling), which were familiar
enough to be the object of a backlash by the early seventeenth century.[1]
Works of this genre advanced the view that 'through purposeful travel, in
which knowledge and profit were made compatible, the active and the
contemplative would come together in the education of the gentleman'.[2]
Thus, too, the pleasures of travel would be comfortably brought under
the rule of self-cultivation. As Owen Felltham put it:

> Some would not allow a man to moue from the shell of his own Countrey. And
> Claudian mentions it as a happinesse, for birth, life and buriall, to be all in a
> Parish. But surely, Travaile fulleth the Man, he hath liu'd but lockt vp in a
> larger Chest, which hath neuer seene but one Land. A Kingdome to the world,
> is like a Corporation to a Kingdome: a man may liue in't like an vnbred man.
> Hee that searcheth forraine Nations, is becomming a Gentleman of the
> world.[3]

But Springlove's urges are not really compatible with these kinds of
claim. In fact, his desire for a 'voluntary' travel stripped either of
necessity or heteronomous ends, and of extraneous burdens, coalesces
into a hankering for the condition of the ambulant beggar. To wander
freely – and liberty is what Springlove invokes so resonantly – requires
one to spurn the accoutrements of 'horse, and man, and money' (1.1.219),
to go on foot with nothing but what can be gleaned from the charity of
others. Beggary gives material form to an ideal of absolute travel freed
even of educational purpose – travel in itself, and for itself. This, for
Springlove, is his sheer humanity: he asks Oldrents to 'retort me naked to
the world / Rather than lay those burdens on me which / Will stifle me. I
must abroad or perish' (1.1.223). The figure of the steward, surveying the

---

1 Lipsius, 1592. See Rubiés, 1995 and Ord, 2007; the most notable riposte is Hall, 1617.
2 Rubiés, 1995 45.
3 Felltham, 1628, 251.

economy of his master's lands from the centre of the household, is thus contrasted sharply with this epitome of an entirely opposed, and thoroughly essentialist, sense of the experience of 'place and air'.

Brome's play does not, though, leave this initial polarity intact. Oldrents' daughters and their suitors, who at first mimic Springlove's valorisation of pure travel, are quickly disenchanted with the reality. Springlove himself turns out to have lost ties to place that stain his 'liberty' with the more melancholy colours of exile. The crew of beggars with whom he associates are only problematically idealised. Such idealisation, of course, serves to romanticise, and thus to obscure, the abject lives of the unsettled poor.[4] Yet in its redemption of beggary, however qualified, it acknowledges the force and interest of an ideal of pure or pedestrian mobility, a pilgrimage which is its own object, running counter to the more settled notions of place and air shaping the corrective measures of the poor laws in both the Stuart kingdoms of Britain. It seeks to describe, as if phenomenologically, what such walking is.

Ben Jonson's 1618 walk was not exactly the kind of 'shifting' hymned, however critically, by his onetime servant and friend in *A Jovial Crew* two decades later. He travelled with the accoutrements denounced as burdensome by the purist Springlove; given their need to transport luggage bulky enough to include a pair of pistols it is possible that the walkers were not only accompanied by a servant but also made use of a packhorse, just as John Taylor did on his own northwards journey that summer – such furnishings are frequently as absent from the narrative of the *Pennyles Pilgrimage* as they are from the 'Foot Voyage', so we cannot rule their presence out on these grounds.[5] Yet we should still bear Brome's speculative isolation of the pedestrian essence of travel in mind, because it encourages us to seek the significance of the 'Foot Voyage' in a number of different perspectives. We need to consider, certainly, whence he took his inspiration and his bearings; we need to look at the meanings to be drawn from tracing this trajectory across the real and symbolic topography of a Jacobean high summer. There is the question, too – and this we shall address in our next chapter – of the walk's footprint in Jonson's future work, insofar as that can be reliably discerned. But Brome's interest in what we have been terming a pure mobility prompts us to keep in mind, at the point of contact between its past, its contexts and its futures, the tripartite process of 'the *walk*, as an

4 Fumerton, 2006, 45; McRae, 2009, 131.
5 *PP*, sig. [A4].

event; the *walker*, as a human subject; and *walking*, as an embodied act'.[6]
We need to remember, in other words, that this is not just a journey, and
is not always to be grasped in such general terms. Hayden Lorimer sees
the focus on these 'constituent elements of this most basic of human
activities' as characteristic of a 'new "walking studies"', a focus on
'pedestrianism as practice'.[7] From here, we can approach the issue of
the significance of Jonson's journey without losing sight of its status as an
event constituted by a walker walking. Indeed, as Tim Cresswell and
Peter Merriman suggest, 'walking as a historic practice, artistic method,
and contemporary philosophical aid appears to connect important
themes which lie at the heart of geography, embodiment, landscape',
and it is the form and nature of Jonson's 'embodied engagement' and the
'spatial stories' it produced that will be our focus.[8]

Both Ian Donaldson and James Knowles have suggested that
Jonson's walk should be understood in the light of comments noted
by Drummond: 'He is to write his foot pilgrimage hither, and call it *A
Discovery*' (*Informations*, l.317).[9] We shall return below to the implications of a 'foot pilgrimage'; here, we need to note that the notion of
'discovery' has the more obviously Jonsonian resonances, down to the
Senecan motto – 'tanquam explorator' – that he inscribed in his
books.[10] It is also, of course, the alternative title given to Jonson's
Timber, his collection of commonplaces. For one passage in this compilation, as editors have noted, he draws on the same Senecan epistle
that may well have furnished him with his title.[11] Here, unsurprisingly,
the notion of discovery is inextricable from the idea of route-finding
and following:

> He who follows another not only discovers nothing, but is not even inves-
> tigating. What then? Shall I not follow in the footsteps of my predecessors? I
> shall indeed use the old road, but if I find one that makes a shorter cut and is
> smoother to travel, I shall open the new road. Men who have made these
> discoveries before us are not our masters, but our guides.[12]

Or, as he put it in his own phrasing, 'they opened the gates, and made the
way, that went before us; but as guides, not commanders' (*Disc.* ll.97–8).
The word 'gates' here evokes its northern and Scots meaning of paths or

---

6 Lorimer, 2011, 19.
7 Lorimer, 2011, 19.
8 Cresswell and Merriman, 2011, 6, 5.
9 Donaldson, 1992, 5; Knowles, 2006, 259, 273; Donaldson, 2011, 26.
10 Donaldson, 2011, 356–7.
11 Jonson, 1985, 735–6n.
12 Seneca, *Epistle* 30.11; Donaldson, 1992, 4–5.

roads, a usage with which Jonson was certainly familiar by 1618, if not before.[13] In his understanding of discovery, routes both follow and make paths; a predecessor might lead him, but Jonson himself is 'tanquam explorator', like a scout, or a guide, picking out pathways in a terrain not yet his own. There were, then, precedents and predecessors stalking this walk, providing Jonson with tracks to follow and leave behind, or coordinates for calculating proximities and distances.

Prominent among them were such mapmakers and chorographers as John Speed, Michael Drayton and William Camden, whose works must have influenced Jonson at several levels. Speed's town and county maps, published in a grand folio edition of 1611, are expressly synoptic, rising up to impossible heights from which a land planted with settlements, parks, walls and buildings can at once be seen. The first map in his book presents a view of the singular 'Kingdome of Great Britaine and Ireland', with complementary – and simultaneously visible – prospects of London and Edinburgh facing each other across the page. In Drayton's *Poly-Olbion*, the first eighteen songs of which were initially printed in 1612, it is the Muse that moves across the face of the kingdom, endowing its rivers with the power of speech. As Andrew McRae has suggested, 'in the influential works of chorographers' such as Camden, 'the perambulation of a county frequently means an authorial glide from one settlement to the next, focusing at each stop on local history and the genealogy of land-owning families...The textual movement maintains the ease of a sweep across an abstract surface.'[14] Such abstraction, though, is often qualified. In his address to his reader, Speed notes that he has beheld the 'beautie and benefits' of the country 'not a farre off, as *Moses* saw *Canaan* from *Pisgah*, but by my owne trauels through euery prouince of *England* and *Wales*'.[15] Camden stressed the important place of 'pedestrian fieldwork' among his methods of enquiry, declaring:

> I have trauailed over all England for the most part, I haue conferred with most skillful observers in each country, I haue studiously read ouer our own countrie writers, old and new, all Greeke and Latine authors which haue once made mention of Britaine. I haue had conference with learned men in other parts of Christendome; I haue beene diligent in the Records of this Realme.[16]

---

13 See his extempore response to Mr Craven: *CWBJ*, 5.349, l.7.
14 McRae, 1999, 47.
15 Speed, 1612, sig. ¶3.
16 *CB*, 'The Author to the Reader'. 'Pedestrian fieldwork' is John Wylie's suggestive description of Berkeley geographer's Carl Sauer's influential fieldwork methodologies (Wylie, 2007, 29).

It has long been argued that Jonson's reworking of such topics as antiquarianism in late plays including *A Tale of a Tub* (1633) owes much to Camden's influence, but that influence may have been realised physically as well as intellectually – the paths followed may, in other words, have been literal as well as metaphorical. Camden's own 'scholarly perambulations' were conducted over many years, and he is known to have taken boy scholars from Westminster School – such as Robert Cotton – with him; it is entirely reasonable to speculate that a young Jonson might either have shared this experience or had access to accounts of such trips.[17] The 1618 voyage with his own companion might in one respect have been a remaking of such a youthful experience. So, insofar as Camden's *Britannia* is read as an intertext for Jonson's own engagements with the Stuart nations and regions, we might also see Camden's method as a reference point for the playwright in his adult writing career.

While such compendious works arise, as their authors insist, from their own mobile encounters with the world thus mapped, the traces of these journeys are not easily to be found within them – the textual movement does not obviously correspond to a route taken. Other precedents, though, allow the path followed to organise the resultant work, thus maintaining the traveller's perspective. Fynes Moryson's extensive *Itinerary* appeared in print in 1617, a decade after the significant publication of Camden's text for the first time with accompanying maps. Part I of the work includes comparisons of the customs and practices of different nations across a range of different headings, and expressly commits itself, in the manner of a guidebook, to 'shewing particularly the number of miles, the soyle of the country, the station of the cities, the descriptions of them, with all monuments in each place worth the seeing, as also the rates of hiring coaches or horses from place to place with each daies expences for diet, horse-meate, and the like'.[18] For the most part, though, this section of the work focuses – as its title might lead us to expect – on accounts of the journeys taken in pursuit of the knowledge thus displayed. Among these journeys is a voyage through Scotland begun in April 1598, which furnishes the reader with a clear narrative of the writer's progress. James Knowles has gone as far as to propose that this section of Moryson's work acted as a guidebook for Jonson when he set out in July 1618, and sees in

---

17 Donaldson, 2011, 27.
18 Moryson, 1617, sig. A1.

Moryson a partial explanation for Jonson's choice of a similar east-wards route.[19]

A more potent precedent, as all recent commentators acknowledge, was James VI and I's 'salmonlyke' return to his native land in the 1617 royal progress north.[20] The 'Foot Voyage' confirms the extent to which Jonson was 'treading in the rut-marks of his monarch's carriages', as Ian Donaldson has put it, following the great north road used by government posts, which was significantly improved for the king's voyage.[21] James travelled north with a substantial entourage: it was expected to consist of 5,000 men and as many horses, although that total was not, in the end, realised. It was nevertheless an especially substantial enterprise, lasting for seven months, but much longer in the planning – the Scottish privy council set preparations in train as early as February 1616.[22] In the months preceding, London was doubt-less busier than usual with discussions of Scottish politics, landscape and culture; the long-standing predominance of Scots courtiers among the personnel of the king's bedchamber would have further emphas-ised this significant note in Westminster political life. We might imagine, then, that Jonson would have been party to the preparations, and not least to those of significant individuals accompanying the king with whom he had direct connections. Most prominent among these were Ludovick Stuart, duke of Lennox and elder brother to Esmé Stuart, Lord D'Aubigny, in whose Blackfriars residence Jonson lodged for some years previously, and William Herbert, earl of Pembroke, an equally long-standing patron.[23] It is perhaps no surprise that Jonson's plan to visit Scotland was first publicly noted by George Garrard in June 1617, at a time when news of the progress sent back by those of his English subjects who had accompanied the king was circulating among the Londoners they left behind.[24] The royal progress comes to the surface of the 'Foot Voyage' at Worksop Manor in the intriguing and otherwise unattested revelation that the 'floor' of the great chamber – most likely, part of the ceiling – 'fell down when the king was there' (ll.164–5), but memories of the journey must still have been fresh in those places where James had been received and lavishly entertained the preceding year.

19 Knowles, 2006, 259.
20 *NP*, 3.309–10.
21 Donaldson, 2011, 35; Knowles, 2006, 259.
22 See McNeill and McNeill, 1996, 38–9.
23 Donaldson, 2011, 29.
24 *CSPD, 1611–18*, 471–3; cf. Donaldson, 2011, 34.

Plotting the route

The gests or stages of royal progresses were often written down and preserved in broadly tabular form, and James's 1617 journey was no exception.[25] Along with a note of dates and places visited, such records usually included some information on distances and the number of nights spent in each place. They thus conform to the kind of 'topological map' of a route found in the written itineraries of the early modern period, those listings of places and distances in geographical order that feature in print from the mid sixteenth century and are also to be found in manuscript sources.[26] The spine of the 'Foot Voyage', too, is such an itinerary, though given in narrative rather than tabular form. The course of the journey during that summer can therefore be traced, reconstructed as an itinerary amenable to tabulation and set beside comparable journeys (Figure 3). The travellers left London on Wednesday 8 July and walked up the old north road as far as Tottenham that evening. The next day they continued along what is now the Tottenham High Road into Hertfordshire. By Saturday 18 July they had reached Stamford; either one or two days later they left the main road at Witham and headed west towards Belvoir Castle. From there they travelled on via Bottesford before rejoining the main road at Newark on Friday 24 July. Resuming their journey the following Tuesday, they once again veered westwards away from the customary route, heading now for Rufford Abbey. Two nights were spent at Rufford before they walked on to Welbeck, which was to be their base for a week. From Welbeck trips were made to Worksop Manor and Bolsover before they set out again on Thursday 6 August, rejoining the main road at Bawtry that evening. They then walked to Wentbridge before detouring again to Pontefract. After a two-night stay there they took the road to York, which they reached on Wednesday 12 August. The following Monday they were underway again, walking to Darlington (the account is silent, alas, on the matter of the shoes Jonson mentioned to Drummond), before arriving in Durham

---

25 The gests of the progress to Berwick, with notes on sources, are included in *NP*, 3.257; an account of the 'Gistis of his Majesties progresse in Scotland' was preserved among the manuscripts of the earls of Mar and Kellie (*HMCMK*, 80). The itinerary through Scotland given in McNeill and McNeill, 1996, 38, would appear to follow Nichols's reconstruction (*NP*, 3.306), and preserves what must be an error: for the king to have travelled in a single day from Dunglass, near Cockburnspath, to Seton Palace via 'Cavard' (i.e. Cavers) near Hawick would have required him to cover well over 75 miles. The 'Gistis' recorded in the Mar and Kellie manuscripts include no such implausible detour.

26 See Delano-Smith, 2006, 35.

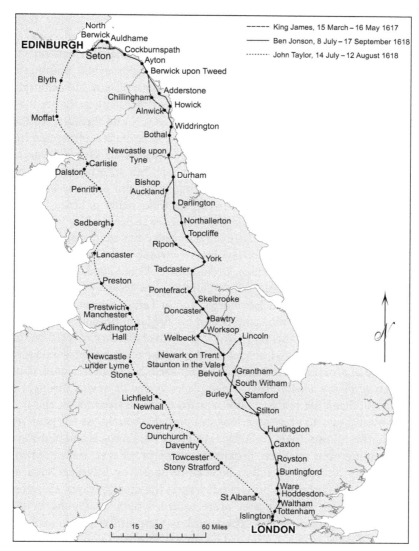

Figure 3 The routes taken by James VI and I, Ben Jonson and John Taylor between London and Edinburgh in 1617 and 1618. Where a separate line is not shown, the king's route coincides with Jonson's.

on Saturday 22 August. They stayed there for three nights, then walked the fourteen miles to Newcastle for a five-day visit. From Newcastle they set out on Sunday 30 August for Bothal Castle, and after a night there journeyed on through coastal Northumberland towards Berwick, arriving on Monday 7 September – almost two months after their departure from London.

Crossing into Scotland they walked to Cockburnspath and on via Dunbar, where they turned northwards and approached Edinburgh through Auldhame, North Berwick, Seton, Preston and Musselburgh, finally arriving on the afternoon of Thursday 17 September. Rather than resting, they visited Edinburgh castle the next day and then crossed the Forth to see Sir George Bruce's celebrated coal mine at Culross and his salt pans at Kincardine, before heading eastwards via Dunfermline to Pettycur. Late on Wednesday 23 September they returned across the Forth from Burntisland to Leith, staying with John Stewart, who has hitherto been erroneously identified as the 'water bailie' of Leith.[27] From there they went back to Edinburgh on Saturday 26 September, 'where my gossip was with all ceremony made burgess'. After that, it seems, they separated, and Jonson disappears from view; the author of the account remained at Euphemia Wilson's house on College Wynd, between the Cowgate and the new university buildings, until Monday 5 October, 'at what time I parted from Edinburgh, and at Leith took boat for Brunt Island, where I met with a ship bound for England' (ll.596–7).

The detail of the itinerary means that the total distance covered on the journey can be estimated, at least roughly. A reasonable guess would give a figure of around 450 miles for the walk itself, although it is hard to be exact: while the account lists all the places visited or passed through, it does not detail the precise roads or paths taken between them, and it is not always easy to determine Jonson's probable course. As Christopher Taylor has shown, there could be a variety of tracks, roads and pathways connecting even relatively proximate towns or villages, each used for different purposes; the route likely to be taken by travellers such as Jonson and his companion was not always the most obvious, the most ancient or the standard post route recorded by John Ogilby in the later seventeenth century.[28] The travellers were also clearly capable of covering 18 miles in a day if need be, on what were no doubt sometimes difficult roads. They walked on forty of the days between their departure from London and their arrival in Edinburgh, so they managed a rough average of 11 miles a day on the road. Given that medieval foot travellers could manage up to 25 miles a day 'over undemanding terrain', it might seem that Jonson and his companion managed a fairly

---

27 See 'Foot Voyage', l.566n.
28 C. Taylor, 1979, 111–52.

unimpressive pace.[29] However, there are few days on which walking was the travellers' sole pastime; on occasion, furthermore, we have enough information to estimate speed, and this tells a somewhat different story. The distance from Bawtry to Doncaster, more than 8 miles, was covered between 'supper' on the evening of Friday 7 August and one o'clock the next morning. They walked the 9½ miles between Tadcaster and York – the route taken can, in this instance, be traced and measured exactly – between six and nine on the morning of 12 August. For this stretch, at least, we can calculate Jonson's walking pace: at nearly 3.2 mph, it compares well with the average preferred walking speed for a modern adult of normal weight, 3 mph.[30] Given this, perhaps we should not assume that Jonson was then quite as corpulent as he is presumed to have been in later life, despite his contemporaneous talk of his 'mountain belly' (*Und.* 9, l.17). Such self-descriptions can perhaps more plausibly be read as instances of comic exaggeration.[31]

To some extent, then, the itinerary of the walk allows us to engage in reasonably detailed and well-informed quantitative analysis, in an epistemic mode that might be thought distant from any that governed the walk as a specifically Jonsonian event. Yet this is not entirely an imposition, either on the walk or on the 'Foot Voyage' account of it, and calculations of time and distance were clearly, on occasion, important. North of York, for example, the travellers initially proposed to visit Sir Henry Frankland's house at Aldwark. 'But as we travelled,' the account says, 'hearing it was out of our way and desiring to take advantage of the fairness of the weather we resolved to go on, and so baited at Tollerton' (ll.316–18), 3 miles east of Aldwark. That day, in fact, they travelled on to Topcliffe – 9 miles further along the road than their planned destination. Moreover, among the gifts bestowed on Jonson during the walk was a surveyor's wheel, crafted, or at least designed, by the mathematician Henry Lukin at Welbeck, 'which driving it before you, would show how

29 Delano-Smith, 2006, 17; citing Ohler, 1989, 107.
30 Rose, Ralston and Gamble, 1994.
31 See also *Und.* 54, where he claims to weigh a mere 2 pounds short of 'full twenty stone'. According to Browning and Kram, 2007, 'most studies' (1633) suggest that people medically classified as obese have a slower preferred walking speed than those of lower weight, although their own work finds otherwise; see also, in this connection, Browning et al., 2006, 391, 393, 396–7. If Jonson had actually weighed 20 stone (127kg or 280lb) at the time of the walk, then even if he was 5ft 10in (178cm) tall – significantly taller than the seventeenth-century northern European average of 5ft 5in (165cm; for this figure, see Steckel, 2004, 216) – he would have had a body mass index of over 40. Assuming a high body-fat percentage, this would be sufficient to classify him in contemporary medical terms as morbidly obese, and may well have had consequences for health and mobility incompatible with the evidence for his walking pace derived from the 'Foot Voyage' (see Lai et al., 2008).

many miles, poles or yards you went, and the just distance from town to town according to our measured miles' (ll.126–8). The account records Lukin demonstrating his invention to Jonson on the road between Welbeck and Worksop, 'to show us the secret and use thereof' (ll.152–3); once instructed, one can imagine Jonson using this instrument to measure his progress, although the 'Foot Voyage' affords it no subsequent mentions. Lukin was tutor to the accomplished mathematician Charles Cavendish, William's younger brother, and his interests and functions in the Cavendish household extended, as the instrument presented to Jonson shows, to surveying and building. Jonson and he collaborated on at least one occasion; his importance both to the family and to the playwright may well be registered in the figure of the 'Mathematician' in the *Cavendish Christening Entertainment*.[32]

The possibilities and demands of surveying, and the geometrical models of space and place it helped to formulate, informed much of the cartographic endeavour of the early modern period. John Norden, the pioneering author of *The Surveyors Dialogue*, was an equally inventive mapmaker, topographer and, in later life, designer of spatially innovative informational aids, such as the distance tables of *An Intended Guyde, for English Travailers* (1625).[33] As McRae has argued, the work of the surveyor was crucial to the production of space in the early modern period, 'offering newly legalistic appreciations of tenurial relationships and rationalistic standards of land measurement'. Surveyors 'challenged notions of land-holding as a bundle of rights and responsibilities, envisaging instead an abstract rural space, pliable to the aspirations of the agrarian improver'.[34] It is perhaps worth noting, however, that the wheel was not one of the surveyor's standard instruments, as Norden's detailed discussion of his methods in Books 3 and 4 of *The Surveyors Dialogue* makes clear.[35] Where the estate surveyor's measurements created a geometrically uniform plan of an abstracted landscape, opening up what Garrett Sullivan has described as a 'problematic rift' between 'a perspective on and an experience of the land', the wheel measured instead the route taken across the surface of the ground.[36] Its distances only make sense in relation to the precise trajectory of an ambulant traveller.

32 Worsley, 2002, I.72–3; *H&S*, 10.700.
33 *ODNB*; Kitchen, 1997; Delano-Smith, 2006, 55–7.
34 McRae, 1999, 50.
35 Norden, 1607, 125–84.
36 Sullivan, 1998, 133.

Elsewhere, too, the walk opened up quantified prospects, albeit in a fairly unsystematic fashion, and probably under the influence of hosts or guides. Most of the houses visited go undescribed, or – like Welbeck – receive only a very partial treatment, but the description of Worksop Manor is unusually extensive and precise:

> We were first brought up to the great chamber, the floor whereof fell down when the king was there, a wonderful fair room; then to the king's chamber, far beyond that, and after to the gallery, who for the bigness and beauty thereof exceedeth most that I have seen. It is fourscore and fifteen of my paces long. There are some eight large windows, in which are set the coats and arms of all the dukes, earls and barons of England.
>
> The house is as goodly as I have seen both for the height, situation and form of building.
>
> (ll.164–71)

In this instance, at least, the visit made by the travellers prompts a need or a desire to measure the proportions of the place encountered, and it is worth noting that the walker's pace is the unit of measurement used – given the function of a long gallery as a place for indoor perambulation, this is perhaps not too surprising. Mary Markham was presumably temporarily resident as housekeeper on behalf of the imprisoned Mary Talbot, countess of Shrewsbury, a function she had performed for her elsewhere, while Sir Thomas Brudenell may only have been visiting his cousin. The building's predominant vacancy, and the guiding perception of a housekeeper, might therefore have invited this distinctively precise mode of encounter. Similarly, the quantitative detail of Sir George Bruce's industrial enterprises at Culross and Kincardine recorded by the writer was presumably provided by Sir George or one of his employees: its closeness in topic and emphasis to the information noted by John Taylor on his visit only a few weeks previously strongly suggests that visitors to the complex were standardly treated to such statistics on production, employment and wages. The information on the Midlands lead trade noted at Bawtry also appears to reflect not only the town's pivotal role in such commerce but also the financial interests and current preoccupations of Jonson's host, Richard Richardson, the Shrewsbury client who was then seeking to safeguard his own monopoly over the vital business of weighing.[37]

While the walk does not appear chiefly to have been an enumerative enterprise, it may well have had a calculatedly commercial dimension. George Garrard's 1617 letter to Sir Dudley Carleton made a point of noting

37 Kiernan, 1989, 235–7.

that 'Ben Jonson is going on foot to Edinburgh and back for his profit'.[38]
The phrase is certainly in part ambiguous – could he be doing it for other
than purely financial gain, perhaps for personal advancement or, even, his
health? But a similar suggestion appears to be made in the verses presented
'To Mr Ben Jonson in his Journey by Mr Craven', probably at Welbeck or
Doncaster.[39] Furthermore, references within the account to high-profile
'subscribers' are an indication that this was indeed an enterprise with a
financial dimension. In Ware, for example, we are told that Sir Robert
Mansell 'subscribed 10 pieces' (l.15); at Belvoir Castle, the earl of Rutland
subscribes 30 pieces, and Lord Willoughby adds a further 10 (ll.56–7).
These, however, are the only subscriptions listed, and the sum of 10 pieces
that Jonson receives from the dignitaries of Newcastle is described as a
'present...for his viaticum' (ll.397–8). So it is not clear whether subscription played much of a part in underpinning or underwriting the walk, or
indeed what his subscribers were expecting to receive for their money.
Here, again, there are precedents and comparators for Jonson's journey. It
is possible that this was a wager journey of a not unfamiliar kind, and
following not just an established pattern but also a familiar northwards
route: in 1589, Sir Robert Carey had won £2,000 for walking from London
to Berwick in twelve days, and, in 'On the Famous Voyage', Jonson refers
to an unknown venturer who 'backwards went to Berwick', again for a bet.
In 1622, Gervase Markham would also be sponsored to travel to the same
destination, this time crossing all rivers and streams by jumping or wading
them and avoiding all bridges.[40] Markham also made sure to bring back
certification from the Berwick mayor to confirm his satisfactory completion of the terms of the wager, but this was not enough to coax payment
from many of those who had given pledges.[41] There are strong indications
in the 'Foot Voyage' that agreed conditions were being observed, and that
similar certification was sought. The public proclamation at the Mercat
Cross in Edinburgh that Jonson 'had performed his journey' suggests
that he wanted his achievement properly and indisputably acknowledged, and the requirement to walk all the way does seem to have been
central to that achievement. The account makes sure to mention those
occasions on which Jonson travelled other than on foot, firstly when he
was 'carried' by Sir William Cavendish from Welbeck to Bolsover
(although the verb itself need not mean anything other than 'escorted',

38 CSPD, 1611–18, 472.
39 CWBJ, 5.349.
40 Donaldson, 2011, 33.
41 ODNB.

the distance and company suggest that the party rode), and secondly when he was taken by coach by Sir Arthur Ingram to visit Archbishop Matthew at Bishopthorpe. On each occasion, he returned to his point of departure before continuing the walk. His consistent pedestrianism is explicitly mentioned a little later on. In the seventeenth century, a ferry carried travellers on the customary route from York to Darlington across the Tees at Neasham. Rather than cross here, Jonson and his companion took a detour over the bridge at Croft-on-Tees instead, thus ensuring that they did not have to take a disqualifying boat ride. As the account puts it, 'We passed Croft bridge, going two miles about because we would not pass Nysam Ferry' (ll.331–3).

So the requirement to walk makes sense, here, as the defining characteristic of a journey undertaken for profit – indeed, it is precisely what makes the journey profitable. Yet the nature of the exchange from which Jonson proposed to benefit, within which his walk *qua* walk functioned as some kind of commodity, remains unclear. In *News from the New World*, Jonson includes some indirect comments which might be read as a complaint that he has not received all the winnings due to him by those with whom he wagered.[42] However, a wager journey – as Jonson well knew – normally required the traveller to lay out a sum on the prospects of their success, and to receive a multiple of that amount from those who accepted the bet on their return. Puntarvolo describes the process in *Every Man Out of his Humour*:

> I do intend, this year of jubilee, to travel; and, because I will not altogether go upon expense, I am determined to put forth some five thousand pound to be paid me five for one, upon the return of myself, my wife, and my Dog from the Turk's court in Constantinople. If all or either of us miscarry in the journey, 'tis gone; if we be successful, why, there will be twenty-five thousand pound to entertain time withal.
>
> (2.2.276–81)

This is exactly how Jonson described the travellers whose exploits are listed in 'On the Famous Voyage': they are 'those that put out moneys on return' (*Epigr.* 133, l.32). It is also possible that Puntarvolo's plan refers not just to a generally known habit but more specifically to the travels of Fynes Moryson and his brother, Henry, in the later 1590s.[43] In his *Itinerary*, Moryson described how Henry had had to wager 'the most part of his small estate', the significant sum of £400, 'to be repaied twelue hundred

---

42 Donaldson, 2011, 34 and 446n.
43 Snuggs, 1936.

pounds vpon his returne…and to lose it if he died in the iourney'.[44] It is
hard to see the subscriptions Jonson receives from Mansell, Rutland and
Willoughby as stages in this kind of transaction: if they were cash sums,
then they came too soon to be 'moneys on return'; if they were in fact
undertakings to pay such a sum on the journey's completion, then it is
perhaps surprising that there is no corresponding mention of any outlay
by Jonson, as the wager would require.

A comparison with John Taylor, whose own journey to Scotland
began only six days after Jonson's, is helpful here.[45] Taylor, too, describes
the finances of his walk in terms of subscription, but for him this is
inextricably tied to the production of a pamphlet detailing his travels,
and he provides aggrieved testimony to the failure of a large number of
his debtors to make good their promises to pay up once the work was
produced.[46] The journey itself, that is to say, is not exactly the commodity in this case. This might imply an early instance of subscription
publication, or 'an entrepreneurial model of discursive production', as
Alexandra Halasz has put it, in which Taylor is both labourer and
capitalist; the resultant pamphlet, which is not for sale via booksellers,
is therefore inscribed 'not in the visible marketplace sites of commodity
sale and purchase but in the financial relations that underwrite the
production and circulation of commodities'.[47] Jonson's comments in
News from the New World, in which the possibility of his 'setting out' –
that is, publishing or circulating what he has written – is said to depend
on whether 'he has all in', might indicate that Jonson, too, envisaged his
walk as labour contributing to the production of a textual commodity for
his subscribers to enjoy. If this was the case, though, in clear contrast
with the 'subscription scenario' staged by Taylor, the writer failed to fulfil
his side of the bargain.[48] Yet Taylor's enterprising domestic journeys
have also been understood on the wager model, following his acknowledged practice in his 1617 voyage through Germany; in the address 'To
the Reader' in *The Scourge of Basenesse* – which mostly reprints his
attack on the bad debtors who failed to pay up after his walk to
Scotland – he describes how he 'gaue out coine… / Which these base

---

44 Moryson, 1617, Part I, 198.
45 For a fuller discussion of Taylor's walk, and the resultant pamphlet, see Sanders, 2013.
46 See, for example, his praise of 'those that haue paid' as 'of that liberall Tribe, / Who freely gaue
    your words, or did subscribe / And were not itch'd with the vain-glorious worme, / To write
    and lye, but promise and performe' (J. Taylor, 1619, sig. B1).
47 Halasz, 2000, 93, 97. The title page of the *Pennyles Pilgrimage* declares that it was printed 'at the
    Charges of the Author'.
48 The phrase is Halasz's: Halasz, 2000, 90.

Mungrels tooke, and promised me / To give me fiue for one, some four, some three'.[49] Evoking what might appear to be a third scenario, Bernard Capp describes those who subscribed as 'sponsors', requiring no initial outlay from the traveller and contributing, instead, to his costs – in which case, the presentation of a copy of a resultant literary work would make this an instance of patronage rather than anything else.[50] Such an approach appears to have been adopted by the Scots traveller William Lithgow, whose exploits deserve more detailed study than they have hitherto received. Lithgow had walked through inland Europe in 1609; a year later, he undertook a forty-day walk from Paris to Rome, before travelling on through Venice and Greece into the heart of the Ottoman empire, ultimately returning to Paris in 1612 via Malta, Sicily, Rome, Barcelona and Bordeaux. His accounts of his travels – first published in London in 1614, reissued in 1616, and appearing in an expanded version seven years later – give little indication of how they were financed, although the resulting publications were the product and property of London stationers in the standard commercial fashion.[51] His 1618 pamphlet, *The Pilgrimes Farewell*, however, was printed at Edinburgh 'at the Expences of the Author', and contains obsequious verse addresses to more than ten prominent Scottish nobles in addition to poems offered to the king (who is addressed as 'Great Pious Paterne, Patrone of Thine owne'),[52] the Prince of Wales and Edmund, Lord Sheffield, President of the Council of the North. It appears to have been intended to solicit donations towards the costs of further planned travels.[53] If Jonson's 'subscribers', too, were really sponsors or donors of this sort, then his failure to give them textual consideration for their 10 or 30 pieces either before or after his journey could have been a problem, assuming – which perhaps we should not – that their subscriptions were more than promises to pay. If they were merely promises, however, then it may be, as the comments in *News from the New World* suggest, that Jonson deftly avoided the awkwardness experienced by Taylor,

49 Capp, 1994, 19, 64–5; J. Taylor, 1624, sig. A5v. See also Clapp, 1931, 217–18.
50 Capp, 1994, 65; see Halasz, 2000, 95.
51 See Lithgow, 1614, 1616 and 1623.
52 Lithgow, 1618, sig. [A4].
53 *ODNB*, William Lithgow. Jonson would undoubtedly have known of Lithgow around the time of his own walk, and not just because of the 1614 and 1616 editions of this traveller's tales. One of the patrons to whom Lithgow dedicated a poem in *The Pilgrimes Farewell* is Sir John Home of North Berwick, who hosted Jonson on his journey; furthermore, two of Jonson's other Scots hosts and companions, Francis Stewart, Lord Bothwell and James Auchmuty, had encountered Lithgow at Naples and Rome during his 1610–12 voyage. See Lithgow, 1618, sig. [E4v]; Lithgow, 1632, 334; Lithgow, 1614, sig. B2v.

Markham and others by effectively annulling, in his failure to provide an immediate or tangible consideration, any transactional dimension inhering in the walk itself. Money received by the poet on or for his walk would then need to be understood in other terms, as gestures within patronage relationships of greater depth and extent, and of longer standing, perhaps, or as charity, gifts, or hospitality. It is notable, in this connection, that Taylor's precisely calculated and defined subscription model was organised around a book recording a 'penniless pilgrimage', in which the journey narrated was accomplished outside the circuits of commercial or financially mediated exchange.

Famous voyages

The uncertainty over the precise place of Jonson's walk within this range of possible models may be connected to a corresponding ambivalence in its relations to other 'famous voyages' of the period. Jonson told Drummond of his fears that 'Taylor was sent along here to scorn him' (*Informations*, l.486), evidently seeing in this contemporaneous journey not just parody but mockery, a malicious joke in which Taylor himself was merely the agent for shadowy rivals or enemies. His concern was presumably that Taylor's ramble would render his own endeavours merely mock-heroic, as if they were of a piece with an absurd or grotesque journey through the London sewers. The roll call of precedents in 'On the Famous Voyage' also includes a clear reference to Thomas Coryate's predominantly pedestrian European travels in 1608, which were the topic of much contemporary comment. His account was published in folio in 1611 as *Coryats Crudities*, with dedicatory verses from a whole host of writers and wits including Jonson – indeed, Jonson was for a long time thought to have had an editorial hand in the book.[54] Coryate even curated his own experience by 'hanging up his shoes proudly in the church at Odcombe for parishioners and pilgrims to wonder at';[55] Jonson's comment to Drummond that his own heavily worn walking shoes 'were appearing like Coryate's' (*Informations*, l.515) shows that this pedestrian predecessor was clearly on his mind as he made his own journey. Yet Coryate had become something of a figure of fun, and much of the commendatory verse prefacing the *Crudities* – Jonson's included – adopted a sometimes harshly comic or mock-heroic

54 Donaldson, 2011, 31.
55 Donaldson, 2011, 31.

tone. Jonson's 'Certain Opening and Drawing Distichs' accompanying the illustrations on the frontispiece gloss these vignettes as moments of humiliation or painful indignity:

> Old hat here, torn hose, with shoes full of gravel,
> And louse-dropping case, are the arms of his travel.
>
> (l.23)

Perhaps recalling this epitome of foot-slogging discomfort, Jonson seems to have been uneasily aware at times that his own committed pedestrianism could bring his otherwise grand tour low, render it absurd, base or bathetic.

It is interesting to note that Jonson should echo himself in sketching out this epitome. The purgatorial shoes worn by Coryate recall a detail of Tucca's description in *Poetaster* of the long-suffering travelling player, who has 'to travel with thy pumps full of gravel...after a blind jade and a hamper, and stalk upon boards and barrel heads to an old cracked trumpet' (3.4.137–9). Jonson's sense of Coryate's mortification, then, and any intimations he also has of his own vulnerability to the same fate, find a correlate in the life on the road lived by the itinerant entertainer. This may have felt like the threat of a return to less secure days. Donaldson speculates that Jonson performed the part of Hieronimo in *The Spanish Tragedy* while on the road with the earl of Pembroke's company in the late sixteenth century, and indeed a reference in Thomas Dekker's *Satiromastix* (1601) implies as much: 'I ha' seen thy shoulders lapped in a player's old cast cloak...and when thou ran'st mad for the death of Horatio, thou borrowd'st a gown of Roscius the stager.'[56] To walk to Edinburgh like this, in other words, was to run the risk of revisiting former indignities in making a comic spectacle of oneself. And the association of such undertakings with players and their peregrinations was not Jonson's alone. Many of Markham's sponsors were actors, playwrights such as Thomas Heywood, or figures connected to the networks around the Red Bull and Bankside theatres.[57] All of this suggests that these events were easily, even readily, understood by contemporaries, through a performative framework, as public and commercial artworks. In his *Itinerary*, Moryson recounted his concerns that the kind of wager journeys he and his brother were undertaking had accumulated

---

56 *Satiromastix*, 1.2.434–81: see Donaldson, 2011, 103, 105. See also Bowers, 1937, 392–3.
57 See *ODNB*; Matthew Steggle there notes that Markham's defaulters included a group of Red Bull actors. Bernard Capp makes a related point, noting among Markham's sponsors Bankside and Clerkenwell individuals from the theatre and printing industries (1994, 19–20).

exactly this kind – the wrong kind – of connotations, and were no longer suitable activities for gentlemen. While he was busy making the necessary arrangements for his voyage, he says, he realised 'that these kind of aduentures were growne very frequent, whereof some were undecent, some ridiculous; and that they were in great part undertaken by bankerouts, and men of base condition', and thus resolved to scale down his plans for financing the journey by this means.[58] Yet he cannot refrain, with the comfort of distance, from offering a critique and a defence:

> All manners of attire came first into the City and Countrey from the Court, which being once receiued by the common people, and by very Stage-players themselues, the Courtiers iustly cast off, and take new fashions...In like sort, many daunces and measures are used in Court, but when they come to be vulgar and to be used upon very stages, Courtiers and Gentlemen think them uncomely to be used; yet is it no reproch to any man who formerly had skill therein. To conclude, (that I may not trouble you with like examples, which are infinite), I say that this manner of giuing out mony uppon these adventures, was first used in Court, and among the very Noble men; and when any of them shewed thereby extraordinary strength, the most censorious approved it, but when any performed a long iourney, with courage and discretion, no man was found who did not more or lesse commend it, according to the condition of the iourney performed. Now in this age, if bankerouts, Stage-players, and men of base condition, have drawne this custome into contempt: I grant that Courtiers and Gentlemen have reason to forbeare it, yet know not why they should be blamed, who have thus put out their mony in another age, when this custome was approved.[59]

Moryson's recognition that wager journeys have become the practice not just of 'men of base condition' in general but specifically of 'stage-players' compares interestingly with Jonson's apparent awareness of the range of social and cultural implications that could be drawn from his own ambulatory performance.

The precedent most apparent to both Moryson and Jonson – even if the latter's walk was not a wager journey in the strictest sense – was undoubtedly the comic actor Will Kemp, formerly of the Lord Chamberlain's Men, who conducted a celebrated dance between London and Norwich over nine days in the summer of 1600. Kemp's was certainly a wager journey – he makes it clear that he 'put out some money to have threefold gaine at my returne' – and was included among Jonson's list of such exploits in 'On the Famous Voyage'.[60] However, it

---

58 Moryson, 1617, Part I, 198.
59 Moryson, 1617, Part I, 199.
60 Kemp, 1600, sig. D2.

was also a public performance, directly drawing on and reinforcing Kemp's status as one of the theatrical stars of the age. He travelled with his tabourer, Thomas Sly, whose music announced his arrival at each staging point on the journey, much as a herald would announce the arrival of a monarch both in real life and on the commercial stages of London. The fact that he was dancing the route in stages also clearly delineated a performative or 'onstage' dimension, as it were, from simple travel. One of the most consistent features of the journey is the presence of crowds of spectators. Kemp has many followers who join him along the way, while at each intermediate destination 'multitudes' come out to meet him. He left London, he says, 'as fast as kinde peoples thronging together would give me leave', while 'many a thousand brought me to Bow'; later in the journey, 'the multitudes were so great at my coming to Burntwood that I had much a doe…to get passage to my Inne', and in one particularly resonant passage a bear-baiting laid on for his delectation is reduced to a soundscape: 'so unreasonable were the multitudes of people, that I could only heare the Beare roare, and the dogges howle'.[61] On occasion he is joined by other vividly depicted performers, including 'a lusty Country lasse' at Sudbury, and a declamatory and finely costumed host at the inn in Rockland. The account of the dance published shortly afterwards is itself designed, Kemp says, to counter false claims put about by 'notable Shakerags', 'the impudent generation of Balladmakers and their coherents'.[62] His dancing progress, in other words, has already taken on an alarmingly independent life in another popular cultural medium. Kemp's own account, addressed as it is to 'the true Ennobled Lady, and his most bountifull Mistris, Mistris Anne Fitton, Mayde of Honour to the most sacred Mayde Royall Queene *Elizabeth*' seeks to retrieve the memory of this performance from such indignities.[63]

This address, maintained as it is throughout the account, makes clear Kemp's own determination to establish high-status associations as the proper context for comprehending and placing his adventure. This is not a manifestation of the comic indignity of the travelling player with his pumps full of gravel: with its gests, followers, crowds and public welcomes, it resembles nothing so much as a royal progress. The generic kinship between this wager journey and a northwards voyage such as Jonson's, with its own echoes of James's 1617 journey, is confirmed by the interesting note of Kemp's meeting at Sudbury with a like-minded

61 Kemp, 1600, sigs. A3v, B1, [A4].
62 Kemp, 1600, sig. [D3].
63 Kemp, 1600, sig. A3.

'Master Foskew, that had before travailed a foote from London to Berwick: who giving me good counsaile to observe temperate dyet for my health, and other advise to be carefull of my company...departed leaving me much indebted to his love'.[64] This exhortation to be careful of one's company might be read as a metagenericc acknowledgement of the generic openness of such journeys – presumably it was all too easy to find yourself among the wrong sort of companions, just as Kemp finds a pair of thieves among his followers at Brentwood, one of them 'a noted Cutpurse, such a one as we tye to a poast on our stage, for all people to wonder at, when at a play they are taken for pilfering'.[65] He too, of course, is set upon the stage of his morris dance for the people to wonder at, and a thief tethered to a post for display to an audience sounds in turn suspiciously like an echo of bear-baiting. To this extent, then, the performed dance and its printed record represent 'a kind of strategic narrativizing by a writer of low rank', in Daryl Palmer's words; appropriating the generic materials proper to the progress, Kemp produces a performance event that seeks to disavow any possible kinship with the merely popular.[66] Despite the long-standing association of stage-players with rogues and vagabonds, his is not the exploit of a 'shakerag'. Yet the problem of 'company', signalled again by Moryson's determination, in turn, to retrieve his own travels from a degrading association with the exploits of stage-players, demonstrates how difficult it must have been to enact a walk that unfolded strictly and purely within the parameters of a particular genre.

It is, though, precisely in its performative aspect, in this sense of the walk as sufficiently spectacular to earn the epithet 'famous', that Jonson's journey comes closest to those of his theatrical and literary contemporaries. Whether or not his was a wager journey in the proper sense, Jonson's insistence on walking all the way from London to Edinburgh and the requirement for his achievement to be certified on completion echo Kemp's arrangements to guarantee the fidelity of his enterprise to the enabling principle that marked it out as a more than ordinary journey, as some kind of spectacle. As well as his tabourer and servant, Kemp was accompanied by George Sprat, whom he describes on at least two occasions in the written account of the morris as an 'overseere'.[67] Sprat's job was to ensure that the journey was completed properly; such

64 Kemp, 1600. sig. B3.
65 Kemp, 1600, sig. B.
66 D. Palmer, 1992, 132.
67 Kemp, 1600, sig. A3.

is the seriousness of that requirement that when Sprat loses sight of
Kemp on a section of his entry into Norwich, and 'would not be deposed
that I had daunst it', the actor retraces his steps so that his overseer can
formally endorse the achievement.[68] Kemp's need for an overseer
implies that those who were laying out wagers on such fantastic voyages
required ocular proof, eyewitness confirmation of the accomplishment.
Sprat's involvement in Kemp's morris raises the possibility that Jonson's
companion was also an eyewitness or overseer of this sort, and that the
'Foot Voyage' account grew out of the need for a full and reliable account
of the journey.[69]

Further generic similarities can be traced. Deploying the same lexicon
of throngs and pressing, for example, Taylor is as keen as Kemp to stress
the crowds who come out to greet him. At the outset of the *Pennyles
Pilgrimage*, he recounts how his departure from London was retarded by
the profusion of the audience that had gathered to see him off:

> Though in the morning I began to goe,
> Good fellowes trooping, flock'd me so
> That make what haste I could, the Sunne was set
> E're from the gates of London I could get.
>
> (*PP*, sig. [A4])

On occasion his spectacular status is emphasised, with crowds gathering
to wonder at him 'as if some Monster sent from the Mogull / Some
Elephant from Affricke I had beene' (*PP*, sig. B2v). In similar vein,
Jonson is 'met with oyez' (ll.29–30) in Caxton, while 'the maids and
young men came out of town to meet us' (ll.25–6) at Royston, a detail
which chimes with Kemp's account of 'the dyvers voyces of the young
men and Maydens, which I should meete at everie myles ende, thronging
by twentie and sometime fortie, yea hundreths in a companie'.[70] Jonson
encounters fireworks and bull-baiting in Newark, just as the townsfolk at
Stratford greet Kemp with bear-baiting (l.87). Crowds, as in Kemp's and
Taylor's texts, are described as presses, throngs, swarms, and, again as in
Kemp's account, they can be a threat and hindrance as much as support:

> We lay at Mr Tatham's, an alderman, to whose house we came the back way
> because all the town was up in throngs to see us. And there was dancing of
> giants, and music prepared to meet us. And notwithstanding we took a byway
> to escape the crowd and staring of the people yet a swarm of boys and others

---

68 Kemp, 1600, sig. D1.
69 See Donaldson, 2011, 40.
70 Kemp, 1600, sig. C3.

> crossed over to overtake us, and pressed so upon us, that we were fain to present our pistols upon them to keep them back, and made them believe we would shoot them to get passage etc.
>
> (ll.254–61)

Taylor indicates at various points on his penniless pilgrimage that word of his coming has gone ahead of him, and that crowds gather and people look out of windows to catch a glimpse. In the 'Foot Voyage', we have similar hints that news travels ahead of Jonson and his companion on the road. A genteel throng gathers to welcome them in York (ll.298–300), while some, such as Parson Rogers on the road to Tollerton, even join them on the way after 'hearing of our passing by' (ll.318–19).

Jonson's arrival in Edinburgh also displays a telling structural conformity with Kemp's conclusion of his journey at Norwich. Kemp arrived at Norwich on the ninth day of his morris, 'being Wednesday of the second weeke'; the multitudes gathering in the city, however, meant that he was advised to delay his dancing entry until another day. The mayor and aldermen 'allotted me time enough not to daunce in till Satterday after':

> Satterday no sooner came, but I returned without the Citty through Saint Giles his gate: and beganne my Morrice where I left at that gate, but I entred in at Saint Stephens gate, where one Thomas Gilbert in name of all the rest of the Cittizens gave me a friendly and exceeding kind welcome.[71]

Jonson's welcome is similarly doubled. The walkers reach the city on the evening of Thursday 17 September, when they too are met by eager crowds: 'The women in throngs ran to see us etc, some bringing sack and sugar, others aquavitae and sugar, etc' (ll.520–1). However, the account records that the voyage was ceremonially completed at the city's Mercat Cross the following morning, with Jonson accompanied up the High Street by a reception committee of civic officials and other local gentry:

> On Friday all these gentlemen with others of the town brought my gossip to the high cross, and there on their knees drank the king's health, testifying in that place that he had performed his journey. My gossip also drank to the bailiff and aldermen and the whole people their health, they being so thick in the street that we could scarce pass by them, they ran in such throngs to have a sight of my gossip. The windows also being full, everyone peeping out of a round hole like a head out of a pillory.
>
> (ll.522–8)

---

71 Kemp, 1600, sig. [C4].

The two accounts reveal the same predominant sense that the spontaneous effusions of a welcoming crowd need to be matched, or overlaid, with the authorised and scheduled formal entry. Both, in other words, echo the conventions of the royal progress as a way of acknowledging and marking fame – even if we cannot easily know what Jonson's fame might have meant to those who gathered in the streets. As with the civic pageant, another genre where this heightened vocabulary of crowds as presses, throngs and multitudes is readily to be found, we need to take care not to reduce spectators to a single entity and to recognise a plurality of meanings and motives both in performing and viewing the walk. But as Jonson surveyed the flowing crowds come to greet him, he might have had cause to think that the generic kinship of his venture both to the wager journeys of popular actors and to the elaborate progress of his royal master was especially visible in such a gathering, and such an occasion.

2

JONSON'S FOOT WORK

The landscape and the way

'A route', Catherine Delano-Smith acutely notes, 'is not a road, nor in itself a physical feature, but a direction, an imaginary line linking a point of departure with a destination. Only its description gives it tangible form in speech or gesture, writing or image.'[1] Jonson's walk was a dynamic and active form of engagement with the landscape, giving it a narrative and linear form that is itself not necessarily identical with the shape of the 'Foot Voyage' account kept by his companion. To read the landscapes of the walk, and the route it traces through them, requires us to attend to what cultural geography describes as the 'geographies of mobility' and 'choreographies of place'.[2] Making sense of the walk might therefore require us to think not just of the wager journey and the royal progress but also of other narrative genres or motifs and performance practices through which its significance might be – might have been – determined. Prominent among these is the pilgrimage, a term adopted for themselves and their expeditions by Taylor and Lithgow, used of Coryate by some of those who penned commendatory verses for his 1611 *Crudities*, and which provided the umbrella under which Samuel Purchas gathered his expanding collections of travel narratives in the second and third decades of the seventeenth century.[3] It is a term applied to Jonson's own adventure both retrospectively by William Drummond (who is perhaps quoting his guest) and, during the journey, by the earl of Rutland.[4] One might also evoke the troubadour tradition of household visitations and a life of performance on the road, the quest structure and adventuring motifs of romance, or pastoral traditions of arboreal

---

1 Delano-Smith, 2006, 32.
2 Cresswell and Merriman, 2011, 4.
3 The first edition of *Purchas His Pilgrimage* appeared in 1613, the last in 1626. See *ODNB*.
4 *Informations*, l.317; 'Foot Voyage', ll.63–4.

sanctuary and escape to the provincial and the regional countryside. All of these ways of understanding the physical and imaginary landscapes through which Jonson and his companion travelled are capable of illuminating aspects of the story of the walk; also relevant, though, is the evocation of more prosaic, material and indeed constructed environments, not least the bricks and mortar of country estates or of inns and hostelries in market towns, and the deer parks, pales and working 'task-scapes' that defined much of the countryside.[5]

Unsurprisingly, forms of passage are significant. Rivers play only a minor and fitful role in the delineation of landscape and journey, in sharp contrast to the emphases of Michael Drayton's *Poly-Olbion*, for example, or Speed's county maps in his *Theatre of the Empire of Great Britain* – even the crossings of such symbolically freighted waterways as the Trent, Tweed and Forth go unremarked. The road itself is important, although the word is never used in the account. The standard term, instead, as should be expected, is 'way', with the account usually detailing occurrences and encounters 'by the way' or 'on the way'. Given the prominence of the 'way' as the site for the walk, it's perhaps unsurprising that the travellers encounter 'the shake-rag errant and his two doxies' near London, and then, near Hoddesdon, 'a lunatic woman [who] met us by the way and went dancing before us', 'a humorous tinker of whom we could not be rid' and 'three minstrels [who] thrust themselves upon us, asking whether we would hear a merry song, which proved to be the life and death of my Lord of Essex' (ll.3, 8–12). Considering that John Taylor fashioned his 1618 journey to Scotland far more in terms of an encounter with the condition of vagrancy, as enshrined in the title of his *Pennyles Pilgrimage*, these meetings with genuine itinerants feature far more visibly in Jonson's narrative than in Taylor's own.[6] Although Taylor's trip was predicated on a mendicant performance, reliant as he was on the hospitality and kindness of friends and strangers for his food and lodging, it is almost as if meeting with real examples of the 'unsettled' communities that Patricia Fumerton has made such an instructive focus of study would have been too destabilising.[7] In this, the 'Foot Voyage' is broader in its embrace of community, and far more akin to Kemp's in its happenstance encounters. The kinds of individual Jonson encounters in the extracts quoted above bear a distinct similarity to the

---

5 This phrase, helpfully suggesting landscape as a worked space rather than a static scene, is unpacked in detail in Ingold, 1993.
6 See more extensive discussion of this topic in relation to Taylor in Sanders, 2013, esp. 19–20.
7 Fumerton, 2006, *passim*.

groupings and voices that populate parish constables' records in the areas through which he travels.

Almost as interesting as this brief string of interactions with figures from the mobile and itinerant communities of early modern England is their disappearance from the account thereafter – was the way suddenly and irrevocably empty of them? Or were they simply no longer considered noteworthy by the writer? Certainly, other chance encounters along the way are noted, including their meeting with the courtiers Davy Wood and James Stewart at Newark, and with the earl of Buccleuch, who comes 'riding in coach' at Doncaster (l.241). In some ways, their appearances on the road echo the mobilities of the shake-rag and his fellows: men such as Wood and Stewart must have been, to some extent, the new denizens of this particular way, high-status itinerants travelling up and down from Lowland Scotland to London in tune with the rhythms of the court year. Indeed, when Jonson is safely berthed at Leith he is joined by David Drummond and Robert Hay, who are then preparing to head for London; Taylor, riding with James Auchmuty from Auldhame a few days later, encounters them at Newcastle, and travels with all three men as far as Topcliffe.[8] Such men could carry news, too: a 1616 letter by Edward Talbot, then resident at Bothal, records how:

> Mr John Ackmoutie, one of the Kynges bedchamber, came post from London of monday was sennight, & sent me word, from the post toune as hee went by: that my brother [i.e. Gilbert, seventh earl of Shrewsbury] could not possibly continewe alyve, any longe time, but was douted everie day by all that was aboute him.[9]

Sometimes, the walkers are joined in their progress by others, but these alignments remain hard to discern. Their meeting with the mysterious Captain Robert Hasell and Captain or Mr Jaques at Ferrybridge is noted (the former was to feature, shortly afterwards, in plans for a large amphitheatre in London, although nothing more of him is known;[10] the account's varying title for the latter makes him hard to identify), and these two 'friends errant' (l.295) are still with them on the road from Tadcaster to York, riding 'fair and soft' (l.280). They appear not to have been entirely welcome company, however, the companion writing that 'although they rid we could not be rid of them' (ll.295–6). Yet they are then to be found accompanying the walkers out of York a few days later,

8 *PP*, sigs. [F4]–G1v.
9 SA, WWM/Str P/20, p.216.
10 Hotson, 1949.

and no indication of a final parting is included; it seems reasonable to suppose that, unwelcome though they might have been, they were with or around Jonson and his companion for the best part of a week. The fact that they, too, are characterised as 'errant' offers another echo of the unsettled life of the vagrant.

Such brief and discontinuous indications that the two walkers were not always travelling alone recur elsewhere. Most enigmatically, there is the 'gossip-in-law', Mr Richardson, who appears unannounced at Tadcaster and then may be with them once again – the account is unclear, as there are several Richardsons in evidence at various points – when they reach Durham. By Durham, in fact, Jonson appears to have collected a troupe of fellow travellers about him – Bishop Neile, the 'Foot Voyage' says, invites him to bring 'all his company' to dinner (l.346). Again, in Fife, we learn that their Dunfermline host 'used my gossip and his company with all freedom and full entertainment' (ll.555–6), but the extent or exact composition of this jovial crew remains unspecified, although the presence of Scottish courtiers can be inferred.[11] Such shimmerings reinforce the sense that the 'Foot Voyage' is a more impressionistic document than its attention to some kinds of detail might lead us to believe.

Garrett Sullivan has written suggestively about the 'relationship between estate and highway' in the early modern 'drama of landscape', examining precisely what links estates, paths, roads and highways in experience and imagination.[12] So if the way is one important vector in the itinerary of the walk as mapped out, performed and experienced, equally significant are the planned and happenstance stopping places enjoyed by the walkers, both the middle-ranking – the inns and post-masters' households that are carefully listed as providing succour and sojourn – and the elite, the estates of noble and gentry families such as the Manners family at Belvoir Castle, the Cavendishes at Welbeck, the archbishops' palaces of Tobie Matthew and Richard Neile at York and Durham, and William Drummond's estate at Hawthornden, Jonson's ultimate 'dwelling-in-travelling' place. We need, then, to make the link in accounts of the walk between the road and what might best be termed the 'micro-geographies of households'.[13] In the Newcastle manuscript, most of the contents of which embody the interests and networks of the

11 See Chapter 3 below.
12 Sullivan, 1998, 159, 162.
13 Strohmayer, 2011, 119. See also Elsky, 2000, and Sanders, 2014. And see Findlay, 2009, on early modern households as sites of theatre.

Cavendish family, we find a verse topography of Cavendish properties written in the early 1620s by Richard Andrews which plots the relations between these houses across a number of different significant dimensions. In the light of Jonson's concentrated round of visits to Rufford, Welbeck, Worksop and Bolsover on his northwards journey it is worth quoting in full:

> Dr Andrewes on houses of Cavendish
>
> Hardwicke for hugenes, Worsope for height,
> Welbeck for vse, and Bolser for sight.
> Worsope for walks, Hardwicke for Hall,
> Welbecke for brew-house, Bolser for all.
> Welbecke a parish, Hardwicke a Court,
> Worsope a pallas, Bolser a Fort.
> Bolser to feast, Welbecke to ride in,
> Hardwicke to thriue, and worsope to bide in.
> Hardwicke good house, Welbecke good keepinge,
> Worsope good walkes, Bolser good sleepinge.
> Bolser new built, Welbecke well mended,
> Hardwicke conceald, and worsope extended.
> Bolser is morne, Welbeck day bright,
> Hardwicke high noone, Worsope good night.
> Hardwicke is nowe, Welbecke will last,
> Bolser will be, and worsope is past.
> Welbecke a wife, Bolser a maide,
> Hardwicke a matron, worsope decaide.
> Worsope is wise, Welbecke is wittie,
> Hardwicke is hard, Bolser is prittie.
> Hardwicke is ritch, Welbecke is fine;
> Worsope is statelie, Bolser diuine.
> Hardwicke a Chest, Welbecke a saddle,
> Worsope a throne, Bolser a Cradle:
> Hardwicke resembles Hampton-court much,
> And worsope windsor, Bolser None-such.
> Worsope a duke, Hardwicke an Earle;
> Welbeck a vicount, Bolser a Pearle:
> The rest ar Iewells of the sheere,
> Bolser the Pendant of the Eare.
> yet an old Abby hard by the way,
> Rufford giue Almes more than all they.[14]

---

14 BL, MS Harley 4955, f.67v.

The houses that define the Cavendish family's place in the topography of the northern Midlands are here repeatedly located in a constellation of related but contrasting qualities. Sometimes the resultant arrangement stresses function or use, sometimes dynastic realities or possibilities, sometimes it mobilises the symbolic or metaphorical. It bears comparison, of course, to the estate poetry of the early modern period, if only to stress the striking particularities of its approach to the reading of the space and time of the properties concerned. To map four such houses is also to trace the connections and traffic between them and, with that, the changing and various meanings of the 'house of Cavendish' in the Midlands landscape.

Just as significant here, though, is the sudden intrusion of a fifth house in the poem's final couplet. As the residence of Jane Talbot, countess of Shrewsbury, Rufford needs to be brought into the space governed by these four points of the Cavendish compass, but it is not given an obvious topographical place within the space thus mapped. Instead, it is celebrated for a single quality, the giving of alms or provision of hospitality, which is uniquely concentrated there and in relation to which the other houses are merely negatively delineated. Such an investment chimes with the terms in which other Cavendish writers, such as William Sampson, also depicted Rufford, thus stressing the topographical form imposed or brought out by the ethos of its owner or occupier.[15] For Jonson and his companion, too, Jane Talbot's Rufford provided 'extraordinary grace and entertainment' (ll.93–4). An instructive contrast can be drawn with the spatial character of the house during the occupation of the previous countess, Mary Talbot, as drawn by Sir John Holles. In June 1611 Holles conducted a search of Rufford, but found little hard evidence of the recusancy he knew the place to be harbouring. In his letter to the lord treasurer he presents a topographical prospect of Catholic conspiracy and duplicity:

> The coming in of the house is exposed to an open plain of the forest that none can come thither but he shall be discovered a mile off flanked also with some lodges of the King's which serve for sentinel: the back part is shouldered with a great woodland country fraught with many scattered granges and all of these inhabited with obstinate recusants, led to that asylum from Derbyshire, Yorkshire, Lincolnshire, etc., and to and fro they continually pass, as in a covert, by many back and trap doors, so as, if the forest way may be called *via regia*, this woodland way is really *via pontificia*.[16]

---

15 Sampson, 1636, 12.
16 *HMCP*, 9.48–9.

Given this sinister landscape, it is no surprise to find the interior of the house described by Holles in similarly alarming terms:

> The house within, a confused labyrinth, underneath all vaults; above, entries, closets, oratories, many stairs down and up, trap doors to issue forth and trap doors to lead into garrets, so as in my search I was never so puzzled in my life.[17]

Religious and political duplicity and danger find obvious architectural, as well as topographical, expression: a single estate can be the locus for intense and spatially articulated foreboding. And then, in what seems like an instant, it can change. The house that was a crooked asylum becomes a uniquely generous nonpareil of charity and hospitality, and secrecy gives way to grace and openness.

Inns, too, punctuate the walk through England from the first night at the Bear in Tottenham to the Nag's Head on Sandhill in Newcastle, taking in such celebrated hostelries as the White Hart at Newark and the George on Coney Street in York. They play a key role as nodal points on the itinerary of the walk, identified as stopping places and 'pauses', to deploy Yi-Fu Tuan's terminology, where stories and events – such as Jonson's drinking competition with his host, William Thornton, and the York parson, Henry Rogers, at Tollerton, or the 'good sport' of John Twentyman at Newark – could unfold.[18] Such pauses are given shape and colour by the hosts who preside over them, as Taylor makes clear in so much of his domestic travel writing, and as the 'Foot Voyage' too cannot help but demonstrate.[19] The hosts and hostesses of the inns in which the travellers stay all serve to characterise the locus of their operations. Also significant, though, was the spacing of the way created by the emergent early modern postal system. The developing network of postmasters, with their associated knowledge of places, times, distances and connections, was something on which Jonson and his co-walker were able to draw, and which also crossed the border into Scotland.[20] At Witham, Northallerton, Darlington and 'Cobersmith' (Cockburnspath) they are accommodated by the postmaster. Sometimes, there is interference or alignment: by 1618, William Folkingham at Stamford was both landlord of the celebrated George Inn and the town's postmaster, while the postmaster of

---

17 *HMCP*, 9.49.
18 Yi-Fu Tuan's formulation is that 'if we think of space as that which allows movement then place is pause; each pause in movement makes it possible for location to be transformed into place' (2001 [1977]), 6.
19 In this connection, it is worth noting the way in which John Taylor seeks to intervene in the reputation of an inn holder at Daventry (PP, sig. B2). See, too, his later attempts to retract his criticisms in the dedicatory epistle to the Daventry host in *A Kicksey-Winsey* (1619, sigs. A3-[A5]).
20 See Brayshay, Harrison and Chalkley, 1998, 265-7.

Darlington, Peter Glover, was the son-in-law of the prosperous innholder Elizabeth Warcup at Topcliffe. By contrast, at Newark, 'we had purposed to lie at Mr Atkinson's, the postmaster's, but Wamble of the Hart subtly anticipated us' (ll.77–9), a scene of conflicting interests that was repeated at Doncaster:

> We came at one of the clock at night to the Hind to Mr Carver's, an alderman and a justice of peace, which Mrs Lovet his neighbour took very grievously because she looked to have had [us], having been by other gentlemen spoken to before and willed to prepare for our entertainment.
>
> (ll.230–4)

Elizabeth Levett was the widow of Richard, alderman and postmaster, who had died only a few months earlier – her irritation and, perhaps, concern at being thus thwarted can easily be imagined. Audible here is the 'grammar' of mobility, or place-making in process; these are the ways in which, as Tim Cresswell terms it, 'places and landscapes are continually practised and performed through the movement and enfolding of a myriad of people and things'.[21] In such complementarity, and such friction, we catch a glimpse of a postal network integrated, not always without remainder, into the spidery web of inns and taverns spread along the main routes of the country.[22] We can see, too, how the way is stitched together from the rhythms of movement and pause that structure the lives both of various kinds of traveller and the hosts and hostesses who labour in time to those very rhythms.

To the walkers travelling through it, the landscape itself was in movement. On their journey from London, Jonson and his companion would have traversed or encountered 'field, forest, fell, fen, marsh, heath, down and *wald*';[23] they would have walked along holloways, Roman roads, tracks, lanes and loans, hugging the coast and moving far inland. The settlements they passed through were marked or known by characteristic activities: post and market towns, villages named after a river crossing, the fortifications at Berwick, the mine at Culross and saltpans of Kincardine, fishermen's bothies at Boulmer and the lead trade at Bawtry, the 'cherry town' of Sherburn 'where all the pins are made' (ll.280–1), 'booting Darlington'.[24] On occasion the landscape was

---

21 Cresswell and Merriman, 2011, 7.
22 On the 'organisation' of knowledge in relation to travel in this period, see McRae, 2009, esp. 67–9.
23 Everitt, 1985, 3.
24 This characterisation of Darlington through one of its predominant trades is given by the military travellers of 1634: *AShS*, 23; Darlington, of course, was where Jonson purchased the shoes of which he spoke to Drummond.

arrayed as a view, often with a grand house or castle providing the focal point. Between Chester-le-Street and Newcastle, the companion records, 'we had by the way a full sight of that stately and well-seated castle of Lumley' (ll.381–2). In Northumberland, near Alnmouth, 'we saw the isle of Coquet which one Blackman, a merchant, had taken etc. By the way we saw Dunstanburgh castle, which had been one of the goodliest in that country' (ll.431–4). On the coast of Lothian, standing out against the backdrop of the Firth of Forth, 'we saw Tantallon, the Earl of Angus's castle by Auldhame' (ll.496–7).

Taylor's account of his journey proclaimed his refusal to let his experience be shaped by a predominating awareness of the significance of landscape, and the genre of chorography which embraced it most expansively. As he put it at the opening of the *Pennyles Pilgrimage*:

> That I should write of Cities scituations,
> Or that of Countries I should make relations:
> Of brooks, crooks, nooks; of riuers, boorns and rills,
> Of mountaines, fountaines, Castles, Towers & hills,
> Of Shieres, and Pieres, and memorable things,
> Of liues and deaths of great commanding Kings:
> I touch not those, they not belong to mee,
> But if such things as these you long to see,
> Lay downe my Booke, and but vouchsafe to reede
> The learned Camden, or laborious Speede.[25]

The aims of the 'Foot Voyage' appear to be discernibly, if not consistently, different. There is surprisingly little detail drawn from Camden, yet the concerns eschewed by Taylor nonetheless shape parts of the picture. The walkers' visit to Staunton in the Vale, between Bottesford and Newark, prompts an explanation of 'Tower guard', the form of land tenure by which the Staunton family held their property from the earls of Rutland, in terms that closely resemble the account of the same peculiarity given by the Leicestershire chorographer William Burton.[26] While staying with Sir Thomas Brudenell and Mary Markham, the travellers and their companions 'all walked over to Worsop town where we visited the old and ruinous abbey founded by Lord Lovetoft, who lieth in the church with Lord Furnivall and Nevill' (ll.177–9). A little further on, near

25 *PP*, sig. A3.
26 Burton, 1622, 9.

Skelbrooke, 'we drank at Robin Hood's well' (l.247). At Pontefract, where 'we visited the castle and whatsoever tasted of antiquity in the town,' the lives and deaths of kings commanded their attention even if some of the details became confused: 'There we saw the chamber where Richard the third was murdered and where H the 8th was c by Culpeper' (ll.263–4). At Warkworth, they saw the earl of Northumberland's 'ancient castle', and 'the strange hermitage' (ll.423, 426). Linguistic diversity also captures their attention. Bolsover Castle, the writer notes, is known as 'Bozer' – a well-attested local pronunciation. 'Worthingsop', the formal if rarely used trisyllabic name, is qualified with 'alias Worsop', a phonetically accurate rendering of the town's more usual appellation. In Northumberland, Boulmer is spelled 'Boomer', again capturing the local pronunciation, while Culross in Fife, the account makes clear, is 'called Curos' (Taylor renders it 'Cooras'),[27] as it is to this day. The 'Foot Voyage' concludes with a list of 'the harbour towns upon the Fife' (a slip for Forth), which, if sometimes garbled, nonetheless captures something of their specificity. Writing Kinghorn as 'King-gorn' and 'Kill gorne' accords with then current spellings in registering both the local iambic pronunciation of the name and its roots in the Gaelic *ceann gorn*, 'head of the bog'.[28] The scribe's 'Auster', in the same list, is an understandable misreading of 'Anster', itself a local pronunciation of Anstruther. This linguistic sensitivity to location is manifested in other ways, too. It is noticeable that the account begins to use the northern form of 'bridge', 'brigg', at 'Wentbrigg' (standardly 'Wentbridge'), just the point where it might be expected to manifest itself. In Scotland, the companion both notes and glosses the word 'inch', 'as they call it, that is, a little island' (l.561); the gloss on 'capper' (App. 1, l.1) in one of the brief supplementary passages appended to the 'Foot Voyage' shows a similar interest in lexical particularity. In the attention to such details paid by the travellers, we see something of chorography's 'inclination to focus on what is *distinctive* about local places', as John Adrian has put it.[29]

Adrian's account of chorography is offered as a counterweight to the view promulgated by critics and historians beginning with Richard Helgerson, in which such scholarly endeavours primarily serve the interests of nation-building.[30] For Adrian, then, the multiplicity acknowledged in the title of Drayton's *Poly-Olbion* is as important as

---

27 *PP*, sig. E1.
28 Taylor and Markus, 2006, 416–17.
29 Adrian, 2011, 21.
30 Helgerson, 1992.

its national perspective.[31] Jonson's walk, however, took itself beyond this particular interplay of the national and the local in crossing the border: unlike all those precedent walkers who had gone as far as Berwick, his express aim and accomplishment was to continue as far as the capital of King James's native land. The surviving gests of James's northward progress in 1617 are themselves broken off at the border: they describe either the itinerary as far as Berwick, or within Scotland.[32] Our sense of the landscape and route of the 'Foot Voyage', in other words, would be incomplete without giving due consideration to the continuities and discontinuities evident in this binational dimension.

British landscapes

Both the Union of the Crowns and James's consequent pursuit of full constitutional union have been the focus of ample scholarly attention in recent decades.[33] The stalling of James's grander plans – largely the result of alarmed opposition in the English parliament, although there were weighty reservations in Scotland too – did not, of course, mean the end of the project: the verdict in Calvin's Case, which confirmed the naturalisation in England of Scots born after the king's accession to his later throne, conceded the fundamental constitutional importance for the southern realm of the coincidence of the two monarchies in James's person. And while the king had tried to tempt his English subjects by talking of the projected union as a 'conquest' of Scotland – though wrought by love, rather than war – in his celebrated speech to parliament in March 1607, they chose not to believe him.[34] This was perhaps in part because the kind of union he had created in the organisation of his court, in the distribution of power and favour, and in his emphasis on aristocratic Scoto-English marriages, spoke not of English dominance, or even of an indifferent or transcendent Britishness, but of the balancing of national claims. Such moves confounded both the English national self-image encouraged by his Tudor predecessors and the hopes for

---

31 Adrian, 2011, 94.
32 *NP*, 3.572; *HMCMK*, 80.
33 See, in particular, Galloway, 1986, Levack, 1987 and A. Nicholls, 1999. The cultural and literary implications and consequences have been addressed in a number of monographs and collections, including Baker and Maley, 2002, Schwyzer and Mealor, 2004, K. Curran, 2009, T. Marshall, 2000 and Kerrigan, 2008.
34 Rhodes, Richards and Marshall, 2003, 307–24.

preferment of many aspirant English nobles and gentlemen.[35] Some of the dismayed or disgruntled responded with violent xenophobia, and Jonson himself was caught up in an incident no doubt arising from inflamed national sensitivities in 1605, when he was accused – as Drummond noted – of 'writing something against the Scots' (*Informations*, ll.207–8) in *Eastward Ho!* The setback was temporary, however, and Jonson was to thrive in helping to craft a symbolic language of British union that drew its strength both from the corporeal facticity of the king himself, and from the elite cross-border marriages that he sought to broker.[36] Indeed, Jonson cultivated and sustained close relationships with Scots contacts and patrons, especially James's own kin, to an extent that has not always been apparent to critics.[37]

His 1618 walk, then, might appear to be a singularly British enterprise, an enactment of union in the embodied terms that James had established for it. In fact, this might be the best sense in which it was any kind of 'pilgrimage', since Edinburgh was not only the Scottish capital – 'Britain's other eye', Jonson apparently called it, in a poem which does not survive (*Informations*, l.318) – but also the birthplace of the king himself. A statue of James had been installed atop the Netherbow Port in 1615, and looked down over Jonson and his companion as they made their formal entry into the city.[38] The chamber in Edinburgh Castle in which he was born can still be seen; its current decorative scheme was painted by James Anderson for the celebrations of his return in 1617.[39] It is hard to believe that Jonson and his companion were not taken there during the visit to the castle they made immediately after the ceremony with which the voyage was completed, even though the account makes no mention of it. The 'Tounis college', founded under royal charter of 1582, had been renamed 'King James's College' at the royal behest in the wake of his 1617 stay: its alumni included William Drummond, and Jonson's interest in its activities was to extend beyond his four-month stay in the city.[40] Furthermore, the extension on to Edinburgh of the traditional wager journey route from London to Berwick, modelled on James's own journeys of 1603 and 1617, would give specific form to what

35 See Cuddy, 1989, and Wormald, 1996. We might note, in this context, that the Robert Colville who preached before Jonson at Culross in September 1618 was brother to James, first Lord Colville, who instigated 'Calvin's' case on behalf of his infant grandson. See *ODNB*, James Colville.

36 K. Curran, 2009, 17–88.

37 Knowles, 2006; Butler, 1995b; Donaldson, 1997, 57–65.

38 Glendinning, 2004, 88–9.

39 Bath, 2003, 242.

40 *CWBJ*, Letter 14; Dalzel, 1862, II.8, 68, 70–1.

at least one panegyrist had already suggested was a British Protestant alternative to the Camino de Santiago, the well-known devotees' path to the shrine of a different, sanctified James in northern Spain.[41] James is a shadowy presence throughout the walk: he was invoked by Jonson and his hosts in healths drunk at Welbeck, Durham and Edinburgh – the first of these a conspicuous gesture of loyalty performed on the anniversary of the Gowrie plot (see l.201n.). His presiding influence is also recalled in memories and echoes of his progress, and evident in the construction at royal command – as the companion was certainly informed – of the King's Manor at York. That the 'John Stewart' who 'appointed my gossip his guest' in Leith should be, as we now know, neither a 'water bailie' nor a ship's captain but the kinsman of King James himself sharpens our sense of a presiding royal influence.[42]

York, of course, was the city of Constantine, a legendary figure who could offer James a sometimes controversial model of Britannic imperium to which he was not always averse, and it is clear that the question of Britain, of the meaning and extent of binational union, was still being posed during Jonson's walk along the *via regia*.[43] One of the incidents in York's own history recalled in a passage appended to the 'Foot Voyage' is the elaborate celebration of the marriage of Henry III's daughter, Margaret, to Alexander III of Scotland, at the Minster on 26 December 1251, an event that was attended by many of the nobility and knights of both kingdoms (App. 3, ll.4–6). The memory of Anglo-Scottish border friction is also evident in the story and relics of Sir David Dunbar encountered at Bothal (App. 3, ll.1–2) and in the legendary details of the earl of Morton's ancestor noted by the companion at Aberdour (ll.561–3). Such friction could be found, too, in the chorographic production of meaningful landscape, despite the apparently generous British inclusiveness seen in the 1607 edition, in particular, of Camden's *Britannia* and John Speed's *Theatre of the Empire of Great Britain*. As Roger Mason has shown, and despite its often Welsh sources, the Britain visible in such works was decidedly Anglocentric: Scotland

---

41 Anon., 1604, 11–12.

42 This identification also illuminates Taylor's use of the spelling 'Stuart' in his mention of Jonson's host, and his description of the poet's companions in Leith as 'Noble-men and Gentlemen that knowes his true worth, and their owne honours' (*PP*, sig. F3v). John and Francis Stewart had been seeking to recover the lands and titles forfeited by their father, the earl of Bothwell; while some of their entitlements were restored to them, the earldom was never regained. Francis Stewart, nonetheless, was often styled – as he is in the 'Foot Voyage' – Lord Bothwell.

43 Pocock, 2005, 72; R. Mason, 1987, 69–70.

was either marginalised or reduced in historical stature relative to its southern neighbour. The work of Scottish historians such as Hector Boece and George Buchanan was belittled or ignored – William Harrison's 'Description of Britain' had been contemptuous of the former, while Camden was dismissive of Buchanan's account of Scotland's ancient history and ignored the uniquely informative chorographic description of its topography and people to be found in the first book of his *Rerum Scoticarum Historia*.[44] Both Buchanan and Boece had insisted on the longevity and continuity of a Scottish kingdom that could be traced back to the mythical king Fergus I, primarily because such a narrative was crucial in the Scottish resistance to English claims to suzerainty over Scotland.[45] These claims based their idea of Britain as an English imperium at least in part on the mythic narrative of British origins advanced by Geoffrey of Monmouth and his followers, according to which the Trojan Brutus had been the original possessor of the whole island; dividing it between his three sons, but giving the realm now transformed into England to the eldest, he established *ab initio* the dependent character of any Scottish kingdom. This narrative had figured in the unionist propaganda of Lord Protector Somerset in the 1540s, and was given renewed life in the work of the Welsh antiquary Humphrey Llwyd in his *Breviary of Britain*, first published in Latin in 1572. Llwyd had been scathing about the alternative narrative of Scottish origins presented by Boece; Buchanan, in turn, vehemently criticised Llwyd's account in his *Historia*.[46] As if in response to these versions of Britain, Buchanan's chorographical account was published, without acknowledgement, in an English translation that appeared first at Edinburgh under the unhelpful title *Certaine Matters Composed Together* in 1594, and then at London, as *Certeine Matters Concerning the Realme of Scotland*, on James's accession to his English throne. Although Camden certainly did not share Llwyd's confidence in the Brutus story, his dismissive attitude to Scottish historical claims was perceived by his critics, and by educated Scots more broadly, as just as objectionable: William Drummond possessed a manuscript copy of an apparently antagonistic tract with the title 'Nuntius Scoto-Britannus, or, a paire of Spectacles for W. Camden, to look upon North-Britain'.[47]

44 R. Mason, 2013, 53. See also R. Mason, 2012.
45 Important accounts of these ideological contentions include R. Mason, 1987, MacColl, 2006, Armitage, 2000, esp. 36–60, and Kidd, 2010.
46 R. Mason, 1987; R. Mason, 2013, 53–4.
47 McDonald, 1971, 224; R. Mason, 2013, 54.

There is ample evidence to indicate that the walkers of 1618, as well as their hosts, might have been sensitive to this conflict over the meaning of British histories. Despite his difficulties over *Eastward Ho!*, Jonson's own deployments of such narratives had often shown an unusual degree of national tact, at least as far as Scotland was concerned: in his contribution to the coronation entertainment of 1604, for example, he coupled his portrayal of London as the new Troy, founded by Brutus, and the 'empire's seat', with the insistence that neither 'the Briton stroke [i.e. rule]' nor 'the Roman, Saxon, Dane, and Norman yoke' could bring about what 'this point of time' – or, to put it another way, a Scottish king – had accomplished, presenting the Jacobean union not as the restoration of an originary and implicitly English empire but as an unprecedented, if prophesied, event (*King's Ent.*, ll.218–20, 277). Such a way of putting it happily conceded Scotland's sovereignty, its status as an unconquered realm, and made the fulfilment of the prophecy of empire a distinctively Scottish achievement. In *The Speeches at Prince Henry's Barriers*, six years later, the Arthurian characters and setting in 'St George's Portico' are redolent of Galfridian patriotic myth, as is the parade of kingly English warriors for whom the name of 'Briton' is glibly appropriated. That one of the most prominent of these 'brave Briton heroes' should be Edward I, *malleus scotorum*, would seem to point towards an evocation of precisely the claims of suzerainty for which Edward himself had mobilised the Brutus story (*Barriers*, l.211). Yet the whole event is in fact presided over by the new Arthur, Prince Henry, who is named Meliadus and styled 'Lord of the Isles', an emphatically Scottish title which here grows, imperially, to embrace the 'fortunate isles' of Britain as a whole (*Barriers*, l.379). This gesture is coupled with a notable exclusion from the list of countries in which 'you may behold... / The conquests got, the spoils, the trophies reared / By British kings': Wales is there lumped in with the 'Low Countries, France, and Spain', while the securing of Ireland, 'that more in title than in fact / Before was conquered', is attributed to 'Royal and Mighty James' himself (*Barriers*, ll.318–20). The inclusion of Wales, conquered by Edward I, serves to stress the ultimate failure of Plantagenet designs on the kingdom omitted from Jonson's list – and therefore, once again, to acknowledge Scotland's own independence even while rehearsing the English imperial theme.

Such British concerns appear again, in a different key, in Jonson's antimasque *For the Honour of Wales*, which was performed at court only five months before he set out on his walk. This featured a trio of Welsh characters who petition James to honour Wales with the kind of visit he had recently paid to Scotland, but whose assertion of Welsh 'honour' is rendered in a distinctly comic register. Here, the retelling of British myth modulates into the characters' search for securely Welsh roots even for the names of Scottish courtiers such as John Auchmuty and Sir Robert Carr. Such an exaggerated insistence on the Welsh origins of Britain parodied the aims of the Galfridian antiquarianism associated with Humphrey Llwyd and could be seen as akin to the 'distinctly fishy historical reasoning' of Shakespeare's Fluellen in *Henry V*.[48] In this context, it is notable that the Welsh attorney of Jonson's antimasque opens his song with the line 'I's not come here to tauk of Brut', while nonetheless reminding his audience that 'the long pedigree of Prince Camber [Brutus's third son, legendary first ruler of Wales]...would fill aull this chamber' (ll.175, 177–8). That Galfridian claims are here being mocked rather than upheld should be clear not only from the apparent etymological violence done in their insistence on a primal British Welshness for all the masquers but also from the mention of 'Cadwallader' as a grander historical and mythic figure than Hercules (l.153). According to Geoffrey of Monmouth, Cadwaladr was the last king of the Britons, the recipient of God's promise that his issue would one day recover their title, and thus a suitably prophetic figure to name before the king of a new, if still somewhat prospective, Britain.[49] Yet the presentation of Cadwaladr was also a noted flaw in Geoffrey's account, and one of 'the means by which the Galfridian tradition was exploded'.[50] To emphasise this character was to highlight the flaws as much as the divinatory possibilities of the Galfridian account of Britain.

There is, too, a Scottish twist to this game of etymological trumps, which makes it more than an exercise in humanist scepticism towards antiquarian narratives of the sort begun by Polydore Vergil and continued by Camden. Having earlier attempted to show that names as diverse as Irwin, Carr, Auchmuty and Abercromby are all really Welsh, thus reinforcing Galfridian assertions of an originary British, or rather Brutish, identity, the three protagonists turn in concluding to consider 'His Madesty's anagrams of Charles James Stuart', the king's full name (ll.307–8). The first such anagram to be aired, and the only one actually taken from the king's name, is borrowed from Camden's *Remains*

---

48 See Schwyzer, 2002, 19.
49 Geoffrey, 1966, 180–4. Cf. *CWBJ*, 5.335.
50 J. Curran, 1997, 286; cf. Floyd-Wilson, 2002, 110.

Figure 4 Detail of the Timothy Pont map of Fife, from Joan Blaeu, *Atlas*, 1654. The map shows some of the places visited by Jonson on his tour through southern Fife. Prospect of Edinburgh at bottom right, showing Arthur's Seat and royal park. © National Library of Scotland.

Concerning Britain, an unsurprisingly non-Galfridian source, and had been used by Jonson previously in *Prince Henry's Barriers*.[51] It is said in the masque to refer to Cadier Arthur, 'Arthur's chair', a site of mythic importance in Brecknockshire mentioned by Camden and to which Evan has already referred earlier in the antimasque (l.56). Yet the anagram itself is constrained to say something slightly different, and in so doing to point elsewhere: James, it suggests, 'Claimes Arthur's Seat' (l.308). As the king, his Scots courtiers and all those who had joined him on his progress six months previously would have known first hand, 'Arthur's Seat' was – and is – the name given to the striking hill to the south-east of Edinburgh that had long sat at the heart of a royal hunting park (see Figure 4).[52] A topographical poem by the humanist scholar and neo-Latin poet John Johnston, included by Camden in the 1607 *Britannia* and subsequently translated for the English edition of 1610, shows Arthur's Seat presiding over a locus of wonder that is emphatically a royal and national capital:

51 Camden, 1605, 153; see also *CWBJ*, 5.341.
52 See Blaeu, 1654, or Blaeu, 2006.

Vnder the rising of an Hill, Westward there shootes one way
A castle high; on th'other side, the Kings house gorgeous gay.
Betweene them both the city stands, tall buildings shew it well,
For arm's [sic], for courage much renown'd, much people therein dwell.
The Scots head city large and faire, the kingdomes greatest part,
Nay, even the Nations kingdome whole well neere, by just desart.
Rare arts and riches: what ones minde can wish is therein found,
Or else it will not gotten be throughout all Scottish ground.
A civill people here a man may see, a Senate graue,
Gods holy lawes with purest light of preachers here yee haue.
In parts remote of Northren clime would any person ween,
That ever these or suchlike things might possibly be seene?
Say Travailer, now after that thou forraine towne hast knowne,
Beholding this, beleevest thou these eies that are thine owne?[53]

Interestingly, Philemon Holland's English translation of *Britannia*, which Jonson consulted when writing *For the Honour of Wales*, rendered the name of the Edinburgh location as 'Arthurs Chaire'; Camden, of course, noted its associations with '*Arthur* the Britaine'.[54] So the story of unitary British origins told by the Welsh characters in the antimasque becomes strangely bivocal: the attempt to trace Scottish names back to Welsh sources and places is thrown into reverse, and a Britannic Arthur is discerned awkwardly within the symbolically dense topography of Scotland's capital. Can Arthur have two seats? Not, presumably, if the prophetic and iconographic truth of the anagram is to be recognised, nor if its point is to mark the recovery of a lost – and, therefore, once possessed – union. In citing some of the more embarrassing or problematic elements in the Galfridian story Jonson may have been aligning himself with the kind of critique of the old stories of Britishness in which Camden had engaged; in giving Arthur an incompatible set of Scottish coordinates, the masque displays a wider and deeper awareness of the conflicting histories of multiple Britains. In this connection, Camden's description of Arthur's Seat as 'an hill with two heads' seems both apposite and uncomfortable.[55]

Taylor, too, despite his declared intention of evading the perspectives and approaches of chorography, would have been aware of this tangle of competing historical claims. Like Jonson, one of his first actions on arrival at Edinburgh is to visit the castle, which he declares in his pamphlet is 'so strongly grounded, bounded, and sounded, that by force of man it can never bee confounded'; it is, in short, 'this

53 *CB*, 'Scotland', 15.
54 *CWBJ*, 5.312; *CB*, 'Scotland', 14–15.
55 *CB*, 'Scotland', 14.

unconquered Castle', a suitable emblem of the legendarily unconquered Scotland in whose capital it sits. At the other end of the Royal Mile, with topographical symmetry, he encounters 'his Majesties Pallace':

> In the inner Court, I saw the Kings Armes cunningly carved in stone, and fixed over a doore aloft on the wall, the red Lyon being the Crest, over which was written this inscription in Latine,
>
> *Nobis haec invicta miserunt, 106. proavi*
>
> I enquired what the English of it was? it was told me as followeth, which I thought worthy to be recorded.
>
> *106. Fore-fathers hath left this to us unconquered.*
>
> This is a worthy and a memorable Motto, and I thinke few Kingdomes or none in the world can truly write the like, that…maugre the strength and pollicie of enemies, that Royall Crowne and Scepter hath from one hundred and seaven descents, keepe still unconquered.[56]

The 'enemies' mentioned but not named here would have to include, of course, those English monarchs who had sought to exert an imperial sovereignty over Scotland, while the 107 kings constitute the unbroken line from Fergus I to James VI as customarily calculated – the core element in the national history given by both Boece and Buchanan, witheringly dismissed by Humphrey Llwyd, and sceptically handled by Camden.[57] The unconquered country that Taylor encounters in its capital, then, has its historical credentials written across the surface and through the impregnable fabric of its built and natural landscape, just as it does in Johnston's topographical poem. Taylor's heavy emphasis on these claims reveals a willingness to take that history, and the version of Britain it implies, on its own assertive terms.

Although there is no similarly stark moment in the 'Foot Voyage', these walkers cannot have evaded the British question. Indeed, a poem surviving in a single manuscript copy suggests that current Anglo-Scottish tensions made their presence felt on at least one occasion. Attributed to 'J. Joshnston' (*sic*), it figures Jonson as an Orpheus descending into the dark ('scotos') hell to England's north:

> Thither went Orpheus, but who can saye
> he tooke the paines to foote itt all the waye
> Perchance he thought itt paine enough to ride
> Thou there out goest him: Then a while abide
> Come take thy hire, before thou further goe
> And play such streines as many years agoe

56 *PP*, sig. D3.
57 R. Mason, 2013, 42, 49.

Drew listening stocks & stones: soe draw with the*e*
those that heart-eate this climes felicitie
unto their natiue home: there staye thy hand.
And if the well knowne sweetnes of this land
Beginne but to reduce them, be not slacke
to send them backe againe, by lookeing backe
As Orpheus did his dead Euridice.[58]

The poem's complaints about parasitic Scots living off England's 'sweet-nes' sound a sourly xenophobic note, as does its fervently expressed desire that they should return whence they came. The suggestion that, in the event of the Scots failing to confine themselves to their own land, Jonson should become an 'iambick' satirist and, like Archilochus and Hipponax, drive his victims to suicide compounds the offence.[59] Its direct address to Jonson might imply that it was presented to him during the northwards leg of his journey; although the 'Foot Voyage' makes no mention of any such occurrence, its silence cannot be taken as evidence that no presentation took place – it is not, after all, a comprehensive record. And there is perhaps a hint of something similar in the labelling of the 10 pieces with which Jonson was presented on his departure north from Newcastle as his 'viaticum' (l.398): while this might well simply mean money to support a traveller, it could also denote the final com-munion received by those passing out of this world.

On another occasion, the account's omissions seem harder to explain. In contrast to Taylor, whose crossing of the border did not, to his surprise, in any way alter his experience of the landscape through which he was moving, Jonson and his companion are participants in a little ceremony north of Berwick organised by Sir William Bowyer:

> After dinner we took our journey, brought out of town with all the knights, gentlemen, mayor and aldermen; two miles out of town was wine ready, where Sir William had sent a company of musketeers who gave us a volley of shot. Sir William could not contain himself from tears when he took his leave.

> (ll.484–8)

---

58 WYAB, MS 32D86/34, 120. First noted in Bland, 2004, Appendix 1. Bland's transcription gives 'fresher' for 'further' in the fifth line quoted above.

59 Bland suggests (2004, 378) that it was written by John Johnston and given by him to Jonson during the latter's stay in Scotland. However, Johnston would not have shared the poem's sentiments, and his death in October 1611 anyway makes this impossible. The poem's preser-vation among the manuscripts of the Yorkshire antiquary John Hopkinson indicates that it might derive from a source close to his friend Nathaniel Johnston, although this latter's father was of Scottish origins, and he himself probably studied at St Andrews (*ODNB*, John Johnston, John Hopkinson, Nathaniel Johnston). The verb 'heart-eat', meaning to envy or covet, is a northern English coinage (*OED*, Heart-eat *v.*).

Bowyer had been captain of the garrison, so this ritual marked the
outermost limit of English military power and political authority –
although it is also worth noting that the walkers were guided to their
first destination on the Scottish side of the border by Sir John Selby, a
fellow Berwick dignitary. What is just as interesting is the somewhat
alienated take on the event proffered by the writer. While there can be no
doubt that this was a ceremony to mark Jonson's passage into Scotland,
the account appears indifferent, almost as if the significance of this toast
and the volley of shot was neither recognised nor questioned. As it
continues into Scotland the account is for the most part untouched by
any indication that it is recording an encounter with a different country.

In one border detail, though, there are signs that Jonson and his
companion may indeed have been aware of some of the chorographical
literature on Scotland, and therefore – perhaps – of the contested landscapes such a literature produced. As we have noted in our introduction
and previous chapter, one of the passages additional to the 'Foot Voyage'
account itself gives a rendering of what it calls 'sleu dogs' language', the
commands and responses that pass between a master and the species of
bloodhound particularly associated with James's 'middle shires'. While
such dogs were kept and used on both sides of the border, they are
singled out in a number of well-known Scottish sources and appear to
have been particularly associated with the southernmost parts of the
northern kingdom. Hector Boece described the sleuth-hound in his
Scotorum Historia, and his account was eventually incorporated into
Holinshed's *Chronicles* in an Anglicised version (App. 2, Title n).
Camden's 1607 *Britannia* incorporated a brief passage from John
Leslie's *De Origine, Moribus et Rebus Gestis Scotorum*, which was originally published in 1578.[60] An interestingly distinctive account of the
breed appeared among a list of 'the most rare and wonderfull things in
Scotland' in *Certaine Matters Composed Together* in 1594, and was
republished in the London edition of this collection in 1603. This
description coupled a spurious etymology of the name 'sleuth hound'
with a focus on the 'words of Art spoken by his Master' in his direction of
the dog. This latter, of course, is also the singular focus of the additional
passage on 'sleu dogs' accompanying the 'Foot Voyage'. While it would
be very difficult to show that the 1618 rendering of 'dogs' language' is
directly shaped or focused by the emphases of this earlier pamphlet, it is
nonetheless suggestive that Jonson's companion should make a detailed

60 Leslie, 1675, 60.

record not just of a local cultural practice that featured particularly prominently in chorographies of Scotland, but of an aspect of that practice that is emphasised in a work drawing extensively on Buchanan's contested history and description of his native land. In this connection, the fact that Jonson owned a copy of Buchanan's *Rerum Scoticarum Historia*, and that it was a gift to him from William Drummond, perhaps assumes a heightened significance.[61]

Writing along the way

Although the 'Foot Voyage' shows relatively little interest in Jonson's writerly life, it can nonetheless help us to see the extent of its impact on his body of work. The walk gave rise, directly, to a range of poems, beginning most revealingly with *Underwood* 53, the recalled occasion of which can be dated to Wednesday 5 August, Jonson's final full day as a guest of Sir William Cavendish at Welbeck. This epigram was nonetheless written a few years later, either drawing on Jonson's vivid memory of this moment from his summer progress or prompted by a textual record such as the 'Foot Voyage' itself (see above, pp. 30–1). Other poems are more obviously products of a particular moment or encounter along the way in 1618. Another of Jonson's works for Cavendish, the prosopopoeiac epitaph on his father (*CWBJ*, 5.350), was the product of his collaboration with John Smithson and, it seems, Henry Lukin, and clearly has its roots in their visit to Bolsover on Tuesday 4 August. As we noted above, the Jonsonian grace surviving in a number of variants dated from 1617 to 1619 was probably the toast to 'the king's health' (l.201) that Jonson uttered at Welbeck and 'entreated *poetica licentia*' (l.370) to pronounce again at dinner with Bishop Neile in Durham. He may well, indeed, have composed, refined and played variations on it during the walk, given the number of companionable dinners and banquets that he attended; it seems likely that the 'Foot Voyage' records only a fraction of the occasions on which the honoured guest was required to say a few words. The account may also provide support for one attribution that has hitherto been treated with scepticism. In a 1649 history of his home town, the Newcastle chorographer William Gray ascribed a verse riddle about the extraordinary tower and crown of St Nicholas's church (now the cathedral), to 'Ben Johnson'.[62] It is a rough

---

61 McPherson, 1974, 32–3.
62 Gray, 1649, 10.

piece, making a mystery of an admired architectural feature, and the attribution was dismissed by Herford and Simpson.[63] It should be noted, however, that the 'free school' Jonson visited on 26 August 1618 had been housed across the churchyard from St Nicholas's until 1607, and still maintained strong connections with the church – indeed, a 'school gallery' was installed within it in 1620.[64] Gray himself had probably studied there in the years immediately preceding Jonson's visit, and he was well connected to the civic leaders who hosted the poet in 1618. His attribution, though late, might have more authority than has hitherto been supposed. A further poem that may have been composed on the walk is the 'Epitaph on Master Philip Gray' (*Und.* 16), who died in late 1615.[65] Jonson stayed at Howick, the Northumberland house in which Philip Grey had lived, as a guest of Randall Fenwick, his brother-in-law. Philip's widow, Margaret, might well be the 'Mrs Gray' who, with Randall Fenwick's wife, Catherine, Philip's sister, accompanied Jonson and his companion on their departure from Howick 'two miles on the way to a loan where her kine fed to give us a merrybub [i.e. a syllabub or posset] for our farewell' (ll.441–2). Such pastoral generosity would certainly make sense as a response to Jonson's own gift of a respectful – if somewhat generic – epitaph for their late husband and brother. Whether Jonson's gesture was purely one of thanks, or whether he had known Philip Grey himself, it is impossible to say for certain. Some of Grey's friends and relatives were Catholics, and Randall Fenwick was on occasion accused of complicity in the Gunpowder Plot, so an association with Jonson in the early years of James's reign is not out of the question.[66]

A more ephemeral incident is captured in the hitherto unplaced exchange between Jonson and 'Mr Craven' recorded in the Newcastle manuscript:

> *To Mr Ben Jonson in his Journey by Mr Craven*
> When wit and learning are so hardly set
> That from their needful means they must be barred,
> Unless by going hard they maintenance get,
> Well may Ben Jonson say the world goes hard.
> *This Was Mr Ben Jonson's Answer of the Sudden*

63 *H&S*, 8.424, 443.
64 *Laws*, 1925, 65.
65 A death date of 1626 has been conjectured by recent editors, but this is not found in Joseph Hunter's *Chorus Vatum*, the source cited by Herford and Simpson, and conflicts with reliable evidence (see note to 'Foot Voyage' l.438; see also *H&S*, 11.59–60; BL, MS Add 24,491, f.18v).
66 *CSPD*, 1611–18, 406; Forster, 1972, 198–9.

Ill may Ben Jonson slander so his feet,
For when the profit with the pain doth meet,
Although the gate were hard, the gain is sweet.

(*CWBJ*, 5.349)

The identity of this 'Mr Craven' has eluded scholars until now. However, the detailed itinerary in the 'Foot Voyage' allows us to make a plausible identification. Among the dignitaries of Doncaster, where Jonson dined with Sir William Anstruther and 'a long table full of gentlemen and ladies', was John Craven, who had matriculated from St John's, Cambridge, in 1588, before moving as a scholar to Trinity; in 1604 he was appointed vicar of Harworth in Nottinghamshire, 7 miles south of his home town.[67] In 1616 he married, as his second wife, Dorothy, widow of one Anthony Armitage; both Armitage and his elder brother, William, featured prominently in Doncaster's governing gentry.[68] 'Master Craven', as he is described in the town records, held property there, and by 1618 also had a lease, through his wife, on Hexthorpe Hall, about a mile to the west.[69] Interestingly, John Craven had been chaplain to Gilbert Talbot, seventh earl of Shrewsbury and William Cavendish's uncle; Harworth, Craven's parish, was a Shrewsbury living.[70] It is likely, therefore, that this is our 'Master Craven', and that the poetic exchange recorded in the Newcastle manuscript took place either at Welbeck, perhaps on the Sunday when Jonson entertained some of the local gentry, or during the banquet hosted by Sir William Anstruther on Saturday 8 August 1618.[71] Given Harworth's close proximity to Bawtry, however, it is also possible that Craven was present during Jonson's entertainment there a day or two previously.

Such a gossamer collection of poems might seem like slim pickings to anyone looking to discern the immediate impact of the walk on Jonson's writing – perhaps, then, the absence of literary concerns or endeavour from the 'Foot Voyage' reflects an indifference that was not that of the companion alone. It is, however, hardly surprising that any work produced on the hoof or *currente calamo* should be brief, fragmentary or

---

67 *AC*; Train, 1961, 91.
68 His first wife, the widow of his predecessor at Harworth, was buried at the parish church in Rotherham; the inscription on her memorial in the 'high quyer' there was transcribed by Roger Dodsworth in 1619, but the year of death that he notes, 1616, must be an error. The memorial does not survive. See Dodsworth, 1904, 10.
69 Blagg, 1914–15, III.42; Brent and Martin, 1994, ll.216–17, 256; DA, AB6/2/16, f.4v.
70 Train, 1961, 90; LP, MS 3201, f.237.
71 BL MS Harl. 4955, f.47v.

unpolished. And Jonson's voyage saw the writing of more substantial pieces, as he himself advertised in the title of *Und.* 9, 'My Picture Left in Scotland', which he gave to Drummond in an autograph copy dated 19 January 1619, and described in a graceful dedication celebrating their friendship as 'a picture of myself'.[72] This copy of the poem is textually very close to one preserved in the Newcastle manuscript under the title 'Verses on his Picture', sharing some distinctive variants not found in other surviving manuscript copies and differing in only two significant readings.[73] Most tellingly, both copies give Jonson's age as 'six and forty years' (l.15), where other manuscript copies and the version printed in the second folio have either 'over six and forty' or 'seven and forty'. Given the two undoubtedly authorial variants, the copy in the Newcastle manuscript must have been taken from an independent source; it appears on the same folio, and seems to have been copied at the same time, as the exchange with Mr Craven, so it might be thought that its source was most probably an autograph copy presented by Jonson to one of his hosts during his 1618 stay with the extended Cavendish–Ogle family, their households or clients. However, the title of the poem in *The Underwood* explicitly associates it with Jonson's time in Scotland, hinting at composition between September 1618 and January 1619, so it is possible that a copy of the recently completed verse was presented to Cavendish or one of his family during or very shortly after Jonson's return journey – about which, of course, we know nothing.

By the time of his departure from Edinburgh in January 1619, as Drummond's *Informations* make clear, Jonson had gleaned enough from his walk and his stay in Scotland to have formulated distinctive plans. In addition to his own account of his 'foot pilgrimage', to be called 'A Discovery', he also had an 'intention to write a fisher or pastoral play, and set the stage of it in the Lomond Lake'; presumably, too, we should take into account the lost poem, perhaps owing something to John Johnston's topographical verses in the 1607 *Britannia*, in which he wrote his praise of Edinburgh (*Informations*, ll.313–14, 318). Loch Lomond was one of Scotland's natural wonders, often picked out in

---

72 NRS, GD18/4312.

73 BL, MS Harley 4955, f.47v; and see the collations for the poem in *CWBJ*, 7.102–3. The differences are the Drummond copy's unique reading 'doubt that' for 'now think' in the Newcastle manuscript (l.2), and 'hundreds' for 'numbers' – a variant found only in the Newcastle manuscript – in line 14. The text printed in the second folio agrees with the Newcastle copy in the first instance, and with the Drummond autograph in the second.

chorographical accounts, and especially noted for a distinctive kind or species of fish, 'very delectable to eat', 'tempestuous waves and surges of the water, perpetually raging without wind', and an island 'that is not corroborate, nor united to the ground, but hath bene perpetually loose; and although it be fertil of good grasse, and replenished with Neat; yet it mooves by the waves of the water, and is transported somtimes toward one point, and other whiles toward an other'.[74] Jonson sought further information on the loch from Drummond, doubtless to furnish him with additional matter for his proposed play. That Loch Lomond was the most notable feature of the historic province of Lennox, from which Jonson's illustrious Stewart patrons took their title, perhaps encouraged Jonson in his research; Camden's description of the province dwelt equally on the loch and the genealogy of the earls and dukes of Lennox.[75]

These may not have been the only Scotocentric writings planned by Jonson at his departure for England, drafts and sketches for which were presumably included with the 'papers of this country' that he promised to send Drummond 'if he died by the way' (*Informations*, l.517). Giving the statement pride of place at the outset of the *Informations*, Drummond records how Jonson 'hath an intention to perfect an epic poem, entitled *Heroologia*, of the worthies of this country roused by fame, and was to dedicate it to his country' (*Informations*, ll.1–2). At least, this is how a modernised text of the Sibbald transcript of Drummond's notes would put it – modern editors, however, amend 'this' to 'his', following the reading given in the somewhat different, abbreviated and independently derived text of the 'Conversations' first printed in 1711.[76] Such a move erases what would have been a challengingly non-Anglocentric, indeed distinctively British, gesture – a verse history of Scotland told through the lives and deeds of its most celebrated figures, addressed to an English audience that was not always interested in, or receptive to, the national claims of those peoples with whom it was required to share the archipelago.[77] The bookseller and writer Henry Holland – whose father, Philemon, had published his translation of Camden's *Britannia* in 1610 – produced his *Heroologia Anglica* in 1620, soon

---

74 ?Monipennie, 1594, sig. K4.
75 *CB*, 'Scotland', 24–6.
76 See *H&S*, 1.132; *CWBJ*, 5.359.
77 As John Kerrigan puts it, 'the "his/this" variant alone educes the British problem' (Kerrigan, 2008, 148).

after Jonson's return home. Holland's work was a decidedly Tudor sequence of biographical sketches in Latin prose and verse, and Jonson may indeed have been moved by the same spirit to write his own 'versified dictionary of national biography', as Ian Donaldson has suggested.[78] But the Scottish possibility should not be ruled out, despite Drummond's later suggestion that Jonson 'thinketh nothing well but what either he himself or some of his friends and countrymen hath said or done' (*Informations*, ll.558–9). While this might be read as an accusation of simple national chauvinism, it is not clear that Jonson's prejudicial views here apply to Englishmen other than poets – indeed, the inclusion of 'he himself' argues in favour of just such a restriction. It might more plausibly be read as the cosmopolitan Drummond's irritation at his guest's metropolitan parochialism in literary matters. And among the books that passed in some way between Drummond and Jonson was a copy of John Johnston's *Inscriptiones Historicae Regum Scotorum*, his sequence of Latin epigrams on all the Scottish kings from Fergus I, which was published at Edinburgh in 1602.[79] Johnston was widely admired, a friend of Justus Lipsius and, as we have seen, a collaborator with William Camden, and had contributed other topographical poems besides his encomium to Edinburgh to the 1607 edition of *Britannia*.[80] His *Inscriptiones* was an accomplished celebration of the Stewart dynasty, though in a 'Buchanan-esque tone' that might not have proved consistently pleasing either to its royal dedicatee or to Jonson.[81] It was published with a fragment of Andrew Melville's epic poem *Gathelus*, which retold Scotland's mythic counterblast to the Galfridian story of Brutus. The *Inscriptiones* was followed a year later by *Heroes ex omni Historia Scotica*, which develops the form of the epigrammatic biographical sketch to stage 'a celebration of contemporary Scottish noblemen and a selection of their illustrious ancestors', furnishing a 'baronial counterweight' to the royal histories of the former work.[82] Interestingly, a copy of this work bearing Drummond's signature on its final leaf has

---

78 Donaldson, 2011, 355–6.
79 McDonald, 1971, 232; now NLS, H.31.a.6. See also Henry Woudhuysen's catalogue of Jonson's library, *CWBJ* Online.
80 Cameron, 1963, xxiii, xxxv, xxxvi, lxiii, lxxv, 64–6 and 330; on Johnston's wider intellectual milieu, see Holloway, 2011.
81 R. Mason, 2013, 49. Jonson's comments to Drummond contain some indirect criticism of Buchanan's approach to verse recitation, which nonetheless show an awareness of, and interest in, the work and practice of this pre-eminent Renaissance scholar. Camden's *Remains* were also a topic of conversation during their encounter. See *Informations*, ll.442–3, 487.
82 R. Mason, 2013, 49.

long been bound together with the copy of the *Inscriptiones* signed, on its title page, by Jonson. Both works are not infrequently found in the one volume, a reflection of their complementarity.[83]

These details testify to the availability and proximity of such materials for Jonson, and perhaps also to Drummond's role in guiding or influencing his engagement with these other British histories. Johnston's work, Buchanan's *Historia* and the *Certaine Matters* in which the focus of 'Canesco' is mirrored all contribute to a historiographical and chorographical perspective on the basis of which, as Roger Mason says, 'the union of the Scottish and English crowns was to be seen, not as a recreation of the empire of Brutus or Constantine or Arthur, but as the conjunction of two historic sovereign states'.[84] It is clear, as we noted above, that Taylor was confronted with this tradition in his encounter with Scotland's unbroken and unconquered monarchical lineage at Holyrood, and Drummond's exchanges of books with Jonson suggest that something similar may have been taking place between them. Given such tutelage, and Jonson's evidently contemporaneous interest in the differences within the history and historiography of ancient Britain, it is far from impossible that the epic he was mulling over at his departure from Edinburgh did indeed turn on an audacious plan to effect a binational alignment of the differing perspectives of 'his country' and 'this country' – as Sibbald's generally careful and accurate transcript would suggest.[85] In this connection, we might well wonder why Jonson subsequently requested that Drummond send him 'the oath which the old valiant knights of Scotland gave when they received the Order of Knighthood'.[86]

If such a work was ever anything more than an editorial misreading, it may have been only a fleeting plan hatched in the warm glow of Scots hospitality. Nonetheless, such a plan makes sense in the context of what we might call the biogeography of Jonson's journey – not just the symbolic movement between two capitals but the broader connotations of the fact of walking.[87] To walk this road was to turn one's back, even if temporarily, on the metaphysics of union as given shape in some of Jonson's court masques, with its obliteration of differences, its magical

---

83 R. Mason, 2013, 49; Woudhuysen, *CWBJ* Online; see, for example, NLS, H.31.a.5; NLS, *NHA*, Q.98.2
84 R. Mason, 1987, 75.
85 For a defence of the reliability and comprehensiveness of the Sibbald transcript, see Ian Donaldson's textual introduction to the *Informations*, *CWBJ* Online.
86 *CWBJ*, Letter f.
87 See Macfarlane, 2012, 32–3, for a relevant discussion of the concept of biogeography.

translations, its preference for topology over topography. To walk this road was to emphasise instead the biomechanics of union, the conjunction of two polities in the lives, circles and movements of all the king's subjects: shifting place and air, pacing out the sometimes difficult dimensions of this distinctively Jacobean proximity. And for James's pensioned poet to come on foot, like a pilgrim, seeking hospitality, reintroduces the symbolism at another level. The expenditure of energy and shoe-leather, the physical sufferings emphasised in his recounting of the voyage, become a sign of Jonson's commitment to seeing the union through 'Britain's other eye', rather than sitting in the empire's seat surveying the landscape with a monocular vision.[88]

Footsteps retraced

We know that Jonson continued to think about his voyage for many years following its completion: in his vituperative poem, 'To his False Friend Mr Ben Jonson', Inigo Jones referred slightingly to Jonson's many repetitions of the 'tedious story' of the foot voyage, so it is reasonable to suppose that it remained for the walker a copious fund of anecdotes and jests.[89] During the summer of 1619 he wrote to Drummond informing him that James had listened approvingly to his story of his exploits and a proposed book (presumably his account of the voyage itself, rather than any of the other works he had been considering); six months later, however, in *News from the New World*, Jonson puts some self-deprecating commentary in the mouth of the Printer:

> one of our greatest poets – I know not how good a one – went to Edinburgh o'foot, and came back. Marry, he has been restive, they say, ever since, for we have had nothing from him; he has set out nothing, I am sure.
>
> (ll.141–3)

One might infer from this that a selective writer's block had beset him. His attempt to write out his 'journey into Scotland sung, with all the adventures' (*Und.* 43, 94–5) was overtaken – as he had been in the voyage itself – by Taylor, whose pamphlet narrative of the *Pennyles Pilgrimage* appeared just months after the two walkers had met in Leith. Jonson's relation of his journey was still apparently not ready for its public when

---

88 *H&S*, 11.385.
89 Donaldson, 2011, 447n.; and see Literary Record, *CWBJ* Online.

the draft was lost in the fire of 1623. But if we look beyond the months immediately following the walk, and beyond the plans explicitly outlined either to Drummond or the king, a more positive picture emerges. Ian Donaldson has acutely observed that 'most of Jonson's works with a rural setting post-date his walk to Scotland', but it can be argued that a more fundamental impact is traceable in Jonson's post-1618 writing, in what geographer John Wylie has referred to in other circumstances as the 'co-scripting of landscape, movement and biography'.[90] Hayden Lorimer and Katrin Lund have written of the ways in which walks are curated and collected.[91] From the writing of their 'day notes' onwards, in the abbreviated form of the 'Foot Voyage' and its pendants, or the papers that Jonson promised to send to Drummond if he failed to make it home, 'hewn [i.e. imperfect, rough-hewn] as they were' (*Informations*, ll.517–18), the poet and his companion can be seen to be curating their walk, and what Lorimer and Lund term the 'cartographies of collection' can be located in many of Jonson's masques and plays produced after 1619.[92]

The New Inn, first acted a decade after Jonson's return from Scotland, performs many manifestations of the mobility that the foot voyage itself either practised or witnessed. Andrew McRae has described this play, with its large cast of aristocrats (known and disguised), servants, coach-drivers, ostlers and inn-workers, as 'sophisticated in its treatment of mobility'.[93] The five acts that unfold within the significant locale of 'The Light Heart', presided over by a jovial host, Goodstock, are a physical realisation on the commercial stage of the ways in which inns acted as significant pauses, stopping places or staging posts on the road networks of early modern England. The 'spatial stories' enabled by the inn-setting relate directly to what cultural geographers have identified as the specific nature of hospitality in the history of mobilities. If, for Yi-Fu Tuan, place is pause, then this kind of hospitality too 'is produced through the negotiation of movement and mooring'.[94] Goodstock is the figure for this in *The New Inn*: his embodiment of hospitality in its commercial form, requiring transactions and reckonings, is expanded to take in other modes when the fifth act reveals that he is in fact an aristocratic estate owner in disguise. In him converge the

---

90 Donaldson, 2011, 27; Wylie, 2007, 208.
91 Lorimer and Lund, 2008, 186, 196n. Although that physical aspect of collection and curation also features in contemporary nature writing organised around the experience of walking: see, for example, the map of 'found things' placed at the start of Macfarlane, 2008.
92 Lorimer and Lund, 2008, 198.
93 McRae, 2009, 134.
94 Moiz and Gibson, 2008, 14.

commercialised space of the inn and the welcome offered by the 'private' house, joined in precisely the rhythm of movement and mooring that Jonson's walking demonstrate a decade or so earlier.

However, Goodstock's symbolic function is expansively transformed when, in an astonishing late revelation, he also presents himself as a traveller who has learned much from those he has met 'on the road':

> I am he
> Have measured all the shires of England over,
> Wales and her mountains, seen those wilder nations
> Of people in the Peak and Lancashire;
> Their pipers, fiddlers, rushers, puppet-masters,
> Jugglers and gypsies, all the sorts of canters,
> And colonies of beggars, tumblers, ape-carriers,
> For to those savages I was addicted,
> To search their natures and make odd discoveries!
>
> (5.5.92–100)

Goodstock/Lord Frampul's use of the language of 'discovery' here links him yet further with Jonson's pedestrian experiment, and recent editors of the play have discerned something quasi-autobiographical in this description of his experiences in the shires and nations during his period of errancy after quitting the family estate. The particular subsections of the community that Goodstock describes here share the itinerant condition, and his listing of their copious 'sorts', even as they are described as 'savages', represents a revaluation of such unsettlement. Goodstock prefigures such characters as Brome's Springlove in his confession of an addiction to travelling – an admission of compulsion that seemingly contradicts his use of the almost anthropological registers of 'discovery' that he also invokes. Such a revaluation, of course, also marks the gypsies of Jonson's 1621 masque for Buckingham, which may themselves have been shaped by the associations between Scots, gypsies and James's own court traced by Mark Netzloff.[95] Such associations are crystallised in the annual gypsy fair conducted from 1559 to 1628 at Roslin glen, in the north Esk valley just below Hawthornden, at which plays were performed.[96] The association of Jonson's writing with such explorations of the social and symbolic power of errancy seems to have been particularly strong: both John Taylor and Izaak Walton, presumably independently, credited him with the authorship of the thematically related play *Beggars Bush*,

95 Netzloff, 2001, esp. 774–7.
96 Netzloff, 2001, 776; Knowles, 2006, 271–2.

although its attribution to John Fletcher in 1647 has not seriously been doubted.[97]

Goodstock's experiences in *The New Inn* evoke the marginal and the itinerant on the roads and highways of England and Wales – workers and beggars, travellers and the destitute. Yet such figures cannot easily be abstracted from the specific forms of landscape and topography, the sense and importance of place implicit in the notion of the 'way'. If the inn as a pause or stopping place can be comprehended as a juncture in travel, the way, like the practice of pilgrimage, continues to imbue travel and its modes with a sense of direction – somewhere to come from, somewhere to get to, and all the places by, past or through which one travels. In the 'Foot Voyage', Jonson's way and its coordination of place through itinerary overlaps and intersects with the topographies of grand estates, adapting itself to their spatial organisations and structuring rhythms. The most spectacular of such intersections is the shaping of the walk around the extended Cavendish estates and households at Rufford, Welbeck, Worksop, Bolsover and beyond, which sets the scene for Jonson's subsequent engagements not only with the family but also with their place in the landscape. He was later to elegise both of the powerful Ogle sisters and perhaps to dramatise something of Cavendish himself in the figure of Lord Lovel in *The New Inn*, while Helen Ostovich has argued that *The Magnetic Lady* honours both of his parents.[98] Later, Jonson undertook two major commissions for Cavendish, authoring entertainments to welcome King Charles I to Welbeck Abbey in 1633 on his progress north for his Scottish coronation (a journey that itself consciously imitated that of his father in 1617) and then to welcome the king and his French queen consort, Henrietta Maria, to Bolsover Castle the following year.

James Knowles has commented on the 'self-conscious localism' of the Welbeck entertainment in particular.[99] There are references within the performance to Cavendish's Wardenship of Sherwood Forest, and the character Fitzale even wears a coat decorated with 'fragments of the forest' (ll.46–7). He is a record-keeper in a chorographical manner, who can report all the stories associated with the key sites in the counties of Derbyshire and Nottinghamshire across which Cavendish's domains extended. In the tilting section of the masque, six hooded knights compete for victory with obvious reference to the Robin Hood narrative and

---

97   J. Taylor, 1637, sig. B2v; Walton, 1655, 164–5. Cf. Bevan, 1983, 452.
98   Raylor, 1999, 435; *CWBJ*, 6.407–11.
99   *CWBJ*, 6.662.

its local links. While the Bolsover masque might seem less obviously 'placed', shaped as it is by the neoplatonism promoted by Henrietta Maria at court, its movements and operations nonetheless anchor it in this Cavendish property. Shifting between interior and exterior domains, between the decorated splendour of the Little Castle to the gardens with their Venus fountain, this masque is wholly 'site-specific', and draws attention to this fact in its closing speeches, where the audience and performers are deictically located 'here in Derbyshire' (l.133). The decision to structure the work around the spatial organisation of the site reveals the understanding, no doubt common to both patron and poet, of topography. By the time of the masque's composition Jonson was aged, and complaining of his immobility; a topographical memory of Bolsover dating back to 1618 may therefore have guided him. This process might have been helped by the possibility that the symbolism of Bolsover was itself shaped by *Pleasure Reconciled to Virtue*, the masque performed at court only months before Jonson's visit to the Little Castle, and which may have been the subject of discussion between Cavendish and Jonson when they met that summer.[100] If this were the case, these men might best be thought of as sharing a text-space, an articulated locus or topos, that was realised in various ways and at different moments during the period of their intellectual and social relationship.

The same may also apply to what is perhaps Jonson's last play, left unfinished at his death. In *The Sad Shepherd* the resonance of place seems to dominate the play, from the dialects spoken to the actions performed. In the printed version of the text we see this detailed tracing of landscape vividly taking place:

> The Scene is Sherwood: consisting of a landscape of forest, hills, valleys, cottages, a castle, a river, pastures, herds, flocks…
>
> (Persons of the Play, 28–31)

It has been suggested that the play owes something to Jonson's lost pastoral, the 'May-Lord', of which he spoke to Drummond in 1618–19 (*Informations*, ll.307–12). Certainly, scholarly speculation has been prompted by the common rural setting, the significant presence of a witch or sorcerer, and the shared character name of Alken. It is possible that the pastoral was a prose or verse romance, rather than a dramatic work; it is also possible that both it and the *Sad Shepherd* were intended for private rather than public stages.[101] Yet there is no mention of a

---

100 Raylor, 1999; Worsley, 2002, I.125–6.
101 *CWBJ*, 5.343–5; Knight, 2005, 129–31; Sanders, 2011, 86.

Robin Hood aspect to the 'May-Lord', so the *Sad Shepherd* must at least have been a significant reworking of any earlier material. Perhaps one of the ways in which Jonson developed it was to bring in a greater degree of specific local reference – he may have taken the sheerly generic or allegorical rural settings of his earlier pastoral and reworked them with particular references to the Midlands landscapes between Belvoir and Welbeck that he brought together in his 1618 progress. This, as well as his debt to Drayton's twenty-sixth song in *Poly-Olbion*, might account for the apparent continuity in the play between the vale of Belvoir and Sherwood Forest, which are actually some miles apart – it was the walk itself, as undertaken, that tied them together.[102]

Nowhere is this localism of the play, its rootedness in the Midlands landscapes that Jonson traversed in 1618, more visible than in its plotlines relating to venison and witchcraft. An epigram 'On Hypocrisy' published in *Witts Recreations* in 1640 declared: 'As Venison in a poor man's kitchin's rare / So Hypocrites and Usurers in Heaven are', and it is interesting to note the automatic, indeed proverbial, association of venison with the elite kitchen space.[103] It is exactly these assumed spatial dynamics of food culture that Maudlin the Papplewick witch in Jonson's play sets out to challenge and subvert through her actions. The discourse of venison is everywhere in Jonson's play, from the detailed description of the performance and attendant rituals of the hunt in Act One (tellingly identified as a 'sport' rather than in terms of food, a fact that will become important later in the play):

> For by his slot, his entries and his port,
> His frayings, fumets, he doth promise sport
> And standing 'fore the dogs.
>
> (1.2.12–14)

The 'slot' is the hoofprint or track that the stag leaves in the ground; 'frayings' refers to the marks left on trees by antlers as the deer scratch off old velvet; and 'fumets' refers to the heavily scented dung of the stag. The array of descriptive terms used here has long been thought to show that Jonson 'knew nothing at first hand about stag-hunting'.[104] This, though, cannot quite be true. To insist thus on the details of the hunt is not only to recall the forest status of Sherwood but also the experience of 1618 – at

---

102 Knight, 2005, 133.
103 Anon., 1640, sig. [I7].
104 *CWBJ*, 7.434; See also Berry, 2001, 14, 214–16. Jonson's freedom with the descriptive language of the hunt here will have to be accounted for in other ways.

Rufford, we learn, with the walkers in attendance, there was 'hunting and a stag killed, and hawking at the poult' (ll.94–5), while at Belvoir Jonson and his companion encountered the earl of Rutland and Lord Willoughby out hunting as they were walking down into the vale below the castle. The grounds of Welbeck Abbey itself accommodated red as well as fallow deer (l.159), and the venison sourced from both kinds of animal is at the heart of the social exchanges in which Jonson participates in the Cavendish estates, and in those over which he presides. By the same token, in his use of northern and Scots dialect terms and forms Jonson might be thought to be concentrating different localities fused together in the experience of the walk in the one locale, without thereby – perhaps paradoxically – stripping them of their local distinctiveness. It is not impossible that the Jonsonian fascination with idiom here draws the memory of the 'dog's language' of the Anglo-Scottish borders recorded in *Canesco* into the Cavendish orbit: hunting is as much a feature of their passage through the Ogle lands of Northumberland as it is of their sojourn in the Midlands.

In *The Sad Shepherd*, the kitchen as well as the forest proves to be a significant offstage space. When the venison, successfully hunted by Marion, has been acquired for the feast in the opening act, the stag's carcass is dispatched there for storage and subsequent preparation. This room will also later become the site for Maudlin's performance of her spells when she afflicts the cook, who is turning the deer-meat on the spit, with a kind of crippling arthritis (2.7.1–5). The kitchen belongs to Robin Hood's woodland household or lodge – and it is significant that he appears to reside in a lodge, since that would have helped knowledgeable early modern audiences to locate this Robin less as a dissident outlaw than as a legal official, the keeper in the forest whose job would come with a residence and certain rights to the venison for which he took duty of care. Robin is a 'woodman' in this play in the sense that he is a forest official working on behalf of the Crown within a defined geographic and administrative domain (in this instance, Cavendish's estates), and this means that he is not stealing from the rich to feed the poor but protecting the resources of the rich against the poaching activities of the local labouring sort. The vocabulary of forest 'walks' in this play, as its recent Cambridge editors have indicated, helps us to see that this Sherwood Forest is not just a romance locale but an administrative unit of the Crown, and therefore very much a product of the Cavendish and Rutland domains that Jonson had experienced directly on his 1618 journey through Nottinghamshire. Indeed, Jonson had shown his understanding of just such arrangements in appointing one of the Markham brothers his 'woodman' (l.134) during his brief spell as Welbeck's very own belated 'May-Lord' that summer.

At the heart of *The Sad Shepherd* lie questions of property and access. These are visibly figured in a battle over contested venison in which Robin is rather uncomfortably positioned as a representative of authority and elite protectionism. Marion, having brought back the stag killed for the feast, is impersonated by Maudlin, who seizes the meat for her own purposes. This rather specific onstage act of poaching provokes a tense discussion of rights. Returned to her own shape, Maudlin revisits Robin's household to 'thank him' for the gift of the venison that he has sent her. Maudlin's significant, though not wholly accurate, claim is that she has shared the seized venison out among her neighbours, a telling attack on the exclusivity of Robin's feast as well as on the life of luxury in which this small minority live in the forest enclave. Addressing Marion, she declares:

> But I knaw ye, a right free-hearted lady,
> Can spare it out of superfluity.
> I have departit it 'mong my good neighbours
> To speak your largesse.
>
> (2.6.36–9)

The use of terms like 'largesse' and 'superfluity', key to the accepted discourse of aristocratic hospitality at this time, is deliberately loaded. Marion, outraged by what she regards as social transgressions, accuses Maudlin of poaching the venison: 'What's ravished from me / I count it worse: as stol'n' (43–4). In truth she is somewhat closer to the reality in this accusation, since Maudlin's claim to any kind of proto-socialist sense of the good of the many is undermined by Scathlock's return with the carcass intact, requisitioned from her home. Unsurprisingly, it appears that she never did intend to distribute it among the needy.

It is this detail that connects the play by a direct line back to Jonson's Belvoir Castle visit in 1618. In March 1619, less than a year after Jonson's visit to the region, the trial and execution of several members of the Flower family had taken place. Their story, one of witchcraft accusations and neighbour testifying against neighbour, was also directly linked to the spaces and activities of Belvoir Castle and its patron-owner, Francis Manners, Earl of Rutland. Joan Flower, the matriarch of the group, and her daughter Margaret were said to have carried out 'damnable practices' against the earl's children.[105] A pamphlet written in support of the Manners family and published after the trial states

---

105 Anon., 1619, title page; see also Honeybone, 2008.

that 'Beauer Castle was a continuall Palace of entertainment and a daily receptacle for all sorts both rich and poor', thereby positioning its resident lord as a scion of hospitality.[106] It also describes how both Joan and Margaret found employment there, Joan as a 'chair-woman' or midwife, and Margaret 'as a continuall dweller in the Castle, looking both to the poultry a-broad and the wash-house within dores'.[107] It seems that Joan was not much liked by her neighbours, and rumours soon spread that she was a 'notorious Witch'.[108] Her daughter was in turn rumoured to be seen bringing illicit provisions from the castle to her mother's home. The connection to the purloined venison of *The Sad Shepherd* seems self-evident. The news of this scandal would have been brewing in the summer of 1618, when Jonson himself visited the castle, and was then hosted by Samuel Fleming, Rutland's chaplain, at Bottesford. It is tempting to speculate that he may have informed himself of the fuller details of the case once these became available in 1619. Certainly, the treatment of the cultural politics of witchcraft in this play has been deemed by several critics to be unusually sensitive and well-drawn.[109]

In the venison and witchcraft plotlines of *The Sad Shepherd*, the errant wanderings of Goodstock the Host in *The New Inn*, and the local particularities of the Welbeck and Bolsover entertainments of the 1630s, we can see the walk and its particular physical, cultural and sociopolitical landscapes resurfacing at later moments in Jonson's writing. This was undoubtedly – to use an appropriate metaphor – a threshold event for Jonson in many ways; the 'Foot Voyage' enables us to trace some of those resonances in all their rich detail. The landscape of early modern practice that emerges provides us in turn with fresh insight into the man who set off on foot from London on that July day in 1618.

---

106 Anon., 1619, sig. C2v.
107 Anon., 1619, sig. C2v. See also Gibson, 1999.
108 Anon., 1619, sig. C3.
109 See Sanders, 2011, 84–100, and Hayes, 1993.

3
SCENES OF HOSPITALITY

'As if they came to entertain us...'

One of the most prominent features of the 'Foot Voyage' is the writer's extraordinary effort to note the names and titles of the many people who hosted, escorted or encountered Jonson on the journey. While much of the other detail of the walk is abbreviated or omitted, this comprehensive enumerative effort reaches across the social spectrum, from earls, countesses, lords, ladies, baronets and knights to members of their households, minor gentry, clerics, aldermen, innkeepers and captains – encompassing, in all, more than 300 people. At times, however inclined to thoroughness, he gives up in the face of a crowd: despite mentioning by name many of the people Jonson met at Welbeck, for example, he can note only that 'diverse gentlemen' (l.140) dined with them on the Sunday; similarly, in Sir William Anstruther's house at Doncaster, he records simply that they 'found a long table full of gentlemen and ladies' (ll.239–40), while he mentions by name just a few of the 'diverse' who came to greet them on their arrival in York (l.298). On occasion, the names recorded are familiar or diminutive, most strikingly in the case of 'Randy' – for Randall – Fenwick in Northumberland, suggesting an easy informality in the relationship between Jonson and his companions here. At times, too, the writer is led into error: a would-be host at Buntingford is given the name Sir John Skinner, although investigation indicates that this is more likely to have been Sir John Caesar; at Ware, Sir Robert Mansell is correctly named on his first appearance but rechristened 'Sir Thomas' ten words later, probably because this was the name and title of Mansell's elder brother, a baronet and courtier. While the first slip suggests that Caesar was entirely unknown to the companion, the second might be thought to betray a degree of familiarity on the writer's part with the circles in which the Mansells moved. Perhaps, though, he was taking his cue from Jonson himself, who certainly knew Sir Robert and was no doubt familiar with his elder brother, too.

What purpose is served by the companion's habit of listing as many people as possible? It is telling to note that so many of these names occur in the amply repeated context of hospitality, one of the most consistently prominent features of the walk as it is recorded in the 'Foot Voyage' – these are, by and large, either Jonson's hosts or his fellow guests. 'While hospitality was often expressed in a series of private actions', Felicity Heal has argued, 'in the sense that it depended on an individual household and a particular host, it was integrated into a matrix of beliefs that were shared and articulated publicly...The duty of generosity was proclaimed from the pulpit, and urged in prescriptive literature. It was seen as one of the foundations of the moral economy.'[1] Yet the worrying possibility of the decay or abandonment of hospitality was also a focus for governmental and moralistic concern, signalled in everything from homilies to proclamations. Hospitality and the social anxieties focused on or through it were also a key concern for Jonson, animating the most notable poems in *The Forest* and developed in epigrams such as 'Inviting a Friend to Supper'. While the range of specific Jonsonian investments in hospitality has been the focus for debate, the centrality of the practice to him is not in any doubt.[2] One of the reasons for this centrality is Jonson's many-layered exploration of the economies of literary circulation and exchange, which are, of course, the economies through which he lives. In much of his work, the liberties, compromises, fidelities and constraints of different forms of writerly life are either explicitly or implicitly addressed, and an often subtle interplay between the performed and the stated, or the saying and the said, is traced or unfurled. Such is certainly the case with his lifelong engagement with the condition of patronage, worked out in relation to a variety of noble and royal masters and mistresses.[3] The practice of hospitality as examined or praised in, for example, 'To Penshurst' or 'To Sir Robert Wroth' positions the Jonsonian speaker as the guest or recipient, a claim which downplays or overlooks the poet's dependence on those praised – indeed, if Jonson was for a time tutor to Sir William Sidney, as has been suggested, then his status at the Penshurst table at the time when the poem was written would at least potentially have been at odds with that arrogated by the praising voice.[4] Yet patronage itself, as Jonson's deft 'Epistle to Sir

1 Heal, 1990, 2.
2 See Celovsky, 2009, for a recent and comprehensive discussion.
3 See M. Butler, 1995a, for an examination of Jonson's handling of this fundamental relationship.
4 Brennan and Kinnamon, 2003; Donaldson, 2011, 285–8.

Edward Sackville' demonstrates so powerfully, was articulated through the language of gifts, those circuits between donor and recipient that also serve to circulate their status. This, too, was a moral economy, or an economy of morality. Jonson privately criticised one of the grandest figures of the early English Jacobean period, the earl of Salisbury, for his failure as a patron: for the aggrieved client, as he told Drummond, Cecil's inadequate hospitality was a prime and telling example of such failure (*Informations*, ll.243–6).

In Heal's account of early modern practice, and in Jonson's Senecan tracing of what he carefully calls – exploiting the semantic openness of translation – both gifts and 'benefits' (*Und.* 13, l.5), the idea that such interactions make sense within a reciprocal economy of giving, and of debt and redemption, remains dominant.[5] Caleb Dalechamp, too, noted the 'manifold Profit wherewith' hospitality was rewarded, the 'increase of goods, honour and good reputation', for 'if any motive can draw our iron hearts to the performance of any vertuous act, it is the loadstone of utilitie'.[6] More recently, Linda Pollock has qualified such an understanding of hospitable acts, arguing that expectations of reciprocity could co-exist comfortably with genuinely affectionate or kindly behaviour: kindness could be the sentiment that animated an action that was of utility to its giver. Acts of hospitality, then, were more than a calculated gesture made with the presumption of commensurate benefit.

Kindness was linked to civility too, in the performance of 'hospitality and courtesy to strangers' enjoined by biblical teachings.[7] The traveller provided a particular test for the moral and affective economies of hospitality, particularly when the person travelling was neither kinsman nor associate. Inviting a friend to supper is one thing; the requirement that the door be opened to strangers might be a rather more difficult demand, and the point at which the hospitable encounter and its failure appear in their ethically starkest form.[8] Here one might be expected to touch most readily on such fundamentals as whether hospitality is freely given or in some way required, completed by some form of reciprocation or operating entirely independent of such considerations. So the ways in which, even in a post-Reformation society officially less accommodating to the pilgrim or the mendicant, the figure of the travelling stranger could reveal the meaning and state of hospitality, were of great interest. John Taylor's *Pennyles Pilgrimage*

5 Heal, 1990, 11, 20–2, 193.
6 Dalechamp, 1632, 82–3.
7 Pollock, 2011, 130, 134, 142, 153.
8 Heal, 1990, 192–222.

documents his testing of different forms of the relationship between guest and host, and while his welcome is often aided by prior acquaintance or a letter of introduction, it is also in places a keen examination of the current viability of the demand for hospitality – as well as, in its textual manifestation, a form of reciprocation or – if need be – payback.[9] Such testing of limits and conceptual structures is also implicit in the 'pure' travel of idealised or idealising vagrants such as Brome's Springlove: in *A Jovial Crew*, as Garrett Sullivan has suggested, 'beggarly travel is finally understood in terms of and as an opportunity for hospitality'.[10]

Jonson and his companion, of course, were not engaging in this kind of pure travel, although – as we have noted – the connotations of travelling by foot tend in this direction and were certainly those of which contemporary commentators were readily aware. The hospitality Jonson received along the way, however, was clearly predominant in his companion's sense of what was worthy of record about the voyage. We hear of 'great entertainment' at Bottesford and Bawtry, 'open entertainments' at Welbeck, 'all freedom and full entertainment' at Dunfermline, and 'extraordinary grace and entertainment' at Rufford (ll.66, 222, 105, 555–6, 94–5). Particular note is made of Jonson's welcome at Worksop Manor, Skelbrooke, York, Berwick upon Tweed and Edinburgh. Dinners and banquets are staged in his honour.[11] Food and, particularly, drink are vital tokens in these exchanges, and the account makes a point of noting not just the kinds of drink offered – which could themselves be markers of esteem, or mark a difference between good hosts and bad – but their occasions. So, a drunken parson at Bottesford insists they try the full range of local ales; a milkmaid prepares a 'merrybub' or syllabub for them in a Northumbrian loan; Sir William Bowyer marks the crossing of the border north of Berwick with a glass of wine; Jonson takes his leave of the earl of Winton at Prestonpans 'with a cup of sack' (l.514). The documentation in the 'Foot Voyage' of the many gifts given and honours done to Jonson also make sense in this accounting of hospitality. There are minor and, sometimes, perplexing gifts, such as the 'forest bill' (l.18) received at Puckeridge and the 'fustian letter' (l.47) sent by William Folkingham at Stamford, or more intriguing donations like Lukin's wheel at Welbeck. Grander ceremonial welcomes and entertainments are provided, including the bull-baiting and fireworks of Newark, the dancing giants of Pontefract, the piper-led evening procession from Bawtry

---

9 Heal, 1990, 210–16.
10 Sullivan, 1998, 191.
11 Cf. the royal requirement that the duke of Wurtemberg should be asked 'either to dinner or a banckett' during his 1608 tour of England: Heal, 1990, 204.

to Doncaster, and the crowds and throngs at various points from Royston to Edinburgh. The account's patchy details of financial transactions also play a part in its documentation of the welcome received by Jonson. Although such references say nothing about the actual costs of undertaking the walk, or any prices paid for board, lodging or logistical support, they do record the careful expenditure of goods in a gift economy in which Jonson is both giver and recipient. While he receives 'subscriptions' from the earl of Rutland and Lord Willoughby at Belvoir, for example, he also gives money to a scullion, while at Newcastle the viaticum tendered to him complements his gift of a piece to the master of the free school. Such an ethic of gift-giving prevailed – to everyone's advantage – over mere commerce at the postmaster's house in Witham, 'where the gentlewoman would give no reckoning, but the bounty of my gossip made it dearer than an inn' (ll.51–3). And as we have noted in our previous chapter, Jonson can sometimes be seen to reciprocate with a toast of his own composition, an extempore verse, a riddle or epitaph, or an autograph copy of one of his finer works. All these dinners, banquets, salutes and presentations constitute elaborate and often public contributions to Jonson's entertainment, in the wider early modern sense – festive performances of hospitality, in which the guest himself will play a full and proper part.

Hosts and patrons

Although the staging of these hospitable scenes is a consistent thread all along the itinerary of the 'Foot Voyage', there is significant variation of kind among Jonson's hosts – indeed, the words 'host' and 'hostess' themselves only occur in relation to innkeepers. Theoretically, lodging in inns enabled the traveller to avoid being caught up in the 'reciprocal pressures' and codes of etiquette involved in staying in a private house.[12] However, as the example of the Witham hostess shows, the companion is as acutely aware as John Taylor of the importance and performance of public hospitality, and judgement is not infrequently pronounced. At Huntingdon, for example, Taylor met with an innkeeper who 'did drinke and beginne Healths like a Horse-leech…In a word, as hee is a Poste, hee dranke poste, striuing and calling by all meanes to make the Reckoning great, or to make vs men of great reckoning.'[13] The traveller's astonished disgruntlement shows that his

12 Heal, 1990, 194–5, 202, 208–9.
13 *PP*, sig. G2.

host had contravened expectations. In this case Taylor's embarrass-
ment was saved by his companion settling the bill; the writer, of course,
had the last laugh, immortalising the innkeeper's incivility in print.
The 'Foot Voyage' expresses rather briefer opinions: at Ware, we learn,
'my fat hostess commended me with a token' (l.16), while at Caxton, by
contrast, 'I fell out with mine hostess' (l.30); John Bate or Bates of
Stamford is described as 'my pleasant host' (l.45), whereas the
unnamed innholder at Chester-le-Street is a 'drunken disordered fellow, but she' – the hostess – 'a good wife' (l.380).

   Jonson's first important encounter with patrons along the way, however, took a somewhat unusual form. At Waltham, the account says, they
were greeted by Lady Mary Wroth, who had come out to meet Jonson
rather than welcoming him to her house at Loughton, 6 miles to the east.
Jonson dedicated the published text of *The Alchemist* to her, and she was
the addressee of several epigrams. While her star was waning somewhat by
1618, she continued to be sufficiently in favour for the king to send her the
gift of a buck in 1621.[14] Her presence at the roadside here may have meant
that she was staying at the time with her kinsman, Lord Edward Denny, at
Waltham Abbey.[15] This salute to Jonson is a mark of respect from the
Sidney family, to be sure, but also an acknowledgement from one of
Jonson's most esteemed, wealthy and powerful patrons, William
Herbert, third earl of Pembroke, Wroth's cousin and, it is generally
agreed, her lover. As Drummond of Hawthornden was to recall, Jonson
claimed that 'every first day of the new year he had £20 sent him from the
earl of Pembroke to buy books'.[16] Pembroke had been Jonson's protector
from the early years of James's reign, when the playwright had dedicated
Sejanus to him, and Pembroke had helped Jonson in his difficulties over
Eastward Ho! 'I must expect, at your Lordship's hand, the protection of
truth and liberty', Jonson wrote in his dedication of the 1616 *Epigrams* to
Pembroke; the volume itself included a conspicuous panegyric to his
patron.[17] Pembroke's appointment as Lord Chamberlain in 1615 made
him even more valuable to Jonson: while his office gave him the responsibility for the royal household's affairs, his role also, crucially, included the
organisation of court entertainments, of masques and plays, and the
licensing of theatres.[18] Despite the political threat posed by the new

14 *Epigr.* 103, 105; *Und.* 47; *CSPD, 1619–23,* 278.
15 *ODNB.*
16 *Informations,* l.375.
17 Letter 8; *Epigr.* ll.11–12; *Epigr.* 102.
18 *ODNB.*

marquis of Buckingham, Pembroke remained one of the most senior and powerful of James's trusted officials. The Pembroke connection is also discernible in the otherwise shadowy trio of 'Mr Ed Kerry, Mr Harbert and Mr Powell' (ll.5–6) who accompanied Wroth that morning. As we noted in our introduction, Sir Henry Herbert, Pembroke's kinsman, was to secure the de facto Mastership of the Revels in 1623 and resided at Woodford, only a few miles from the Wroth estate; Jonson's connection to the family is attested in an epigram to Henry's elder brother Edward, Lord Herbert of Cherbury.[19] Their brother George, the poet, was at Cambridge in 1618, but occasionally visited his mother in London; either he or Henry might have been the Mr Herbert or Harbert at Waltham, although it should be noted that there are other plausible candidates.[20] Pembroke's burgeoning political network, built to counter-act Buckingham's influence in the 1620s, was to include several members of the Herbert family, with George himself sitting as an MP in 1624–5. One of Pembroke's other clients, and MP for Portsmouth in 1625, was Sir Benjamin Rudyerd, to whom Jonson had already addressed three epigrams.[21]

A more obviously hospitable encounter took place further along the way, when Jonson and his companion left the post route to travel to Belvoir castle, where they stayed for a number of nights as the guests of Francis Manners, sixth earl of Rutland. The 'Foot Voyage' reveals that they were there lodged in the oldest part of the castle, Staunton Tower, but little else about the visit – it seems that a bout of illness excluded the companion from events, and he made no attempt to fill in the gaps in the narrative caused by his absence. However, the companion makes up for this by providing such a detailed account of their stay on the estates and among the extended networks of William Cavendish, his mother and his aunt. Between them they held properties including the abbeys of Rufford and Welbeck in Nottinghamshire, the manor of Pontefract in Yorkshire's West Riding, and estates and lands up the Northumbrian coast. The hospitable embrace of this family provided grand lodgings, guidance and entertainment for much of the walk

19 *Epigr.* 106.
20 Herbert, 1941, 367–70, 457. The abbreviated first name given to Mr 'Kerry' here – presumably a Carey or similar – might actually belong to Mr Herbert. If so, then he might be Edward Herbert, of the Montgomery branch of the family, another Pembroke client who was called to the bar in 1618. This Edward was later to marry the widow of the courtier Thomas Carey. See HP04.
21 *Epigr.* 121, 122, 123; V. Rowe, 1935, 242–56; O'Farrell, 2011, 161, 193–5.

Figure 5 Detail of the John Speed map of Nottinghamshire, from *Theatre of the Empire of Great Britaine*, 1612. The area shown includes Jonson's route from Kneesall (bottom right) to Bawtry ('Bantre', top) via Rufford ('Rughforde'), Edwinstow, Welbeck Abbey, Worksop Manor ('The Maner') and Hodsock Priory ('Hodsoks'). To the south-west of Bawtry is Harworth, the parish of John Craven (see p.157). © Cambridge University Library.

between the Trent and the Tweed; its earliest intimations were perhaps registered at Newark, where the 'gentlemen of the country, especially the Markhams' (l.84) kept Jonson company for around three days. They may have included Gervase Markham, who – as we have noted above – would undertake his own walk north in 1622.[22] Gervase's branch of the Markham family had held the manor of Cotham, just south of Newark, but by 1616 had sold it to Sir Charles Cavendish of Welbeck. His heir, Sir William, had probably inherited a residual relationship with the Markhams along with their former lands. It is possible, however, that these men might have been from the Ollerton branch of the family, whose estates lay towards Rufford. Thomas Markham of Ollerton had been an affiliate of the seventh earl of Shrewsbury, and associated with the Shrewsburys' properties of Rufford and Worksop. His widow, Mary, and several of their sons were to welcome Jonson to Worksop Manor a few days later.

Jonson's first host after Newark was Jane Talbot (née Ogle), countess of Shrewsbury, widow of the recently deceased eighth earl and aunt to William Cavendish. In contrast to Mary, impoverished widow of the seventh earl, Gilbert, Jane was a wealthy Protestant, possessing the castles of Bothal and Ogle in Northumberland through her Ogle inheritance.[23] She was well known for the hospitality she provided at Rufford, and the 'Foot Voyage' presents a suitably Jonsonian image of a large and well-ordered household, including the gentlemen attendants, lawyers and land agents who run her affairs and provide educated company. Their entertainment included a day spent hunting and hawking, with a stag killed for their benefit. The gracious image of the lady and her aristocratic world in the 'Foot Voyage' honoured both Jane Talbot and her guest, a fact Jonson's companion was keen to emphasise: such entertainment can be read as the performance of precisely the role that royal proclamations sought to rekindle in the wayward hearts of early Stuart nobility and gentry. But Jane Talbot was not as secure as this apparently entrenched and seamlessly noble scene implied. Although a substantial heiress, she was in 1618 enmeshed in legal battles over the estate of her deceased brother-in-law, Gilbert. Sir William Cavendish, son of her sister Catherine, was an executor of the late earl's will.[24] It was being disputed by the husbands of Gilbert's three daughters, the earls Thomas of Arundel and William of Pembroke, and Lord Ruthin. Substantial quantities of both money and land were at stake. Just before his death in February 1618, Jane's husband had been fighting to recover annuities of about £17,000 from the estate that had been

22 *ODNB*.
23 *HMCS*, 19.3.
24 NA, DD4P/46/6.

blocked by these nobles.[25] Jane also risked losing Rufford to another of Gilbert's sisters, the impoverished Grace, in a separate action.[26] So while she fulfilled the role of beneficent hostess, Jane Talbot needed support to counter the powerful sway of the earls of Pembroke and Arundel at court. Jonson's own court connections, and perhaps even his ties to Pembroke, might well have added a layer of 'utility' to such generosity – after all, despite travelling on foot, Jonson came not as a mendicant but as the king's poet, a royal pensioner, and a figure of genuine and evident fame. His presence might therefore be thought an opportunity for hosts with something to prove or a suit to pursue, as well as a chance for the display of proper hospitality. The countess may have hoped that a good impression would be communicated through Jonson to influential figures in the royal household, and ultimately to his master, the king.

If the countess of Shrewsbury's generosity to Jonson was noteworthy, it was evidently surpassed by the hospitality provided by Sir William Cavendish and his mother at Welbeck. We see Jonson being forwarded along the Shrewsbury–Ogle–Cavendish network, the countess giving 'charge of my gossip' (l.96) to one of Sir William's servants as they walked the 12 miles from Rufford to Welbeck Abbey. At Welbeck the travellers were to be offered all 'open entertainments', including food and lodgings, but also the personal attention and courtesy of Sir William himself. The guided tour they received from their host on their arrival, his subsequent escorting of Jonson to see the 'delicate little house' (l.193) of Bolsover, and the riding display to which the poet was memorably treated, all demonstrate the substantial investment made by Cavendish in this visit. Again, the account at points shadows the registers of Jonsonian estate poetry – on a walk through the park at Welbeck 'a herd of huge grown stags made towards us as if they came to entertain us' (ll.159–60), thus recalling the 'seasoned deer' of Penshurst, given by the personified park itself to its lord 'When thou wouldst feast, or exercise thy friends' (*For.* 2, ll.20–1), or the 'loud stag' hunted on the Wroth estate at Durrants (*For.* 3, l.22). The most exceptional of Cavendish's hospitable gestures, however, is his investiture of Jonson with his own lordly status at his departure for Rufford on the second day of his guest's visit. Such extraordinary liberality recalls the zenith of hospitality as set out in a central passage of 'To Penshurst', where the poem describes how the host's generosity transforms his guest into a version of himself:

25 *WP*, no. 50.
26 NA, DD/SR/225/158.

Where comes no guest but is allowed to eat,
Without his fear, and of thy lord's own meat:
Where the same beer and bread, and self-same wine,
That is His Lordship's, shall be also mine.
And I not fain to sit (as some, this day,
At great men's tables) and yet dine away.
Here no man tells my cups; nor, standing by,
A waiter, doth my gluttony envy;
But gives me what I call, and lets me eat;
He knows below he shall find plenty of meat.
Thy tables hoard not up for the next day,
Nor, when I take my lodging, need I pray
For fire, or lights, or livery: all is there,
As if thou, then, wert mine, or I reigned here...

                              (*For.* 2, ll.61–74)

Cavendish's actions switch the grammatical mood of this passage, making the subjunctive indicative in actually appointing Jonson the master of Welbeck in his absence. 'Which authority [Jonson] did as freely put in execution' (l.132), the account says, the new master throwing open the wine cellar and commanding a buck to be killed, inviting guests to dinner and appointing men to positions in his 'household'. 'Mr Steward with other gentlemen would not be persuaded to sit but wait' (ll.140–1), the companion notes, the servants ceremonially acknowledging Jonson's transformed status. Half of a second buck was then sent, at Jonson's command, to Sir Thomas Brudenell at Worksop. Venison was a 'status food', 'the most gift-ascribed of all items of consumption', with strong elite associations and further removed from commercial exchange than other comestibles.[27] Jonson was later to be offered a buck by Sir Gervase Clifton and received one from the countess of Shrewsbury on his arrival at Pontefract; that he could order the slaughter of fallow deer from the Welbeck deer park establishes his temporary powers in the most visible of ways. Thus, even at what must still have been an early stage in their relationship, Cavendish allowed Jonson the 'unusual degree of licence' evident in their later exchanges.[28] It was a freedom in which Jonson clearly revelled, and in which he could live out the triumph of his own vision of hospitality.

The question of motive remains, however. Was this kindness or fondness on the part of the Cavendishes, or might there have been

27 See Heal, 2008, 55–62, quotation at 57.
28 N. Rowe, 1994, 200.

other considerations in play? William had succeeded his father in April 1617, and had now – as the account makes clear – also secured a very advantageous marriage to Elizabeth Bassett at his mother's behest.[29] His position, however, was not secure: the moment was one of both opportunity and danger. As we have seen, he was embroiled in his dispute over Gilbert Talbot's will with the powerful earls of Pembroke and Arundel, worrying about the retrieval of around £17,000 owed to his family by the estate. He was also nervous about any residual liabilities for which he, as executor, might be responsible. Pembroke and Arundel wanted him to surrender his executorship, in order for them to settle the estate in their own favour. In a memo to himself written earlier in 1618, Cavendish noted, 'the Lords will bee wonderfull ernest with mee aboute partinge with the exseqetorship wherin I must bee excedinge carfull uppon what termes I doe itt, because itt keepes mee safe & upright agaynst ther malice or uniust procedinges'.[30] His anxieties over the earls' considerably greater influence at court were evident, fearing 'theyr power woulde over bowe uss'. But Sir William was open to negotiation in his desire to secure 'the Honor off A Viscounte' and was offering to give up his executorship in return for the earls' efforts to procure him a title – a difficult labour of negotiation that eventually bore fruit in his elevation to the title of Lord Mansfield in 1620.[31]

Jonson's visit may well have been an element in Cavendish's plan to seize the opportunities presented by this climacteric moment. Its ostensible purpose appears to have been the collaboration with John Smithson on the monument to Sir Charles Cavendish in the church at Bolsover, where Sir William and his mother – to whom the monument is credited in its inscription – were seeking to establish a family mausoleum of the kind which his Midlands neighbours, the earls of Rutland, had established at Bottesford.[32] It is not impossible that the walk itself and elements in its itinerary grew from this commission: Sir Charles Cavendish had died only two months before George Garrard reported Jonson's plan for his northwards journey, and while Jonson's visit to the church at Bottesford was no doubt partly an act of piety towards the memory of his patron, Elizabeth Sidney, countess of Rutland, whose monument was then under construction, it might also have been a preparation for the Bolsover commission.[33]

29 Worsley, 2002, I.186.
30 UNL, Pw 1/553; NA, DD/4P/46/10. See also Worsley, 2002, I.183–6.
31 UNL, Pw 1/554; BL, MS Add 70,499, ff.95, 99, 104.
32 On the elder Lady Cavendish's leading role in this, see Worsley, 2002, I.186.
33 See 'Foot Voyage', note to ll.60–1.

In displaying his inheritance and his aspirations to their guest, treating him with filial reverence to stories of his father's achievements and triumphs, and putting both house and provisions at his disposal, Cavendish was most probably showing himself and his view of his ancestral dignity and honour to best advantage, hoping that Jonson could help to bolster his claim to the kind of standing in society best reflected in titles and royal favour. As should be clear, though, this was not Sir William's scheme alone: that his mother was integral to the whole project is symbolically evident from the account's emphatic doubling of the grand gesture, Mr Carnaby sent back from Rufford to Welbeck to convey the message 'that my lady', too, and in case Jonson was in any doubt, 'resigned all power and authority to him to do what he pleased' (ll.144–5). In August 1619, the king did visit Welbeck, knighting William's brother, Charles, and his lawyer, Edward Richardson, both of whom are mentioned in the 'Foot Voyage'. James was to grace the estate with his presence again when on progress in August 1624.[34] Jonson's subsequent writing in the Cavendish interest and for Cavendish occasions testifies to the mutual benefit, and the loyalty, generated by the understanding apparently cemented during this week at Welbeck: for Jonson, Cavendish was to become 'next the King, my best patron', while the playwright was in turn to figure himself as Cavendish's 'truest beadsman and most thankful servant'.[35] At Welbeck we see this relationship finding its form through an elaborate performance of hospitality in which the preferences, ideals and aspirations of both patron and client found compelling expression.

Civic sociability

As we have noted, an Ogle–Cavendish network sustained Jonson long after he had departed from Welbeck. Between Hodsock and Pontefract, and again between Newcastle and Berwick, his hosts were kinsmen or clients of Sir William Cavendish or, just as usually, Jane, countess of Shrewsbury. North of Bothal, the companion is careful to note how Lady Mary Widdrington, 'being sent for to her only sister, my lady Lampton… lying then extreme sick…hearing my gossip Jonson was a coming would not stir till she saw him, deferring her going two days only to give my gossip entertainment' (ll.410–14). Cousins to Jane and Catherine Ogle, the Widdringtons were either keen or requested to continue the solicitude

34 *NP*, 4.994.
35 *CWBJ*, Letters 16 and 17.

shown to Jonson by their kinsfolk further south. A party led by Sir Henry Widdrington collected Jonson from Bothal Castle with the aim of escorting him on his way, 'and quit his horses and went on foot with us, Mr Carnaby the elder and Mr Johnson, the countess of Shrewsbury's chaplain doing the like, and Mr Randall Fenwick doing the like' (ll.407–9). Once again, hunting was arranged for their entertainment. Once again, dining and drinking punctuated the procession.

Jonson and his companion were also afforded an impressive welcome by other hosts along the way. In York, he was given the honour of being taken in a coach to enjoy the celebrated hospitality of Tobie Matthew, the archbishop, at his Bishopthorpe palace, while the companion notes two complementary aspects of bishop Neile's generosity to Jonson at Durham, both of which show 'My lord using him with all the love and respect that could be':

> the plenty of meat, variety of dishes and state of service was such as I saw not the like since our coming forth. But that which exceeded all the rest was my lord's extraordinary and strange freedom and familiarity with my gossip, and his grace and favour for his sake to us.
>
> (ll.348–52)

The account's sometimes awed documentation of the beneficence bestowed by noble patrons and senior clerics, however, runs the risk of overshadowing the entertainment the travellers received from the civic leadership of many of the towns through which they passed. Such hospitality, taking place outside Jonson's patronage relationships and away from the familiar topography of the noble estate, might seem less eye-catching or familiar, but it is a crucial component of the walk as recorded.

As a member of the Tylers' and Bricklayers' Company in London, Jonson was no stranger to this civic world. He was initially made free of the company in 1594; while his membership lapsed for a number of years, the company appears to have celebrated his return to the fold in 1611, with 10s 8d spent 'for wine and sugar for Benjamin Jonson'.[36] The theatrical profession relied on the structures of the London liveried companies to facilitate its business, with apprentice players bound to freemen just as John Catlin was bound to Jonson in 1612. To a poet or a player, guild or company membership brought both a particular kind of social status and the possibility of work, as Jonson well knew.[37]

---

36 Donaldson, 2011, 89.
37 Donaldson, 2011, 89–90; Kathman, 2004, 16, 31, 32.

Jonson's civic connections, of course, were necessarily metropolitan. What is perhaps most remarkable about his reception in the urban communities of the 'Foot Voyage' is the alacrity with which he was greeted in towns far from London. The extent of the hospitality offered suggests that he was already well known in such places, at least by reputation and status; no doubt, too, his own company membership afforded him recognition from such civic elites. By the 1600s, almost all the towns and cities that granted him a civic reception had received royal charters of incorporation or equivalent status; they were known as corporations or boroughs in England, and burghs in Scotland. Their charters gave these towns judicial, political and trading privileges, and in doing so cemented in place an oligarchy of those who had gained membership of merchant companies or craft guilds and the accompanying status of freeman, burgess or citizen. Although these communities gave protection to all those included, they nonetheless excluded the less fortunate or prosperous from any part in local government. As Laura Stewart observes of Edinburgh, there was 'an acute awareness that those who governed came from an exclusive social group, unrepresentative of the bulk of the urban population'.[38]

Each of these communities had its corporate structure laid out in its charter. In Huntingdon the civic affairs were run by the bailiffs and burgesses on a common council of twenty-four, some of whom kept Jonson 'continual company' (l.35) for two nights; in 1630 they formed themselves into a new style of mayor, aldermen and burgesses on a council reduced to twelve members, concentrating power in the hands of the 'better Burgesses'.[39] Newark was reorganised in 1625, with its previous government by one alderman and twelve assistants giving way to a more familiar structure of mayor and aldermen. The use of the plural 'aldermen' to describe Newark's civic leadership in the 'Foot Voyage' may indicate that this reform was merely the formal recognition of a terminological change that had already taken place in practice, although the records of the corporation sustain the official designations.[40] In Durham, the city was governed by 'a body politic and corporate' of a mayor, twelve aldermen and twenty-four common burgesses on a common council, with powers to hold borough courts.[41] In Doncaster the structure was similar, but the mayor and one alderman were

38 L. Stewart, 2006, 23.
39 HLA, H26/17, ff.1–2, 6.
40 See NA, DC/NW/3/1/1, and C. Brown, 1879, 65.
41 DCRO, Du 1/1/3; DA, AB 10/8.

also justices of the peace, with one of whom Jonson made 'good sport' (l.243) at dinner. In Scotland, the equivalent of the mayor was the provost, assisted by a council of twelve burgesses, who unlike in England – and *pace* the terminology used in the 'Foot Voyage' – were called councillors or magistrates rather than aldermen. Four of them were elected bailiffs each year. On the day before Jonson was made an honorary burgess in Edinburgh, the council nominated those standing for election to such office for 1618–19. James Ainslie, the burgess charged with arranging Jonson's banquet, was a bailiff in 1617–18.[42] Jonson's request to Drummond of Hawthornden to send him information 'touching the government of Edinburgh', shows him to have been exploring how this type of local government worked in Scotland, with its distinct system of civic representation in the Convention of Royal Burghs.[43]

Jonson's works, it has been argued, often reflected his 'long-term ruminations' on 'notions of community' and commonwealth.[44] The civic officials who hosted him in 1618 were keenly aware of their place within their urban communities, the maintenance of their power depending on the preservation of reputations and social status.[45] Boroughs and corporations were sometimes described as little 'commonwealths' in the early modern period, each one being 'a Common wealth among themselves'; they were the 'gathering together of society and men' so 'that they might in all things live the more commodiously together and frame themselves a Commonwealth', thus creating what Phil Withington has termed 'city commonwealths'.[46] With that name came its humanist associations with the concepts of *communitas*, civic duty and virtue, in which the responsibility to provide hospitality for one another and for the stranger was rooted. A city commonwealth was also meant to be an Aristotelian political 'community of equals, aiming at the best life possible', to the benefit of all, governors and governed alike.[47] In the most oligarchic of England's boroughs, those excluded from civic benefits would have been unlikely to see things this way. Within the civic community, however, it was supposed that 'no other officer of the [Crown] or other [had] authority to entermeddle amongst them'.[48] In its election of its own council, and its legal protection from some jurisdictions, such an

42 L. Stewart, 2006, 5–6, 23, 341–2.
43 Letter 14, ll.9–10; MacDonald, 2007, 5–9.
44 Sanders, 1998, 182–3.
45 Braddick, 2001, 171–3.
46 Withington, 2005, 10–11, quoting Thomas Wilson and Henry Manship.
47 Aristotle, 1996, 176.
48 Manship, quoted by Withington, 2005, 11.

incorporated town could be viewed as employing some republican ideals of local government within a wider monarchical context.

In their concern to conserve, and sometimes to extend, their privileges, these civic communities were necessarily anxious to establish good relations with the king in whose hands the guarantee of their status ultimately lay. James's arrival on the English throne in 1603 had worried civic officials, who rushed to get his confirmation of their charters of incorporation. His progress north in 1617 had provided an opportunity for some of them to press their town's case, prompting displays of ostentatious civic hospitality by some of the same men who were to welcome Jonson a year later. Gilded or enamelled silver bowls were presented to James at cities and towns including Lincoln, York, Ripon and Durham; at Newcastle he was given 'a great standing Bowl, to the value of an hundred Jacobuses, and an hundred marks in gold', while at Edinburgh he received 'ane purse contening five hundreth double angellis laid in a silver basing double overgilt'.[49] At Doncaster, the king was given £50, with over £40 paid to the attendant ushers, grooms and trumpeters. Further money was laid out on behalf of a Mr Hepburn, a 'gentleman usher to the kinge' on his return from Scotland, for his charges at Mr Carver's, where Jonson was also to stay.[50] At Durham, the connection between what was being given and what was sought was explicitly made. 'Most gratious Soueraigne what vnspeakable ioy is this your highnes presence', said the mayor, before reminding James that he 'found this Cyttie inabled with diuers liberties, and priviledges, [which you] gaue vnto vs the same againe, and afterwards of your Gracious bountie confirmed them'; therefore, he continued, 'we humblie beseech your Ma[jes]tie conteynue your favour…And in token of our loue and Loyaltie' he delivered the 'siluer boule guilt' with Durham's emblem, the cow, engraved upon it. Before the king had ridden 40 yards further, an apprentice delivered the same message in verse.[51]

So Jonson was received in a series of little commonwealths on his way north: as well as at Huntingdon, Newark, Doncaster, Durham and Edinburgh, the presence of civic officers or 'the chief of the town' is clearly registered in Bawtry, Pontefract, Newcastle and Berwick, while the honour of burgess was conferred on both Jonson and his companion at Dunfermline. In all of these places, the civic leaders took a primary role in the provision of the hospitality that the 'Foot Voyage' is so concerned to

49 *NP*, 3.262, 270, 274, 277, 280, 317.
50 DA, AB6/2/159, pp.4–5, 10.
51 DCA, DU 1/4/4: ff.21–2; *NP*, 3.277.

document. While it was virtuous for a gentleman to be hospitable in the country, civic virtue was to be found in entertainment offered to visitors, whether strangers or high dignitaries, by civic officials.[52] If, as Withington observes, the 'public service of private citizens is a fundamental virtue', the hospitality which fulfilled that ideal was to be encouraged and, further, venerated.[53] Less obviously moral, but nonetheless important, was the need felt by early modern officials to maintain the reputation on which their authority was based. Furthermore, they were anxious to uphold the collective reputation of their town and its civic dignity. In their honorable reception of visitors, officials showed 'a sensitivity to the collective honour of the corporation', and indeed 'reputation-enhancing gestures were even more mandatory in the civic world than in the countryside'.[54] The ritualised entertainment extended by English and Scottish civic commun- ities to King James the previous year, the staged royal entries into towns, and the offering of gold and silver were undertaken not only to honour the king but also to maintain the dignified reputation of each town or city and its governors. As William Lithgow wrote of Edinburgh, the 'Prouost, Bailies, Counsel, Senate graue, / Stood plac'd in ra[n]ks, their King for to receaue', 'Glistring in Golde, most glorious to the eye...In richest Veluet Gownes'; they were a 'splendant Throng'.[55]

Such hospitality is readily visible in the 'Foot Voyage', with leaders welcoming Jonson and keeping him company for many hours at a time. Indeed, the Merchant Adventurers of Newcastle who entertained Jonson were also members of the Hostmen's Company, whose traditional role had been to offer hospitality to 'strangers', generally those merchants arriving at its quays.[56] The provision of lodging, food and drink was perhaps the most fundamental requisite of such entertainment, a basic constituent of sociability. The interaction between Jonson and his civic hosts repeatedly involved the ritualised ceremony of drinking and feast- ing incumbent on both under laws of civility and conviviality that Jonson himself, in his own domains, sought to codify.[57] In Dunfermline, where Jonson and his companion 'drank hard, with some six more, and were made burgesses', the linkage between the act of drinking and the cere- monial granting of civic status was made explicit. In sharing their drink, Jonson was being included within their exclusive circle, in both social

52 Heal, 1990, 2–5, 23–4, 99–101; Pollock, 2011, 130–1, 139, 153.
53 Withington, 2005, 54.
54 Braddick, 2001, 166–87; Heal, 1990, 300–2.
55 Lithgow, 1618, sigs. E3v–4.
56 HR, xiii, xxviii–xxix; Newton, 2006, 38.
57 CWBJ, 5.418–21; O'Callaghan, 2004, 41; O'Callaghan, 2007, 1, 77, 168.

and civic spheres.[58] This necessarily distanced those outside that circle, distinguishing the drinkers of burnt wine, claret and fine hollock from those beneath them in the ale-houses, a contrast neatly captured in William Marshall's engraving, 'The Lawes of Drinking', prefaced to Richard Brathwaite's *Solemne Joviall Disputation*.[59]

Music is another frequently encountered component in the entertainment offered to Jonson by his civic hosts. It was described as a 'civil necessity', 'for the better attaynynge [of] the knowledge of a publike weale' in the musical and social harmony it brought.[60] In Durham, Jonson was woken by the shawms of the town's waits, paid by the corporation to perform at official occasions or to honour a noted guest.[61] 'Preamble' was to refer to such 'town-music' in Jonson's *Tale of A Tub* (1.4.24). Will Kemp had been equally honoured on his arrival in Norwich at the conclusion to his dance from London, admiring 'their excellency in wind instruments' that 'refreshed my weariness'.[62] At Pontefract, the walkers found 'music prepared to meet us' (ll.256–7), anchoring the spectacular scenes of dancing giants and pressing crowds. The practised and extravagant hospitality of the Newcastle elite was legendary: nine years after Jonson's visit, Christopher Wandesford was to complain that 'Mr Maior's greate peces of beife and the profuse intertainment we had from the gentlemen in those parts...indaingered our healths more then the Spaniards did our coastes.'[63] So the music and forty-year-old hollock with which Jonson was entertained at the house of William Bonner – a Hostman of long standing – may not have been an unaccustomed treat for an honoured guest. Such generosity, however, no doubt called for a response – hence Jonson's gift of money to the master of the town's free school, and the possibility that he flattered them with an extempore riddle honouring the church of St Nicholas. Hence, too, their reciprocal gift at his departure, ensuring that the economies of hospitality visible to Jonson in the Sidney estates and at Welbeck were also affirmed in urban and mercantile contexts.

Nonetheless, the spatial organisation of such urban economies could differ from those performed in the houses of noblemen. In England, Jonson was almost always to stay in inns when the guest of the leadership of a town, rather than in the houses of his hosts, where other kinds of

58 Shepard, 2005, 112, 120.
59 O'Callaghan, 2007, 67–70; Brathwaite, 1617.
60 Case, 1586, 71; Marsh, 2010, 44–5.
61 Marsh, 2010, 115–30; Brayshay, 2005, 436–7.
62 Kemp, 1600, sig. C4v.
63 WP, 263.

entertainment might be provided. This was not, however, a sign of derogation or disrespect. There was instead an established practice in England (unlike Scotland and mainland Europe) whereby civic officials tended to come to the visitor in his commercial lodgings to feast and drink with him, with the town council picking up the bills both for this and, sometimes, for his lodging. In Scotland, where such inns were lacking, private hospitality was preferred.[64] We can hazard the cost of Jonson's time at the Hind in Doncaster from the 15s 10d that the council there paid its innkeeper, William Carver, an alderman and former mayor, for Mr Hepburn's charges in 1617. It would probably have included the provision of adequate libations, such as the 'gallan of Claret, a potle of sack, a potle of white wine for my Lords grace of yorke & a quarte of Claret & suger for Mr Maior' the previous year.[65]

Mr Carver's inn was used by those travelling on official business, as well as private travellers such as Jonson. Inns throughout England's provincial towns provided spaces, as Michelle O'Callaghan observes of London taverns, for 'the formation of elite communal identities through sociable activity that brought together civil gentlemen'.[66] Jonson stayed in Newcastle at the Nag's Head, a renowned fine stone inn on Sandhill, which was run by Leonard Carr, another Merchant Adventurer, who hosted the Barber Surgeons' and Chandlers' Company's annual dinner, providing music, wine and tobacco.[67] At Buntingford the petty sessions were held at the George, where Jonson probably stayed, and in Doncaster Jonson's host had also looked after the judges at the Lent assizes of 1617, the council reimbursing him over £9.[68] It appears, therefore, that Jonson was staying almost without exception at the finest inns in each town. The 'Foot Voyage' also shows us how deftly Jonson could manage the opportunities presented by each hospitable scene. In Pontefract, unusually, he stayed in an alderman's own house; this private hospitality, in contrast to the civic-funded entertainment at the inns, changed the structure of the host–guest relationship and loosened its underlying rules. He had also received the gift of a buck from the countess of Shrewsbury and already dispatched half of it to his previous host at Skelbrooke. These circumstances, and the particularly elaborate welcome he had received here, might help to explain why Jonson then

64 Heal, 1990, 202–3, 304.
65 DA, AB6/2/159, 10, 15.
66 O'Callaghan, 2004, 37.
67 REED, Newc, 150–1.
68 Falvey and Hindle, 2003, 48n.; DA, AB6/2/159, 16.

inverted the normal practice, inviting 'the whole town to his venison' (l.273) and paying – as the account notes precisely – 41s for the wine. Once again, we see the guest becoming a host, affirming the equilibrium of the moral economy evidenced in functioning hospitality.

Courtly companions

As we have noted, Jonson enjoyed particularly elaborate civic hospitality in Edinburgh. He was, in fact, honoured twice: first, in the ceremonial completion of the walk at the Mercat Cross on Friday 18 September and, second, in the conferral of the honour of burgess on him at a banquet eight days later. Details of this latter event have been known to scholars since David Masson explored the city archives more than a century ago, but the 'Foot Voyage' clarifies the motives behind its organisation. When 'the town of Edinburgh' communicated their invitation to Jonson, they expressed the hope that this honour would 'make him amends for his no fuller entertainment when he was there before, excusing the same by the absence of many of them' (ll.578–82). The invitation was repeated, in person, by James Ainslie, one of the new bailiffs and the man who was to host the ensuing dinner.

When Ainslie went to Leith to see Jonson, he was visiting his own house – at least, he was the owner of the tenement in which Jonson was lodging. But the person who had assumed the role of host here – who had, as the account puts it, 'appointed my gossip his guest' (l.567) – was not a civic dignitary at all. The tenement's occupier was instead a kinsman of King James himself, a younger son of the Stewart earl of Bothwell, James's cousin, whose reckless political ambitions had led to his being stripped of his lands and titles. While Jonson had received hospitality from patrons, towns and primates in England, once he entered Scotland he found himself closer to the court and his king than he had been since Waltham or Royston. It is tempting to think of this as paradoxical, but that would be to overlook the distinctive binationality of Jacobean courtly politics and culture that we have already had occasion to emphasise.

John Stewart and his elder brother in Leith were in fact only the last in a lengthy queue of Scots courtiers who had the care of Jonson. The James Baillie who met him near Dunbar was a Receiver of the Crown Rents; he had been a key official in preparing for the royal progress the previous year, procuring adequate comforts such as the 'sueit wynes and beir [to] be provydit from London' and furnishings brought from Whitehall. Baillie spent well over £50,000 on the king's behalf for his three months' stay in Scotland and was rewarded for 'his grit paines & traveilis in making his Ma: provisionis' with the considerable sum of £3,600 in June 1617. In 1618 he invested that in his landholdings around Dunbar, and it was here, at Lochend, that he welcomed Jonson on the way towards Edinburgh.[69] From here the walkers passed on to the house of the Auchmuty family at Auldhame, near Tantallon. John Auchmuty was the eldest of three brothers in royal service; he was Master of the King's Wardrobe in Scotland and, like Baillie, had been involved in the organisation of the 1617 progress; he had also performed in Jonson's *Irish Masque* in 1613, and in his *Pleasure Reconciled* and *For the Honour of Wales* at the beginning of 1618.[70] Unlike his brothers and fellow courtiers, Alexander and James, John is not mentioned by name in the 'Foot Voyage', although this should not necessarily be taken to mean that he was absent. Further evidence suggests otherwise: in July 1619, Jonson presented a gift of a book to Auchmuty, 'as the pledge of my thankfulnesse' for 'the hospitable fauors / I receiud of him in Scotland / and else where'.[71] If this shows 'the care with which Jonson cultivated the London-based Scottish entourage', as James Knowles rightly suggests, it also demonstrates a keen and no doubt mutual awareness in evidence throughout the walk of the requirement for reciprocity brought about by such 'hospitable fauors'.[72]

In the 'Foot Voyage', we see these courtiers managing Jonson's reception in Lowland Scotland. Alexander and James Auchmuty accompanied him from Auldhame to North Berwick, where Jonson stayed with the hospitable Sir John Home; Home offered Jonson an extraordinary welcome, arranging for him to walk up into the fields where the reapers 'circled him and danced round about him' (l.507) to the sound of bagpipes. At North Berwick 'came Mr William Ramsey and two gentlemen more from Edinburgh of purpose to meet my gossip' (ll.502–3), indicating that word of Jonson's approach had been sent ahead. This William Ramsay was in all likelihood a long-standing groom of the bedchamber, and possibly the brother of John Ramsay, viscount Haddington, whose lands lay on Jonson's route.[73] Accompanied now by Sir John Home and his sons,

---

69 McNeill and McNeill, 1996, 47–9; *RPCS*, 11.16, 25, 61, 255–6, 511; NRS, E124/10/125; E21/84, f.67; *RMS*, 7. no. 1808.
70 Bath and Craig, 2010, 282–7, *CWBJ*, 1.cxliv.
71 *CELM*, JnB 758; Knowles, 2006, 267.
72 Knowles, 2006, 267.
73 TNA, LC5/50, p.36.

Jonson went on his way with the aim of meeting Ramsay at Prestonpans; he had presumably ridden back towards Edinburgh to organise Jonson's next lodging. His efforts were in vain, however, as Jonson was 'waylaid' (l.510) by George Seton, third earl of Winton, and pressed into staying the night at his grand residence, Seton Palace.

Most strikingly, Jonson's arrival at Edinburgh on the evening of Thursday 17 September was managed by courtiers, rather than the city's leaders. 'At the town's end,' the account says, 'Mr William Ramsey, Mr [James] Heatley, Mr Alexander Stewart, and Mr Alexander Dunsire met us' (ll.517–19) and escorted the walkers to their lodgings. All these men were Scottish members of the king's household in London, and it is highly probable that Jonson and they were known to each other. In their eagerness to furnish him with a suitable welcome to Edinburgh (for they will have had to kick their heels at the foot of the Canongate until he appeared), we can perhaps detect the wishes of their royal master. These same courtiers then accompanied Jonson on his formal entry into the city the following day and may even have escorted him on the brief tour of Fife on which he immediately embarked. At Dunfermline he lodged with John Gibb, one of the king's oldest servants, and his sons; John held a house in the formerly monastic buildings adjoining the palace.[74] The Gibbs 'used my gossip and his company with all freedom and full entertainment' (ll.555–6), perhaps indicating the presence of the gaggle of other courtiers. They reappear, too, at the house of John Stewart in Leith – as at Welbeck, Jonson was left in possession during the master's absence, and he once again took full advantage to dispense some hospitality of his own. There is, though, a twist here: when Taylor stayed in Leith he was hosted by Bernard Lindsay, groom of the bedchamber and occupant of the King's Wark, which was the customary resort of significant visitors to the port.[75] In stopping instead at Stewart's residence nearby, Jonson was playing a significant variation on the normal practice. Proximity to the court was here complemented, or complicated, by proximity to a branch of the royal house itself.

Others of Jonson's hosts in Scotland are more shadowy presences in the account, though important figures in the country's cultural, economic and political life. He enjoyed the generous hospitality of Sir George Bruce at Culross and, like other guests, toured the famous coalmine and

74 Gibb, 1874, I.313–14.
75 *PP*, sig. D3v; Arnot, 1779, 572.

neighbouring saltpans. His host at Seton, George, third earl of Winton, was a diligent member of the Scottish privy council; the king had also stayed at Winton's 'magnificent seat' as he approached Edinburgh in 1617, where Drummond's 'Forth Feasting' – a work that Jonson admired – was recited before him.[76] Winton's earldom brought him the headship of the extensive Seton family and its related landholdings. The family was then enjoying significant power and influence through the chancellorship of Winton's uncle, Alexander Seton, earl of Dunfermline. As the king's most senior Scottish official, Dunfermline had had the ultimate responsibility for the smooth running of King James's progress around Scotland the previous summer. In September 1618, however, he was at the royal palace of Dunfermline, fulfilling his additional duties as the queen's agent in her regality. The privy council in Edinburgh sent several letters to him there that September, and it is possible that one of these may have contained news of Jonson's arrival; the chancellor and his countess received the poet at the palace only four days after his entry into Edinburgh.[77] King James had stayed with Dunfermline twice in the July of the previous year.[78] Jonson was subsequently to ask Drummond for details of the 'inscriptions at Pinkie', the earl's house near Edinburgh; Drummond supplied details of Mary Queen of Scots' embroidered bed-hangings, which may then have been kept there, but Jonson is usually thought to have been referring to the famous neo-Stoic painted ceiling in the house's long gallery.[79] Dunfermline, a learned humanist, had commissioned this large work, composed of over twenty emblematic scenes, and had an important hand in its composition. As Michael Bath has detailed, it was replete with references to works with which Jonson would have been familiar, and in which he shared an interest.[80] The two men must have had much to discuss, and it seems likely that Jonson visited Dunfermline at Pinkie when the earl returned to his duties in Edinburgh that October.

Cross purposes

The impression conveyed by the 'Foot Voyage' is that Jonson and his companion passed smoothly and serenely through the hands of their

---

76 *NP*, 3.306, 307n; *Informations*, ll.78–9.
77 NRS, E21/85, ff.34v, 35.
78 *HMCMK*, 80.
79 Letter 14; Bath, 2007, 73–6, 84.
80 Bath, 2003, 79–103; Bath, 2013.

many hosts during their northwards progress. There are few obvious signs of friction, even where – as at Seton – arrangements were made or changed at short notice. Yet, as we have already had reason to observe, the expectation that the performance of hospitality might conceal a heteronomous moment or ulterior motive encourages us to regard such apparently smooth functioning, the seemingly unproblematic circulation of honour, with a degree of suspicion. When John Stewart ostentatiously took Jonson into his house in Leith, was this hospitable gesture also a calculating one? Did he do it out of a sense of proximity to Jonson's royal master, as his kinsman? Or was it instead borne out of his awareness of the continuing distance between the family of the disgraced Bothwell, pardoned but not yet restored to much by way of titles or estates, and the king against whom he had raised his hands? It would make sense both as Stewart's performance of his duty as the monarch's kinsman and as an attempt to curry favour with a well-kent figure who might have useful influence at court. It would make sense too, of course, as neither, or both, of these things.

If the account requires us to conjecture motive, it does sometimes hint at possible conflicts or rivalries in the performance of hospitality between different kinds of would-be host. From what the companion records, it appears that the offer of a burgess dinner at Edinburgh derived, at least in part, from a sense that the civic dimension had been insufficiently emphasised at Jonson's courtier-dominated arrival in the city. Ainslie also offers Jonson 'his house to remain in as long as he pleased' (ll.586–7), although it seems from the burgh accounts that Jonson was back in Leith by 6 October.[81] The differences between Elizabeth Levett and William Carver over Jonson's arrival at Doncaster might be thought to be rivalries within the town's governing elite, although it is also possible that we see in the instructions given to Levett by some mysterious 'other gentlemen' (l.233) the arranging hand of another kind of host. There appears to have been something of a tussle over the guest, too, at Durham, where John Richardson entreated Neile 'for Mr Jonson's company to supper', but the bishop 'by no means would spare him' (l.363). Richardson was clerk to the palatinate chancery until his dismissal shortly after Jonson's visit; as one of the previous bishop's men, he had fallen foul of the incoming Neile.[82] Richardson was also on the Commission for Charitable Uses, which brought him together with Durham councillors in the

---

81 ECA, Burgh of Edinburgh, Bailies' Accounts, Unlaws and Extents, 1564–1689, p. 617.
82 Foster, 1987, 189–90, 200.

administration of bequests to the town; in his correspondence with them he signed himself their 'very loving friend'.[83] He was also caught up in an ongoing dispute between the bishop and the city over its representation in parliament: in 1620, a group of citizens and gentry, including Richardson's son, petitioned the king for the right to send two burgesses for the city and two knights for the shire to parliament, in an attempt to counter the palatinate's restraints on their parliamentary representation.[84] In dining with the bishop, and lodging in town, Jonson was at the sometimes fractious interface between ecclesiastical and civic interests.

Even where there is apparent harmony in the hospitality provided, underlying tensions might be discernible. At Newcastle, for example, Lionel Maddison, the mayor, invited Jonson to dinner; yet he was also 'lovingly used' there by Andrew Boyd, one of James's Scots courtiers, who had danced in *The Irish Masque* of 1613.[85] As the account bluntly puts it, Boyd was then 'in suit with the town for an impost upon coal' (l.386); indeed, he was attempting to use the favour he enjoyed with the king to muscle in on the vital Newcastle coal trade, much to the annoyance and alarm of the local merchants and Hostmen.[86] Clearly, Boyd's presence in Newcastle and his evident kindness to Jonson were understood by those present in the context of this rivalry, although it seems that their differences merely spurred the parties on to grander displays of welcome and honour. Similar differences might be visible at Pontefract: it is noticeable that Jonson's entertainment here was organised by the aldermen, rather than by the officers of the countess of Shrewsbury, despite her long association with the town and the proximity of Pontefract New Hall, her local estate. In the late sixteenth and early seventeenth centuries, relations between the aldermen of Pontefract and the earls of Shrewsbury were sometimes strained, with the latter losing their hold over the corporation.[87] Given the noble associations of venison, the buck presented to Jonson by the agents of the countess might be seen as an attempt to stage her own welcome to the town, trumping the generosity of the civic authorities; it might, too, have been her agents who prompted Elizabeth Levett to make her ultimately abortive preparations for Jonson's arrival. From this perspective, Jonson's

---

83 DCA, Du 6/3/1, f.12.
84 DCA, Du 1/4/4, f.23v; Foster, 1987, 180–1, 186.
85 *CWBJ*, 1.cxliv.
86 *CSPD, 1611–18*, 351, 556.
87 J. Hunter, 1828–31, 1.21.

decision to share his venison with 'the town' at a dinner he hosted looks like an effort at integration or reconciliation. The presence of an honoured guest could perhaps soothe, as well as rouse, social rivalries; if so, a further performance of hospitality would presumably be an obvious way to attempt to do so, especially one hosted by the honoured guest himself.

That Jonson could act as host even during his foot voyage, though, raises a question. What kind of host was he? At Pontefract, it is his generosity with venison and wine that seems most noteworthy to the companion; in Leith, he invites his courtier friends to spend a day with him, entertains a somewhat indistinct member of the Hamilton family, and joins Lord Bothwell on a trip out hawking – from the *Pennyles Pilgrimage* we learn, too, that he gave Taylor a considerable sum, as if he were now in a position to emulate the generosity that the earl of Rutland and Newcastle's civic elite, among others, had shown to him. In this role, on the evidence that we have, he appears comfortably at home. At Welbeck, by contrast, a greater degree of self-consciousness is in evidence. Having played the part of lord of the manor and bountiful host in the real master's absence, Jonson varies his role on his arrival back at Welbeck from a brief stay with Brudenell:

> Presently upon our return the ladies came, whom Mr Jonson welcomed to his house, and at supper bid them want nothing, for if they did it was not his fault. Chafed at the table for lights, and checked the waiters because there was no more new bread, which freedom of his mingled with a great deal of mirth much delighted the ladies.
>
> (ll.187–91)

When assuming the role of generous host, then, Jonson also acted it out in parody or pastiche, modulating his portrayal of bounty with the display of traits such as irascibility. In this performance he stages his own versions, from both sides, of the encounter between master and servant, host and guest, patron and client. It chimes, therefore, as we suggested at the outset of this chapter, with the concerns about such relationships addressed in much of Jonson's writing. His consciously comic inhabitation of the roles required for the enactment of hospitality points also to the scope for reflexivity or distancing within those encounters, a willingness to mount a *critical* staging of a scene of hospitality, in which this vital social practice might be assessed, judged or ironised. The account says that Jonson's free and mirthful performance here 'much delighted' Lady Catherine and Lady Elizabeth, as if fulfilling one of the celebrated Horatian requirements for poetry set out in Jonson's favourite passage from the *Ars Poetica*.[88] Yet there would clearly be the chance for a pedagogic 'profit' here, too, for reflections on the nature of hospitality, and on its imbrication with patronage relationships, social rivalries, and the varying practices and aspirations of town, court and country. Both in his Welbeck performance and on the walk in general, in other words, Jonson takes the chance to stage the social dynamics of a commonwealth, much as the 'field-poet' Scribble does in Act Four of Brome's *A Jovial Crew*.[89] The beggars of this play are able to 'present a commonwealth...with all her branches and consistencies' (4.2.179–80) at least in part because they live at a critical distance from the rooted realm. If Taylor's *Pennyles Pilgrimage* was a test of hospitality, as Heal suggests, and through that a proof or test of commonweal itself, then Jonson – in the fruitfully ambivalent roles of special guest, mock-host, poet and walker – configured his northern journey to fulfil a not dissimilar function in a different register, and in his own characteristic style.

88 'Horace, Of the Art of Poetry', ll.477–8; see *CWBJ*, 7.50.
89 The description is Vincent's: 'Phoebus', he says, 'inspires / As well the beggar as the poet laureate' (4.2.136–7).

PRINTED WORKS CITED

See also List of Abbreviations

ADAMSON, DONALD. 2008. 'A Coal Mine in the Sea: Culross and the Moat Pit', *Scottish Archaeological Journal*, 30. 161–99.

ADAMSON, JOHN. 1618. *Ta Ton Mouson Eisodia: The Muses Welcome to the High and Mighty Prince Iames...* Edinburgh.

ADRIAN, JOHN. 2011. *Local Negotiations of English Nationhood, 1570–1680*. London.

ANDERSON, A. O. Ed. 1908. *Scottish Annals from English Chroniclers, AD 500 to 1286*. London.

ANDERSON, PATRICK. 1618. *The Colde Spring of Kinghorne Craig*. Edinburgh.

ANON. 1500. *The Boke of Cokery*. London.

ANON. 1604. *Northerne Poems*. London.

ANON. 1605. *Ratseis Ghost, or the Second Part of his Madde Prankes and Robberies*. London.

ANON. 1606. *A True and Perfect Relation of the Proceedings at the Seuerall Arraignments of the Late Most Barbarous Traitors*. London.

ANON. 1608. *The Great Frost*. London.

ANON. 1619. *The Wonderful Discouerie of the Witchcrafts of Margaret and Phillip Flower, Daughters of Ioan Flower neere Beuer Castle: Executed at Lincolne, March 11 1618*. London.

ANON. 1640. *Witts Recreations: Selected from the Finest Fancies of Modern Muses*. London.

ANON. 1645. *The Great Feast at the Inthronization of the Reverend Father in God, George Neavill*. London.

ARISTOTLE. 1996. *The Politics and the Constitution of Athens*. Ed. Stephen Everson. Cambridge.

ARMITAGE, DAVID. 2000. *The Ideological Origins of the British Empire*. Cambridge.

ARNOT, HUGO. 1779. *The History of Edinburgh*. Edinburgh.

ATKINSON, J. A. 1993. Ed. *Darlington Wills and Inventories 1600–1623*. Surtees Society, 201.

AUBREY, JOHN. 1898. *Brief Lives*. Ed. Andrew Clark. 2 vols. Oxford.

AVITY, PIERRE D'. 1615. *The Estates, Empires, & Principallities of the World*. London.

AYLMER, GERALD. 1961. *The King's Servants: The Civil Service of Charles I, 1625–1642*. New York.

BACON, FRANCIS. 1824. *The Works of Francis Bacon. In 10 Volumes*. Vol. IV. London.

BAILLIE, JOHN. 1801. *An Impartial History of the Town and County of Newcastle-upon-Tyne and its Vicinity*. Newcastle.

BAKER, DAVID and WILLY MALEY. 2002. Eds. *British Identities and English Renaissance Literature*. Cambridge.

BALL, W. W. ROUSE and J. A. VENN. 1911–16. *Admissions to Trinity College, Cambridge*. 5 vols. London.

BANNERMAN, W. B. 1914–15. Ed. *The Registers of St Mary le Bow, Cheapside, All Hallows, Honey Lane, and of St Pancras, Soper Lane, London*. Harleian Society Register Series, 44–5.

BARBER, B. J. 1994. 'The Corporation and the Community', in B. J. Barber et al. *Doncaster: A Borough and its Charters*. Doncaster.

BARCLAY, WILLIAM. 1618. *The Nature and Effects of the New-Found Well at Kinghorne*. Edinburgh.

BARKER, NICOLAS and DAVID QUENTIN. 2006. *The Library of Thomas Tresham & Thomas Brudenell*. Roxburghe Club.

BARRETT, ROBERT. 2009. *Against All England: Regional Identity and Cheshire Writing, 1195–1656*. Notre Dame.

BATH, MICHAEL. 2003. *Renaissance Decorative Painting in Scotland*. Edinburgh.
 2007. 'Ben Jonson, William Fowler and the Pinkie Ceiling', *Architectural Heritage*, 18. 73–86.
 2013. 'Philostratus Comes to Scotland: A New Source for the Pictures at Pinkie', *Journal of the Northern Renaissance*, 5.

BATH, MICHAEL and JENNIFER CRAIG. 2010. 'What Happened to Mary Stuart's Bed of State?' *Emblematica*, 18. 279–88.

BAUMANN, WOLF-RUDIGER. 1990. *The Merchants Adventurers and the Continental Cloth-Trade (1560s–1620s)*. Berlin.

BAWCUTT, N. 1996. Ed. *The Control and Censorship of Caroline Drama: The Records of Sir Henry Herbert, Master of the Revels, 1623–73*. Oxford.

BEDWELL, WILLIAM. 1631. *The Turnament of Tottenham*. London.

BELLAMY, C. VINCENT. 1965. *Pontefract Priory Excavations, 1957–1961*. Thoresby Society, 49.

BENNETT, MARTIN. 2005. Ed. *Society, Religion and Culture in Seventeenth-Century Nottinghamshire*. Lewiston and Lampeter.

BERGERON, DAVID. 1999. *King James and Letters of Homoerotic Desire*. Iowa City.

BERRY, EDWARD. 2001. *Shakespeare and the Hunt: A Cultural and Social Study*. Cambridge.

BEVAN, JONQUIL. 1983. 'Stage Influences in *The Compleat Angler*', *Review of English Studies*, 34. 452–7.

BEVERIDGE, DAVID. 1885. *Culross and Tulliallan, or Perthshire on Forth*. 2 vols. Edinburgh.

—— 1888. *Between the Ochils and Forth*. Edinburgh.

BIDWELL, WILLIAM and MAIJA JANSSON. 1992. Eds. *Proceedings in Parliament 1626*. Vol. II: *House of Commons*. Woodbridge.

BLAEU, JOAN. 1654. *Theatrum orbis terrarum, sive atlas novus pars quinta*. Amsterdam.

—— 2006. *The Blaeu Atlas of Scotland*. Edinburgh.

BLAGG, THOMAS. 1914–15. Gen ed. *Yorkshire Marriage Registers*. 4 vols. London.

BLAND, MARK. 2000. '"As far from all Reuolt": Sir John Salusbury, Christ Church MS 184 and Ben Jonson's First Ode', *English Manuscript Studies*, 8. 443–78.

—— 2004. 'Ben Jonson and the Legacies of the Past', *Huntington Library Quarterly*, 67. 371–400.

BLOMEFIELD, FRANCIS. 1806. *An Essay towards a Topographical History of the County of Norfolk*. Vol. V. London.

BLOUNT, THOMAS. 1656. *Glossographia: or a Dictionary, interpreting all such Hard Words. . .as are now used in our Refined English Tongue*. London.

—— 1661. *Glossographia: or, A Dictionary, interpreting all such Hard Words of Whatsoever Language now used in our Refined English Tongue*. Second edn. London.

BOECE, HECTOR. 1540. *Heir Beginnis the Hystory and Croniklis of Scotland*. Edinburgh.

BOGG, EDMUND. 1904. *Two Thousand Miles in Wharfedale*. London.

BOND, EDWARD. 1974. *Bingo: Scenes of Money and Death*. London.

BOUTELL, CHARLES. 1863. *Heraldry, Historical and Popular*. London.

BOWERS, FREDSON. 1937. 'Ben Jonson the Actor', *Studies in Philology*, 34. 392–406.

BRADDICK, MICHAEL. 2001. 'Administrative Performance: The Representation of Authority in Early Modern England', in Michael Braddick and John Walter, eds. *Negotiating Power in Early Modern Society: Order, Hierarchy and Subordination in Britain and Ireland*. Cambridge. 166–87.

BRATHWAITE, RICHARD. 1617. *A Solemne Joviall Disputation*. London.

—— 1638. *Barnabees Journall*. London.

BRAYSHAY, MARK. 2005. 'Waits, Musicians, Bearwards and Players: The Inter-urban Road Travel and Performances of Itinerant Entertainers in Sixteenth- and Seventeenth-Century England', *Journal of Historical Geography*, 31. 430–58.

BRAYSHAY, MARK, PHILIP HARRISON and BRIAN CHALKLEY. 1998. 'Knowledge, Nationhood and Governance: The Speed of the Royal Post in Early Modern England', *Journal of Historical Geography*, 24. 265–88.

BRENNAN, MICHAEL. 1988. *Literary Patronage in the English Renaissance*. London.

BRENNAN, MICHAEL and NOEL KINNAMON. 2003. 'Robert Sidney, "Mr Johnson", and the Education of William Sidney at Penshurst', *Notes and Queries*, 50. 430–7.

BRENT, ANDREW and GEOFFREY MARTIN. 1994. Eds. *Doncaster Borough Courtier: A Transcription*. Doncaster.

BRIDGEMAN, ORLANDO and J. P. EARWAKER. 1899. *A Genealogical Account of the Family of Aldersey of Aldersey and Spurstow Co. Chester*. London.

BRIGG, WILLIAM. 1902. Ed. *The Parish Registers of Aldenham, Hertfordshire, 1559–1659*. St Albans.

—— 1917. Ed. *Yorkshire Fines for the Stuart Period*. Vol. II: *12–22 Jas. I, 1614–1625*. Yorkshire Archaeological Society, 58.

BROME, RICHARD. 1659. *Five New Playes*. London.

—— 1968. *A Jovial Crew*. Ed. Ann Haaker. London.

BROWN, CORNELIUS. 1879. *The Annals of Newark-upon-Trent*. London.

BROWN, KEITH. 1994. 'The Vanishing Emperor: British Kingship and its Decline, 1603–1707', in Mason, 1994, 58–87.

BROWN, SARAH. 2003. *York Minster: An Architectural History*. Swindon.

BROWNING, RAYMOND and RODGER KRAM. 2007. 'Effects of Obesity on the Biomechanics of Walking at Different Speeds', *Medicine and Science in Sports and Exercise*, 39. 1632–41.

BROWNING, RAYMOND, EMILY A. BAKER, JESSICA A. HERRON and RODGER KRAM. 2006. 'Effects of Obesity and Sex on the Energetic Cost and Preferred Speed of Walking', *Journal of Applied Physiology*, 100. 390–8.

BURKE, BERNARD. 1859. *Vicissitudes of Families and other Essays*. Second edn. London.

BURKE, JOHN. 1833–8. *A Genealogical and Heraldic History of the Commoners of Great Britain and Ireland*. 4 vols. London.

BURKE, VICTORIA and MARIE-LOUISE COOLAHAN. 2005. 'The Literary Contexts of William Cavendish and his Family', in Bennett, 2005, 115–41.

BURTON, WILLIAM. 1622. *The Description of Leicester-Shire*. London.

BUTLER, EDWARD. 1951. *The Story of British Shorthand*. London.

BUTLER, MARTIN. 1995a. '"Servant but not Slave": Ben Jonson at the Jacobean Court', *Proceedings of the British Academy*, 90. 65–93.

—— 1995b. 'Sir Francis Stewart: Jonson's Overlooked Patron', *Ben Jonson Journal*, 2. 101–27.

CAIUS, JOHN. 1576. *Of English Dogges, the Diversities, the Names, the Natures and the Properties*. London.

CALDER, ISABEL MACBEATH. 1934. *The New Haven Colony*. New Haven.

—— 1957. Ed. *Activities of the Puritan Faction of the Church of England, 1625–33*. London.

CALTHROP, M. M. C. 1916. *Recusant Roll No. 1, 1592–3, Exchequer, Lord Treasurer's, Remembrancer, Pipe Office Series.* Catholic Record Society, 18.

CAMDEN, WILLIAM. 1605. *Remaines of a Greater Worke, concerning Britaine.* London.

CAMERON, JAMES. 1963. Ed. *Letters of John Johnston and Robert Howie, c.1565–c.1645.* Edinburgh.

CAPP, BERNARD. 1994. *The World of John Taylor the Water Poet, 1578–1653.* Oxford.

CARLISLE, NICHOLAS. 1826. *Collections for a History of the Ancient Family of Bland.* London.

CASE, JOHN. 1586. *The Praise of Musicke.* London.

CAVENDISH, MARGARET. 1667. *The Life of the Thrice Noble, High and Puissant Prince William Cavendishe, Duke, Marquess and Earl of Newcastle.* London.

CAVENDISH, WILLIAM. 1677. *The Triumphant Widow, or, the Medley of Humours.* London.

CELOVSKY, LISA. 2009. 'Ben Jonson and Sidneian Legacies of Hospitality', *Studies in Philology*, 106.

CHANDLER, JOHN. 1999. Ed. *Travels through Stuart Britain: The Adventures of John Taylor.* Stroud.

CHAUNCY, SIR HENRY. 1826. *The Historical Antiquities of Hertfordshire.* 2 vols. London.

CLAPP, SARAH. 1931. 'The Beginnings of Subscription Publication in the Seventeenth Century', *Modern Philology*, 29. 199–24.

CLARK, PETER. 1983. *The English Alehouse: A Social History, 1200–1830.* London.

CLARKE, A. W. H. 1942. Ed. *The Register of St Mary Magdalen, Milk Street, 1558–1666, and St Bassishaw, London. Part I: 1538–1625.* Harleian Society Register Series, 72.

CLAY, JOHN. 1906. Ed. *The Parish Registers of Ledsham, 1539–1812.* Publications of the Yorkshire Parish Register Society, 26.

CLIFFORD, ANNE. 2003. *The Diaries of Lady Anne Clifford.* Ed. D. J. H. Clifford. Stroud.

COLES, ELISHA. 1677. *An English Dictionary.* London.

COLVIN, H. M. 1963–82. Ed. *The History of the King's Works.* 6 vols. London.

COOK, ROBERT BEILBY. 1909. *The Parish Registers of St Martin's, Coney Street, York. 1557–1812.* Yorkshire Parish Register Society Publications, 36.

COOKE, WILLIAM. 1868. Ed. *Students Admitted to the Inner Temple, 1571–1625.* London.

COOPER, J. P. 1973. Ed. *Wentworth Papers, 1597–1628.* Camden Society, fourth ser., 12.

CORBET, RICHARD. 1955. *The Poems of Richard Corbett.* Ed. Jack Bennett and Hugh Trevor-Roper. Oxford.

COWLING, GEOFFREY. 1968. *The History of Easingwold and the Forest of Galtres.* Huddersfield.

CRESSWELL, TIM and PETER MERRIMAN. 2011. Eds. *Geographies of Mobilities: Practices, Spaces, Subjects.* Aldershot.

CROFT, PAULINE. 2000. 'The Catholic Gentry, the Earl of Salisbury and the Baronets of 1611'. In Lake and Questier, 2000, 262–81.

CROSS, CLAIRE. 1967. 'Achieving the Millennium: The Church in York during the Commonwealth', in G. J. Cuming, ed. *Studies in Church History vol. IV: The Province of York.* Leiden. 122–42.

CUDDY, NEIL. 1989. 'Anglo-Scottish Union and the Court of James I, 1603–1625', *Transactions of the Royal Historical Society,* 39. 107–24.

CURRAN, JOHN. 1997. 'Royalty Unlearned, Honor Untaught: British Savages and Historiographical Change in Cymbeline', *Comparative Drama,* 31. 277–303.

CURRAN, KEVIN. 2009. *Marriage, Performance, and Politics at the Jacobean Court.* Farnham.

DALECHAMP, CALEB. 1632. *Christian Hospitalitie Handled Common-place-wise in the Chappel of Trinity Colledge in Cambridge.* Cambridge.

DALZEL, ANDREW. 1862. *History of the University of Edinburgh from its Foundation.* 2 vols. Edinburgh.

DAVIES, ROBERT. 1880. *Walks Through the City of York. . . Edited by his Widow.* London.

　　　1883. *Historical Notices of the Edifice called the King's Manor, Situate near the Walls of the City of York.* York.

DEKKER, THOMAS. 1615. *The Cold Yeare. 1614 A Deepe Snow.* London.

DELANO-SMITH, CATHERINE. 2006. 'Milieus of Mobility', in James Akerman, ed. *Cartographies of Travel and Navigation.* Chicago. 16–68.

DENNISON, E. PATRICIA and SIMON STRONACH, 2007. *Historic Dunfermline: Archaeology and Development.* Dunfermline.

DOBSON, R. B. 1996. *Church and Society in the Medieval North of England.* London.

DOBSON, R. B. and JOHN TAYLOR. 1976. *Rhymes of Robin Hood: An Introduction to the English Outlaw.* London.

DODSWORTH, ROGER. 1904. *Yorkshire Church Notes, 1619–1631.* Ed. J. W. Clay. Yorkshire Archaeological Society Record Series, 34.

DONALDSON, IAN. 1992. *Jonson's Walk to Scotland.* Edinburgh.

　　　1997. *Jonson's Magic Houses.* Oxford.

　　　2011. *Ben Jonson: A Life.* Oxford.

DRAKE, FRANCIS. 1736. *Eboracum, or the History and Antiquities of the City of York.* London.

DUGDALE, WILLIAM. 1854. *Visitation of the County of Yorke.* Ed. Robert Davies. Surtees Society, 36.

DUNBAR, JOHN. 2013. *Epigrammaton Ioannis Dunbari Megalo-Britanni.* Ed. Jamie Reid Baxter and Dana F. Sutton. Rev. edn. The Philological Museum. http://www.philological.bham.ac.uk

DUPPA, BRIAN. 1638. Ed. *Jonsonus Virbius, or the Memorie of Ben Johnson Revived.* London.

EDDISON, EDWIN. 1854. *History of Worksop, with. . . sketches of Sherwood Forest.* London.

ELLER, IRWIN. 1841. *The History of Belvoir Castle.* London.

ELSKY, MARTIN. 2000. 'Microhistory and Cultural Geography: Ben Jonson's "To Sir Robert Wroth" and the Absorption of Local Community in the Commonwealth', *Renaissance Quarterly*, 53. 500–28.

ENOS, CAROL. 2004. 'Catholic Exiles in Flanders and As You Like It; or, What If You Don't Like It at All?', in Richard Dutton, Alison Findlay and Richard Wilson, eds. *Theatre and Religion: Lancastrian Shakespeare.* Manchester. 130–42.

EVERITT, ALAN. 1985. *Landscape and Community in England.* London.

FALVEY, HEATHER and STEVE HINDLE. 2003. Eds. *'This Little Commonwealth': Layston Parish Memorandum Book, 1607–c.1650 and 1704–c.1747.* Hertfordshire Record Society, 19.

FELLTHAM, OWEN. 1628. *Resolves, or Excogitations. A Second Centurie.* London.

FINDLAY, ALISON. 2009. *Playing Spaces in Early Women's Drama.* Cambridge.

FLETCHER, REGINALD. 1901. Ed. *Pension Book of Gray's Inn, 1569–1669.* London.

FLOYD-WILSON, MARY. 2002. 'Delving to the Root: *Cymbeline*, Scotland, and the English Race', in Baker and Maley, 2002.

FORSTER, ANN. 1960. Ed. 'Durham Entries on the Recusants' Roll 1636–7', in *Miscellanea. Vol. III.* Surtees Society, 175.

1972. 'The Real Roger Widdrington', *Recusant History*, 11. 196–205.

FOSTER, ANDREW. 1976. 'The Function of a Bishop: The Career of Richard Neile, 1562–1640', in O'Day and Heale, 1987, 33–54.

1987. 'The Struggle for Parliamentary Representation for Durham, 1600–1641', in Marcombe, 1987, 176–201.

2000. 'Archbishop Neile Revisited', in Lake and Questier, 2000, 159–78.

FOSTER, JOSEPH. 1875. Ed. *The Visitation of Yorkshire. . .1584/5. . .to Which is Added the Subsequent Visitation Made in 1612.* London.

FOWLER, JOSEPH. 1903. Ed. *Rites of Durham: being a Description of all the Ancient Monuments, Rites and Customes belonging or beinge within the Monastical Church of Durham before the Suppression; written in 1593.* Surtees Society, 107.

FOWLER, WILLIAM. 1914. *The Works of William Fowler.* Ed. Henry W. Meikle. Vol. I. Edinburgh.

FOX, ADAM. 2000. *Oral and Literate Culture in England, 1500–1700.* Oxford.

FOX, GEORGE. 1827. *The History of Pontefract in Yorkshire.* Pontefract.

FUMERTON, PATRICIA. 2006. *Unsettled: The Culture of Mobility and the Working Poor in Early Modern England.* Chicago.

'GALLOBELGICUS'. 1629. *Wine, Beere and Ale, Together by the Eares.* London.

GALLOWAY, BRUCE. 1986. *The Union of England and Scotland, 1603–1608.* Edinburgh.

GASCOIGNE, GEORGE. 1575. *The Noble Arte of Venerie or Hunting.* London.

GAUDRIAULT, RAYMOND. 1995. *Filigranes et autres caractéristiques des papiers fabriqués en France aux XVIIe et XVIIIe siècles.* Paris.

GEDDIE, JOHN, 1908. 'The Sculptured Stones of Edinburgh: The Dean Group', *The Book of the Old Edinburgh Club,* 1. 77–135.

GENT, THOMAS. 1730. *The Ancient and Modern History of the Famous City of York.* York.

GEOFFREY OF MONMOUTH. 1966. *The History of the Kings of Britain.* Trans. Lewis Thorpe. Harmondsworth.

GIBB, GEORGE. 1874. *The Life and Times of Robert Gib Lord of Carribber.* 2 vols. London.

GIBSON, MARION. 1999. *Reading Witchcraft: Stories of Early English Witchcraft.* London.

GIROUARD, MARK. 1962. 'The Smythson Collection of the Royal Institute of British Architects', *Architectural History,* 5. 23–184.

    1983. *Robert Smythson and the Elizabethan Country House.* New Haven and London.

GLENDINNING, MILES. 2004. *The Architecture of Scottish Government.* Dundee.

GRANGER, J. 1824. *A Biographical History of England, from Egbert the Great to the Revolution.* Fifth edn. 6 vols. London.

GRAY, WILLIAM. 1649. *Chorographia: or a Survey of Newcastle Upon Tyne.* London.

GRAZEBROOK, GEORGE and JOHN PAUL RYLANDS. 1889. Eds. *The Visitation of Shropshire taken in the year 1623 by Robert Tresswell.* Publications of the Harleian Society, 28–9. London.

GREEN, ROGER, P. H. BURTON and D. J. FORD. 2012. *Scottish Latin Authors in Print up to 1700: A Short Title List.* Supplementa Humanistica Lovaniensia, 30.

GRELL, OLE PETER. 2011. *Brethren in Christ: A Calvinist Network in Reformation Europe.* Cambridge.

GRIFFITH, JOHN. 1914. *Pedigrees of Anglesey and Carnarvonshire Families, with their Collateral Branches in Denbighshire, Monmouthshire and Other Parts.* Horncastle.

HAHN, THOMAS G. 2000. Ed. *Robin Hood in Popular Culture: Violence, Transgression, and Justice.* Woodbridge.

HAKLUYT, RICHARD. 1599. *The Principal Nauigations, Voyages, Traffiques and Discoueries of the English Nation made by Sea or Ouer-land.* London.

HALASZ, ALEXANDRA. 2000. 'Pamphlet Surplus: John Taylor and Subscription Publication', in Arthur Marotti and Michael Bristol, eds. *Print, Manuscript, and Performance: The Changing Relations of the Media in Early Modern England.* Columbus. 90–102.

HALL, JOHN. 1892. *A History of South Cave and of other Parishes in the East Riding of the County of York.* Hull.

HALL, JOSEPH. 1617. *Quo Vadis? A Just Censure of Travel as it is Commonly Undertaken by the Gentlemen of Our Nation.* London.

HALLEN, ARTHUR. 1878. 'Notes on the Secular and Ecclesiastical Antiquities of Culross', *Proceedings of the Society of Antiquaries of Scotland,* 12. 245–53.

HAMMER, PAUL. 1999. *The Polarisation of Elizabethan Politics: The Political Career of Robert Devereux, 2nd Earl of Essex, 1585–1597.* Cambridge.

HANNAY, MARGARET. 2010. *Mary Sidney, Lady Wroth.* Aldershot.

HARGROVE, W. 1818. *History and Description of the Ancient City of York.* 2 vols. York.

HARINGTON, SIR JOHN. 1591. *Orlando Furioso in English Heroical Verse.* London.

—— 1804. *Nugae Antiquae, being a Miscellaneous Collection of Original Papers.* 2 vols. London.

—— 1962. *Sir John Harington's A New Discourse of a Stale Subject, Called the Metamorphosis of Ajax.* Ed. Elizabeth Story Donno. London.

HARRIS, ALEXANDER. 1879. *The Œconomy of the Fleete.* Ed. Augustus Jessop. Camden Society, 25.

HARRIS, BRIAN. 2006. *Guide to Churches and Cathedrals.* London.

HARVEY, C. H. and JOHN MACLEOD. 1930. Eds. *Calendar of Writs Preserved at Yester House, 1166–1625.* Scottish Record Society, 55.

HASLER, P. W. 1981. Ed. *The History of Parliament: The House of Commons 1558–1603.* Woodbridge.

HAYES, TOM. 1993. *The Birth of Popular Culture: Ben Jonson, Maid Marian, and Robin Hood.* Pittsburgh.

HEAL, FELICITY. 1990. *Hospitality in Early Modern England.* Oxford.

—— 2008. 'Food Gifts, the Household and the Politics of Exchange in Early Modern England', *Past and Present,* 199. 41–70.

HEATH, JOHN. 1619. *The House of Correction: or, Certain Satyricall Epigrams.* London.

HEATON, GABRIEL. 2010. *Writing and Reading Royal Entertainments.* Oxford.

HEAWOOD, EDWARD. 1930. 'Paper Used in England after 1600: 1. The Seventeenth Century to c.1680', *The Library,* fourth ser., 11. 263–99.

HELGERSON, RICHARD. 1992. *Forms of Nationhood: The Elizabethan Writing of England.* Chicago.

HENDERSON, EBENEZER. 1879. *The Annals of Dunfermline and Vicinity.* Glasgow.

HERBERT, GEORGE. 1941. *The Works of George Herbert.* Ed. F. E. Hutchison. Oxford.

HESLOP, DAVID. 1993. *Historic Buildings in Pontefract at 7–9 Corn Market and Swales Yard.* Pontefract.

HEY, DAVID. 1981. *Buildings of Britain 1550–1750: Yorkshire.* Ashbourne.

HOBBES, THOMAS. 1997. *The Correspondence*. Ed. Noel Malcolm. Vol. II: *1660–1679*. Oxford.

HODGSON, JOHN. 1832. *A History of Northumberland in three parts: part II, vol. II*. Newcastle.

HOLINSHED, RAPHAEL. 1577. *The Firste Volume of the Chronicles of England, Scotlande, and Irelande*. London.

HOLLOWAY, ERNEST. 2011. *Andrew Melville and Humanism in Renaissance Scotland 1545–1622*. Leiden.

HONEYBONE, MICHAEL. 2008. *Wicked Practise and Sorcerye: the Belvoir Witchcraft Case of 1618*. Buckingham.

HOPPIT, JULIAN. 1993. 'Reforming Britain's Weights and Measures, 1660–1824', *English Historical Review*, 108. 82–104.

HOTSON, LESLIE. 1949. 'The Projected Amphitheatre', *Shakespeare Survey*, 2. 24–35.

HOWELLS, B. E. 1967. *A Calendar of Letters Relating to North Wales, 1533–circa 1700*. Cardiff.

HOWELL, JAMES. 1650. *Epistolae Ho-Elianae. Familiar Letters*. London.

HUGHES, HELEN. 2010. 'Interdisciplinary Collaboration to Understand and Recreate the Splendour of the Marble Closet at the Little Castle Bolsover', *Multidisciplinary Conservation: A Holistic View for Historic Interiors*. ICOM-CC Interim Meeting. Rome.

HUNTER, JOSEPH. 1828–31. *South Yorkshire: The History and Topography of the Deanery of Doncaster in the Diocese and County of York*. 2 vols. London.

HUNTER, WILLIAM KING. 1858. *History of the Priory of Coldingham*. Edinburgh.

INGOLD, TIM. 1993. 'The Temporality of Landscapes', *World Archaeology*, 25. 152–74.

INGOLD, TIM and JO LEE VERGUNST. 2008. Eds. *Ways of Walking: Ethnography and Practice on Foot*. Aldershot.

ISHAM, SIR GYLES. 1951. Ed. *The Correspondence of Bishop Brian Duppa and Sir Justinian Isham, 1650–1660*. Publications of the Northamptonshire Record Society, 17.

JAQUES, FRANCIS. 1990. *The Queen of Corsica*. Ed. H. D. Janzen. Malone Society Reprints.

JESSE, GEORGE. 1866. *Researches into the History of the British Dog*. 2 vols. London.

JOHNSTON, NATHANIEL. 1835. 'History of the Family of Foljambe', Part II, in his *Collectanea Topographica et Genealogica*. Vol. II. London. 68–90.

JONSON, BEN. 1970. *Ben Jonson: Selected Masques*. Ed. Stephen Orgel. New Haven. *Ben Jonson*. 1985. Ed. Ian Donaldson. Oxford.

KATHMAN, DAVID. 2004. 'Grocers, Goldsmiths, and Drapers: Freemen and Apprentices in the Elizabethan Theater'. *Shakespeare Quarterly*, 55. 1–49.

KELLIHER, HILTON. 1993. 'Donne, Jonson, Richard Andrew and the Newcastle Manuscript', *English Manuscript Studies*, 4. 134–73.

2000. 'Francis Beaumont and Nathan Field: New Records of their Early Years', *English Manuscript Studies*, 8. 1–42.

KEMP, WILLIAM. 1600. *Kemps Nine Daies Wonder*. London.

KERRIGAN, JOHN. 2008. *Archipelagic English: Literature, History and Politics 1603–1707*. Oxford.

KIDD, COLIN. 2010. 'The Matter of Britain and the Contours of British Political Thought', in David Armitage, ed. *British Political Thought in History, Literature and Theory, 1500–1800*. Cambridge. 47–66.

KIERNAN, D. 1989. *The Derbyshire Lead Industry in the Sixteenth Century*. Derbyshire Record Society, 14.

KING, ANN. 1996. Ed. *Muster Books for North and East Hertfordshire, 1580–1605*. Hertfordshire Record Society, 12.

KING, THOMAS. 1814a. *Catalogue of the Library of the Reverend John Price*. London.

1814b. *Bibliotheca Curiosa: Supplement to Thos King, junr's. Catalogue, including the Reserved Part of the Library of the Reverend John Price*. London.

KITCHEN, FRANK. 1997. 'John Norden (c.1547–1625): Estate Surveyor, Topographer, County Mapmaker and Devotional Writer', *Imago Mundi*, 49. 43–61.

KNIGHT, STEPHEN. 2005. '"Meere English flocks": Ben Jonson's *The Sad Shepherd* and the Robin Hood Tradition', in Helen Phillips, ed. *Robin Hood: Medieval and Post-Medieval*. Dublin. 129–44.

KNOWLES, JAMES. 2006. 'Jonson in Scotland: Jonson's Mid-Jacobean Crisis', in Takashi Kozuka and J. R. Mulryne, eds. *Shakespeare, Marlowe, Jonson: New Directions in Biography*. Aldershot. 259–77.

LAI, P., A. LEUNG, A. LI and M. ZHANG. 2008. 'Three-dimensional gait analysis of obese adults', *Clinical Biomechanics*, 23: Suppl. 1. S2–6.

LAING, DAVID. 1858. Ed. *A Catalogue of the Graduates in the Faculties of Arts, Divinity, and Law, of the University of Edinburgh since its Foundation*. Edinburgh.

LAKE, PETER and MICHAEL QUESTIER. 2000. Eds. *Conformity and Orthodoxy in the English Church, c.1560–1660*. Woodbridge.

LAWS, ARTHUR. 1925. *Schola Novocastrensis: A Biographical History of the Royal Free Grammar School of Newcastle-upon-Tyne*. Vol. I. Newcastle-upon-Tyne.

LEECH, CLIFFORD. 1947. 'Francis Jaques: Author of the Queen of Corsica', *Durham University Journal*, new ser., 8. 111–19.

LELAND, JOHN. 1770. *Joannis Lelandi Antiquarii de Rebus Britannicis Collectanea*. Ed. Thomas Hearne. Vol. VI. London.

1906–10. *The Itinerary of John Leland, in or about the Years 1535–1543*. Ed. Lucy Toulmin Smith. 5 vols. London.

LESLIE, JOHN. 1675. *De Origine, Moribus & Rebus Gestis Scotorum*. London.

1888–95. *The Historie of Scotland*. Trans. James Dalrymple. 2 vols. Edinburgh.

LEVACK, BRIAN. 1987. *The Formation of the British State: England, Scotland and the Union, 1603–1707*. Oxford.

LINCOLN'S INN. 1896. *The Records of the Honorable Society of Lincoln's Inn*. Vol. I: *Admissions from AD 1420 to AD 1799*. London.

LIPSIUS, JUSTUS. 1592. *A Direction for Travailers*. Trans. Sir John Stradling. London.

LISTER, JOHN. 1917. *The History of Shibden Hall: The Waterhouse Family*. Transactions of the Halifax Antiquarian Society, 205.

LITHGOW, WILLIAM. 1614. *A Most Delectable and True Discourse of an Admired and Painefull Peregrination from Scotland*. London.

1616. *A Most Delectable and True Discourse of an Admired and Painefull Peregrination from Scotland*. Second edn. London.

1618. *The Pilgrimes Farewell to his Native Countrey of Scotland*. Edinburgh.

1623. *A Most Delectable and True Discourse of an Admired and Painefull Peregrination from Scotland*. Third edn. London.

1632. *The Totall Discourse, of the Rare Adventures, and Painefull Peregrinations of Long Nineteene Yeares Travayles, from Scotland, to the most Famous Kingdomes in Europe, Asia, and Affrica*. London.

LORIMER, HAYDEN. 2011. 'Walking: New Forms and Spaces for Studies of Pedestrianism', in Cresswell and Merriman, 2011, 19–33.

LORIMER, HAYDEN and KATRIN LUND. 2008. 'A Collectable Topography: Walking, Remembering and Recording Mountains', in Ingold and Vergunst, 2008, 185–200.

LOXLEY, JAMES. 2009. 'My Gossip's Foot Voyage: A Recently Discovered Manuscript Sheds New Light on Ben Jonson's Walk to Edinburgh', *Times Literary Supplement*, 5554.

MACCAFFREY, WALLACE. 1960. 'Talbot and Stanhope: An Episode in Elizabethan Politics', *Historical Research*, 33. 73–85.

MACCOLL, ALAN. 2006. 'The Meaning of "Britain" in Medieval and Early Modern England', *Journal of British Studies*, 45. 248–69.

MACDONALD, ALAN. 2007. *The Burghs and Parliament in Scotland, c.1550–1651*. Aldershot.

MACFARLANE, ROBERT. 2008. *The Wild Places*. London.

2012. *The Old Ways: A Journey on Foot*. London.

MACGIBBON, DAVID and THOMAS ROSS. 1887–92. Eds. *The Castellated and Domestic Architecture of Scotland, from the Twelfth to the Eighteenth Century*. 5 vols. Edinburgh.

MACKENZIE, ENEAS. 1827. *A Descriptive and Historical Account of the Town and County of Newcastle upon Tyne*. 2 vols. Newcastle.

MADDISON, A. R. 1902–4. Ed. *Lincolnshire Pedigrees*. Harleian Society Publications, 50–2.

MAINS, BRIAN and ANTHONY TUCK. 1986. Eds. *Royal Grammar School, Newcastle upon Tyne: A History of the School in its Community*. Stocksfield.

MAITLAND, RICHARD. 1829. *The History of the House of Seytoun to the Year 1559, with the Continuation by Alexander Viscount Kingston to 1687*. Glasgow.

MARCOMBE, DAVID. 1987. Ed. *The Last Principality: Politics, Religion and Society in the Bishopric of Durham, 1494–1660*. Nottingham.

MARKHAM, CLEMENTS. 1873. 'The Genealogy of the Markhams', *Herald and Genealogist*, 7. 318–35.

1913. *Markham Memorials*. 2 vols. London.

MARKHAM, DAVID. 1854. *A History of the Markham Family*. London.

MAROTTI, ARTHUR. 1995. *Manuscript, Print and the English Renaissance Lyric*. London and New York.

MARSH, CHRISTOPHER. 2010. *Music and Society in Early Modern England*. Cambridge.

MARSHALL, GEORGE. 1871. Ed. *The Visitations of the County of Nottingham in the years 1569 and 1614*. Harleian Society, 4.

MARSHALL, TRISTAN. 2000. *Theatre and Empire: Great Britain on the London Stages under James VI and I*. Manchester.

MARTIN, CHARLES TRICE. 1904–5. Ed. *Middle Temple Records: Minutes of Parliament, 1501–1703*. 3 vols. London.

MASON, ROGER. 1987. 'Scotching the Brut: Politics, History and National Myth in Sixteenth-Century Britain', in Roger Mason, ed. *Scotland and England, 1286–1815*. Edinburgh. 60–84.

1994. Ed. *Scots and Britons: Scottish Political Thought and the Union of 1603*. Cambridge.

2012. 'From Buchanan to Blaeu: The Politics of Scottish Chorography 1582–1654', in Caroline Erskine and Roger Mason, eds. *George Buchanan: Political Thought in Early Modern Britain and Europe*. Aldershot.

2013. '*Certeine Matters Concerning the Realme of Scotland*: George Buchanan and Scottish Self-Fashioning at the Union of the Crowns', *Scottish Historical Review*, 92. 38–65.

MASON, W. H. 1915. 'Note on a 16th-Century Ring', *Transactions of the Thoroton Society*, 19. 153–5.

MASSINGER, PHILIP. 1632. *The Maid of Honour*. London.

MASSON, DAVID. 1893. 'Ben Jonson in Edinburgh', *Blackwood's Edinburgh Magazine*, 154. 790–804.

MASTORIS, STEPH. 1998. 'A Newly Discovered Perambulation Map of Sherwood Forest in the Early Seventeenth Century', *Transactions of the Thoroton Society*, 102. 79–92.

MAY, STEVEN. 1980. Ed. 'The Poems of Edward De Vere, Seventeenth Earl of Oxford, and of Robert Devereux, Second Earl of Essex', *Studies in Philology: Texts and Studies*, 77:5.

MCDONALD, ROBERT. 1971. *The Library of William Drummond of Hawthornden*. Edinburgh.

MCKEAN, CHARLES. 2004. *The Scottish Chateau*. Rev. edn. Stroud.

MCNEILL, WILLIAM and PETER MCNEILL. 1996. 'The Scottish Progress of James VI', *The Scottish Historical Review*, 75. 38–51.

MCPHERSON, DAVID. 1974. 'Ben Jonson's Library and Marginalia: An Annotated Catalogue', *Studies in Philology*, 71. 5.

MCRAE, ANDREW. 1999. 'The Peripatetic Muse: Internal Travel and the Cultural Production of Space', in Gerald Maclean, Donna Landry and Joseph Ward, eds. *The Country and the City Revisited*. Cambridge. 41–57.

2009. *Literature and Domestic Travel in Early Modern England*. Cambridge.

METCALFE, WALTER. 1886. Ed. *The Visitations of Hertfordshire. . .with Hertfordshire Pedigrees*. Harleian Society, 22.

MEYRICK, SAMUEL RUSH. 1846. Ed. *Heraldic Visitations of Wales and Part of the Marches*. 2 vols. Llandovery.

MILLER, WILLIAM E. 1959. 'Samuel Fleming, Elizabethan Clergyman', *Library Chronicle* (Pennsylvania), 25. 61–79.

MILLS, DAVID. 1989. 'William Aldersey's "History Of The Mayors Of Chester"', *REED Newsletter*, 14. 2–10.

MOIZ, JENNI GERMANN and SARAH GIBSON. 2008. Eds. *Mobilizing Hospitality: The Ethics of Social Relations in a Mobile World*. Aldershot.

MONIPENNIE, JOHN. 1594. *Certaine Matters Composed Together*. Edinburgh.

MONTGOMERIE, ALEXANDER. 2000. *Poems*. Ed. David J. Parkinson. 2 vols. Edinburgh.

MORFILL, W. R. and F. J. FURNIVALL. 1873. Eds. *Ballads from Manuscripts*. 2 vols. Ballad Society.

MORYSON, FYNES. 1617. *An Itinerary. . .Containing his Ten Yeares Travell Through the Twelve Dominions*. London.

MOUL, VICTORIA. 2010. *Jonson, Horace and the Classical Tradition*. Cambridge.

MOWL, TIMOTHY. 1993. *Elizabethan and Jacobean Style*. London.

MURRAY, HUGH and IAN PATTISON. 2000. *Monuments in York Minster*. York.

NETZLOFF, MARK. 2001. '"Counterfeit Egyptians and Imagined Borders: Jonson's *The Gypsies Metamorphosed*', *ELH*, 68. 763–93.

NEWTON, DIANA. 2006. *North-East England, 1569–1625: Governance, Culture and Identity*. Woodbridge.

2013. 'St Cuthbert: Durham's Tutelarie Deitie', *Recusant History*, 31. 439–59.

NICHOLLS, ANDREW. 1999. *The Jacobean Union: A Reconsideration of British Civil Policies under the Early Stuarts*. Westport.

NICHOLLS, CHARLES. 1992. *The Reckoning*. London.

NICOLSON, JOSEPH and RICHARD BURNS. 1777. *Antiquities of Cumberland and Westmorland*. 2 vols. London.

NORDEN, JOHN. 1607. *The Surveyors Dialogue*. London.

O'CALLAGHAN, MICHELLE. 2004. 'Tavern Societies, the Inns of Court and the Culture of Conviviality in Early Seventeenth-Century London', in Adam Smyth, ed. *A Pleasing Sinne: Drink and Conviviality in Seventeenth-Century England*. Cambridge. 37–51.

2007. *The English Wits: Literature and Sociability in Early Modern England*. Cambridge.

O'DAY, ROSEMARY and FELICITY HEAL. 1976. Eds. *Continuity and Change: Personnel and Administration of the Church of England*. Leicester. 33–54.

O'FARRELL, BRIAN. 2011. *Shakespeare's Patron: William Herbert, Third Earl of Pembroke, 1580–1630*. London.

OGILBY, JOHN. 1675. *Britannia, or the Kingdom of England and Dominion of Wales Actually Survey'd*. London.

OGLE, SIR HENRY ASGILL. 1902. *Ogle and Bothal: or, A History of the Baronies of Ogle, Bothal, and Hepple, and of the Families of Ogle and Bertram*. Newcastle.

OHLER, NORBERT. 1989. *The Medieval Traveller*. Trans. Caroline Hillier. Woodbridge.

ORD, MELANIE. 2007. 'Returning from Venice to England: Sir Henry Wotton as Diplomat, Pedagogue and Italian Cultural Connoisseur', in Thomas Betteridge, ed. *Borders and Travellers in Early Modern Europe*. Aldershot. 147–67.

ORNSBY, GEORGE. 1877. Ed. *Selections from the Household Books of the Lord William Howard of Naworth Castle, 1612–40*. Surtees Society, 68.

OSBORN, JAMES. 1957. 'Ben Jonson and the Eccentric Lord Stanhope', *Times Literary Supplement*, 2862.

PAINTING STUBBS, CLARE. 2011. 'Abraham Fleming: Writer, Cleric and Preacher in Elizabethan and Jacobean London'. Unpublished PhD thesis. University of London.

PALMER, DARYL. 1992. *Hospitable Performances: Dramatic Genre and Cultural Practices in Early Modern England*. West Lafayette.

PALMER, W. M. 1927. *Notes on Cambridgeshire Villages, No. 2, Caxton. Repr. from Cambridge Chronicle*. Cambridge.

PARSONS, EDWARD. 1834. *The Civil, Ecclesiastical, Literary, Commercial and Miscellaneous History of Leeds, Halifax, Huddersfield, Bradford, Wakefield, Dewsbury, Otley and the Manufacturing District of Yorkshire*. Vol. I. Leeds.

PATON, HENRY. 1905. Ed. *The Register of Marriages for the Parish of Edinburgh, 1595–1700*. Scottish Record Society, 27.

     1911. Ed. *Parish Register of Dunfermline, 1561–1700*. Scottish Record Society, 44.

PEARMAN, REV. A. J. 1889. 'The Chutes of Bethersden, Appledore and Hinxhill', *Archaeologia Cantiana: Transactions of the Kent Archaeological Society*, 13. 55–71.

PERCEVEL, RICHARD. 1599. *A Dictionarie in Spanish and English*. London.

PEVSNER, NIKOLAUS. 1979. *The Buildings of England: Nottinghamshire*. Second edn, rev. Elizabeth Williamson. Harmondsworth.

PHILLIPS, HELEN. 2000. 'Forest, Town and Road: The Significance of Places and Names in Some Robin Hood Texts', in Hahn, 2000, 197–214.

POCOCK, J. G. A. 2005. *The Discovery of Islands*. Cambridge.

POLLOCK, LINDA. 2011. 'The Practice of Kindness in Early Modern Elite Society', *Past and Present*, 211. 121–58.

POYNTER, F. N. L. 1947. 'Notes on a Late Sixteenth-Century Ophthalmic Work in English', *The Library*, fifth ser., 2. 173–9.

PREST, W. R. 1986. *The Rise of the Barristers: A Social History of the English Bar, 1590–1640*. Oxford.

PRESTWICH, MENNA. 1966. *Cranfield: Politics and Profits under the Early Stuarts*. Oxford.

PULLEIN, CATHARINE. 1915. *The Pulleyns of Yorkshire*. Leeds.

PULLEIN, THOMAS. 1608. *Ieremiahs Teares, or A Sermon Preached in York-Minster vpon Trinity Sunday, in the yeare of our Lord, 1604*. London.

PUREY-CUST, A. P. 1890. *The Heraldry of York Minster*. Leeds.

RAINE, JAMES. 1852. *The History and Antiquities of North-Durham*. London.

RAY, JOHN. 1674. *A Collection of English Words, Not Generally Used*. London.

     1691. *A Collection of English Words, Not Generally Used*. Second edn. London

RAYLOR, TIMOTHY. 1999. '"Pleasure Reconciled to Virtue": William Cavendish, Ben Jonson and the Decorative Scheme of Bolsover Castle', *Renaissance Quarterly*, 52. 402–39.

REID-BAXTER, JAMIE. 2006. 'Elizabeth Melville's Letters', *Notes and Queries*, 53. 525–8.

RHODES, NEIL, JENNIFER RICHARDS and JOSEPH MARSHALL. 2003. Eds. *King James VI and I: Selected Writings*. Aldershot.

ROBERTS, IAN. 1990. *Pontefract Castle*. Wakefield.

ROBERTSON, J. and D. J. GORDON. 1954. Eds. 'A Calendar of Dramatic Records in the Books of the Livery Companies of London, 1485–1640', in *Collections (Malone Society)*. Vol. III. 101.

ROGERS, ALAN. 1983. *The Book of Stamford*. Buckingham.

ROSE J., H. J. RALSTON and J. G. GAMBLE. 1994. 'Energetics of Walking', in J. Rose and J. G. Gamble, eds. *Human Walking*. Second edn. Baltimore. 45–72.

ROWE, NICK. 1994. '"My Best Patron": William Cavendish and Jonson's Caroline Drama', *The Seventeenth Century*, 9. 197–212.

ROWE, VIOLET. 1935. 'The Influence of the Earls of Pembroke on Parliamentary Elections, 1625–41', *English Historical Review*, 1. 242–56.

ROWLEY, WILLIAM. 1632. *A New Wonder, a Woman Never Vext*. London.

RUBIÉS, JOAN PAU. 1995. 'Christianity and Civilization in Sixteenth-Century Ethnological Discourse', in Henriette Bugge and Joan Pau Rubiés, eds. *Shifting Cultures: Interaction and Discourse in the Expansion of Europe*. Münster. 35–60.

RYLANDS, J. PAUL and F. C. BEAZLEY. 1918. *The Monuments of Bunbury Church*. Privately printed.

SAMPSON, WILLIAM. 1636. *Virtus Post Funera Vivit, or, Honour Tryumphing over Death*. London.

SAMUELS, JOHN, F. CHARLES, ADRIAN HENSTOCK and PHILIP SIDDALL. 1996. '"A Very Old and Crasey Hous": The Old White Hart Inn, Newark, Nottinghamshire', *Transactions of the Thoroton Society*, 100. 19–54.

SANDERS, JULIE. 1998. *Ben Jonson's Theatrical Republics*. Basingstoke.

2011. *The Cultural Geography of Early Modern Drama, 1620–1650*. Cambridge.

2013. 'The *Pennyles Pilgrimage* of John Taylor: Poverty, Mobility and Performance in Seventeenth-Century Literary Circles', *Rural History*, 24. 9–24.

2014. 'Geographies of Performance in the Early Modern Midlands', in Susan Bennett and Mary Polito, eds. *Performing Environments: Site-specificity in Medieval and Early Modern Drama*. London. 119–39.

SCHWYZER, PHILIP. 2002. 'British History and "The British History": The Same Old Story?', in Baker and Maley, 2002, 11–23.

SCHWYZER, PHILIP and SIMON MEALOR. 2004. Eds. *Archipelagic Identities: Literature and Identity in the Atlantic Archipelago, 1550–1800*. Aldershot.

SCOT, SIR JOHN. 1872. *The Staggering State of Scottish Statesmen from 1550–1650*. Ed. Charles Rogers. Edinburgh.

1888. *Berwick-upon-Tweed: The History of the Town and Guild*. London.

SCOTT, WALTER. 1805. *The Lay of the Last Minstrel, a Poem*. Second edn. Edinburgh.

SEDDON, P. R. 1975. Ed. *Letters of John Holles, 1587–1637*. Vol I. Nottingham. Thoroton Society Record Series, XXXI.

1980. 'Marriage and Inheritance in the Clifton Family during the Seventeenth Century', *Transactions of the Thoroton Society*, 84. 33–41.

SENNING, CALVIN. 1983. 'Piracy, Politics, and Plunder under James I: The Voyage of the Pearl and its Aftermath, 1611–1615', *Huntington Library Quarterly*, 46. 187–222.

SETON, GEORGE. 1882. *Memoir of Alexander Seton, Earl of Dunfermline*. Edinburgh.

SHAW, WILLIAM. 1908. *Calendar of Treasury Books, 1669–72*. London.

SHEARER, ANDREW. 1951. *Extracts from the Burgh Records of Dunfermline in the 16th and 17th Centuries*. Dunfermline.

SHEPARD, ALEXANDRA. 2005. "'Swil-bols and Tos-pots': Drink Culture and Male Bonding in England, c.1560–1640', in Laura Gowing, Michael Hunter and Miri Ruben, eds. *Love, Friendship and Faith in Europe, 1300–1800*. Basingstoke. 110–30.

SIMPSON, PERCY. 1895. 'Thomas Palmer', *Notes and Queries*, Ser. 8. No. 8 (Issue 196). 243–4.

SKINNER, SIR JOHN. 1604. *Rapta Tatio: The Mirrour of His Maiesties Present Gouernment*. London.

SMART, PETER. 1643. *A Short Treatise of Altars, Altar-furniture, Altar-cringing, and Musick of all the Quire, Singing-men and Choristers*. London.

SNUGGS, H. L. 1936. 'Fynes Moryson and Jonson's Puntarvolo', *Modern Language Notes*, 51. 230–4.

SOMERVILE, WILLIAM. 1735. *The Chace*. London.

SOTHEBY's (London), 1986. *English Literature and History: Thursday 18 December 1986*. London.

SPEED, JOHN. 1612. *The Theatre of the Empire of Great Britaine*. London.

STAUNTON, GEORGE WILLIAM and F. M. STENTON. 1911. *The Family of Staunton of Staunton, Nottinghamshire*. Newark.

STECKEL, RICHARD. 2004. 'New Light on the "Dark Ages"', *Social Science History*, 28. 211–29.

2012. 'Charles Chester, Scurrilous Jester'. Unpublished paper.

STEGGLE, MATTHEW. 2004. *Richard Brome: Place and Politics on the Caroline Stage*. Manchester.

STEWART, A. M. 1979. Ed. *The Complaynt of Scotland*. Scottish Text Society.

STEWART, LAURA. 2006. *Urban Politics and the British Civil Wars*. Leiden.

STOW, JOHN. 1633. *Survey of London*, rev. and cont. Anthony Munday. London.

STROHMAYER, ULF. 2011. 'Bridges: Different Conditions of Mobile Possibilities', in Cresswell and Merriman, 2011, 119–35.

SULLIVAN, GARRETT. 1998. *The Drama of Landscape: Land, Property and Social Relations on the Early Modern Stage*. Stanford.

SUMMERS, NORMAN. 1972. 'Old Farm, Kneesall', *Transactions of the Thoroton Society*, 76. 17–25.

SUTTON, C. N. 1902. *Historical Notes of Withyham, Hartfield and Ashdown Forest, Together with the History of the Sackville Family*. Tunbridge Wells.

TADCASTER HISTORICAL SOCIETY. 2005. *Tadcaster: Manor Court Rolls 1498–1599*. Tadcaster.

TAYLOR, CHRISTOPHER. 1979. *Roads and Tracks of Britain*. London.

TAYLOR, JOHN. 1619. *A Kicksey-Winsey, or a Lerry Come-Twang*. London.

1622. *A Very Merry Wherry-Ferry-Voyage: or Yorke for my Money*. London.

1624. *The Scourge of Basenesse*. London.

1636. *The Honorable, and Memorable Foundations, . . . within Ten Shires and Counties of this Kingdome*. London.

1637. *A Funerall Elegie, in Memory of that Rare, Famous and Admired Poet, Mr Benjamin Jonson*. London.

1639. *Part of this Summer's Travels, or News from Hell, Hull and Halifax*. London.

TAYLOR, KATE. 1998. *Wakefield District Heritage*. 2 vols. Wakefield.

TAYLOR, SIMON and GILBERT MARKUS. 2006. *The Place-Names of Fife*. Vol. I: *West Fife between Leven and Forth*. Donington.

THOROTON, ROBERT. 1790. *The Antiquities of Nottinghamshire*. Ed. John Throsby. Second edn. 3 vols. Nottingham.

TIGHE, WILLIAM. 1986. 'A Nottinghamshire Gentleman in Court and in Country: The Career of Thomas Markham of Ollerton (1530–1607)', *Transactions of the Thoroton Society*, 90. 30–45.

TILLBROOK, MICHAEL. 1987. 'Arminianism and Society in County Durham', in Marcombe, 1987, 202–26.

TOOMER, GERALD. 2009. *John Selden: A Life in Scholarship*. 2 vols. Oxford.

TOPSELL, EDWARD. 1607. *The Historie of Four-Footed Beasts*. London.

TRAIN, K. S. S. 1961. *Lists of the Clergy of North Nottinghamshire*. Thoroton Society Record Series, XX.

TRICOMI, ALBERT H. 1977. 'Identifying Sir Gervase Clifton, the Addressee of Marston's Letter, 1607', *Notes and Queries*, 24. 202–3.

TROLLOPE, ANDREW. 1890. *An Inventory of the Church Plate of Leicestershire*. Leicester.

TUAN, YI-FU. 2001 [1977]. *Space and Place: The Perspective of Experience*. Minneapolis.

TUCK, RICHARD. 1986. 'Civil Conflict in School and Town, 1500–1700', in Mains and Tuck, 1986, 1–38.

TURBERVILLE, A. S. 1938–9. *A History of Welbeck Abbey and its Owners*. 2 vols. London.

UPTON, ANTHONY. 1961. *Sir Arthur Ingram, c.1565–1642: A Study of the Origins of an English Landed Family*. Oxford.

WAKE, JOAN. 1954. *The Brudenells of Deene*. Second edn. London.

WALTON, IZAAK. 1655. *The Compleat Angler*. Second edn. London.

WARK, KEITH ROBERTS. 1971. *Elizabethan Recusancy in Cheshire*. Chetham Society Publications, third ser., 19.

WARRICK, JOHN. 1899. *The History of Old Cumnock*. Paisley.

WELDON, ANTHONY. 1650. *The Court and Character of King James*. London.

WELFORD, RICHARD. 1884-7. *History of Newcastle and Gateshead.* 3 vols. Newcastle.

WERNHAM, R. B. 1984. *After the Armada: Elizabethan England and the Struggle for Western Europe, 1588–1595.* Oxford.

WHATLEY, CHRISTOPHER. 1984. *'That Important and Necessary Article': The Salt Industry and its Trade in Fife and Tayside c.1570–1850.* Dundee.

WHITE, ROBERT. 1875. *Worksop, The Dukery, and Sherwood Forest.* Worksop.
     1904. *The Dukery Records.* Worksop.

WILKINS, JOHN. 1668. *An Essay towards a Real Character, and a Philosophical Language.* London.

WILLIAMSON, GEORGE. 1889. *Trade Tokens Issued in the Seventeenth Century in England, Wales and Ireland.* London.

WILLIS, BROWNE. 1755. *The History and Antiquities of the Town, Hundred, and Deanery of Buckingham.* London.

WITHINGTON, PHIL. 2005. *The Politics of Commonwealth: Citizens and Freemen in Early Modern England.* Cambridge.

WOOD, MARGUERITE. 1931. Ed. *Extracts from the Records of the Burgh of Edinburgh, 1604–26.* Edinburgh.

WOODHOUSE, ADRIAN. 1999. 'A Newly Identified Estate Plan by John Smithson, 1608', *Transactions of the Thoroton Society*, 103.

WOOLGAR, CHRISTOPHER. 2001. 'Fast and Feast: Conspicuous Consumption and the Diet of the Nobility in the Fifteenth Century', in Michael Hicks, ed. *Revolution and Consumption in Late Medieval England.* Woodbridge. 7–25.

WORMALD, JENNY. 1996. 'James VI, James I and the Identity of Britain', in Brendan Bradshaw and John Morrill, eds. *The British Problem c.1534–1707: State Formation in the Atlantic Archipelago.* London. 148–71.

WORSLEY, LUCY. 2002. 'The Architectural Patronage of William Cavendish, First Duke of Newcastle, 1593–1676'. 2 vols. Unpublished DPhil thesis. University of Sussex.
     2007. *Cavalier: A Tale of Chivalry, Passion and Great Houses.* London.

WOUDHUYSEN, H. R. 1996. *Sir Philip Sidney and the Circulation of Manuscripts 1558–1640.* Oxford.

WYLIE, JOHN. 2007. *Landscape.* London.

ZUPKO, RONALD. 1985. *A Dictionary of Weights and Measures for the British Isles: The Middle Ages to the Twentieth Century.* American Philosophical Society. Philadelphia.

INDEX